Art History II

Art History II

Edited by Bruce Schwabach

Published by SUNY OER Services
Milne Library
State University of New York at Geneseo
Geneseo, NY 14454

Distributed by State University of New York Press

ISBN: 978-1-64176-048-5

This book was produced using Pressbooks.com, and PDF rendering was done by PrinceXML.

Contents

About This Book   15

Chapter 1: Introduction

Chapter 1 Overview   3
Key Learning Items   5
What is Art? Form and Content   7
The Skill of Describing   8
Art as Concept   9
Art & Context   10
Representation & Abstraction   11
Why Is That Important?   12
Why Is This Art?   13
Interpreting Contemporary Art   14
Iconographic Analysis: Understanding Iconography   15
Formal Analysis: Understanding Visual Form   16
Art History Terms   17

Chapter 2: Proto-Renaissance (1300–1400)

Chapter 2 Overview   21
Key Learning Items   22
Cimabue   24
Giotto's Arena Chapel   25
Ognissanti Madonna   28
Duccio, Maesta   29
Lorenzetti's Palazzo Pubblico Frescos   31
Simone Martini's Annunciation   32

Chapter 3: 1400–1500—Art in Northern Europe

Chapter 3 Overview   35

Key Learning Items	37
Introduction to the Renaissance in Italy and the North	39
Sluter's Well of Moses	40
Holy Thorn Reliquary	41
Introduction to Flanders	42
Campin's Merode Altarpiece	44
Jan van Eyck's Ghent Altarpiece	47
Arnolfini Portrait	48
Hugo van der Goes	49
Van der Weyden's Deposition	50
The Unicorn in Captivity	51

Chapter 4: 1400–1500—Art in Italy

Chapter 4 Overview	55
Key Learning Items	57
Florence in the Early Renaissance	59
Orsanmichele	61
Bruelleschi & Ghiberti, The Sacrifice of Isaac	62
Linear Perspective	64
Early Applications of Linear Perspective	65
Donatello's Works	67
Contrapposto	69
Masaccio's Tribute Money	71
Masaccio's Holy Trinity	74
Fra Angelico's The Annunciation	76
Piero della Francesca's Portraits of the Duke and Duchess of Urbino	77
Botticelli's Birth of Venus	78
Introduction to Venice	79
Bellini's St. Francis	83
Mantegna's Works	84

Chapter 5: 1500–1600—High Renaissance and Mannerism in Italy

Chapter 5 Overview	87
Key Learning Items	89
Art and Science in the Renaissance	91
Toward the High Renaissance	93
Leonardo da Vinci Introduced	96
Virgin of the Rocks	99
The Last Supper	101
Mona Lisa	105

Michelangelo Introduced   108
Pietà   110
David   111
Moses   113
Sistine Chapel Ceiling   117
Sistine Chapel: Last Judgment   124
Marriage of the Virgin   127
Madonna of the Goldfinch   128
School of Athens   129
Saint Peter's Basilica   131
Giorgione, The Tempest   133
Titian, Bacchus & Ariadne   134
Titian, Venus of Urbino   135
Veronese, Feast in the House of Levi   136
Tintoretto, The Origin of the Milky Way   140
Introduction to Mannerism   141
Parmigianino's Madonna of the Long Neck   142
El Greco's Adoration of the Shepherds   143

Chapter 6: 1500–1600—The Age of Reformation: Northern Renaissance Art

Chapter 6 Overview   147
Key Learning Items   149
Introduction to the Protestant Reformation   151
Dürer's Four Apostles   153
Self-Portrait 1500   154
What Is a Print?   155
Dürer's Prints   156
Bosch's Last Judgment   157
Cranach's Adam and Eve   158
Holbein's The Ambassadors   159
Portrait of Henry the VIII   160
Bruegel's The Dutch Proverbs   161

Chapter 7: 1600–1700—Baroque Art in Italy

Chapter 7 Overview   165
Key Learning Items   167
Introduction to the Baroque   169
Baroque Art in Italy   175
Bernini's David   177
Bernini's St. Peter's Square   180

Bernini's Ecstasy of St. Teresa   181

Caravaggio's Deposition   184

Caravaggio's Calling of St. Matthew   187

Caravaggio and His Followers   189

Gentileschi   190

Carracci's Ceiling of the Farnese Palace   191

Chapter 8: 1600–1700—Baroque Art in Flanders, Dutch Republic, Spain and France

Chapter 8 Overview   195

Key Learning Items   197

Baroque Terms Explained   199

Rubens, Elevation of the Cross   200

Rubens, Arrival of Marie de Medici   203

Rubens, The Consequences of War   204

Vermeer, Young Woman with a Water Pitcher   206

Vermeer, The Glass of Wine   207

Vermeer and the Camera Obscura   208

Rembrandt, Bathsheba at her Bath   209

Rembrandt, The Three Crosses   210

Rembrandt's Self-Portraits   211

Hal's Malle Babbe   212

Vanitas Painting Explained   213

Dutch Genre Painting Explained   214

Las Meninas   215

Louis XIV & Versailles   216

Poussin, Landscape with St. John   219

Le Nain, Peasant Family in an Interior   220

Chapter 9: 1700–1800—The Age of Enlightenment

Chapter 9 Overview   223

Key Learning Items   225

Age of Enlightenment   227

Rococo Explained   230

Fragonard's The Swing   231

Boucher's Madame de Pompadour   233

Introduction to Neo-Classicism   234

David's Oath of the Horatii   236

David's Death of Marat   239

Antonio Canova   241

Benjamin West   245

William Hogarth 248

John Singleton Copley 253

Copley's Watson and the Shark 255

Gilbert Stuart 257

Chapter 10: 1800–1848 — Industrial Revolution Part I

Chapter 10 Overview 263

Key Learning Items 265

Introduction to Romanticism 267

Liberty Leading the People 269

Scene of the Massacre at Chios 272

Death of Sardanapalus 273

Understanding Delacroix's Painterly Techniques 276

Napoleon Bonaparte Visiting the Plague-Stricken in Jaffa 278

Raft of the Medusa 280

Portraits of the Insane 281

Grand Odalisque 286

Third of May, 1808 288

Sleep of Reason Produces Monsters 292

Saturn Devouring One of His Sons 295

Constable, The Haywain 296

Turner, Slave Ship 299

Hudson River School 300

The Oxbow 301

Chapter 11: 1848–1907 — Industrial Revolution Part II

Chapter 11 Overview 307

Key Learning Items 310

Becoming Modern 312

Introduction to Early Photography 315

Louis Daguerre 319

Timothy O'Sullivan 321

Introduction to Realism 324

Courbet, The Stone Breakers 326

Bonheur, Plowing in the Nivernais 328

Millet, The Gleaners 329

Degas, The Dance Class 330

Degas, At the Races in the Countryside 331

Manet, Luncheon on the Grass (Le Dejeuner sur l'herbe) 332

Manet, Olympia 333

Manet, A Bar at the Folies-Bergere   334

Garnier, Paris Opera   335

Introduction to Impressionism   337

Monet, Gare St. Lazare   340

Monet, Rouen Cathedral Series   341

Caillebotte, Paris Street; Rainy Day   342

Cassatt, In the Loge   343

Cassatt, The Child's Bath   345

Morisot, The Mother and Sister of the Artist   346

Renoir, Moulin de la Galette   347

Post-Impressionism Explained   348

Seurat, La Grande Jatte   349

Van Gogh, Self-Portrait Dedicated to Paul Gauguin   350

Van Gogh, The Bedroom   353

Van Gogh, Self-Portrait with Bandaged Ear   354

Cezanne, Basket of Apples   359

Cezanne, The Large Bathers   362

Gauguin, Vision After the Sermon   363

Gauguin, Spirit of the Dead Watching   364

Toulouse-Lautrec, At the Moulin Rouge   368

Gaudi, Sagrada Familia   369

Fin-de-siecle Explained   371

Klimt, The Kiss   372

Munch, The Storm   373

Rodin, Gates of Hell   374

Emanuel Leutze, Washington Crossing the Delaware   375

Eakins, The Gross Clinic   378

Homer, The Life Line   381

John Singer Sargent, Madame X   382

Whistler, Nocturne in Black and Gold   384

Chapter 12: 1907–1960—Age of Global Conflict Part I

Chapter 12 Overview   389

Key Learning Items   392

Introduction to Fauvism   394

Matisse, Bonheur de Vivre   397

Matisse, The Red Studio   402

Kirchner, Street, Dresden   404

Kandinsky, Composition VII   405

Schiele, Seated Male Nude   406

Picasso, Still Life with Chair Caning   407

Picasso's Early Works   410

Picasso, Les Demoiselles d'Avignon   413

Picasso, Guitar   418

Picasso, Guernica   419

Braque, The Portuguese   420

Braque, The Viaduct at L'Estaque   422

Duchamp, Fountain   425

Arp, Untitled   426

Klee, Twittering Machine   427

An Introduction to Futurism   428

Three Futurists   431

Malevich   432

Mondrian, Composition No. II   433

Modigliani, Young Woman in a Shirt   434

Maholy-Nagy   435

Chapter 13: 1907–1960—Age of Global Conflict Part II

Chapter 13 Overview   439

Key Learning Items   442

Man Ray, The Gift   444

Giacometti, The Palace at 4 a.m.   448

Giacometti, The City Square   449

Magritte, The Treachery of Images   450

Dali, The Persistence of Memory   451

Dali, Metamorphosis of Narcissus   452

House of Art   454

George Bellows   459

Grant Wood, American Gothic   460

Georgia O'Keeffe   461

Edward Hopper, Nighthawks   462

Frida Kahlo and Diego Rivera   465

Origins of Abstract Expressionism   466

Impact of Abstract Expressionism   471

Pollock, One: Number 31, 1950   472

Pollock's Painting Techniques   473

Rothko, No. 3/No. 13   474

Rothko's Painting Technique   475

Newman, Onement 1   476

de Kooning, Woman I   477

Robert Motherwell   478

Jasper Johns   480

Rauschenberg   481

Introduction to Photography   482

Cartier-Bresson   486

Brancusi, Bird in Space   487

Frank Lloyd Wright, Guggenheim Museum   488

Mies van der Rohe, Seagram Building   489

Chapter 14: 1960–Now—Age of Post-Colonialism Part I

Chapter 14 Overview   493

Key Learning Items   495

Introduction to Contemporary Art   497

Diane Arbus   498

Cindy Sherman   499

Francis Bacon   500

Lucian Freud   501

Louise Bourgeois   502

Warhol, Gold Marilyn Monroe   504

Warhol, Campbell's Soup Cans   507

Oldenburg, Floor Cake   508

Lichtenstein, Rouen Cathedral Set V   509

Ed and Nancy Kienholz   510

Richter, Uncle Rudi   511

Richter, The Cage Paintings   513

Donald Judd   514

Dan Flavin   516

Robert Morris   517

Eva Hesse, Untitled   519

Eva Hesse, Untitled (Rope Piece)   520

Introduction to Performance Art   521

Joseph Beuys, Fat Chair   525

Chapter 15: 1960–Now—Age of Post-Colonialism Part II

Chapter 15 Overview   529

Key Learning Items   531

Understanding Installation Art   533

Vito Acconci   534

Mary Kelly   536

Robert Smithson   539

Bruce Nauman   542

Damien Hirst   544

Art in the Twenty-First Century   545
Ai Weiwei   546

About This Book

Your Art History II textbook is a compilation of articles written by instructors for universities around the country. The entire compilation is provided free of charge online through a Creative Commons license. You can access or even copy all the material here, for your own reference, even after the semester ends.

Different Versions

An electronic version is made available via your course in Blackboard, through the College Library, and at https://courses.lumenlearning.com/suny-arthistory2/. You may also purchase a physical copy at the College Bookstore. The electronic version has access to multimedia content including video, slideshows, and interactive activities. The print version will have all the same reading material, but not include the multimedia content.

This text is printed in monotone to save cost. To see the true beauty and range of colors, go online to the web version of the text.

About the Author

There are many different authors; look to the "Licenses and Attributions" section at the end of each chapter to identify contributors. This compilation was edited by Bruce Schwabach at Herkimer County Community College.

Bruce Schwabach taught studio art, and art history for over 35 years at Herkimer College of SUNY. He also is an early advocate of the SUNY Learning Network, promoting online learning.

With an BFA from SUNY New Paltz, and an MFA from Pennsylvania State University, he is a nationally recognized painter, and photographer.

Recently his photograph, "Ponderosa Pines in Yosemite National Park", was on view at The National Botanical Gardens in Washington, DC.

Currently, Schwabach is one of the SUNY OER panelists promoting open-sourced learning on SUNY campuses.

Chapter 1: Introduction

Chapter 1 Overview

What You'll Learn To Do: Navigate the history and language of art.

Chapter 1 will serve as an introduction to the History of Art. We will cover some important art historical concepts and terms. It is imperative to understand the "language" of Art History in order to evaluate works of art.

Learning Activities

The learning activities for this module include:

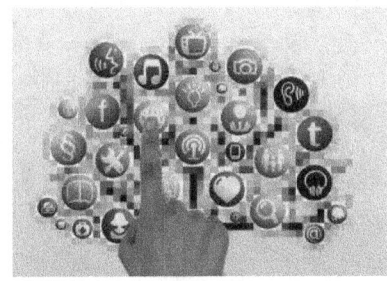

- **Complete:** Orientation to Distance Learning
- **Review:** Key Learning Items

An Introduction to Art

- **Read:** What is Art? Form and Content
- **Watch:** The Skill of Describing (3:42)
- **Watch:** Art as Concept (10:07)
- **Watch:** Art & Context (10:26)
- **Watch:** Representation & Abstraction (8:28)
- **Watch:** Why Is That Important? (12:17)
- **Watch:** Why Is This Art? (7:08)
- **Watch:** Interpreting Contemporary Art (7:48)
- **Read:** Iconographic Analysis: Understanding Iconography
- **Read:** Formal Analysis: Understanding Visual Form
- **Watch:** Art History Terms (4:04)

Attributions

- Art History II. **Provided by**: Extended Learning Institute of Northern Virginia Community College. **Located at**: http://eli.nvcc.edu/. **License**: *CC BY: Attribution*

Public domain content

- Image of Finger . **Authored by**: geralt. **Located at**: https://pixabay.com/en/finger-touch-hand-structure-769300/. **License**: *Public Domain: No Known Copyright*

Key Learning Items

Learning Objectives

After successful completion of this module, you will be able to:

- Understand and apply the basic concepts and terminology of Art History as a discipline
- Investigate and apply the fundamental questions we ask when looking at an art object
- Discuss, collaborate, and generate understanding as to the meaning of works of art and architecture

Key Questions to Ask

While you are reviewing the content of this module, consider the following questions:

- What year was the artwork created?
- What is going on in history when the artwork was created?
- How should I look at art?
- How should I describe art?
- What is the special language that is used to describe art?

Key Vocabulary Terms

- form
- content
- representation
- abstraction
- medium/media

- oil

- prints

- woodcuts

- engravings

- tempera

- patronage

- donors

- iconography

Here are links to art history glossaries that will help you better understand the above key vocabulary terms.

- ArtLex: Art Dictionary

  - http://www.artlex.com/

- About.com: Art History

  - http://arthistory.about.com/od/glossary/l/bl_Art-Glossary.htm

- Artcyclopedia: A Guide to Fine Art

  - http://www.artcyclopedia.com/

Attributions

CC licensed content, Original

What is Art? Form and Content

Click on the link below to view the website "What is the Definition of Art?" on About Education. This website will help provide you with a working definition of "art." As you read the article, you will notice that there isn't a concise way to define art; art has many moving parts and means something slightly different to every person.

- What is the Definition of Art?
  - http://arthistory.about.com/cs/reference/f/what_is_art.htm

The Skill of Describing

This video helps you understand why the skill of describing is so essential to understanding and appreciating art.

- https://youtu.be/h_pWZBOR4ec

Attributions

All rights reserved content

Art as Concept

This video is a conversation with Sal Khan & Steven Zucker about regarding the artist, Duchamp, and the art movement, Dada, examining art as a concept.

> The only definition of "readymade" published under the name of Marcel Duchamp ("MD" to be precise) [is found] in Breton and Eluard's Dictionnaire abrégé du Surréalisme: "an ordinary object elevated to the dignity of a work of art by the mere choice of an artist."
>
> —Hector Obalk

- https://youtu.be/MRv20I13vqM

Marcel Duchamp, In Advance of the Broken Arm, 1964, fourth version, after lost original of November 1915 (The Museum of Modern Art)

Attributions

Art & Context

Sal Khan, Steven Zucker, and Beth Harris discuss art and its context using Monet's *Cliff Walk at Pourville* and Malevich's *Suprematist Composition: White on White* to illustrate their points.

- https://youtu.be/2aUFB9hQncQ

Works Discussed

Claude Monet, *Cliff Walk at Pourville*, 1882, oil on canvas, 66.5 cm × 82.3 cm (26 1⁄8 in × 32 7⁄16 in), (Art Institute of Chicago).

Kazmir Malevich, *Suprematist Composition: White on White*, 1918, oil on canvas, 79.4 cm × 79.4 cm (31 1/4 in × 31 1/4 in), (Museum of Modern Art, New York City).

Representation & Abstraction

Sal Khan, Beth Harris & Steven Zucker discuss representation and abstraction in art; they take a look at Millais's *Ophelia* and Newman's, *Vir Heroicus Sublimus.*

- https://youtu.be/8-5DTsl1V5k

Works Discussed

John Everett Millais, *Ophelia*, 1851–52, oil on canvas, 76.2 cm × 111.8 cm (30.0 in × 44.0 in), (Tate Britain, London).

Barnett Newman, *Vir Heroicus Sublimus*, 1950–51, oil on canvas, 242.3 cm × 541.7 cm (95 3⁄8 in × 213 1⁄4 in), (Museum of Modern Art, New York City).

Attributions

Why Is That Important?

Sal Khan, Steven Zucker, and Beth Harris discuss the things that make art important using Pollock's *Number 1A, 1948* to illustrate their points.

- https://youtu.be/NT0SHjOowLA

Jackson Pollock, *Number 1A, 1948*, 1948, oil paint, 5′ 8″ x 8′ 8″, (The Museum of Modern Art).

Attributions

CC licensed content, Shared previously

Why Is This Art?

Steven Zucker and Sal Khan try to answer why something is qualified as art. They use Andy Warhol, *Campbell's Soup Cans* to illustrate their points.

- https://youtu.be/SdbOrNLcC0I

Andy Warhol, *Campbell's Soup Cans*, 1962, synthetic polymer paint on thirty-two canvases, each 20 × 16 inches (50.8 × 40.6 cm), (The Museum of Modern Art).

Attributions

CC licensed content, Shared previously

Interpreting Contemporary Art

Beth Harris, Sal Khan and Steven Zucker discuss the Damien Hirst sculpture, *The Physical Impossibility of Death in the Mind of Someone Living*, and issues of interpretation.

- https://youtu.be/uDuzy-t7GDA

Damien Hirst, *The Physical Impossibility of Death in the Mind of Someone Living*, 1991, tiger shark, glass, steel, 5% formaldehyde solution, 213 cm × 518 cm × 213 cm (84 in × 204 in × 84 in).

Attributions

CC licensed content, Shared previously

Iconographic Analysis: Understanding Iconography

In iconographic analyses, art historians look at the icons or symbols in a work to discover the work's original meaning or intent. To accomplish this kind of analysis, they need to be familiar with the culture and people that produced the work. Click on the link below to view the article "Iconographic Analysis" by Marjorie Munsterberg on her website *Writing About Art*.

- "Iconographic Analysis" by Marjorie Munsterberg
  - http://writingaboutart.org/pages/iconographicanalysis.html

Attributions

Formal Analysis: Understanding Visual Form

Formal analysis is exactly what it sounds like: an analysis of the work's form. This kind of analysis focuses on structure, materials, and composition rather than the culture the work came from. Click on the link below to view the article "Formal Analysis" by Marjorie Munsterberg on her website *Writing About Art*.

- "Formal Analysis" by Marjorie Munsterberg

  ◦ http://writingaboutart.org/pages/formalanalysis.html

Art History Terms

This visual art glossary defines art categories, styles, and terms while giving examples of each term.

- https://youtu.be/b2gWJTjgd1c

Chapter 2:
Proto-Renaissance
(1300–1400)

Chapter 2 Overview

What You'll Learn To Do: Understand the artistic period known as the Proto-Renaissance and its impact on art history.

In Chapter 2 we will delve into the beginning of the Renaissance. We will cover what is known as the Proto-Renaissance. It is imperative to understand these early beginnings of the Renaissance in order to see how art evolves in later centuries.

Learning Activities

The learning activities for this module include:

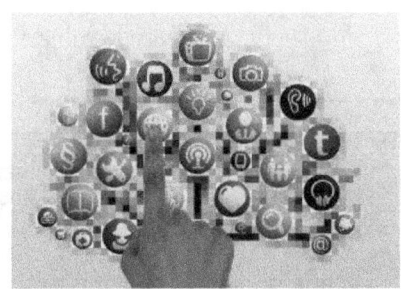

- **Review:** Key Learning Items

Florence

- **Watch:** Cimabue (7:29)
- **Read:** Giotto's Arena Chapel (includes four videos: 4:56, 10:13, 5:41, and 6:22)
- **Watch:** Ognissanti Madonna (4:04)

Siena

- **Read:** Duccio, Maesta (includes two videos: 6:23 and 4:09)
- **Watch:** Lorenzetti's Palazzo Pubblico Frescos (10:17)
- **Watch:** Simone Martini's Annunciation (4:33)

Attributions

Key Learning Items

After successful completion of this module, you will be able to:

- Understand and apply the concepts and terminology of the earliest Renaissance art
- Investigate and apply the fundamental questions we ask when looking at art objects from the Proto-Renaissance
- Discuss, collaborate, and generate understanding as to the meaning of Proto-Renaissance art
- Assess and evaluate the beginnings of Renaissance art

While you are reviewing the content of this module, consider the following questions:

- What is the Proto-Renaissance?
- How does the Proto-Renaissance differ from the Renaissance?
- Why is Giotto considered the father of Western painting?
- What changes begin to occur in art during the Proto-Renaissance?

Key Vocabulary Terms

- narrative cycle
- fresco
- buon (true) fresco
- secco fresco
- trompe l'oeil

- register

- chiaroscuro

- lapis lazuli

- monumental

- naturalism

- iconography

- symbolism

Here are links to art history glossaries that will help you better understand the above key vocabulary terms.

- ArtLex: Art Dictionary

  ○ http://www.artlex.com/

- About.com: Art History

  ○ http://arthistory.about.com/od/glossary/l/bl_Art-Glossary.htm

- Artcyclopedia: A Guide to Fine Art

  ○ http://www.artcyclopedia.com/

Attributions

CC licensed content, Original

Cimabue

Dr. Beth Harris and Dr. Steven Zucker provide a description, historical perspective and analysis of Cimabue's *Maesta of Santa Trinita*.

- https://youtu.be/_alU-o_qDt8

Cimabue, *Maesta of Santa Trinita*, 1280–1290, tempera on panel, 151 1/2 × 87 3/4″ (385 × 223 cm), (Uffizi, Florence).

External Link
View this painting up close in the Google Art Project: • https://www.google.com/culturalinstitute/asset-viewer/maesta-of-santa-trinita/uQHfVH5CnUN-hxA?projectId=art-project

Attributions

CC licensed content, Shared previously

Giotto's Arena Chapel

Late Medieval or Proto-Renaissance

The Renaissance does not have a start date. Its origins are often located around 1400 but as early as the late 1200s we see changes in painting and sculpture that lay the foundation for what we will come to recognize as the Renaissance. Some scholars call this early period the "Late Gothic"—a term which refers to the late Middle Ages, while other people call it the "Proto-Renaissance"—the beginnings of the Renaissance. In any case, a revolution is beginning to take place in the early 1300s in the way people think about the world, the way they think about the past, and the way they think about themselves and their relationship with God.

Giotto: The father of Western Painting

The artist who takes the biggest step away from the Medieval style of spiritual representation is Giotto. You could say, in fact, that Giotto changed the direction of art history. Giotto is perhaps best known for the frescos he painted in the Arena Chapel. They were commissioned by a wealthy man named Enrico Scrovegni, the son of a well-known banker (and banker himself). According to the Church, *usury* (charging interest for a loan) was a sin, and so one of Enrico's motivations for building the chapel and having it decorated by Giotto may have been to atone for the sin of usury.

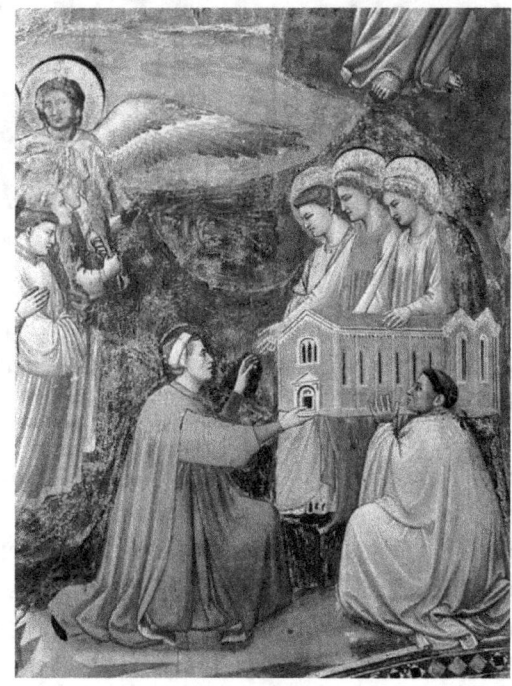

Figure 1. Enrico in the Last Judggment

Commissioning works of art for churches was a very common way of doing "good works" which could help earn one's way into Heaven. We can see Enrico himself in a fresco of the *Last Judgment* on the west wall of the chapel, on the side of the blessed (or the elect)—those whom Christ has chosen to go to Heaven. He is shown kneeling, giving a symbolic model of the Arena chapel itself to the Virgin Mary and the Virgin of Charity and the Virgin Annunciate (to whom the chapel was dedicated). In fact, on March 25—the Feast of the Annunciate Virgin—sunlight enters one of the side windows and falls directly on the figure of Enrico Scrovegni.

Figure 2 gives us a sense of what it feels like to be a tourist visiting the Arena Chapel. Because frescos are painted directly on the wall, they can't easily be moved and put in a museum (unless you take the whole wall!). So, most frescos are still in the spaces that the artists created them for, and the patrons commissioned them for. Having the work of art in its original context helps us to understand its meaning for the people of the 14th century.

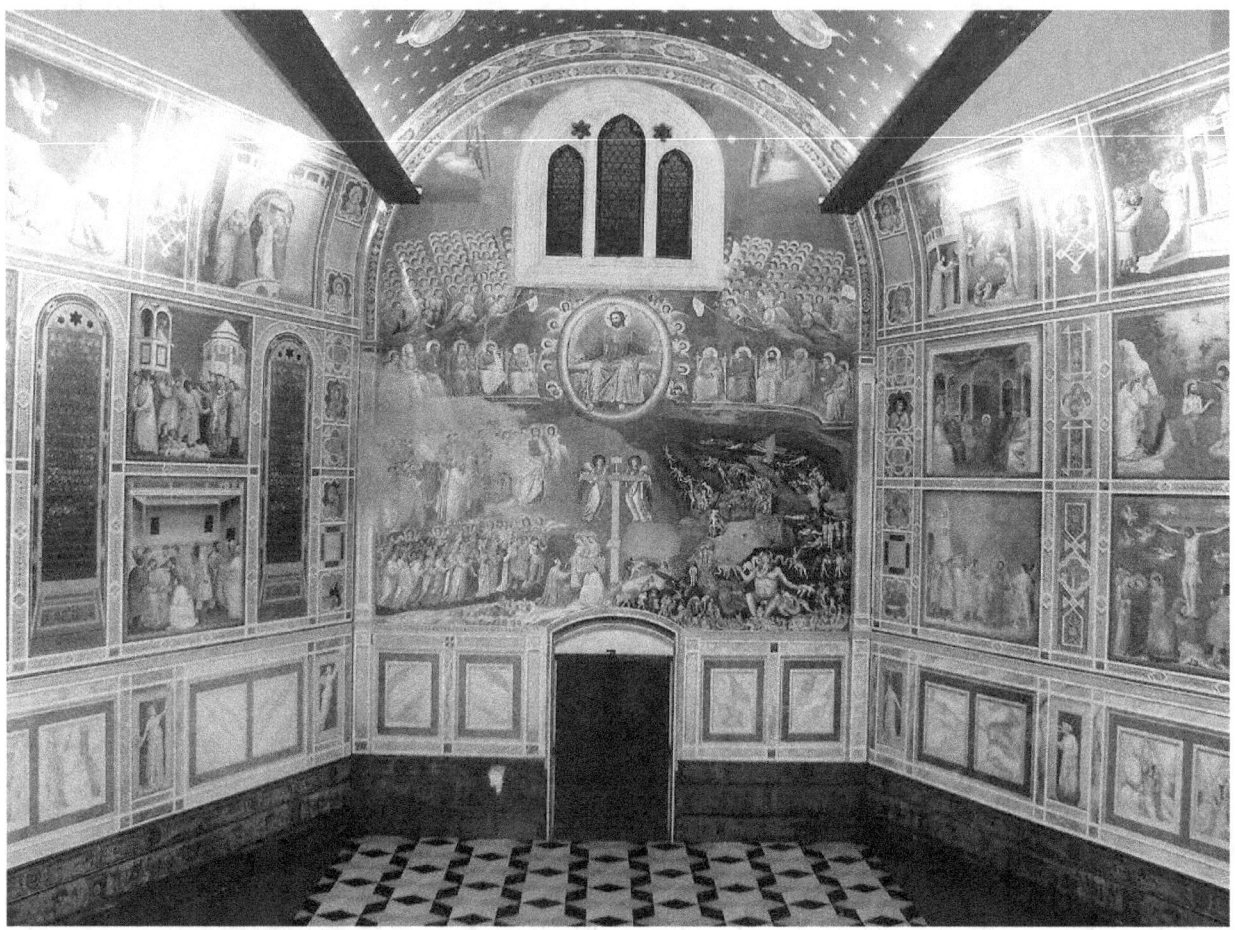

Figure 2. Model of Capella degli Scrovegni, which is a church in Padua, Italy. This reproduction on the scale of 1:4.

Looking at this photo, you can see that there are numerous separate paintings in the chapel (the Lamentation is one of them. Giotto covered the walls with scenes from the Lives of Joachim and Anna (Mary's parents) and Christ himself.

Rather like a comic book without words, Giotto tells the story of Christ and his parents through pictures. Why? Because most of the population of Europe was illiterate at this time. Most people couldn't read the bible for themselves (Bibles were rare and expensive—there was no printing press and so each was copied by hand). Instead, people learned the stories of the Bible—stories that would help them get to heaven—by hearing the words of the priest in the church on Sunday, and by looking at the paintings and sculptures.

The frescoes in the Arena Chapel tell the story of Mary and Christ on the long walls. By the altar, Giotto painted the *Annunciation*, and at the other end, on the entrance wall, the *Last Judgment*.

Video Tour

- **Giotto, Arena (Scrovegni) Chapel (part 1)**
  - ◦ https://youtu.be/47QgqdeSi0U
- **Giotto, Arena (Scrovegni) Chapel (part 2)**
  - ◦ https://youtu.be/I356lV1v8Bc
- **Giotto, Arena (Scrovegni) Chapel (part 3)**
  - ◦ https://youtu.be/RbBQN0Wt_wY
- **Giotto, Arena (Scrovegni) Chapel (part 4)**
  - ◦ https://youtu.be/6z_Kjsn8VLI

Attributions

CC licensed content, Shared previously

Ognissanti Madonna

Dr. Beth Harris and Dr. Steven Zucker provide a description, historical perspective, and analysis of Giotto's *The Ognissanti Madonna*.

- https://youtu.be/P9s3YA-glNk

Giotto, *The Ognissanti Madonna*, 1306–10, tempera on panel, 128 x 80 1/4″ (325 x 204 cm). Painted for the Church of Ognissanti, Florence

---

External Link

View this painting up close in the Google Art Project:

- https://www.google.com/culturalinstitute/asset-viewer/the-ognissanti-madonna/OgE-RDjvff-y6g?projectId=art-project

---

Attributions

Duccio, Maesta

During this period, and for hundreds of years, Italy was not a unified country, but rather was divided into many small countries we call city-states. Florence, Siena, Milan, Venice—these were essentially independent nations with their own governments—and they were at war with each other. These city-states also had independent cultures with their own distinct styles in painting and sculpture. Siena had a unique style that emphasized decorative surfaces, sinuous lines, elongated figures and the heavy use of gold. Duccio was the founder of the Sienese style and his work was quite different from the Florentine painter Giotto. Giotto emphasized a greater naturalism—creating figures who are more monumental (large, heavy and with a greater sense of accurate proportion) and a greater illusion of three-dimensional space.

Contemporaneous description of the procession that brought this painting to Siena Cathedral (or Duomo):

At this time the altarpiece for the high altar was finished and the picture which was called the "Madonna with the large eyes" or Our Lady of Grace, that now hangs over the altar of St. Boniface, was taken down. Now this Our Lady was she who had hearkened to the people of Siena when the Florentines were routed at Monte Aperto, and her place was changed because the new one was made, which is far more beautiful and devout and larger, and is painted on the back with the stories of the Old and New Testaments. And on the day that it was carried to the Duomo the shops were shut, and the bishop conducted a great and devout company of priests and friars in solemn procession, accompanied by the nine signiors, and all the officers of the commune, and all the people, and one after another the worthiest with lighted candles in their hands took places near the picture, and behind came the women and children with great devotion. And they accompanied the said picture up to the Duomo, making the procession around the Campo, as is the custom, all the bells ringing joyously, out of reverence for so noble a picture as this. And this picture Duccio di Niccolò the painter made, and it was made in the house of the Muciatti outside the gate aStalloreggi. And all that day persons, praying God and His Mother, who is our advocate, to defend us by their infinite mercy from every adversity and all evil, and keep us from the hands of traitors and of the enemies of Siena.[1]

- https://youtu.be/2fijnNzktDI

Duccio, *Maesta* (front), 1308–11 (Museo dell'Opera Metropolitana del Duomo, Siena)

- https://youtu.be/w6Tgu14VSLY

Duccio, *Maesta* (back), 1308–11 (Museo dell'Opera Metropolitana del Duomo, Siena)

1. English translation: Charles Eliot Norton, *Historical Studies of Church-Buildings in the Middle Ages: Venice, Siena, Florence* (New York: Harper & Brothers, 1880), 144–45; Italian text: G. Milanesi, *Documenti per la storia dell'arte senese* (Siena: 1854, I), 169

Attributions

CC licensed content, Shared previously

Lorenzetti's Palazzo Pubblico Frescos

Dr. Beth Harris and Dr. Steven Zucker provide a description, historical perspective, and analysis of Lorenzetti's *Allegory of Good Government, Effects of Good Government in the City and the Country*, and *Allegory and Effects of Bad Government in the City and the Country.*

- https://youtu.be/jk3wNadYA7k

Ambrogio Lorenzetti, *Allegory of Good Government, Effects of Good Government in the City and the Country*, and *Allegory and Effects of Bad Government in the City and the Country*, Siena c. 1337–40, fresco, Sala della Pace (Hall of Peace) also know as the Sala dei Nove (the Hall of the Nine), 7.7 × 14.4 meters (room), Palazzo Pubblico, Siena

Attributions

CC licensed content, Shared previously

Simone Martini's Annunciation

Dr. Beth Harris and Dr. Steven Zucker provide a description, historical perspective, and analysis of Simone Martini's *Annunciation*.

- https://youtu.be/7PsgPJoGWig

Simone Martini, *Annunciation*, 1333, tempera on panel, 72 1/2 × 82 5/8″ or 184 × 210 cm. (Uffizi, Florence)

Attributions

Chapter 3: 1400–1500—Art in Northern Europe

Chapter 3 Overview

What You'll Learn To Do: Examine Northern Renaissance art and understand its impact on art history as a whole.

In Chapter 3 we will examine Northern Renaissance art. We will look at how artists like van Eyck contributed to the development of Western art. It is imperative to understand Northern Renaissance art in order to see how it impacted later artistic developments.

Learning Activities

The learning activities for this module include:

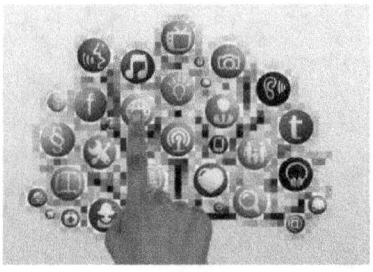

- **Review:** Key Learning Items

Introduction

- **Watch:** Introduction to the Renaissance in Italy and the North (10:25)

Burgundy

- **Watch:** Sluter's Well of Moses (4:51)
- **Read:** Holy Thorn Reliquary (includes a video: 2:44)

Flanders

- **Read:** Introduction to Flanders
- **Read:** Campin's Merode Altarpiece (includes a video: 5:46)
- **Watch:** Jan van Eyck's Ghent Altarpiece (two videos: 5:17 and 7:22)
- **Watch:** Arnolfini Portrait (7:11)
- **Watch:** Hugo van der Goes (3:47)
- **Watch:** Van der Weyden's Deposition (7:08)

- **Watch:** The Unicorn in Captivity (5:56)

Attributions

CC licensed content, Original

- Art History II. **Provided by**: Extended Learning Institute of Northern Virginia Community College. **Located at**: http://eli.nvcc.edu/. **License**: *CC BY: Attribution*

Public domain content

- Image of Finger. **Authored by**: geralt. **Located at**: https://pixabay.com/en/finger-touch-hand-structure-769300/. **License**: *Public Domain: No Known Copyright*

Key Learning Items

Learning Objectives

After successful completion of this module, you will be able to:

- Understand and apply the concepts and terminology of Northern Renaissance art
- Investigate and apply the fundamental questions we ask when looking at art objects from this movement
- Discuss, collaborate, and generate understanding as to the meaning of Northern Renaissance art
- Assess and evaluate the impact of Northern Renaissance art on the continued evolution of Western art

Key Questions to Ask

While you are reviewing the content of this module, consider the following questions:

- What are the unique characteristics of Northern Renaissance painting?
- How does Northern Renaissance painting differ from Renaissance art in Italy?
- When and where do we first see the widespread use of oil paint?

Key Vocabulary Terms

- oil paint
- relic
- reliquary
- triptych
- altarpiece
- polypych

- tapestry

- iconography

- symbolism

Here are links to art history glossaries that will help you better understand the above key vocabulary terms.

- ArtLex: Art Dictionary
    - http://www.artlex.com/

- About.com: Art History
    - http://arthistory.about.com/od/glossary/l/bl_Art-Glossary.htm

- Artcyclopedia: A Guide to Fine Art
    - http://www.artcyclopedia.com/

Attributions

CC licensed content, Original

Introduction to the Renaissance in Italy and the North

Here is an introduction to the Renaissance, which means *rebirth:*

- https://youtu.be/kzhuZmzoX5o

Sluter's Well of Moses

Dr. Beth Harris and Dr. Steven Zucker provide a description, historical perspective, and analysis of Claus Sluter's, *The Well of Moses*. The prophets depicted include: Moses, David, Jeremiah, Zachariah, Daniel, and Isaiah.

- https://youtu.be/xdIVZrr_8tI

Claus Sluter (with Claus de Werve), *The Well of Moses*, 1395–1405 (calvary finished 1399, prophets 1402–05, painted by Jean Malouel c. 1402), Asnières stone with gilding and polychromy, slightly less than 7 meters high, originally close to 13 meters with cross. Located on the grounds of the former Chartreuse de Champmol, a Carthusian monastery in Dijon, France established by Philip the Bold, Duke of Burgundy.

Attributions

Holy Thorn Reliquary

In this video, Neil MacGregor discusses the Holy Thorn Reliquary at the British Museum, video embedded with permission of the British Museum

- https://youtu.be/0Xxm2SGuGTk

Holy Thorn Reliquary (made in Paris for Jean, Duc de Berry), c. 1390s, gold, enamel, ruby, pearl, sapphire, and rock crystal, 30 × 14.2 × 6.8 cm (British Museum, London)

This sumptuous reliquary holds a single thorn from the crown of thorns bought by King Louis IX in Constantinople in 1239. The price was 135,000 livres, an enormous sum that speaks to the importance placed on this relic, believed to have been used to mock Christ during his trials and crucifixion. The remainder of the crown of thorns is in the Cathedrale Notre Dame de Paris. Jean, Duke of Berry was the brother of Charles V, the king of France. The goldsmith has not been identified. It is interesting to note that a copy of this original had been secretly substituted and had remained undetected in the royal Viennese collection for decades.

A relic is an object, often a portion of a saint's body or clothing, that is ascribed with spiritual power. During the medieval era, relics were enormously important economic engines that could draw pilgrims to a church that held them in search of the blessings they were thought to bestow. A reliquary is a decorated container for a relic.

Introduction to Flanders

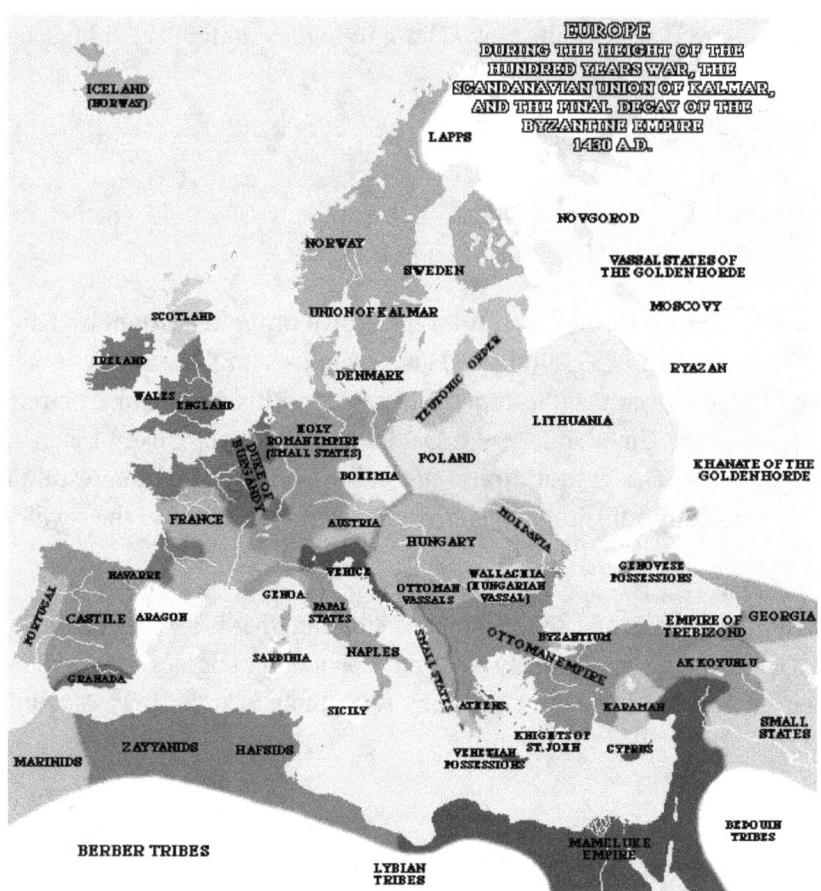

Figure 1. A map of Europe in 1430.

We often think of the Renaissance as an entirely Italian phenomenon, but in northern Europe, in an area known as Flanders (which is the northern portion of Belgium today) there was also a Renaissance. Though profoundly different, the Italian and Northern Renaissances shared a similar interest in the natural world, and recreating the illusion of reality in their paintings and sculptures.

Figure 1 shows a map of Europe in the fifteenth century. The area in Northern Europe that is dark red is Flanders, which was controlled by the Dukes of Burgundy (in France) during this time period, and we call the art and culture of this area Flemish.

Like Florence, Flanders encompassed an area with rich industrial and banking cities that allowed a large middle class population to flourish. The court of the Dukes of Burgundy were the most important patrons during this time, but newly wealthy private citizens also commissioned art as part of a growing interest in private meditation and prayer. They also commissioned portraits in growing numbers.

Classical Antiquity?

The fact that we are far from Italy tells us something about the character of the Northern Renaissance. The Renaissance in Italy was, in part, a rebirth of the art and culture of Ancient Greece and Rome. In Northern Europe we're far from the important centers of Ancient Greek and Roman culture, and so the Renaissance in the North is not a rebirth of Ancient Greek and Roman culture the way it was in Florence.

Oil Paint

Though the medium of oil paint had been in use since the late middle ages, the artists of the North were the first to exploit what this medium had to offer. Using thin layers of paint, called glazes, they creating a depth of color that was entirely new, and because oil paint can imitate textures far better than fresco or tempera, it was perfectly suited to creating that illusion of reality that was so important to Renaissance artists and patrons . In contrast to oil paint, tempera dries quickly and to create an illusion of three dimensional form, the paint has to be applied in short thin brushstrokes, like cross-hatching. In the Northern Renaissance, we see artists making the most of oil paint—creating the illusion of light reflecting on metal surfaces or jewels, and textures that appear like real fur, hair, wool or wood.

Campin's Merode Altarpiece

The *Merode Altarpiece* is one of the great masterpieces of Northern Renaissance art. The use of objects from the material world to symbolize spiritual ideas, the effort to make the divine accessible to us and part of our world, and the attention to clarity and detail—at the expense of creating a coherent space—are all basic characteristics of the Northern Renaissance style. The first thing you'll notice about the *Merode Altarpiece* (located in New York City in the Cloisters, part of the Metropolitan Museum of Art) is that it is not one painting, but three connected paintings, in this case measuring four feet across by two feet high. This is called a **triptych** (the prefix "tri" means three, as in tricycle). Artists today still use this popular format for a painting. The three panels are connected by hinges (like on a door) so that triptychs usually could open and close. This was important because altarpieces, like this one, were usually closed or covered until the Mass was performed in front of them.

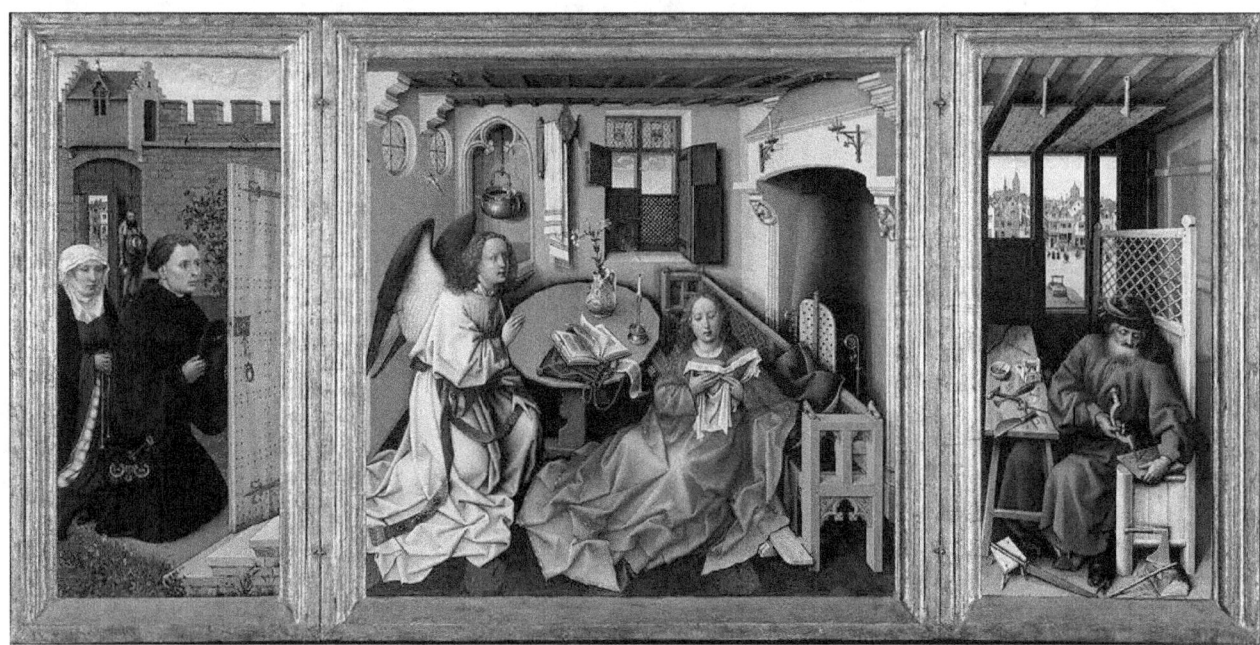

Figure 1. Robert Campin, Merode Altarpiece, oil on oak panel, 1425-28 (Metropolitan Museum of Art)

External Link

View this painting up close in the Google Art Project:

- https://www.google.com/culturalinstitute/asset-viewer/annunciation-triptych-merode-altarpiece/2gH9uXVRR_p-vQ?projectId=art-project

Left Panel: Donors

In the panel on the far left, we see the patrons or donors who commissioned this painting. In Flanders, a new middle class of bankers and merchants were commissioning works of art, and wanted images that brought the divine into their own world.

Center Panel: The Annunciation

In the center we see the Annunciation, a common subject in the Middle Ages, in the Renaissance and after. Here the Angel Gabriel announces (hence the title "Annunciation") to Mary that she is about to conceive the Christ child. The Holy Spirit, which impregnates Mary, appears coming through one of the windows on the right in form of a small image of Christ carrying the cross on his back.

Right Panel: St. Joseph

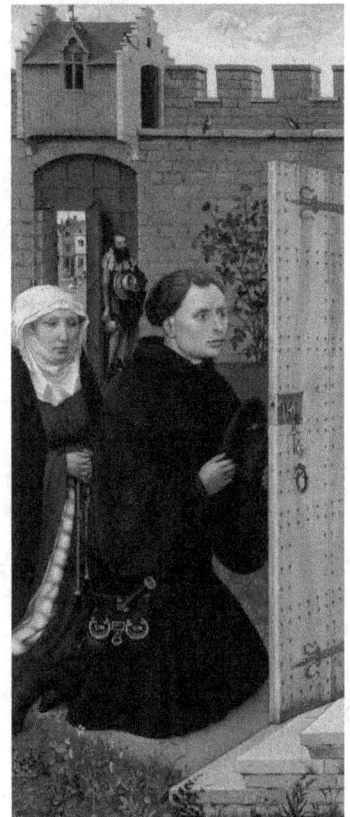

Figure 2. The donors

The panel on the far right depicts St. Joseph (Mary's husband), who was a carpenter by trade. He is shown in his carpenter's shop. Here is one of the amazing characteristics of Northern Renaissance art. Nearly every item that we see in the Merode Altarpiece—even though is looks like an ordinary object—is really a religious symbol. For example, the tools that Joseph is working with are a symbol of the Passion of Christ, the lilies symbolize Mary's virginity, and the candle that has just been extinguished tells us that this is the moment when God takes human form, and his exclusively divine nature is gone. The material world is imbued with spiritual meaning, with the divine. This is one of the defining characteristics of Northern Renaissance art. But it is not only in their paintings that the people of Flanders used everyday objects to symbolize spiritual ideas; this was a part of their way of thinking.

A Closer Look at the Central Panel

Let's look carefully at the central panel of the Merode Altarpiece.

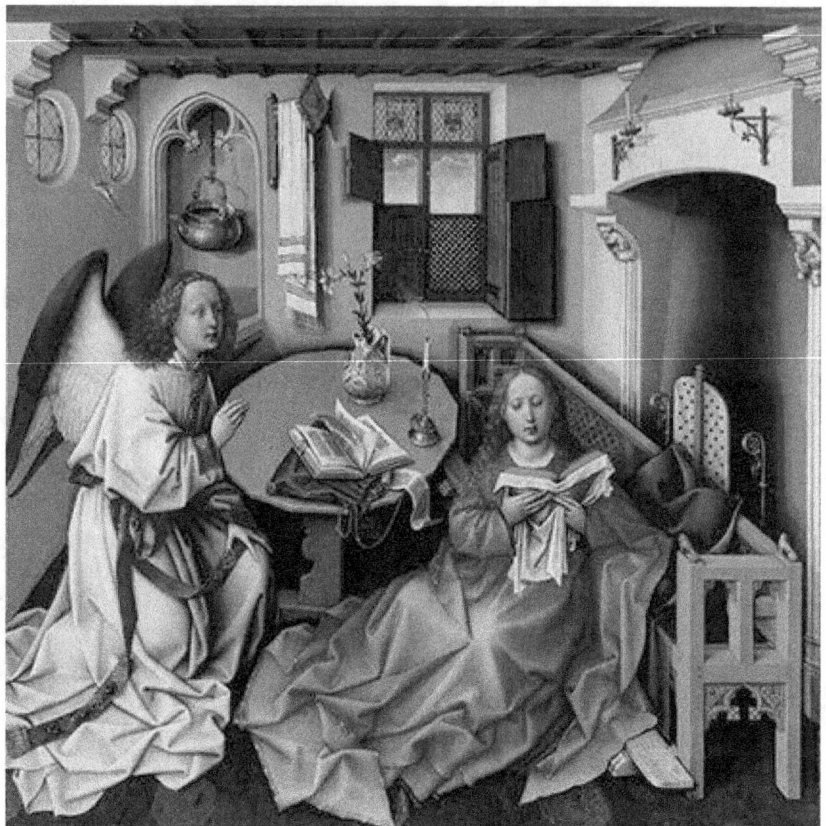

Figure 3. Center panel, the Annunciation

First, notice that the figures have no halos! We can definitely see knees pressing though the drapery. But can we really get a sense of a whole naked body underneath? Do the bodies of Mary and the Angel make sense? Are they in realistic proportion? Does the drapery flow in a way that makes sense? And what about the space? We definitely have an illusion of space, but does the space make sense? How about the table? The shape of the room? There is NO linear perspective here, and NO real study of the human body. The artists of the Northern Renaissance could make their paintings look very real in terms of details—but overall, the space and the body don't look entirely real. This is a very different kind of realism than we saw in the Italian Renaissance. In the Italian Renaissance, their realism was based on the use of science (anatomy) and math (linear perspective and geometry). The realism of the Northern Renaissance was NOT based on science and math, but it WAS based on a very close observation of the world.

- https://youtu.be/WdDzs70Txjs

Attributions

Jan van Eyck's Ghent Altarpiece

Dr. Beth Harris and Dr. Steven Zucker provide a description, historical perspective, and analysis of Jan van Eyck's Ghent Altarpiece.

First, we look at it when it's closed:

- https://youtu.be/udgNvPpDb2I

And now when it's open:

- https://youtu.be/JVhwinCiELI

Jan van Eyck, Ghent Altarpiece, completed 1432, oil on wood, 11′ 5″ × 7′ 6″ (Saint Bavo Cathedral, Ghent, Belgium).

Arnolfini Portrait

Dr. Beth Harris and Dr. Steven Zucker provide a description, historical perspective, and analysis of Jan Van Eyck's *The Arnolfini Portrait*.

- https://youtu.be/9ODhKqFaugQ

Jan Van Eyck, *The Arnolfini Portrait*, tempera and oil on wood, 1434 (National Gallery, London).

Attributions

CC licensed content, Shared previously

Hugo van der Goes

Dr. Beth Harris and Dr. Steven Zucker provide a description, historical perspective, and analysis of Hugo van der Goes's *The Adoration of the Kings (Monforte Altar)*.

- https://youtu.be/B0eHEo-f6fc

Hugo van der Goes, *The Adoration of the Kings (Monforte Altar)*, c. 1470, oil on oak, 147 x 242 cm (Gemäldegalerie, Staatliche Museen zu Berlin)

External Link
View this painting up close in the Google Art Project: • https://www.google.com/culturalinstitute/asset-viewer/the-adoration-of-the-kings-monforte-altar/rAHnypStsAfV2g?projectId=art-project

Attributions

CC licensed content, Shared previously

Van der Weyden's Deposition

David Drogin and Beth Harris provide a description, historical perspective, and analysis of Rogier van der Weyden's *Deposition*.

- https://youtu.be/SLf_oAkngP4

Rogier van der Weyden, *Deposition*, c. 1435 (Prado, Madrid)

The Unicorn in Captivity

Dr. Beth Harris and Dr. Steven Zucker provide a description, historical perspective, and analysis of *The Unicorn in Captivity*.

- https://youtu.be/26WASJHF46A

The Unicorn in Captivity (one of seven woven hangings popularly known as the *Unicorn Tapestries* or the *Hunt of the Unicorn*), 1495–1505, South Netherlandish, wool, silk, silver, and gilt (The Cloisters, The Metropolitan Museum of Art)

External Link

View this painting up close in the Google Art Project:

- https://www.google.com/culturalinstitute/asset-viewer/the-unicorn-in-captivity-from-the-unicorn-tapestries/6QHwPO4q4grNtA?projectId=art-project

---

Attributions

Chapter 4:
1400–1500—Art in Italy

Chapter 4 Overview

What You'll Learn To Do: Examine Italian Renaissance art and its impact on art history.

In Chapter 4 we will examine Italian Renaissance art. We will look at how artists like Donatello contributed to the development of Western art. It is imperative to understand Italian Renaissance art in order to see how it impacted later artistic developments.

Learning Activities

The learning activities for this module include:

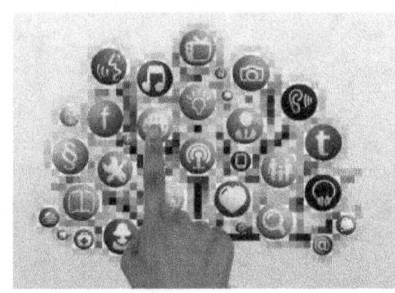

- **Review:** Key Learning Items

Florence

- **Read:** Florence in the Early Renaissance
- **Watch:** Orsanmichele (4:52)
- **Read:** Bruelleschi & Ghiberti, The Sacrifice of Isaac (includes a video: 5:24)
- **Watch:** Linear Perspective (4:15)
- **Read:** Early Applications of Linear Perspective
- **Watch:** Donatello's Works (four videos: 7:23, 5:34, 4:33, and 5:40)
- **Read:** Contrapposto
- **Read:** Masaccio's Tribute Money (includes a video: 8:03)
- **Read:** Masaccio's Holy Trinity (includes a video: 8:36)
- **Watch:** Fra Angelico's The Annunciation (11:36)
- **Read:** Fra Filippo Lippi (includes a video (3:56)
- **Watch:** Piero della Francesca's Portraits of the Duke and Duchess of Urbino (3:57)
- **Watch:** Botticelli's Birth of Venus (3:59)
- **Read:** Alberti

Venice

- **Read:** Introduction to Venice
- **Watch:** Bellini's St. Francis (8:22)
- **Watch:** Mantegna's Works (two videos: 4:41)

Attributions

CC licensed content, Original

- Art History II. **Provided by**: Extended Learning Institute of Northern Virginia Community College. **Located at**: http://eli.nvcc.edu/. **License**: *CC BY: Attribution*

Public domain content

- Image of Finger. **Authored by**: geralt. **Located at**: https://pixabay.com/en/finger-touch-hand-structure-769300/. **License**: *Public Domain: No Known Copyright*

Key Learning Items

Key Questions to Ask

While you are reviewing the content of this module, consider the following questions:

- Why was Florence such an important city for the development of Renaissance art?
- What did early Renaissance art look like?
- What were some of the key developments in Renaissance art?
- How did Renaissance art look different from earlier art?

Key Vocabulary Terms

- linear perspective
- vanishing point
- orthogonals
- horizon line
- contrapposto

- idealized

- free-standing sculpture

- classical architecture

- coffers

- columns

- pediment

- entablature

- pilasters

- barrel vault

- Ionic capital

- Corinthian capital

- fluting

Here are links to art history glossaries that will help you better understand the above key vocabulary terms.

- ArtLex: Art Dictionary

    ○ http://www.artlex.com/

- About.com: Art History

    ○ http://arthistory.about.com/od/glossary/l/bl_Art-Glossary.htm

- Artcyclopedia: A Guide to Fine Art

    ○ http://www.artcyclopedia.com/

Attributions

CC licensed content, Original

Florence in the Early Renaissance

The Renaissance really gets going in the early years of fifteenth century in Florence. In this period, which we call the Early Renaissance, Florence is not a city in the unified country of Italy, as it is now. Instead, Italy was divided into many city-states (Florence, Milan, Venice etc.), each with their own form of government.

Now, we normally think of a Republic as a government where everyone votes for representatives who will represent their interests to the government (remember the pledge of allegiance: "and to the republic for which it stands…"). However, Florence was a Republic in the sense that there was a constitution which limited the power of the nobility (as well as laborers) and ensured that no one person or group could have complete political control (so it was far from our ideal of everyone voting, in fact a very small percentage of the population had the vote). Political power resided in the hands of middle-class merchants, a few wealthy families (such as the Medici, important art patrons who would later rule Florence) and the powerful guilds.

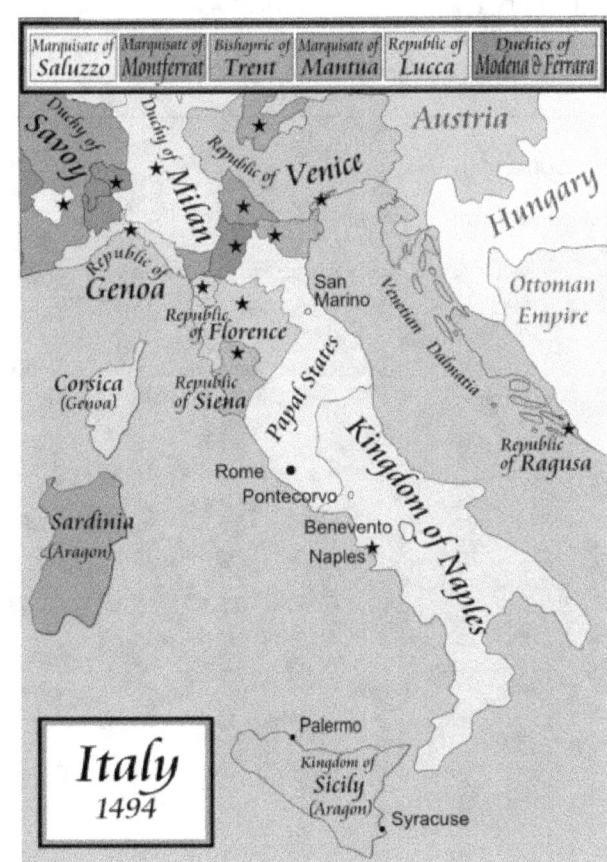

Figure 1. Map of Italy in 1494

Why Florence?

So, why did the extraordinary rebirth of the Renaissance begin in Florence? There are several answers to that question: Extraordinary wealth accumulated in Florence during this period among a growing middle and upper class of merchants and bankers. With the accumulation of wealth often comes a desire to use it to enjoy the pleasures of life—and not an exclusive focus on the hereafter.

Florence saw itself as the ideal city state, a place where the freedom of the individual was guaranteed, and where many citizens had the right to participate in the government (this must have been very different than living in the Duchy of Milan, for example, which was ruled by a succession of Dukes with absolute power) In 1400 Florence was engaged in a struggle with the Duke of Milan. The Florentine people feared the loss of liberty and respect for individuals that was the pride of their Republic.

Luckily for Florence, the Duke of Milan caught the plague and died in 1402. Then, between 1408 and 1414 Florence was threatened once again, this time by the King of Naples, who also died before he could successfully conquer Florence. And in 1423 the Florentine people prepared for war against the son of the Duke of Milan who had threatened them earlier. Again, luckily for Florence, the Duke was defeated in 1425. The Florentine citizens interpreted these military "victories" as signs of God's favor and protection. They imagined themselves as the "New Rome"—in other words, as the heirs to the Ancient Roman Republic, prepared to sacrifice for the cause of freedom and liberty.

> **Important!** The Florentine people were very proud of their form of government in the early 15th century (as we are of our democracy). A republic is, after all, a place that respects the opinions of individuals, and we know that individualism was a very important part of the Humanism that thrived in Florence in the 15th century.

Attributions

CC licensed content, Shared previously

- Florence in the Early Renaissance. **Authored by**: Dr. Beth Harris and Dr. Steven Zucker. **Provided by**: Khan Academy. **Located at**: https://web.archive.org/web/20140215025423/http://smarthistory.khanacademy.org/Florence.html. **License**: *CC BY-NC-SA: Attribution-NonCommercial-ShareAlike*

- Italy 1494 v2. **Authored by**: Capmo and MapMaster. **Located at**: https://commons.wikimedia.org/wiki/File:Italy_1494_v2.png. **License**: *CC BY-SA: Attribution-ShareAlike*

Orsanmichele

Dr. Beth Harris and Dr. Steven Zucker provide a description, historical perspective, and analysis of Orsanmichele in Florence.

- https://youtu.be/-V51ZjxFeH4

Orsanmichele, Florence, 1349 loggia (1380–1404 upper stories).

Attributions

Bruelleschi & Ghiberti, The Sacrifice of Isaac

Dr. Beth Harris and Dr. Steven Zucker provide a description, historical perspective, and analysis of Brunelleschi' and Ghiberti's competition panels.

- https://youtu.be/uvgBSJPiQ8Y

Filippo Brunelleschi & Lorenzo Ghiberti, *Sacrifice of Isaac*, competition panels, Baptistery doors, gilded bronze relief, 1401-2 (Bargello, Florence)

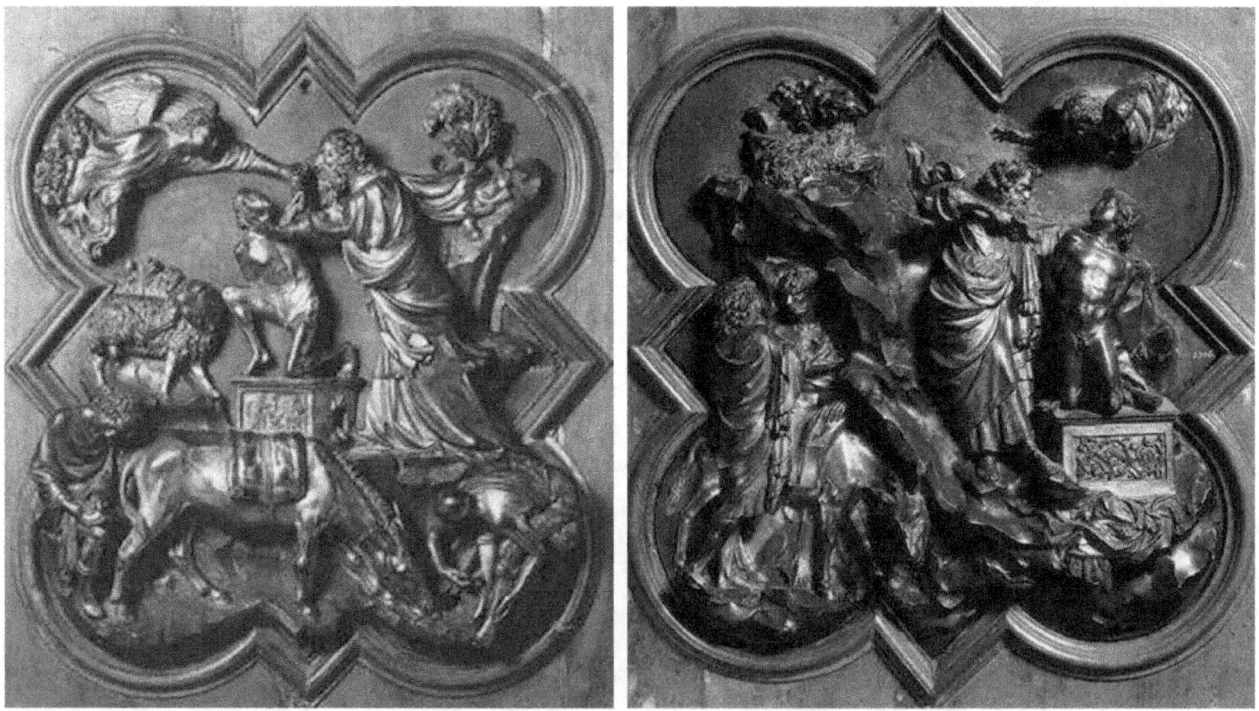

Figure 1. (left) Brunelleschi's competition piece; (right) Ghiberti's competition piece

The Baptistry

There are three buildings that mark the spiritual center of Florence, the Cathedral (with its dome by Brunelleschi), the bell tower (or campanile, designed by Giotto and decorated with reliefs by Andrea Pisano), and the Baptistery. The Baptistery is a sixth or seventh century octagonal building with three entrances and was particularly beloved by the citizens of Florence, who had been baptized there for centuries.

The Commission for the Doors

In 1401, the cloth merchant's guild decided to commission a second set of doors for the Florence Baptistery.

The major guilds of Florence had considerable power and were often responsible for maintaining and developing the city's major public buildings—the cloth merchant's guild was the most powerful among the guilds.

One set of doors had already been created by Andrea Pisano and were completed in 1360. Two panels survive from the competition for the second set, Brunelleschi's entry and Ghiberti's entry. Ghiberti won by a narrow margin.

The Historic Context

And to set the scene—just when the competition was announced, the city-state of Florence was threatened with invasion by the Duke of Milan—their powerful arch enemy. But in 1402, the Duke of Milan died suddenly, and Florence was spared.

In the aftermath, Florence experienced an enormous sense of civic pride—including pride in being a Republic where its citizens lived freely. They saw themselves as the heir to the ancient Roman republic and the golden age of Athens in the fifth century BCE.

Linear Perspective

Dr. Beth Harris and Dr. Steven Zucker provide an introduction to Filippo Brunelleschi's experiment regarding linear perspective (c. 1420) in front of the Baptistry in Florence.

- https://youtu.be/bkNMM8uiMww

Attributions

CC licensed content, Shared previously

Early Applications of Linear Perspective

Representing the Body

What renaissance artists had clearly achieved through the careful observation of nature, including studies of anatomical dissections, was the means to recreate the 3-dimensional physical reality of the human form on 2-dimensional surfaces. In part, the key to this achievement lay in understanding the underlying, hidden structure of the human body which then enabled the artist to produce realistic representations of what he saw on the flat surface of a wall (in the case of frescoes) or on a wooden panel or paper (in the case of drawings).

Artists in the early 15th century had learned to portray the human form with faithful accuracy through careful observation and anatomical dissection, and in 1420 Brunelleschi's experiment provided a correspondingly accurate representation of physical space. Antonio Manetti, Brunelleschi's biographer, writing a century later, describes the experiment based on careful mathematical calculation.

Perspective and Architecture

It seems reasonable that Brunelleschi devised the method of perspective for architectural purposes—he is said by Manetti to have made a ground plan for the Church of Santo Spirito in Florence (1434–82) on the basis of which he produced a perspective drawing to show his clients how it would look after it was built. We can compare this drawing with a modern photo of the actual church. Download this video clip (http://www.mcm.edu/academic/galileo/ars/ars.mpeg) to watch a crossfade back and forth between the original perspective drawing and the modern photograph. It is clear how effective the new technique of mathematical perspective was in depicting spatial reality.

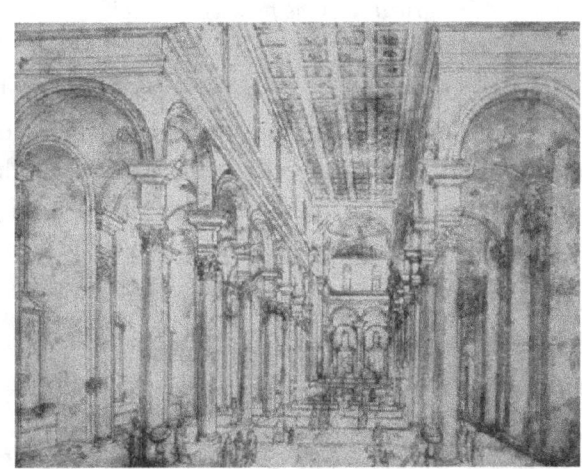

Figure 1. The Church of Santo Spirito

The Body in Space

But this was just the beginning. Ten years later, the painter Masaccio applied the new method of mathematical perspective even more spectacularly—in the fresco *The Holy Trinity,* where the barrel vaulted ceiling is incredible in its complex, mathematical use of perspective.

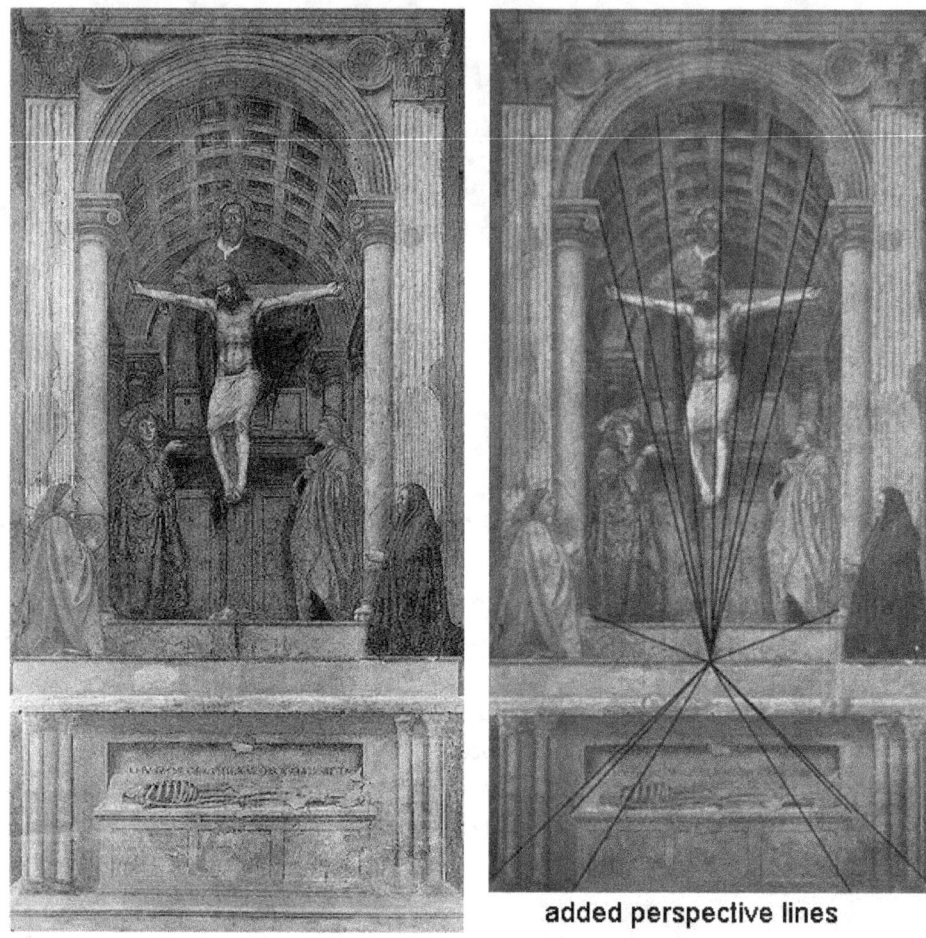

added perspective lines

Figure 2. (left) Masaccio, Holy Trinity, 1427, fresco (Santa Maria Novella, Florence); (right) Here lines overlay Masaccio's actual geometric framework to make clear the structure of the perspective itself.

From the geometry it is actually possible to work backwards to accurately measure and reconstruct the full 3-dimensional space that Masaccio depicts, illustrating exactly, Brunelleschi's interest in being able to translate schemata directly between two and three-dimensional spaces. It was not long before a decisive step was taken by Leon Battista Alberti, who published a treatise on perspective, *Della Pitture (or On Painting),* in 1435. Once Alberti's treatise was published, knowledge of perspective no longer had to be passed on by word of mouth. For some it became a matter of consuming artistic, even philosophical interest.

Attributions

CC licensed content, Shared previously

- Early Applications of Linear Perspective. **Authored by**: Dr. Joseph Dauben. **Provided by**: Khan Academy. **Located at**: https://web.archive.org/web/20140215023927/http://smarthistory.khanacademy.org/applications-of-linear-perspective-in-the-renaissance.html. **License**: *CC BY-NC-SA: Attribution-NonCommercial-ShareAlike*

Donatello's Works

Dr. Beth Harris and Dr. Steven Zucker provide a description, historical perspective, and analysis of several of Donatello's works: *David*, *Saint Mark*, *Feast of Herod*, and *Equestrian Monument of Gattamelata*.

David

- https://youtu.be/6kUUJJV_MNA

Donatello, *David*, bronze, late 1420s to the 1460s, likely the 1440s (Museo Nazionale del Bargello, Florence)

Saint Mark

- https://youtu.be/A8GQfq3U96M

Donatello, *St. Mark*, 1411–13, marble, 93″ (236 cm), Orsanmichele, Florence

Feast of Herod

- https://youtu.be/J9_ouZpBknM

Donatello, *Feast of Herod*, panel on the baptismal font of Siena Cathedral, Siena, Italy, Gilded bronze, 1423–27.

Equestrian Monument of Gattamelata

- https://youtu.be/6dWHPHELCKU

Donatello, *Equestrian Monument of Gattamelata* (Erasmo da Narni), 1445–53, bronze, 12 feet, 2 inches high, Piazza del Santo, Padua

- Donatello, David. **Authored by**: Dr. Steven Zucker and Dr. Beth Harris. **Provided by**: Khan Academy. **Located at**: https://www.khanacademy.org/humanities/renaissance-reformation/early-renaissance1/sculpture-architecture-florence/v/donatello-david-bronze-c-1440s. **License**: *CC BY-NC-SA: Attribution-NonCommercial-ShareAlike*

- Donatello, Saint Mark. **Authored by**: Dr. Steven Zucker and Dr. Beth Harris. **Provided by**: Khan Academy. **Located at**: https://www.khanacademy.org/humanities/renaissance-reformation/early-renaissance1/sculpture-architecture-florence/v/donatello-st-mark-1411-13. **License**: *CC BY-NC-SA: Attribution-NonCommercial-ShareAlike*

- Donatello, Feast of Herod. **Authored by**: Dr. Steven Zucker and Dr. Beth Harris. **Provided by**: Khan Academy. **Located at**: https://www.khanacademy.org/humanities/renaissance-reformation/early-renaissance1/sculpture-architecture-florence/v/donatello-feast-of-herod-1423-27. **License**: *CC BY-NC-SA: Attribution-NonCommercial-ShareAlike*

- Donatello, Equestrian Monument of Gattamelata. **Authored by**: Dr. Beth Harris and Dr. Steven Zucker. **Provided by**: Khan Academy. **Located at**: https://www.khanacademy.org/humanities/renaissance-reformation/early-renaissance1/sculpture-architecture-florence/v/donatello-equestrian-monument-of-gattamelata. **License**: *CC BY-NC-SA: Attribution-NonCommercial-ShareAlike*

Contrapposto

Anatomy and Spirituality in the Middle Ages

The medieval jamb sculptures are almost completely symmetrical—that is one side of their body is nearly identical to the other side. They look stiff, rigid, and incapable of movement. They don't seem to belong to our world—and they're not supposed to. They're suupposed to look other-worldly and spiritual and were made for the doorway of a church. They are also expressionless, and lacking in individuality.

Their bodies match the shape of the columns that they are attached to, and because they are attached, they are NOT free-standing. Their drapery does not reveal the forms of their bodies very much. In addition, the figures are elongated. This sculpture reveals the intense spirituality of the Middle Ages: the figures sense the unimportance of the material world, and the importance of things we can't see or touch—the soul, heaven and God.

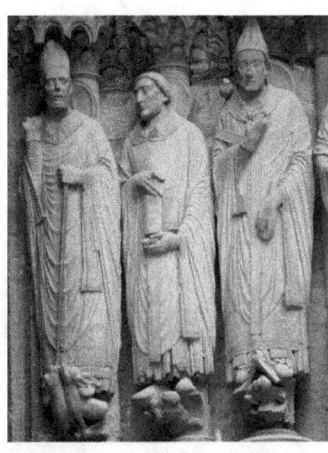

Figure 1. The jamb statue at the Cathedral of Chartres.

Contrapposto and Classical Greece

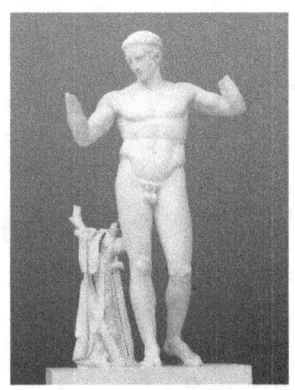

Figure 2. Diadumenos, National Archaeological Museum of Athens

Our Ancient Greek sculpture, on the other hand, **is** free-standing—he was not made to fit on architecture. The artist was obviously much more concerned with the anatomy of the body. The figure is idealized (nude, athletic, young, beautiful proportions). The ancient Greeks invented the position that this sculpture is standing in. The positionis called contrapposto. Contrapposto means weight shift, and we can see that the figure has his weight shifted onto his right leg, while his left leg is bent.

The figure is asymmetrical—different on the different sides of his body. As a result of contrapposto, this figure looks as though it can move, and it looks so much more alive! This sculpture tells us about Greek Humanism and their sense of the enormous potential of the human mind and the beauty of the human body.

Attributions

Masaccio's Tribute Money

Dr. Beth Harris and Dr. Steven Zucker provide a description, historical perspective, and analysis of Masaccio's *The Tribute Money*.

- https://youtu.be/oDPNSPbjzQ8

Masaccio, *The Tribute Money*, 1427, fresco, 247 cm × 597 cm (97.2 in × 235 in), (Brancacci Chapel, Santa Maria del Carmine, Florence).

The Tribute Money is one of many frescos painted by Masaccio (and a lesser artist Masolino) in the Brancacci chapel. All of the frescos tell the story of the life of St. Peter (considered to be the first Pope). The story of the Tribute Money is told in three separate scenes within the same fresco. This way of telling an entire story in one painting is called a continuous narrative.

A Story Unfolds

In this fresco, a Roman tax collector (in a short orange tunic and no halo) demands tax money from Christ and the twelve apostles who don't have the money to pay. Christ (centrally located, wearing a pink robe gathered in at the waist, with a blue toga-like wrap) points to the left, and says to Peter "so that we may not offend them, go to the lake and throw out your line. Take the first fish you catch; open its mouth and you will find a four-drachma coin. Take it and give it to them for my tax and yours." Christ has performed a miracle by making the money needed to pay the tax collector appear in the mouth of a fish. These two things are shown in the same image, *even though they happen at different moments*. Thus, in the center of the fresco (scene 1), we see the tax collector demanding the money, and Christ instructing Peter. On the far left (scene 2), we see Peter kneeling down and removing money from the mouth of a fish, and on the far right (scene 3), St. Peter pays the tax collector.

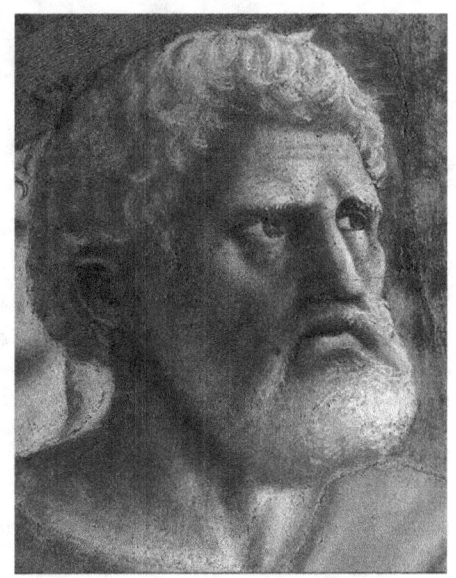

Figure 1. Peter in the central scene

In the fresco, the tax collector appears twice, and St. Peter appears three times (you can find them easily if you look for their clothing).

We are so used to one moment appearing in one frame (think of a comic book, for example) that the unfolding of the story within one image (and out of order!) seems very strange to us. But with this technique, which was also used by the ancient Romans, Masaccio is able to make an entire drama unfold on the wall of the Brancacci chapel.

In the central, first scene, the tax collector points down with his right hand, and holds his left palm open, impatiently insisting on the money from Christ and the apostles. He stands with his back to us, which creates the illusion of three dimensional space in the image. Like Donatello's *St. Mark* from Orsanmichele in Florence, he stands naturally, in contrapposto, with his weight on his left leg, and his right knee bent. The apostles (Christ's followers) look worried and anxiously watch to see what will happen. St. Peter (wearing a large deep orange colored toga draped over a blue shirt) is confused, as he seems to be questioning Christ and pointing over to the river, but he also looks like he is willing to believe Christ.

The gestures really help to tell the story. Peter seems confused. Christ is saying, go to the lake and get the money from the mouth of a fish to pay the tax collector, and Peter looks like he is in total disbelief.

And the tax collector looks upset. He stands in contrapposto and seems to say, "look, no special deals for you guys. You have to pay your taxes right now." He has his back turned to us (which helps to create an illusion of space) and you can see his mouth open and palm out, like he wants the money!

Only Christ is completely calm because he is performing a miracle.

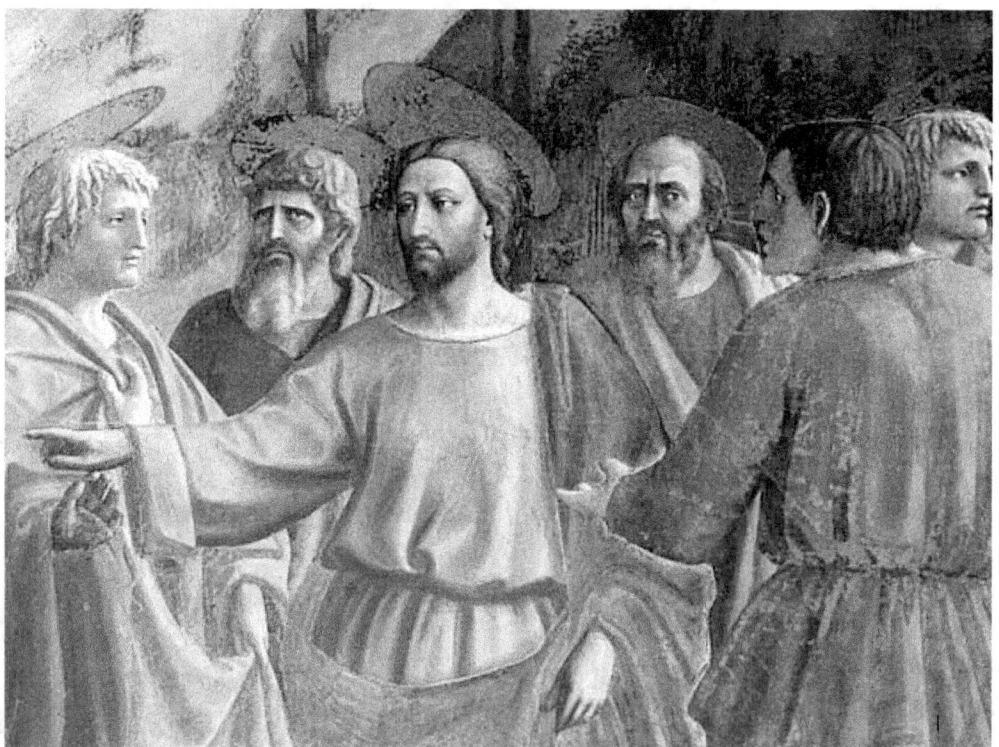

Figure 2. Christ as he directs Saint Peter

Look down at the feet—how the light travels through the figures, and is stopped when it encounters the figures, and so the figures cast shadows (do you see them there on the ground?).

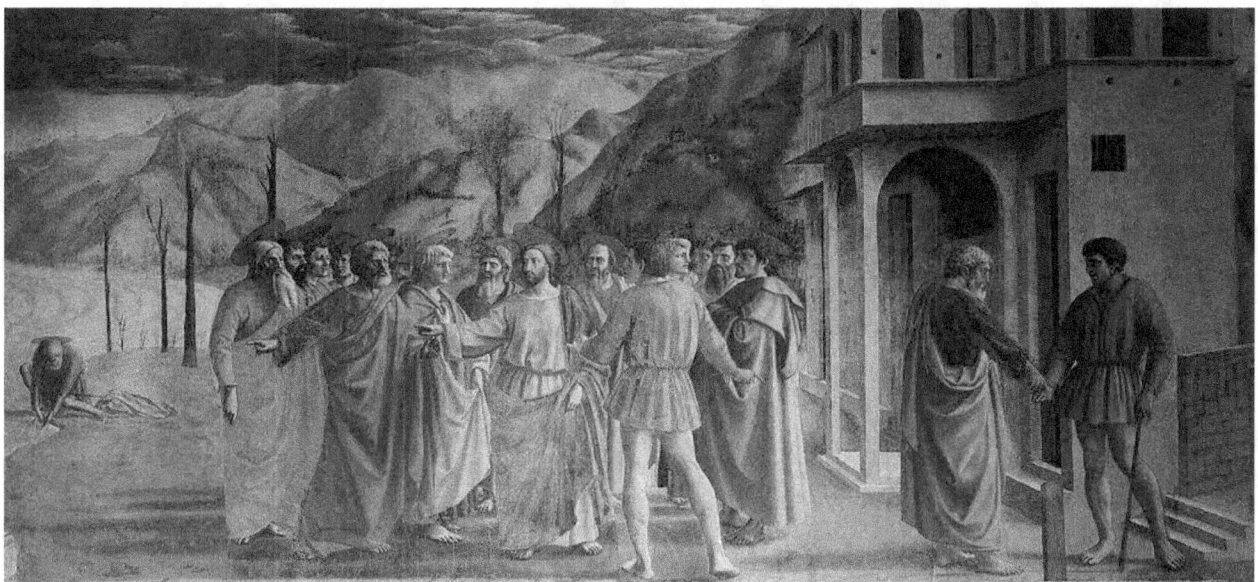

Figure 3. Masaccio, The Tribute Money, fresco, 1427 (Brancacci Chapel, Santa Maria del Carmine, Florence)

Masaccio is the first artist since classical antiquity to paint cast shadows. What that does is make the fresco so much more real—it is like the figures are really standing out in a landscape, with the light coming from one direction, and the sun in the sky, hitting all the figures from the same side and casting shadows on the ground. For the first time, there is almost a sense of weather!

Attributions

CC licensed content, Shared previously

Public domain content

Masaccio's Holy Trinity

Dr. Beth Harris and Dr. Steven Zucker provide a description, historical perspective, and analysis of Masaccio's *Holy Trinity*.

- https://youtu.be/Kl4Dcj9o570

Masaccio, *Holy Trinity*, c. 1427, Fresco, 667 × 317 cm, (Santa Maria Novella, Florence).

The *Holy Trinity*

Masaccio was the first painter in the Renaissance to incorporate Brunelleschi's discovery in his art. He did this in his fresco called the *Holy Trinity*, in Santa Maria Novella, in Florence.

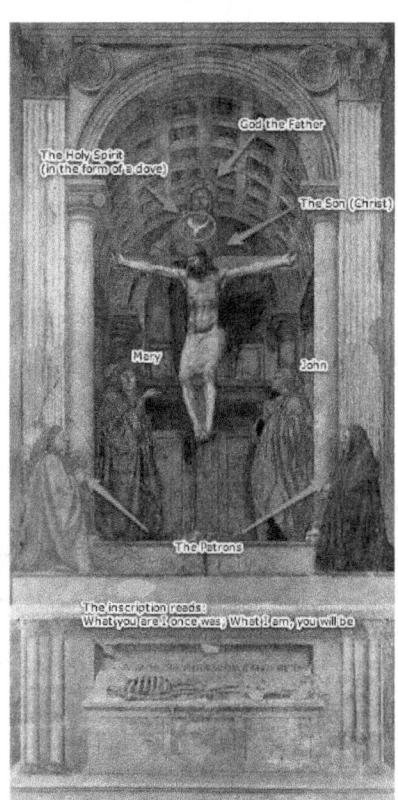

Figure 1. Holy Trinity with labels

Have a close look at the painting (figure 1) and look back at a perspective diagram in figure 2 of Early Applications of Linear Perspective. You see the orthogonals in the lines that form the coffers in the ceiling of the barrel vault (look for diagonal lines that appear to recede into the distance). Because Masaccio painted from a low viewpoint, as though we were looking up at Christ, we see the orthogonals in the ceiling, and if we traced all of the orthogonals the vanishing point would be below the base of the cross.

My favorite part of this fresco is God's feet. Actually, you can only really see one of them. ??Think about this for a moment. God is standing in this painting. Doesn't that strike you as odd just a little bit? This may not strike you all that much when you first think about it because our idea of God, our picture of God in our minds eye—as an old man with a beard—is very much based on Renaissance images of God. So, here Masaccio imagines God as a man. Not a force or a power, or something abstract, but as a man. A man who stands—his feet are foreshortened, and he weighs something and is capable of walking! In medieval art, God was often represented by a hand, just a hand, as though God was an abstract force or power in our lives, but here he seems so much like a flesh and blood man. This is a good indication of Humanism in the Renaissance.

Masaccio's contemporaries were struck by the palpable realism of this fresco, as was Vasari who lived over one hundred years later. Vasari wrote that "the most beautiful thing, apart from the figures, is the barrel-vaulted ceiling drawn in perspective and divided into square compartments containing rosettes foreshortened and made to recede so skillfully that the surface looks as if it is indented."

The Architecture

One of the other amazing things about this painting is the use of **classical architecture** (from ancient Greece and Rome). Masaccio borrowed much of what we see from ancient Roman architecture, and may have been helped by Brunelleschi. Study thediagram below and make sure you can identify the differentarchitectural elements. If you want to read more about these terms lookin the glossary in the back of your book.

- **Coffers**—the indented squares that decorate the ceiling

- **Column**—a round, supporting element in architecture. In this painting we see an attached column.

- **Pilasters**—a shallow, flattened out columns attached to a wall—it is only decorative, and has no supporting function

- **Barrel Vault**—vault means ceiling, and a barrel vault is a ceiling in the shape of a round arch

- **Iconic and Corinthian Capitals**—a capital is the decorated top of a column or pilaster. An**ionic** capital has a scroll shape (like the ones on the attached columns in the painting), and a **Corinthian** capital has leaf shapes.

- **Fluting**—the vertical, indented lines or grooves that decorated the pilasters in the painting. Fluting could also be used on a column

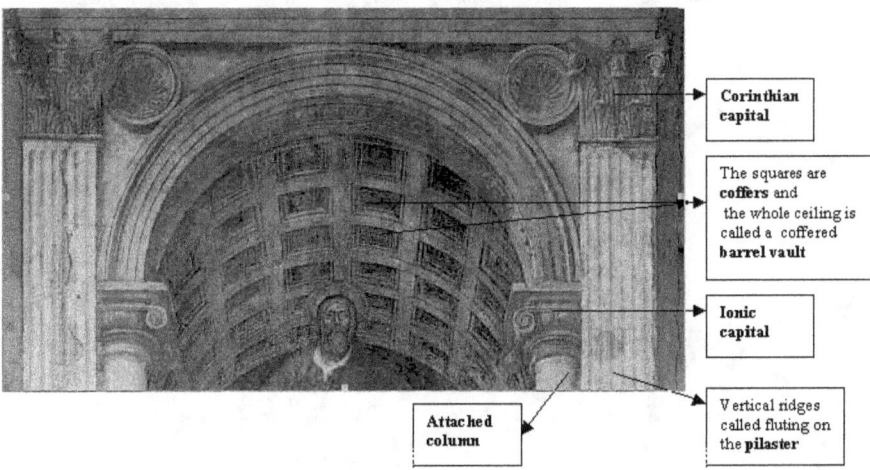

Figure 2. Architecture in the Holy Trinity.

Attributions

CC licensed content, Shared previously

- Masaccio's Holy Trinity. **Provided by**: Khan Academy. **Located at**: https://web.archive.org/web/20140215025859/http://smarthistory.khanacademy.org/holy-trinity-santa-maria-novella-florence.html. **License**: *CC BY-NC-SA: Attribution-NonCommercial-ShareAlike*

Fra Angelico's The Annunciation

Dr. Beth Harris and Dr. Steven Zucker provide a description, historical perspective, and analysis of Fra Angelico's *The Annunciation*.

- https://youtu.be/3B-V_pG3HPQ

Fra Angelico, *The Annunciation*, c. 1438–47, fresco, 230 × 321 cm (Convent of San Marco, Florence).

Attributions

CC licensed content, Shared previously

Piero della Francesca's Portraits of the Duke and Duchess of Urbino

Dr. Beth Harris and Dr. Steven Zucker provide a description, historical perspective, and analysis of Piero della Francesca's *Portraits of the Duke and Duchess of Urbino, Federico da Montefeltro and Battista Sforza*.

- https://youtu.be/XIkryXkz8a4

Piero della Francesca, *Portraits of the Duke and Duchess of Urbino, Federico da Montefeltro and Battista Sforza*, 1467–72, tempera on panel, 47 × 33 cm (Galleria degli Uffizi, Florence)

Attributions

CC licensed content, Shared previously

Botticelli's Birth of Venus

Dr. Beth Harris and Dr. Steven Zucker provide a description, historical perspective, and analysis of Botticelli's *The Birth of Venus*.

- https://youtu.be/tdp22elrY7s

Sandro Botticelli, *The Birth of Venus*, 1483–85, tempera on panel, 68 × 109 5/8″ (172.5 × 278.5 cm), Galeria degli Uffizi, Florence

Attributions

Introduction to Venice

Venice—Another World

Petrarch, the fourteenth-century Tuscan poet, called Venice a *mundus alter* or "another world," and the city of canals really is different from other Renaissance centers like Florence or Rome.

Venice is a cluster of islands, connected by bridges and canals, and until the mid-nineteenth century the only way to reach the city was by boat. In the fifteenth and sixteenth centuries, Venice suffered numerous outbreaks of the plague and engaged in major wars, such as the War of the League of Cambrai. But it also boasted a stable republican government led by a *Doge* (meaning "Duke" in the local dialect), wealth from trade, and a unique location as a gateway between Europe and Byzantium.

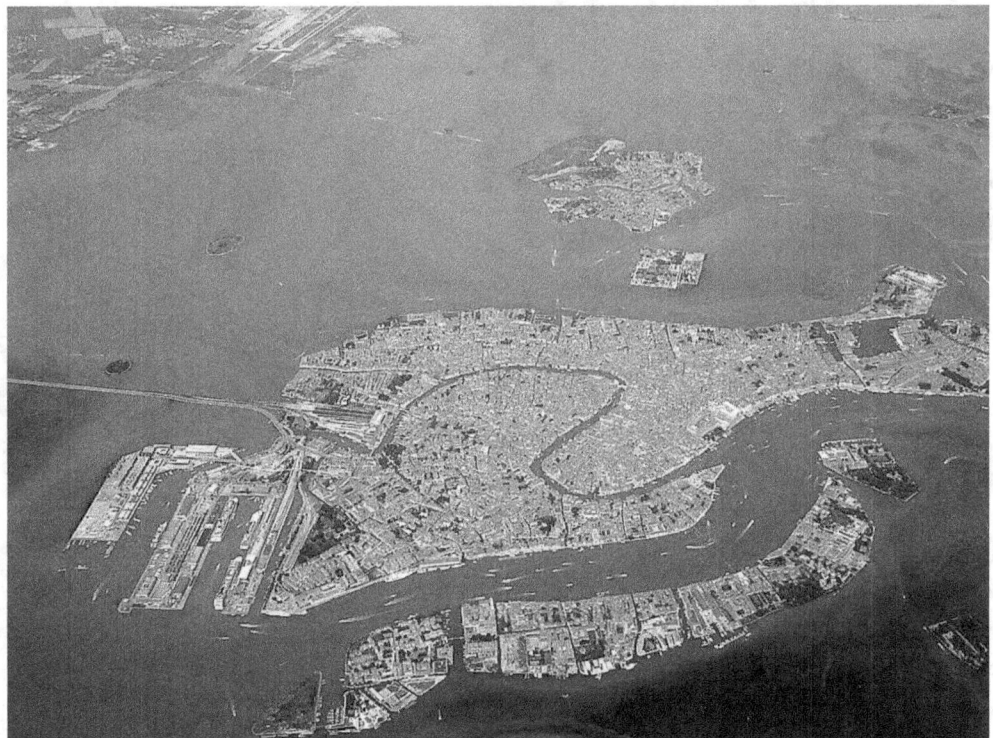

Figure 1. Bird's-eye-view of Venice

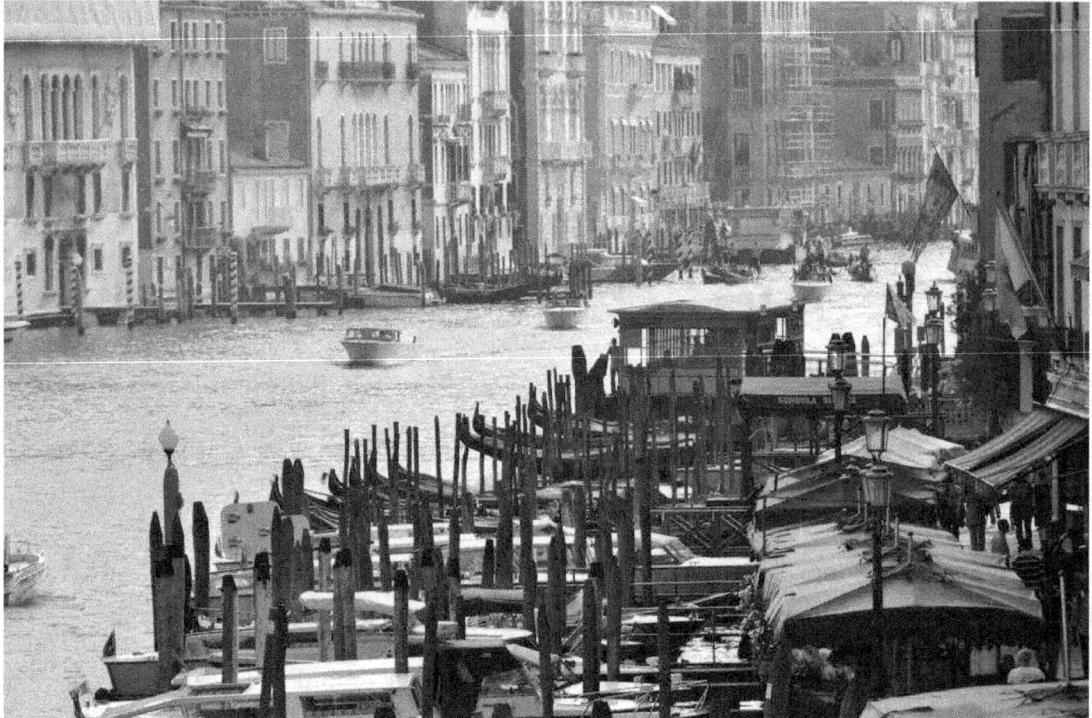

Figure 2. The Grand Canal in modern Venice

The Venetian Style

Painting in Early and High Renaissance Venice is largely grouped around the Bellini family: Jacopo, the father, Giovanni and Gentile, his sons, and Andrea Mantegna, a brother-in-law. Giorgione may have trained in the Bellini workshop and Titian was apprenticed there as a boy.

The Bellinis and their peers developed a particularly Venetian style of painting characterized by deep, rich colors, an emphasis on patterns and surfaces, and a strong interest in the effects of light.

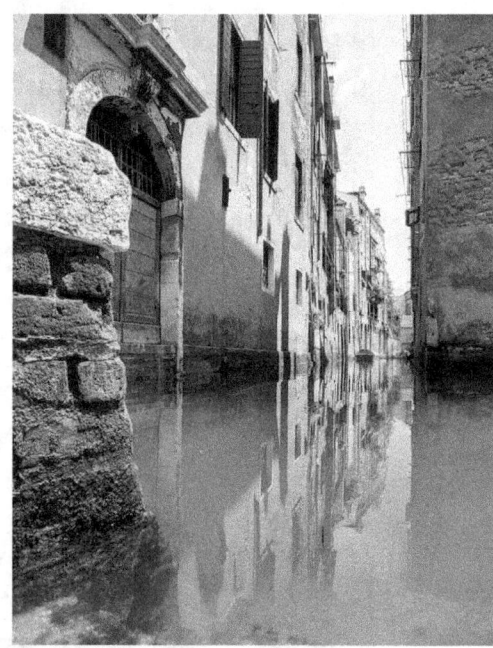

While Venetian painters knew about linear perspective and used the technique in their paintings, depth is just as often suggested by gradually shifting colors and the play of light and shadow. Maybe Venetian painters were inspired by the glittering gold mosaics and atmospheric light in the grand Cathedral of San Marco, founded in the 11th century? Or maybe they looked to the watery cityscape and the shifting reflections on the surfaces of the canals?

Figure 3. The reflections in a canal in Venice

Oil Paint

The Venetian trade networks helped to shape local painting practices. Ships from the East brought luxurious, exotic pigments, while traders from Northern Europe imported the new technique of oil painting. Giovanni Bellini combined the two by the 1460s–70s. In the next few decades, oil paint largely supplanted tempera, a quick-drying paint bound by egg yolk that produced a flat, opaque surface. (Botticelli's *Birth of Venus* is one example of tempera paint).

To achieve deep tones, Venetian painters would prepare a panel with a smooth white ground and then slowly build up layer-upon-layer of oil paint. Since oil dries slowly, the colors could be blended together to achieve subtle gradations. (See this effect in the rosy flush of the *Venus of Urbino's* cheeks by Titian or in the blue-orange clouds in Giorgione's *Adoration of the Shepherds*.) Plus, when oil paint dries it stays somewhat translucent. As a result, all of those thin layers reflect light and the surface shines. Painting conservators have even found that Bellini, Giorgione, and Titian added ground-up glass to their pigments to better reflect light.

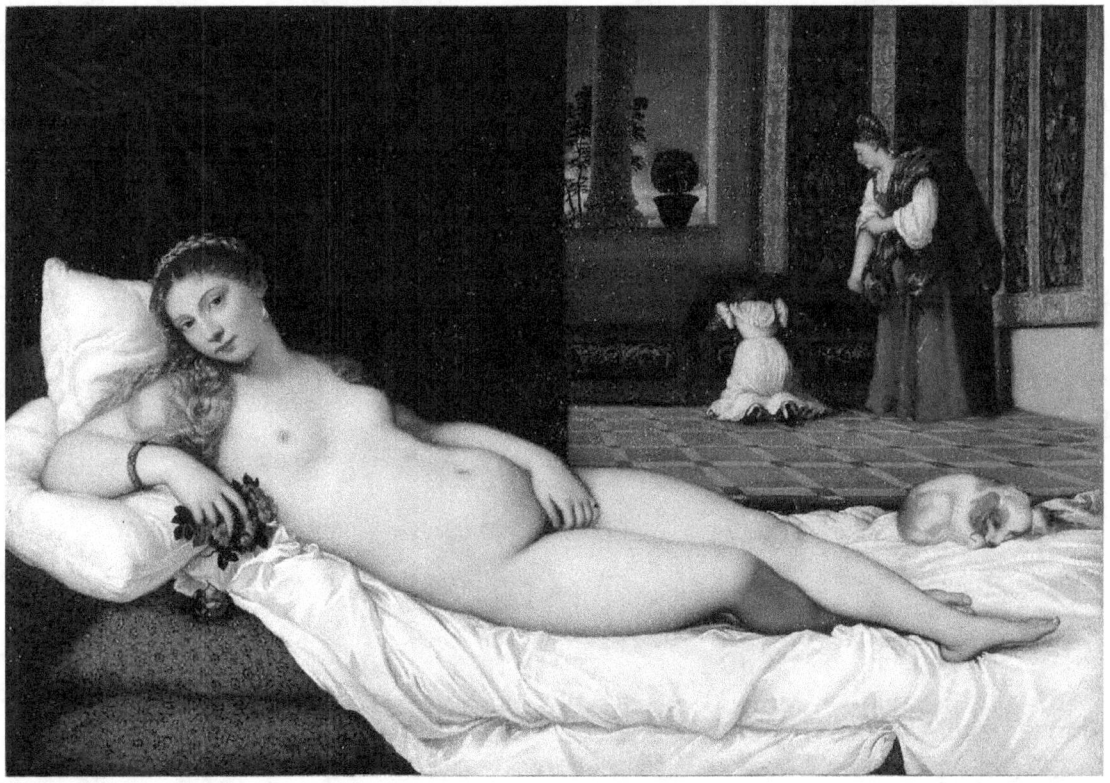

Figure 4. Titian, Venus of Urbino, 1538, oil on canvas, 119.20 × 165.50 cm (Galleria degli Uffizi, Florence)

Venetian Painting in the Sixteenth Century

Over the next century Venetian painters pursued innovative compositional approaches, like asymmetry, and they introduced new subjects, such as landscapes and female nudes. The increasing use of pliable canvas over solid wood panels encouraged looser brushstrokes. Painters also experimented more with the textural differences produced by thick versus thin application of paint.

In the Late Renaissance Titian's mastery was rivaled by Tintoretto and Veronese. Each attempted to out-paint the other with increasingly dynamic and sensual subjects for local churches and international patrons. (Phillip II of Spain was particularly enamored with Titian's mythological nudes.) The trio transformed saintly stories into relatable human drama (Veronese's *The Dream of St. Helena*), captured the wit and wealth of portrait subjects (Titian's *Portrait of a Man*), and interpreted nature through mythological tales (Tintoretto's *The Origin of the Milky Way*).

Attributions

CC licensed content, Shared previously

- **Venice. Authored by**: Dr. Heather A. Horton. **Provided by**: Khan Academy. **Located at**: https://web.archive.org/web/20140215043451/http://smarthistory.khanacademy.org/venice.html. **License**: *CC BY-NC-SA: Attribution-NonCommercial-ShareAlike*

- Venice as seen from the air 01. **Authored by**: Chris 73. **Provided by**: Wikimedia Commons. **Located at**: https://commons.wikimedia.org/wiki/File:Venice_as_seen_from_the_air_01.jpg. **License**: *CC BY-SA: Attribution-ShareAlike*

- Hotel Ca' Sagredo - Grand Canal - Rialto - Venice Italy Venezia. **Authored by**: gnuckx. **Located at**: https://flic.kr/p/8yRaEG. **License**: *CC BY: Attribution*

- Down to the waterline. **Authored by**: Carlos Andru00e9s Reyes. **Located at**: https://flic.kr/p/uvaXHG. **License**: *CC BY: Attribution*

Public domain content

- Venere di Urbino. **Authored by**: Tiziano. **Located at**: https://commons.wikimedia.org/wiki/File:Tiziano_-_Venere_di_Urbino_-_Google_Art_Project.jpg. **License**: *Public Domain: No Known Copyright*

Bellini's St. Francis

Dr. Beth Harris and Dr. Steven Zucker provide a description, historical perspective, and analysis of Giovanni Bellini's *Saint Francis in the Desert*.

- https://youtu.be/STs6h1qUSGs

Giovanni Bellini, *Saint Francis in the Desert*, c. 1480, oil and tempera on poplar, 124.5 × 141.9 cm (The Frick Collection, New York).

External Link

View this work up close on the Google Art Project:

- https://www.google.com/culturalinstitute/asset-viewer/st-francis-in-the-desert/egGQB5gOZujX4g?projectId=art-project

Attributions

Mantegna's Works

Dr. Beth Harris and Dr. Steven Zucker provide a description, historical perspective, and analysis of two of Andrea Mantegna's works: *Dead Christ* and *Saint Sebastian*.

Dead Christ

- https://youtu.be/XGZvvQ8BmjY

Andrea Mantegna, *Dead Christ*, c. 1480–1500,tempera on canvas (Pinacoteca di Brera, Milan)

Saint Sebastian

- https://youtu.be/y1_N1GAsS5I

Andrea Mantegna, *Saint Sebastian*, oil on wood panel, c. 1456–59 (Kunsthistorisches Museum, Vienna)

Chapter 5:
1500–1600–High Renaissance and Mannerism in Italy

Chapter 5 Overview

What You'll Learn To Do: Examine High Renaissance and Mannerist art and their influence on later art history.

In Chapter 5 we will examine High Renaissance and Mannerist art. We will look at how artists like Michelangelo contributed to the development of Western art. It is imperative to understand High Renaissance and Mannerist art in order to see how it impacted later artistic developments.

Learning Activities

The learning activities for this module include:

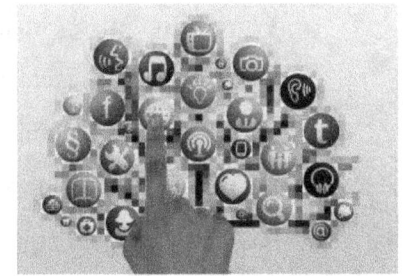

- **Review:** Key Learning Items

The Renaissance

- **Read:** Art and Science in the Renaissance
- **Read:** Toward the High Renaissance

Leonardo da Vinci

- **Read:** Leonardo da Vinci Introduced (includes a video: 3:17)
- **Read:** Virgin of the Rocks (includes a video: 5:37)
- **Read:** The Last Supper (includes a video: 7:39)
- **Read:** Mona Lisa (includes a video: 8:38)

Michelangelo

- **Read:** Michelangelo Introduced
- **Watch:** Pietà (3:38)
- **Read:** David (includes a video: 5:39)
- **Read:** Moses (includes a video: 4:11)

- **Read:** Sistine Chapel Ceiling (includes a video: 6:46)

- **Read:** Sistine Chapel: Last Judgment (includes a video: 7:28)

Raphael

- **Watch:** Marriage of the Virgin (5:03)

- **Watch:** Madonna of the Goldfinch (3:26)

- **Read:** School of Athens (includes a video: 10:41)

- **Watch:** Alba Madonna (6:55)

Bramante

- **Watch:** Tempietto (6:00)

- **Read:** Saint Peter's Basilica (includes a video: 4:27)

Venetian Painting

- **Review:** Introduction to Venetian Painting

- **Watch:** Giorgione, The Tempest (5:54)

- **Watch:** Bellini & Titian, Feast of the Gods (3:04)

- **Watch:** Titian, Bacchus & Ariadne (3:30)

- **Read:** Titian, Madonna of the Pesaro Family (includes a video: 7:05)

- **Watch:** Titian, Venus of Urbino (4:01)

- **Read:** Veronese, Feast in the House of Levi (includes a video: 6:09)

- **Watch:** Tintoretto, The Origin of the Milky Way (5:18)

Mannerism

- **Read:** Introduction to Mannerism

- **Watch:** Parmigianino's Madonna of the Long Neck (4:43)

- **Watch:** Bronzino and the Mannerist Portrait (10:29)

- **Watch:** El Greco's Adoration of the Shepherds (4:09)

Attributions

Key Learning Items

Learning Objectives

After successful completion of this module, you will be able to:

- Understand and apply the concepts and terminology of High Renaissance and Mannerist art
- Investigate and apply the fundamental questions we ask when looking at art objects from this movement
- Discuss, collaborate, and generate understanding as to the meaning of High Renaissance and Mannerist art
- Assess and evaluate the impact of High Renaissance and Mannerist art on the continued evolution of Western art

Key Questions to Ask

While you are reviewing the content of this module, consider the following questions:

- What are the characteristics of the High Renaissance?
- How does Michelangelo's approach to creating art differ from Raphael and da Vinci?
- What role did Humanism play in the High Renaissance?
- How is Venetian art different from art produced in central Italy?
- What are the characteristics of Mannerism?

Key Vocabulary Terms

- Humanism
- sfumato
- pietà

- ignudi

- sibyls

- tempietto

- Greek cross

- basilica

- central plan church

- Mannerism

Here are links to art history glossaries that will help you better understand the above key vocabulary terms.

- ArtLex: Art Dictionary

    ◦ http://www.artlex.com/

- About.com: Art History

    ◦ http://arthistory.about.com/od/glossary/l/bl_Art-Glossary.htm

- Artcyclopedia: A Guide to Fine Art

    ◦ http://www.artcyclopedia.com/

Attributions

CC licensed content, Original

Art and Science in the Renaissance

Renaissance artists had contributed greatly to man's knowledge by the time Galileo was doing his first work at Pisa. The humanist artists of the Italian renaissance had performed their own dissections to promote the study of anatomy, they had invented mathematical perspective to make possible the accurate, realistic portrayal of physical space. The literary humanists had managed to revive all sorts of classics, in particular the works of Plato. Christopher Columbus had directly challenged the limits to the finite European world of Ptolemy's geography. In short, the bounds of human knowledge were expanding at a rapid rate.

Thus it comes as no surprise that Italian artists of Galileo's day responded favorably, even enthusiastically, to the new discoveries that science itself was making. It was Galileo's friend, Lodovico Cigoli, who incorporated the latest discoveries of his telescope, hot off the press in Galileo's *Siderius Nuncius* (1610) in his own version of the *Assumption of the Virgin*, painted just two years later in

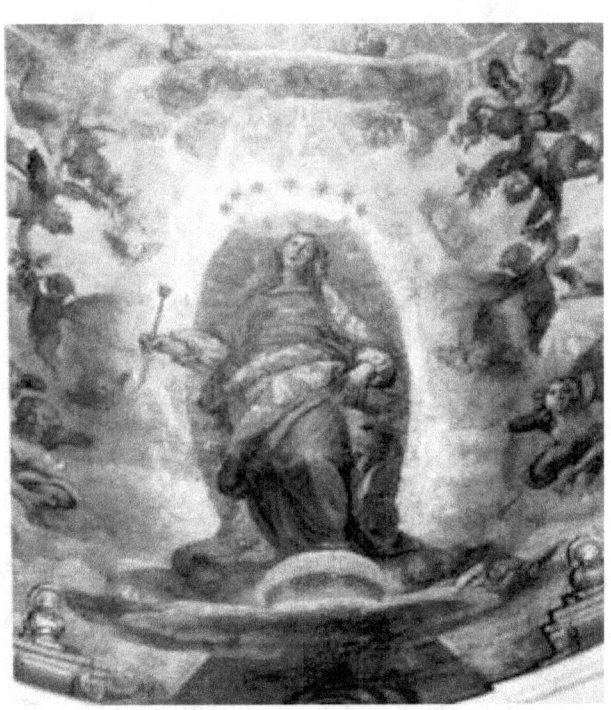

Figure 1. Ludovico Cigoli, Assumption of the Virgin, Pauline Chapel, Santa Maria Maggiore (1612)

1612. In Cigoli's painting, notice the treatment of the moon at the Virgin's feet—rendered as though it were seen though the telescope, exactly as Galileo had recorded it in his own pen and ink drawing only a few years earlier.

Mathematics is the Language of Nature

In closing, how can we draw together all of the diverse strands of renaissance artistic realism, especially Brunelleschi's discovery of perspective, with Galileo's experiments on acceleration and his analysis of projectile motion?

It is clear that renaissance artists were seeking a new world, thanks in part to mathematics and the new perspective, literally, that mathematics provided. Galileo not only inherited this perspective, but a philosophical sense as well that had been inspired by renaissance philosophers (especially Neoplatonists), namely that the underlying reality of the world we perceive is essentially mathematical.

This was exactly the point made in Riccioli's dramatic depiction of the hand of God (figure 2), creating the world according to mathematical principles, number and weight and measure written clearly on his fingers to make no mistake about the inherent, essential mathematical character of the physical world.

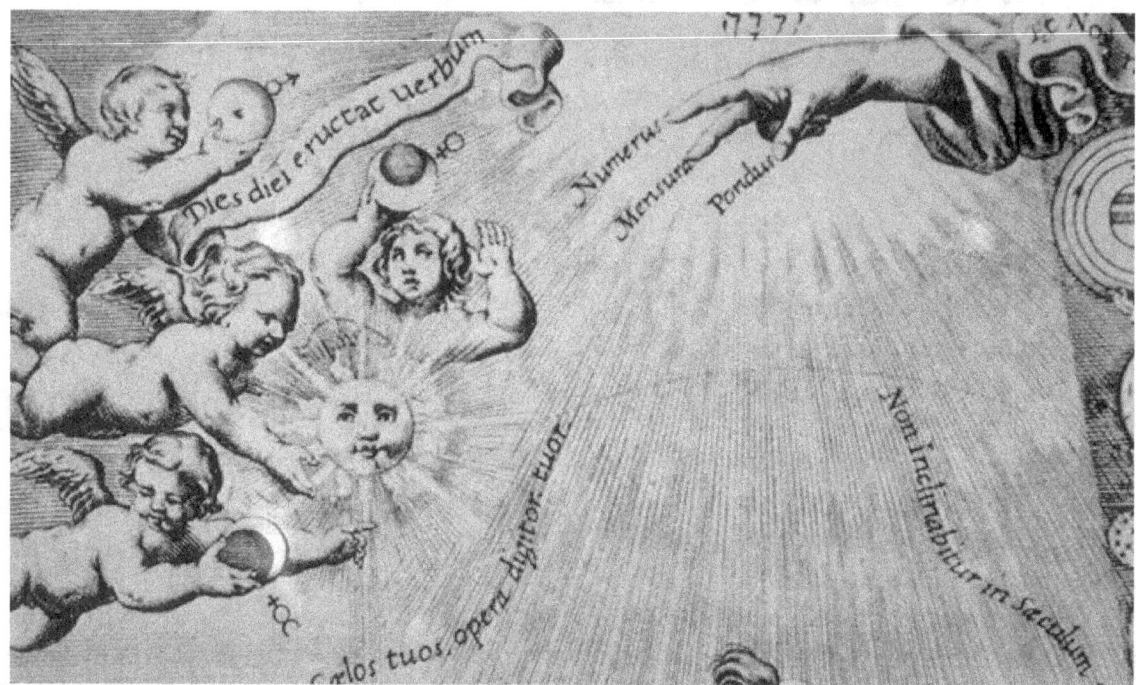

Figure 2. G.B. Riccioli, Almagestum Novum (1651)

Renaissance artists and architects had already succeeded in translating physical space into the mathematical terms of proportion and perspective to produce works that tricked the eye and rivaled nature.

Galileo used mathematics with equal skill to reveal the underlying structure of physical space and motion to show that these, too, could be reduced to mathematical analysis. In connecting physical space and real motion—which could be observed experimentally—with the ideal and uniform change of his neoplatonic, mathematical world, Galileo also serves to bridge the early stages of the scientific revolution in Europe—and figures like Copernicus and Kepler—with the later unifying achievements of Descartes, Newton and Leibniz.

Thus in a very direct way, it was mathematics that not only facilitated the art of renaissance perspective, but provided the key as well to Galileo's New Science of Nature. In both cases, the essence of physical reality was understood in terms that could be reduced to basic mathematical principles.

Attributions

Toward the High Renaissance

The High Renaissance is just that—the height of the Renaissance! When you think of the Renaissance, the names that come to mind are probably the artists of this period: Leonardo and Michelangelo, for instance. When many people think of the greatest work of art in the Western world, they think of Michelangelo's *Sistine Ceiling*. This is a period of big, ambitious projects.

The High Renaissance versus the Early Renaissance

So, what exactly is the High Renaissance, and how is it different from the Early Renaissance? As the Humanism of the Early Renaissance grows, a problem begins to develop. Have a look again at Fra Filippo Lippi's *Madonna and Child with Angels* (figure 1). We see in this painting an image of the Madonna and Christ Child that has become so real, the figures so human, that we can hardly tell that these are spiritual figures (except for the faint shadow of a halo). On the other hand, we have seen that in the Middle Ages, if you want to make your figure spiritual then you sacrifice its realism.

Its almost as if there is this feeling in the Early Renaissance that if you want to be spiritual, then your painting can't look real, and if you want it to be real, then it loses some spirituality. It has to be one or the other. Well, Leonardo da Vinci comes along, and basically says—you don't have to make that choice. It's not either/or. Leonardo is able to create figures who are physical and real—just as real as Lippi's or Masaccio's figures and yet they have an undeniable and intense spirituality at the same time. So we can say that Leonardo unites the real and spiritual, or soul and substance.

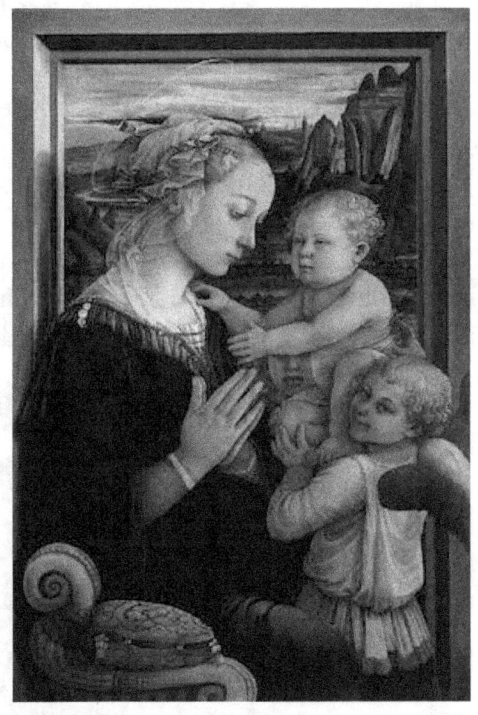

Figure 1. Fra Filippo Lippi, *Madonna and Child with Angels*

The best way to see this is in the *Baptism of Christ* by Verrocchio (figure 2), who Leonardo was apprenticed to when he was young.

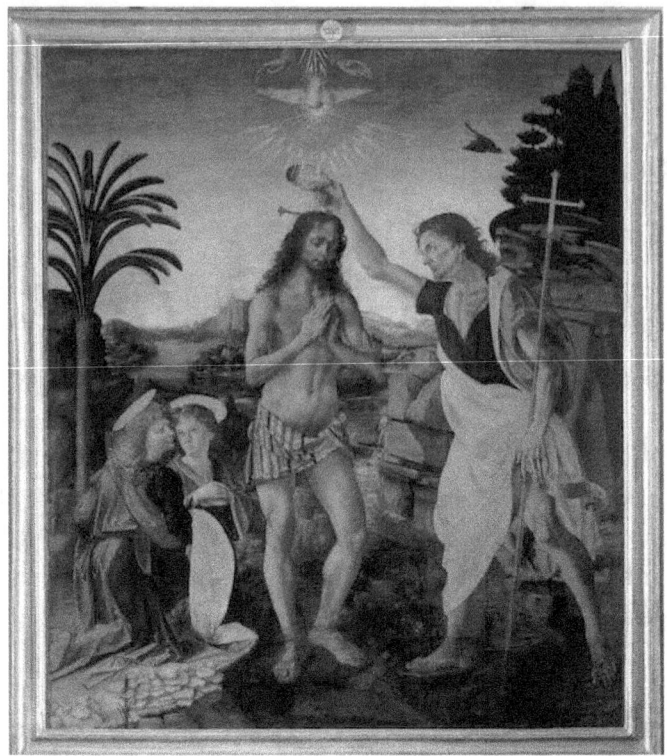

Figure 2. Andrea del Verrocchio (with Leonardo), Baptism of
Christ, 1470–75, oil and tempera on panel, 70 3/4 × 59 3/4
inches or 180 × 152 cm (Galleria degli Uffizi, Florence)

Verocchio asked Leonardo to paint one of the angels in his paining of the *Baptism of Christ,* that we see here. Can you tell which angel is Leonardo's?

One angel should look more like a boy—that's the Early Renaissance angel (the one painted by Verrocchio) and the other angel should look like a High Renaissance angel, like a spiritual figure—truly like an angel sent by God from heaven (that's Leonardo's angel).

Can you tell which one is by Leonardo? Take a minute and look closely.

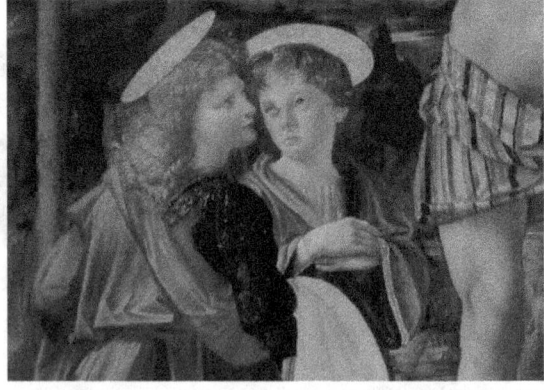

Figure 3. Leonardo and Verocchio's angels

It's the angel on the left. Leonardo's angel is ideally beautiful and moves in a graceful and complex way, twisting to the left but raising her head up and to the right. Figures that are elegant and ideally beautiful are a key characteristic of the High Renaissance.

Attributions

CC licensed content, Shared previously

Leonardo da Vinci Introduced

> The heavens often rain down the richest gifts on human beings, but sometimes they bestow with lavish abundance upon a single individual beauty, grace and ability, so that whatever he does, every action is so divine that he distances all other men, and clearly displays how his greatness is a gift of God and not an acquirement of human art. Men saw this in Leonardo.
>
> —Vasari, on Leonardo

Dr. David Drogin discusses Leonarda da Vinci's Letter to the Duke of Milan.

- https://youtu.be/URcpchlTNBY

Leonardo's Early Life & Training

Leonardo was born illegitimate to a prominent Tuscan family of potters and notaries. He may have traveled from Vinci to Florence where his father worked for several powerful families including the Medici. At age seventeen, Leonardo reportedly apprenticed with the Florentine artist Verrocchio. Here, Leonardo gained an appreciation for the achievements of Giotto and Masaccio and in 1472 he joined the artists' guild, Compagnia di San Luca. Because of his family's ties, Leonardo benefited when Lorenzo de' Medici (the Magnificent) ruled Florence. By 1478 Leonardo was completely independent of Verrocchio and may have then met the exiled Ludovico Sforza, the future Duke of Milan, who would later commission the Last Supper.

Leonardo in Milan

Four years later, Leonardo arrived in Milan bearing a silver lyre (which he may have been able to play), a gift for the regent Ludovico from the Florentine ruler, Lorenzo the Magnificent. Ludovico sought to transform Milan into a center of humanist learning to rival Florence.

Leonardo flourished in this intellectual environment. He opened a studio, received numerous commissions, instructed students, and began to systematically record his scientific and artistic investigations in a series of notebooks. The archetypal "renaissance man," Leonardo was an unrivaled painter, an accomplished architect, an engineer, cartographer, and scientist (he was particularly interested in biology and physics). He was influenced by a variety of ancient texts including Plato's Timaeus, Ptolemy's Cosmography, and Vitruvius's On Architecture. Leonardo is credited with having assisted Luca Pacioli with his treatise, Divina Proportione (1509). Joining the practical and the theoretical, Leonardo designed numerous mechanical devices for battle, including a submarine, and even experimented with designs for flight.

In a now famous letter, Leonardo listed his talents to the Duke, focusing mostly on his abilities as a military engineer. The letter begins:

> Having until now sufficiently studied and examined the experiments of all those who claim to be experts and inventors of war machines, and having found that their machines do not differ in the least from those ordinarily in use, I shall make so bold, without wanting to cause harm to anyone, as to address myself to Your Excellency to divulge my secrets to him, and offer to demonstrate to him, at his pleasure, all the things briefly enumerated below.

In ten short paragraphs, Leonardo enumerated the service he could perform for the Duke — he said (among other things) that he could build bridges, tunnels, fortresses, and "make siege guns, mortars and other machines, of beautiful and practical shape, completely different from what is generally in use."

What might seem amazing to us is that it is not until the very last paragraph that Leonardo mentions art, and he mentions it so modestly! Here is what he wrote:

> In time of peace, I believe I am capable of giving you as much satisfaction as anyone, whether it be in architecture, for the construction of public or private buildings, or in bringing water from one place to another. Item, I can sculpt in marble, bronze or terracotta; while in painting, my work is the equal of anyone's.

Return to Florence, then France

In 1489, Leonardo secured a long awaited contract with Ludovico and was honored with the title, "The Florentine Apelles," a reference to an ancient Greek painter revered for his great naturalism. Leonardo returned to Florence when Ludovico was deposed by the French King, Charles VII. While there, Leonardo would meet the Niccolò Machiavelli, author of The Prince and his future patron, François I. In 1516, after numerous invitations, Leonardo traveled to France and joined the royal court. Leonardo died on May 2, 1519 in the king's chateau at Cloux.

Leonardo's Death and the Changing Status of the Artist

> Finally, having grown old, he remained ill many months, and, feeling himself near to death, asked to have himself diligently informed of the teaching of the Catholic faith, and of the good way and holy Christian religion; and then, with many moans, he confessed and was penitent; and although he could not raise himself well on his feet, supporting himself on the arms of his friends and servants, he was pleased to take devoutly the most holy Sacrament, out of his bed. The King, who was wont often and lovingly to visit him, then came into the room; wherefore he, out of reverence, having raised himself to sit upon the bed, giving him an account of his sickness and the circumstances of it, showed withal how much he had offended God and mankind in not having worked at his art as he should have done. Thereupon he was seized by a paroxysm, the messenger of death; for which reason the King having

risen and having taken his head, in order to assist him and show him favour, to then end that he might alleviate his pain, his spirit, which was divine, knowing that it could not have any greater honour, expired in the arms of the King. (Vasari)

This story is a good indication of the changing status of the artist. Leonardo, who spent the last years of his life in France working for King Francis I, was often visited by the King! Remember that the artist was considered only a skilled artisan in the Middle Ages and for much of the Early Renaissance.

In the High Renaissance, beginning with Leonardo, we find that artists are considered intellectuals, and that they keep company with the highest levels of society. Quite a change! All of this has to do with Humanism in the Renaissance of course, and the growing recognition of the achievement of great individuals (something virtually unheard of in the Middle Ages!). Artists in the Early Renaissance insisted that they should in fact be considered intellectuals because they worked with their brains as well as with their hands. They defended this position by pointing to the scientific tools that they used to make their work more naturalistic (scientific naturalism): the study of human anatomy, of mathematics and geometry, of linear perspective. These were clearly all intellectual pursuits!

Look closely at the self-portrait in figure 1. Isn't it clear that Leonardo thought of himself as a thinker, a philosopher, an intellectual?

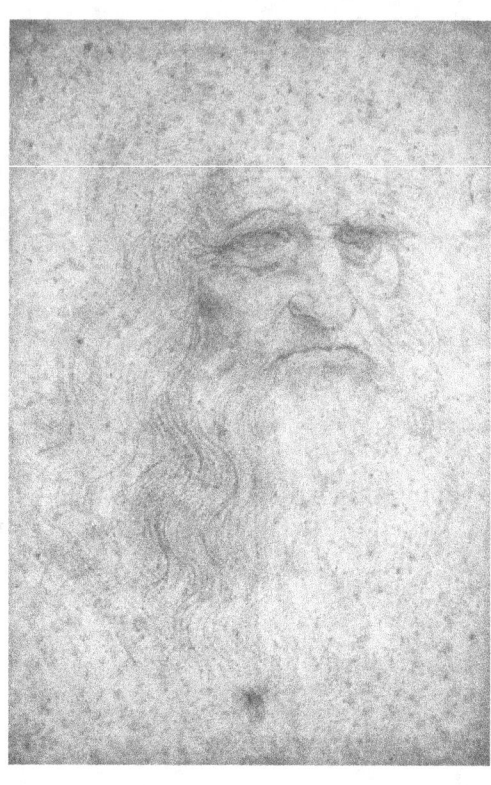

Figure 1. Leonardo da Vinici, Self-Portrait

Leonardo's Naturalism

Ancient Greek physicians dissected cadavers. The early church's rejection of the science of the classical world, along with the possibility of bodily resurrection led to prohibitions against dissection. Both Leonardo and Michelangelo performed them—probably exclusively on the bodies of executed criminals. According to his own count, Leonardo dissected 30 corpses during his lifetime.

Attributions

CC licensed content, Shared previously

- Leonardo da Vinci. **Provided by**: Khan Academy. **Located at**: https://web.archive.org/web/20140215031907/http://smarthistory.khanacademy.org/leonardo-notebooks.html. **License**: *CC BY-NC-SA: Attribution-NonCommercial-ShareAlike*

Virgin of the Rocks

Dr. Beth Harris and Dr. Steven Zucker provide a description, historical perspective, and analysis of Leonardo da Vinci's *The Virgin of the Rocks*.

- https://youtu.be/94xKRkCHlv0

Leonardo da Vinci, *The Virgin of the Rocks*, c. 1491–1508, oil on panel, 189.5 × 120 cm (The National Gallery, London)

Two Versions

There are two versions of Leonardo's *Virgin of the Rocks*. Figure 1 (located in Paris) is Leonardo's original *Virgin of the Rocks* (c. 1483–86) in the Louvre. The other is in London and is the subject of the video you just watched. These two paintings are a good place to start to define the qualities of the new style of the High Renaissance. Leonardo painted both in Milan, where he had moved from Florence.

Normally when we have seen Mary and Christ (in, for example, paintings by Lippi and Giotto), Mary has been enthroned as the queen of heaven. Here, in contrast, we see Mary seated on the ground. This type of representation of Mary is referred to as the Madonna of Humility. Mary has her right arm around the infant Saint John the Baptist who is making a gesture of prayer to the Christ child. The Christ child in turn blesses St. John. Mary's left hand hovers protectively over the head of her son while an angel looks out and points to St. John. The figures are all located in a fabulous and mystical landscape with rivers that seem to lead nowhere and bizarre rock formations. In the foreground we see carefully observed and precisely rendered plants and flowers.

We immediately notice Mary's ideal beauty and the graceful way in which she moves, features typical of the High Renaissance.

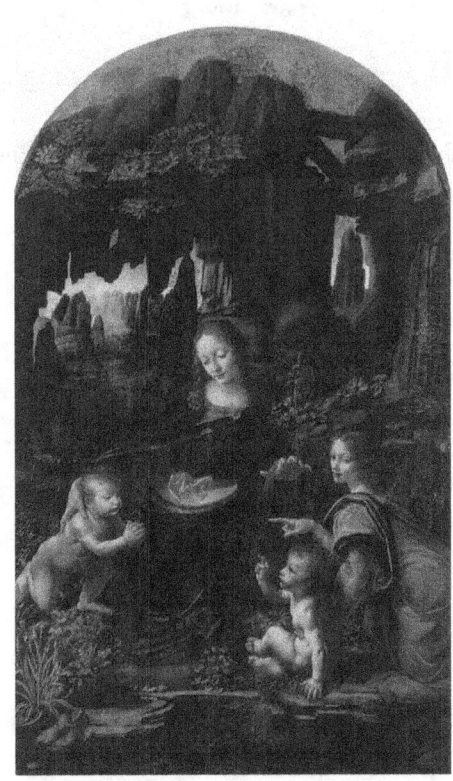

Figure 1. Leonardo da Vinci, *Virgin on the Rocks*

This is the first time that an Italian Renaissance artist has completely abandoned halos. We saw how Fra Filippo Lippi reduced the halo to a narrow ring around Mary's head. Clearly the unreal, symbolic nature of the halo was antithetical to the realism of the Renaissance. It was, in a way, a necessary holdover from the Middle Ages: how else to indicate a figure's divinity?

But Leonardo found another way to indicate divinity — by giving the figures ideal beauty and grace. After all, we would never mistake this group of figures for an ordinary picnic, the way the Lippi's painting of the Madonna and Child with Angels almost looks like a family portrait. We are clearly looking at a mystical vision of Mary, Christ, John the Baptist and an angel in heaven.

The Unified Composition

If we look closely we can see that Leonardo grouped the figures together within a geometric shape of a pyramid (I say pyramid instead of triangle because Leonardo is very concerned with creating an illusion of space—and a pyramid is three dimensional). He also has the figures gesturing to each other and looking at each other. Both of these innovations serve to unify the composition. This is an important difference from paintings of the Early Renaissance where the figures often looked separate from each other. Sometimes this is referred to as a unified composition.

Another way to think about this is to go back to our discussion of Leonardo's angel in his teacher's painting. There, we talked about the more complex pose of the body of Leonardo's angel. Remember this is the High Renaissance, and things that artists were just learning how to do in the Early Renaissance (like contrapposto) are now easy for the artists of the High Renaissance.

As a result, they can do more with the body—make it more complex, more elegant and more graceful. Similarly, the compositions of the paintings of the High Renaissance are more complex and sophisticated than the compositions of the Early Renaissance. Figures interact more, groups of figures are united into pyramidal compositions.

Attributions

CC licensed content, Shared previously

- Leonardo's Virgin of the Rocks. **Provided by**: Khan Academy. **Located at**: https://web.archive.org/web/20140215032932/ http://smarthistory.khanacademy.org/leonardo-virgin-of-the-rocks.html. **License**: *Public Domain: No Known Copyright*

The Last Supper

Leonardo imagined, and has succeeded in expressing, the desire that has entered the minds of the apostles to know who is betraying their Master. So in the face of each one may be seen love, fear, indignation, or grief at not being able to understand the meaning of Christ; and this excites no less astonishment than the obstinate hatred and treachery to be seen in Judas.

—Georgio Vasari, *Lives of the Artists*, 1568; translated by George Bull

St. Andrew, with his long grey beard, lifts up his hands, expressing the wonder of a simple-hearted old man. St. James Minor . . . lays his hand on the shoulder of St. Peter—the expression is, 'Can it be possible? Have we heard aright?' Bartholomew at the extreme end of the table, has risen perturbed from his seat; he leans forward with a look of eager attention, the lips parted he is impatient to hear more.

—Mrs. Anna Jameson, *Sacred and Legendary Art*, 1848

Dr. Beth Harris and Dr. Steven Zucker provide a description, historical perspective, and analysis of Leonardo da Vinci's *Last Supper*.

- https://youtu.be/iV6_wTrkd70

Leonardo da Vinci, *Last Supper*, 1498, tempera and oil on plaster (Santa Maria della Grazie, Milan)

Subject

The subject of the *Last Supper* is Christ's final meal with his apostles before Judas identifies Christ to the authorities who arrest him. The Last Supper, a Passover Seder, is remembered for two events:

Christ says to his apostles "One of you will betray me," and the apostles react, each according to his own personality. Referring to the Gospels, Leonardo depicts Philip asking "Lord, is it I?" Christ replies, "He that dippeth his hand with me in the dish, the same shall betray me." (Matthew 26) We see Christ and Judas simultaneously reaching toward a plate that lies between them, even as Judas defensively backs away.

Christ blessed the bread and said to the apostles "Take, eat; this is my body" and he blessed the wine and said "Drink from it all of you; for this is my blood of the covenant, which is poured out for the forgiveness of sins" (Matthew 26). These words are the founding moment of the sacrament of the Eucharist.

Iconography

Leonardo's *Last Supper* is dense with symbolic references.

- **Apostles.** Attributes identify each apostle. Judas Iscariot is recognized both as he reaches to toward a plate beside Christ (Matthew 26) and because he clutches a purse containing his reward for identifying Christ to the authorities the following day. Peter, who sits beside Judas, holds a knife in his right hand. This foreshadows that Peter will sever the ear of a soldier as he attempts to protect Christ from arrest.

- **Neo-Platonism.** The balanced composition is anchored by an equilateral triangle formed by Christ's body. He sits below an arching pediment that if completed, traces a circle that would perfectly enclose the triangle. These ideal geometric forms refer to the renaissance interest in Neo-Platonism. In his allegory, "The Cave," the Ancient Greek philosopher Plato emphasized the imperfection of the earthly realm. Geometry, used by the Greeks to express Heavenly perfection, has been used by Leonardo to celebrate Christ as the embodiment of heaven on earth. Neo-Platonism is an element of the humanist revival that reconciles aspects of Greek philosophy with Christian theology.

- **Paradise.** Leonardo rendered a verdant landscape beyond the windows. Often interpreted as paradise, it has been suggested that this heavenly sanctuary can only be reached through Christ.

- **Trinity.** The twelve apostles are arranged as four groups of three and there are also three windows. The number three is often a reference to the Holy Trinity in Catholic art. In contrast, the number four is important in the classical tradition (e.g. Plato's four virtues).

Compared to the Same Subject Painted by Early Renaissance Artists

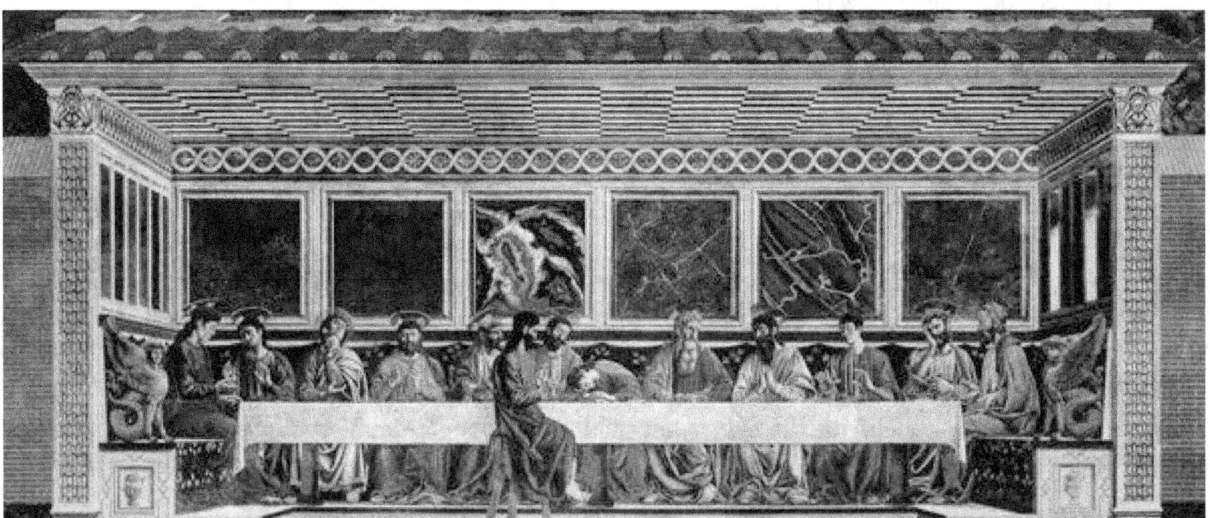

Figure 1. Andrea del Castagno, Last Supper (1447)

Andrea del Castagno's *Last Supper* (1447) is typical of the Early Renaissance. The use of linear perspective in combination with ornate forms such as the sphinxes on the ends of the bench and the marble paneling tend to detract from the spirituality of the event. In contrast, Leonardo simplified the architecture, eliminating unnecessary and distracting details so that the architecture can instead amplify the sense of spirituality. The window and arching pediment even suggest a halo. By crowding all of the figures together, Leonardo uses the table as a barrier to separate the spiritual realm from the viewer's earthly world. Paradoxically, Leonardo's emphasis on spirituality results in a painting that is more naturalistic than Castagno's.

Condition

The Last Supper is in terrible condition. Soon after the painting was completed on February 9, 1498 it began to deteriorate. By the second half of the sixteenth century Giovan Paulo Lomazzo stated that, "the painting is all ruined." Over the past five hundred years the painting's condition has been seriously compromised by its location, the materials and techniques used, humidity, dust, and poor restoration efforts. Modern problems have included a bomb that hit the monastery destroying a large section of the refectory on August 16, 1943, severe air pollution in postwar Milan, and finally, the effects of crowding tourists.

Because Leonardo sought a greater detail and luminosity than could be achieved with traditional fresco, he covered the wall with a double layer of dried plaster. Then, borrowing from panel painting, he added an undercoat of lead white to enhance the brightness of the oil and tempera that was applied on top. This experimental technique allowed for chromatic brilliance and extraordinary precision but because the painting is on a thin exterior wall, the effects of humidity were felt more keenly, and the paint failed to properly adhere to the wall.

There have been seven documented attempts to repair the *Last Supper*. The first restoration effort took place in 1726, the last and most extensive was completed in 1999. Instead of attempting to restore the image, the last conservation effort sought to arrest further deterioration and where possible, uncover Leonardo's original painting. Begun in 1977 and comprising more than 12,000 hours of structural work and 38,000 hours of work on the painting itself, this effort has resulted in an image where approximately 42.5% of the surface is Leonardo's work, 17.5% is lost, and the remaining 40% are the additions of previous restorers. Most of this repainting is found in the wall hangings and the ceiling.

Condition Statistics

- Number of years after its completion that deterioration was noted: 18
- Number of bombs that have hit the refectory: 1
- Number of years needed to complete the recent conservation project: 22
- Number of years that Leonardo needed to complete the painting: 4
- Number of research studies produced during conservation project: 60
- Number of hours spent on the conservation project: 50,000
- Percentage of the surface that is lost: 17.5
- Percentage of the surface painted during the seven previous restorations: 40

- Percentage of the surface that was painted by Leonardo: 42.5

Attributions

CC licensed content, Shared previously

Mona Lisa

Beth Harris and Sal Khan provide a description, historical perspective, and analysis of Leonardo da Vinci's *Mona Lisa*.

- https://youtu.be/3kQ_p2EZX4Q

Leonardo da Vinci, *Mona Lisa*, c. 1503–05, oil on panel 30-1/4 × 21 inches (Musée du Louvre)

Portraits Were Once Rare

We live in a culture that is so saturated with images, it may be difficult to imagine a time when only the wealthiest people had their likeness captured. The weathy merchents of Renaissance Florence could commission a portrait, but even they would likely only have a single portrait painted during their lifetime. A portrait was about more than likeness, it spoke to status and position. In addition, portraits generally took a long time to paint, and the subject would commonly have to sit for hours or days, while the artist captured their likeness.

The Most Recognized Painting in the World

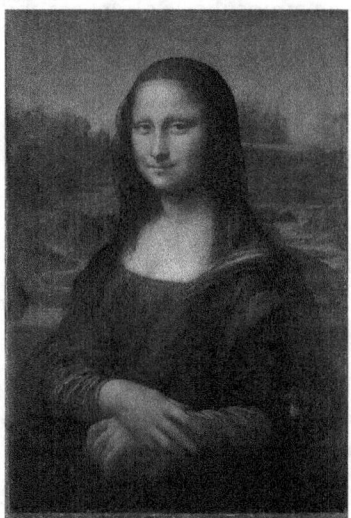

Figure 1. Leonardo da Vinci,
Mona Lisa

The Mona Lisa was originally this type of portrait, but over time its meaning has shifted and it has become an icon of the Renaissance, the most recognized painting in the world. The *Mona Lisa* is a likely a portrait of the wife of a Florentine merchant, and so her gaze would have been meant for her husband. For some reason however, the portrait was never delivered to its patron, and Leonardo kept it with him when he went to work for Francis I, the King of France.

The *Mona Lisa*'s mysterious smile has inspired many writers, singers, and painters. Here's a passage about the *Mona Lisa*, written by the Victorian-era writer Walter Pater:

> We all know the face and hands of the figure, set in its marble chair, in that circle of fantastic rocks, as in some faint light under sea. Perhaps of all ancient pictures time has chilled it least. The presence that thus rose so strangely beside the waters, is expressive of what in the ways of a thousand years men had come to desire. Hers is the head upon which all "the ends of the world are come," and the eyelids are a little weary. It is a beauty wrought out from within upon the flesh, the deposit, little cell by cell, of strange thoughts and fantastic reveries and exquisite passions. Set it for a moment beside one of those white Greek goddesses or beautiful women of antiquity, and how would they be troubled by this beauty, into which the soul with all its maladies has passed!

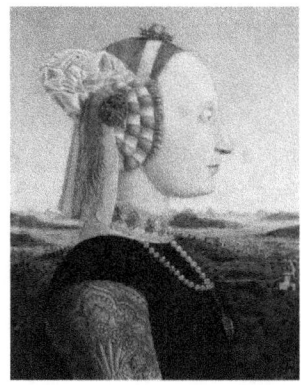

Figure 2. Piero della Francesca, Portrait of Battista Sforza (c. 1465–66)

Early Renaissance artist, Piero della Francesca's *Portrait of Battista Sforza* (figure 2) is typical of portraits during the Early Renaissance (before Leonardo); figures were often painted in strict profile, and cut off at the bust. Often the figure was posed in front of a birds-eye view of a landscape.

A New Formula

With Leonardo's portrait, the face is nearly frontal, the shoulders are turned three-quarters toward the viewer, and the hands are included in the image. Leonardo uses his characteristic sfumato—a smokey haziness, to soften outlines and create an atmospheric effect around the figure.

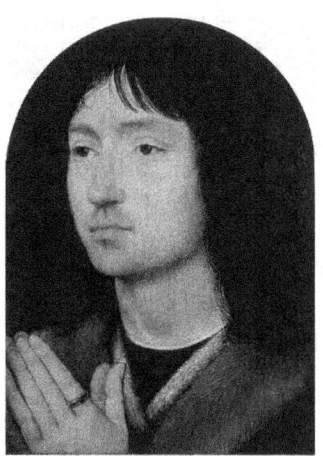

Figure 3. Hans Memling Portrait of a Young Man at Prayer (c. 1485–94)

When a figure is in profile, we have no real sense of who she is, and there is no sense of engagement. With the face turned toward us, however, we get a sense of the personality of the sitter.

Northern Renaissance artists such as Hans Memling (see figure 3) had already created portraits of figures in positions similar to the *Mona Lisa*. Memling had even located them in believable spaces. Leonardo combined these Northern innovations with Italian painting's understanding of the three dimensionality of the body and the perspectival treatment of the surrounding space.

A Recent Discovery

An important copy of the *Mona Lisa* was recently discovered in the collection of the Prado in Madrid. The background had been painted over, but when the painting was cleaned, scientific analysis revealed that the copy was likely painted by another artist who sat beside Leonardo and copied his work, brush-stroke by brush-stroke. The copy gives us an idea of what the *Mona Lisa* might look like if layers of yellowed varnish were removed.

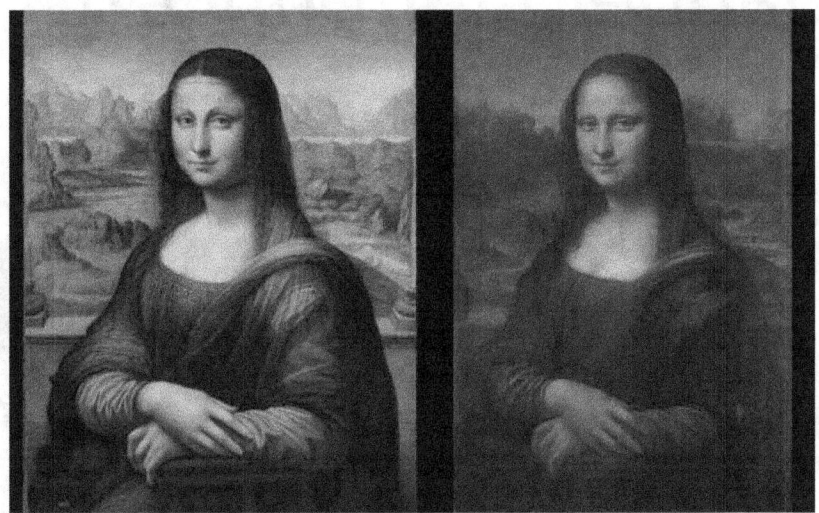

Figure 4. Comparing the copy to the original Mona Lisa.

Attributions

CC licensed content, Shared previously

- Leonardo's MonaLisa. **Provided by**: Khan Academy. **Located at**: https://web.archive.org/web/20140215032805/http://smarthistory.khanacademy.org/leonardo-mona-lisa.html. **License**: *CC BY-NC-SA: Attribution-NonCommercial-ShareAlike*

Michelangelo Introduced

Michelangelo was known as *il divino,* (in English, "the divine one") and it is easy for us to see why. So much of what he created seems to us to be super-human.

When Michelangelo was in his late 20s, he sculpted the 17-foot tall *David*. This colossus seemed to his contemporaries to rival or even surpass ancient Greek and Roman sculpture. *David,* and his later sculptures such as *Moses* and the *Slaves,* demonstrated Michelangelo's astounding ability to make marble seem like living flesh and blood. So much so, it is difficult to imagine that these were created with a hammer and chisel.

In painting, if we look at the ceiling of the Sistine Chapel in Rome, with its elegant nudes and powerful seated figures, and the now-iconic image of the *Creation of Adam,* Michelangelo set a new standard for painting the human figure, one in which the body was not just an actor in a narrative, but emotionally and spiritually expressive on its own.

And then there is his architecture, where Michelangelo reordered ancient forms in an entirely new and dramatic ways.

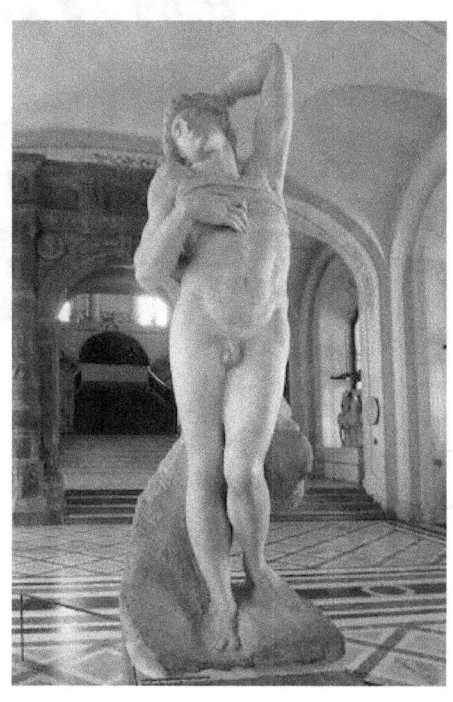

Figure 1. Michelangelo, Dying Slave, 1513–15 (Louvre)

It is no wonder then too, that Vasari, who knew Michelangelo, would write about how Michelangelo excelled in all three arts: painting, sculpture and architecture:

> The great Ruler of Heaven looked down and . . . resolved . . . to send to earth a genius universal in each art. . . . He further endowed him with true moral philosophy and a sweet poetic spirit, so that the world should marvel at the singular eminence of his life and works and all his actions, seeming rather divine than earthy.

Michelangelo was also poet. In the poem below, Michelangelo gives us a sense of the co-existence in his art of a love of both the human (particularly male) body and God.

Sculpture, the first of arts, delights a taste
Still strong and sound: each act, each limb, each bone

Are given life and, lo, man's body is raised,

Breathing alive, in wax or clay or stone.

But oh, if time's inclement rage should waste,

Or maim, the statue that man builds alone,

Its beauty still remains, and can be traced Back to the source that claims it as its own.

Attributions

CC licensed content, Shared previously

- Michelangelo: Sculptor, Painter, Architect and Poet. **Provided by**: Khan Academy. **Located at**: https://web.archive.org/web/20140215023806/http://smarthistory.khanacademy.org/michelangelo.html. **License**: *CC BY-NC-SA: Attribution-NonCommercial-ShareAlike*

Pietà

Dr. Beth Harris and Dr. Steven Zucker provide a description, historical perspective, and analysis of Michelangelo's *Pietà*.

- https://youtu.be/JbWGusfynCw

Michelangelo, *Pietà*, marble, 1498–1500 (Saint Peter's Basilica, Rome)

The Pietà was a popular subject among northern european artists. It means Pity or Compassion, and represents Mary sorrowfully contemplating the dead body of her son which she holds on her lap. This sculpture was commissioned by a French Cardinal living in Rome.

Look closely and see how Michelangelo made marble seem like flesh, and look at those complicated folds of drapery. It is important here to remember how sculpture is made. It was a messy, rather loud process (which is one of the reasons that Leonardo claimed that painting was superior to sculpture!). Just like painters often mixed their own paint, Michelangelo forged many of his own tools, and often participated in the quarrying of his marble—a dangerous job.

When we look at the extraordinary representation of the human body here we remember that Michelangelo, like Leonardo before him, had dissected cadavers to understand how the body worked.

David

Dr. Beth Harris and Dr. Steven Zucker provide a description, historical perspective, and analysis of Michelangelo's *David*.

- https://youtu.be/-oXAekrYytA

Michelangelo, *David*, marble, 1501–04, marble, 517 cm (Galleria dell'Accademia, Florence)

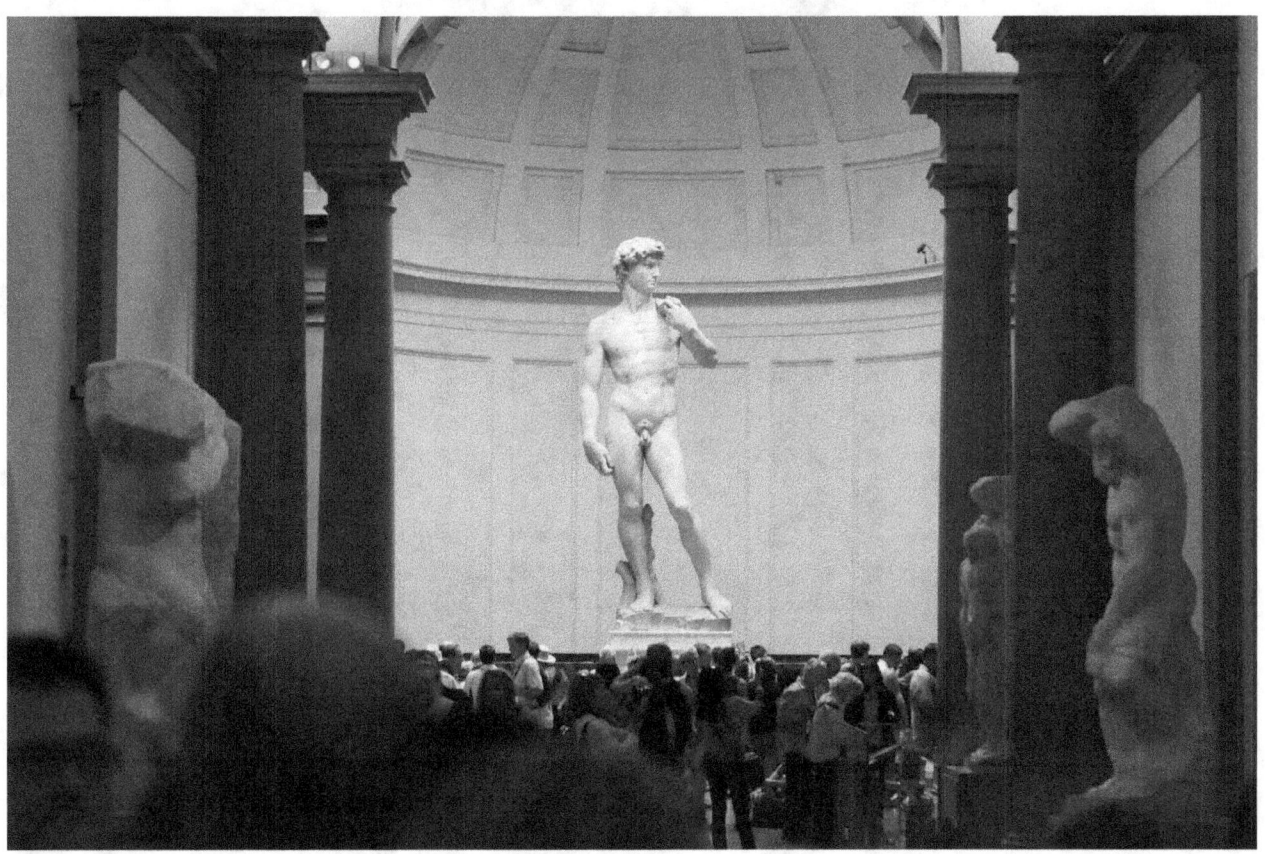

Figure 1. View of Michelangelo's David, and unfinished figures emerging from their marble blocks in the Galleria dell'Accademia, Florence

The Board of Works for the Cathedral of Florence commissioned Michelangelo to sculpt David from an enormous block of marble left over from another project. It was commissioned with the idea that it would stand in a niche on one of the cathedral's tribunes, way up high. When Michelangelo was finished, they realized that it was far too beautiful to be placed up high, and so it was decided to build a base for the sculpture and to place it right in front of the main government building of Florence (like putting it outside the capital building in Washington DC).

His perfect beauty reminds me of Pico della Mirandola, who imagines God saying to man at the creation: "Thou shalt have the power out of thy soul's judgment to be reborn into the higher forms which are divine."

Here is Vasari's description of David,

> Nor has there ever been seen a pose so easy, or any grace to equal that in this work, or feet, hands and head so well in accord, one member with another, in harmony, design, and excellence of artistry.
>
> —Translated by Gaston du C. de Vere

Michelangelo's David stands nearly 17 feet tall!

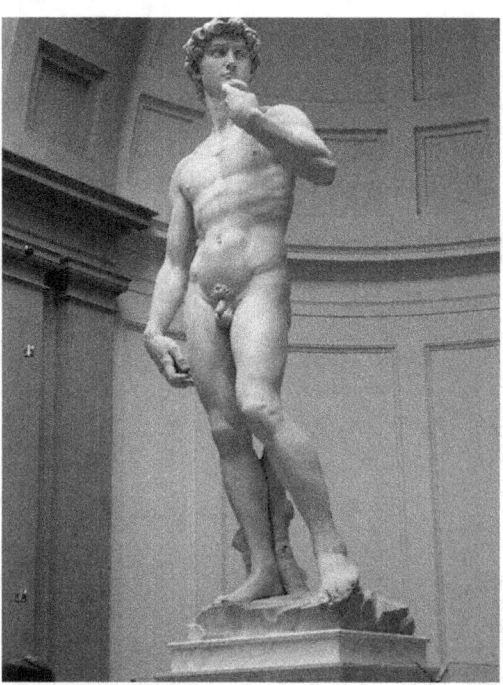

Figure 2. Michelangelo, David

Remember that the biblical figure of David was special to the citizens of Florence—he symbolized the liberty and freedom of their republican ideals, which were threatened at various points in the fifteenth century by the Medici family and others. Watch a video about the importance of the figure of David for Florence.

Attributions

Moses

Dr. Beth Harris and Dr. Steven Zucker provide a description, historical perspective, and analysis of Michelangelo's *Moses*.

- https://youtu.be/pnBbFIxCIGw

Michelangelo, *Moses*, marble, c. 1513–15 (San Pietro in Vincoli, Rome)

The Tomb of Pope Julius II

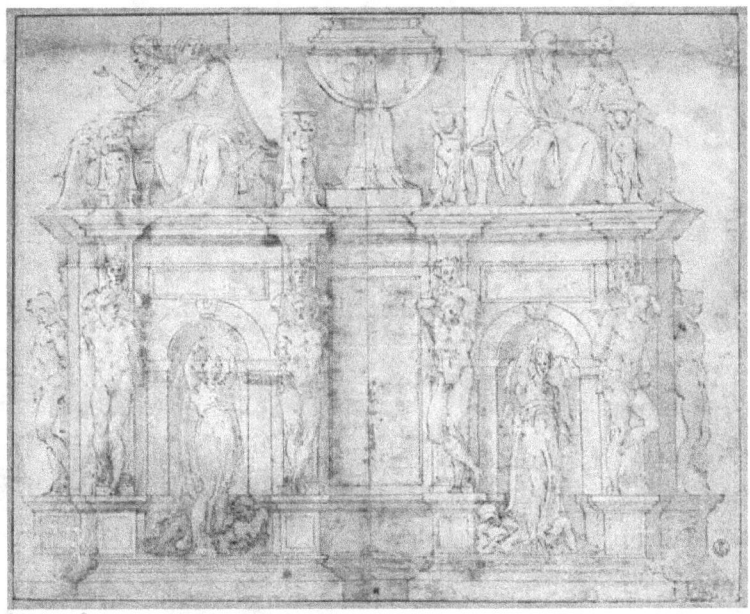

Figure 1. Sketch of the proposed tomb.

When Michelangelo had finished sculpting *David*, it was clear that this was quite possibly the most beautiful figure ever created—exceeding the beauty even of Ancient Greek and Roman sculptures. Word of *David* reached Pope Julius II in Rome, and he asked Michelangelo to come to Rome to work for him. The first work Pope Julius II commissioned from Michelangelo was to sculpt his tomb (Pope Julius II's tomb that is).

This may seem a bit strange to us today, but great rulers throughout history have planned fabulous tombs for themselves while they were still alive to ensure that they will be remembered forever (think of the Pharaohs in Egypt having the Pyramids built). When Michelangelo began the tomb of Pope Julius II his ideas were quite ambitious. He planned a two-story-high structure that would be decorated with over 20 sculptures (each of these over life size—see figure 1). This was more than one person could do in a lifetime!

Of course, Michelangelo was never able to finish the entire tomb. Not least because of Pope Julius himself, who asked Michelangelo to stop working on it and to paint the ceiling of the Sistine Chapel (but that's another story). Michelangelo eventually completed a much scaled-down version of the tomb after trouble from the heirs of Pope Julius II (and this is what can be seen today in San Pietro in Vincoli, in Rome).

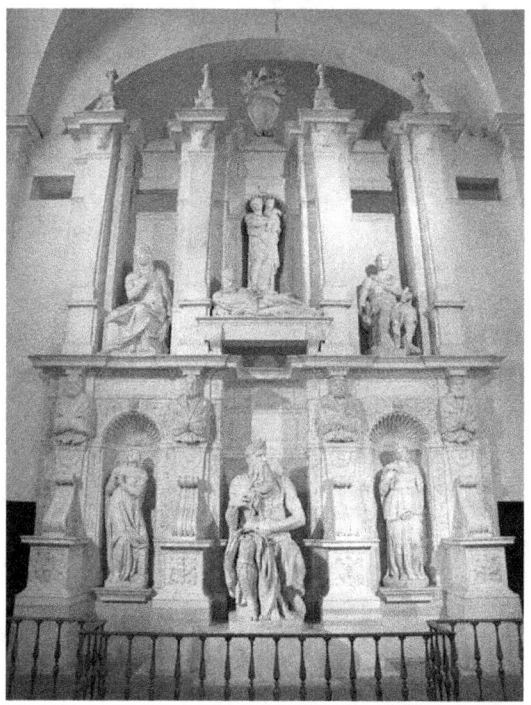

Figure 2. Michelangelo, Moses, marble, 1515 (San Pietro in Vincoli, Rome)

Moses is an imposing figure—he is nearly eight feet high sitting down! He has enormous muscular arms and an angry, intense look in his eyes. Under his arms he carries the tablets of the law—the stones inscribed with the Ten Commandments that he has just received from God on Mt. Sinai.

In this story from the Old Testament book of Exodus, Moses leaves the Israelites (who he has just delivered from slavery in Egypt) to go to the top of Mt. Sinai. When he returns he finds that they have constructed a golden calf to worship and make sacrifices to—they have, in other words, been acting like the Egyptians and worshipping a pagan idol.

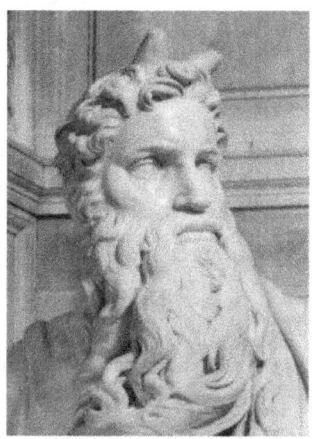

Figure 3. Moses (detail)

One of the commandments is "Thou shalt not make any graven images," so when Moses sees the Israelites worshipping this idol and betraying the one and only God who has, after all, just delivered them from slavery, he throws down the tablets and breaks them. Here is the passage from the Old Testament:

15 Then Moses turned and went down the mountain. He held in his hands the two stone tablets inscribed with the terms of the covenant. They were inscribed on both sides, front and back.

16 These stone tablets were God's work; the words on them were written by God himself.

17 When Joshua heard the noise of the people shouting below them, he exclaimed to Moses, "It sounds as if there is a war in the camp!"

18 But Moses replied, "No, it's neither a cry of victory nor a cry of defeat. It is the sound of a celebration."

19 When they came near the camp, Moses saw the calf and the dancing. In terrible anger, he threw the stone tablets to the ground, smashing them at the foot of the mountain.

We can see the figure's pent-up energy. The entire figure is charged with thought and energy. It is not entirely clear what moment of the story Michelangelo shows us, is he about to rise in anger after seeing the Israelites worshiping the golden calf? He has the tablets with the ten commandments on them under his right arm. Creating an interesting seated figure is not an easy thing to do!

Figure 4a shows a seated figure sculpted by Donatello. It really lacks the power and life of Michelangelo's sculpture, doesn't it?

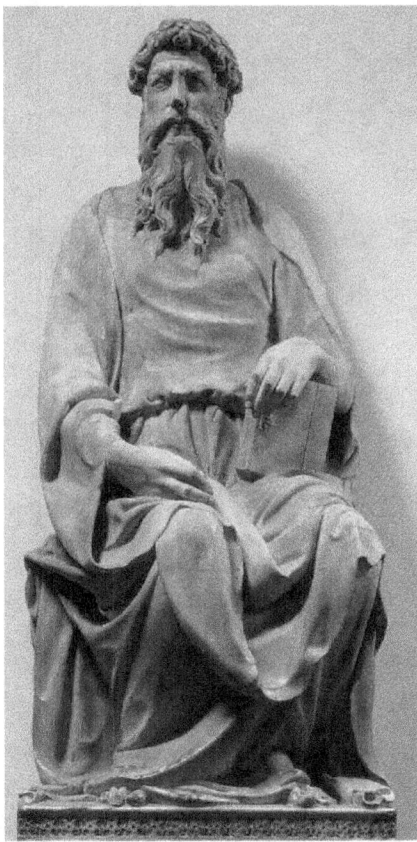 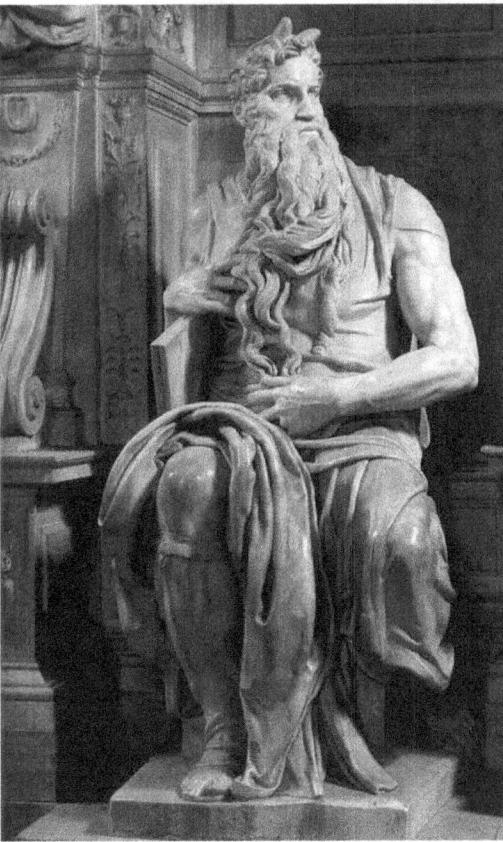

Figure 4. (a) Donatello, St. John, marble, ca. 1408–15 (Museo dell'Opera del Duomo, Florence); (b) Moses seated at the tomb

Think about how you're sitting right now at the computer. Perhaps your legs are crossed, as mine are as I write this. What about if you were not at the computer? And what to do with the hands? You can see that this could be a rather uninteresting position. Yet Michelangelo's Moses has energy and movement in the entire figure. (Look at Figure 4b.)

First of all, you'll see that Moses is not just sitting down; his left leg is pulled back to the side of his chair as though he is about to rise. And because this leg is pulled back, his hips also face left. Michelangelo, to create an interesting, energetic figure where the forces of life are pulsing throughout the body, pulls the torso in the opposite direction. And so his torso faces to his right. And because the torso faces to the right, Moses turns his head to the left, and then pulls his beard to the right.

Michelangelo has created a figure where one part of the body turns in the opposite direction from another part. This creates a dynamic figure—we have a clear sense of the prophet and his duty to fulfill God's wishes. You have probably noticed that Moses has horns. This comes from a mistranslation of a Hebrew word that described Moses as having rays of light coming from his head.

Attributions

CC licensed content, Shared previously

Sistine Chapel Ceiling

Dr. Beth Harris and Dr. Steven Zucker provide a description, historical perspective, and analysis of Michelangelo's *Ceiling of the Sistine Chapel*.

- https://youtu.be/PEE3B8Fsuc0

Michelangelo, *Ceiling of the Sistine Chapel*, fresco, 1508–1512 (Vatican City, Rome)

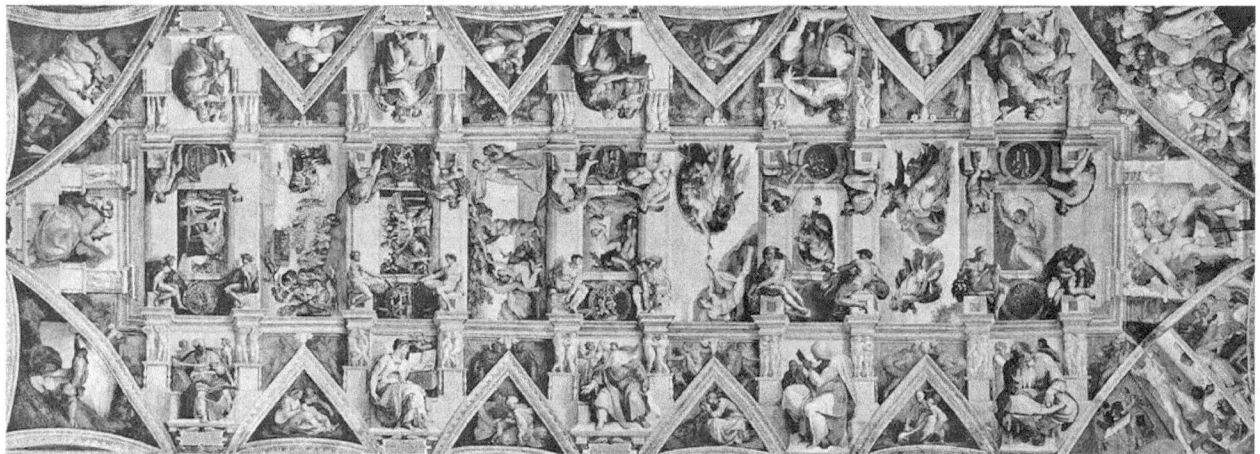

Figure 1. Michelangelo, Sistine Chapel Ceiling (center only), 1508–12 (Vatican, Rome)

Visiting the Chapel

To any visitor of Michelangelo's Sistine Chapel, two features become immediately and undeniably apparent: 1) the ceiling is really high up, and 2) there are a lot of paintings up there.

Because of this, the centuries have handed down to us an image of Michelangelo lying on his back, wiping sweat and plaster from his eyes as he toiled away year after year, suspended hundreds of feet in the air, begrudgingly completing a commission that he never wanted to accept in the first place.

Fortunately for Michelangelo, this is probably not true. But that does nothing to lessen the fact that the frescoes, which take up the entirety of the vault, are among the most important paintings in the world.

Figure 2. The interior of the Sistine Chapel showing the ceiling in relation to the other frescoes.

For Pope Julius II

Michelangelo began to work on the frescoes for Pope Julius II in 1508, replacing a blue ceiling dotted with stars. Originally, the pope asked Michelangelo to paint the ceiling with a geometric ornament, and place the twelve apostles in spandrels around the decoration.

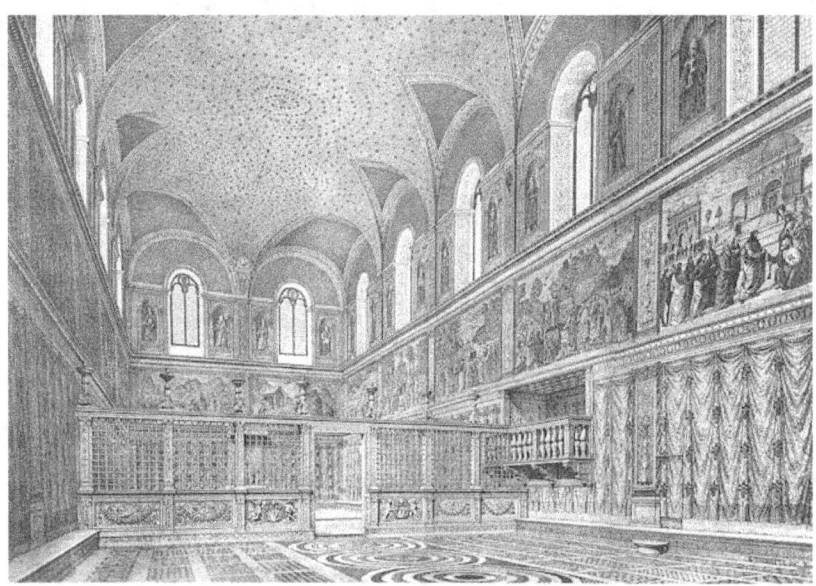

Figure 3. Reconstruction of the chapel prior Michelangelo's frescos.

Michelangelo proposed instead to paint the Old Testament scenes now found on the vault, divided by the fictive architecture that he uses to organize the composition.

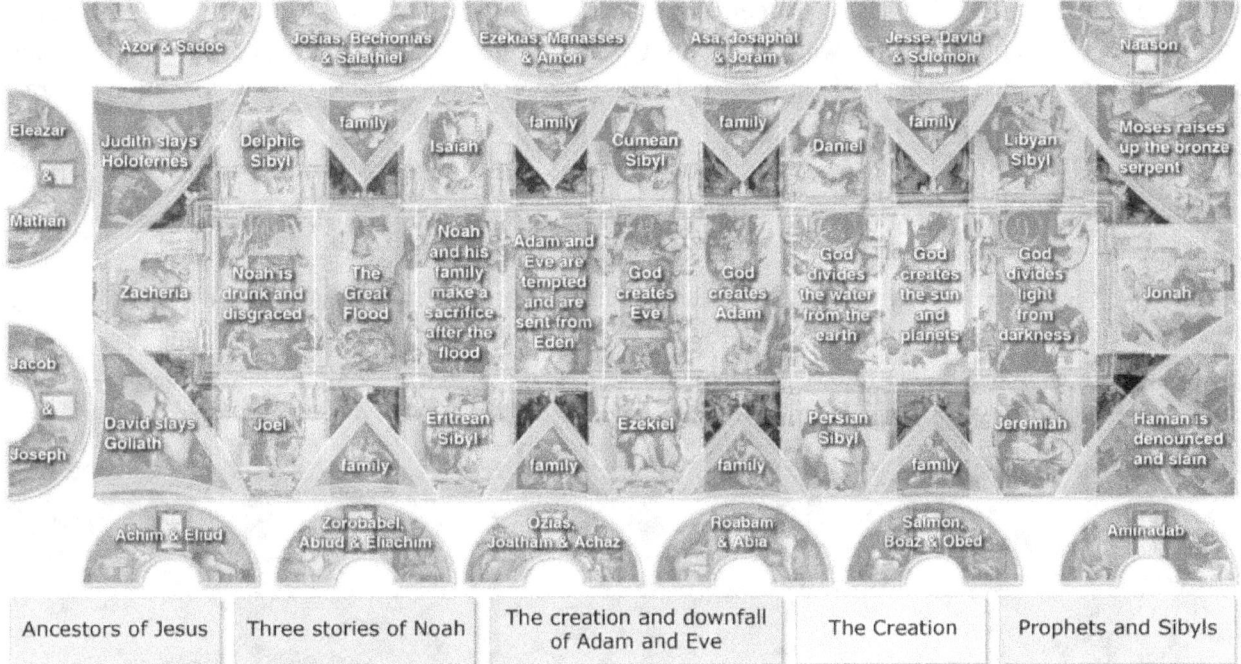

Figure 4. Sistine Chapel ceiling diagram

The Subjects of the Frescoes

The narrative begins at the altar and is divided into three sections. In the first three paintings, Michelangelo tells the story of *The Creation of the Heavens and Earth*; this is followed by *The Creation of Adam and Eve* and the *Expulsion from the Garden of Eden*; finally is the story of *Noah and the Great Flood*.

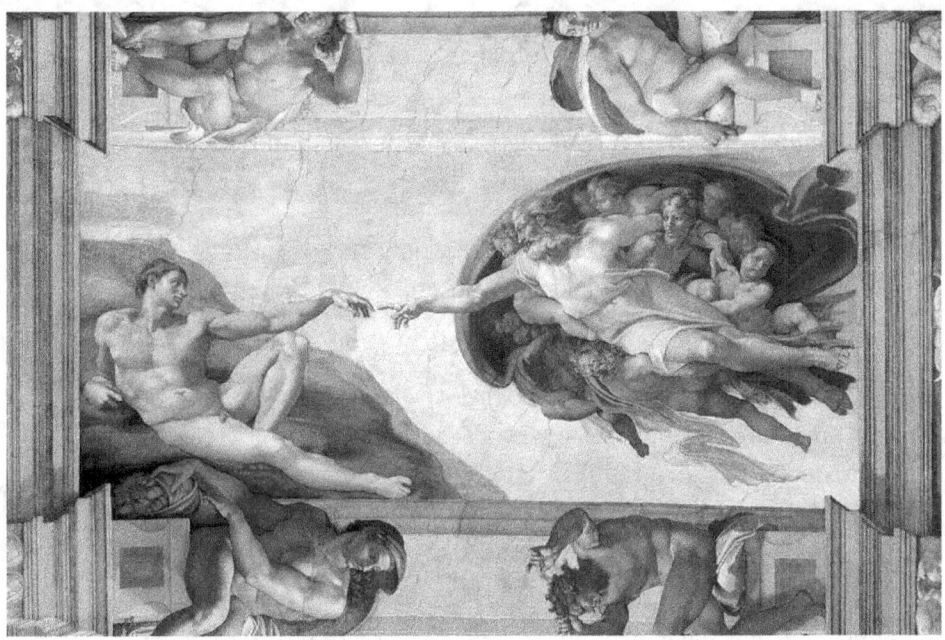

Figure 5. Michelangelo, The Creation of Adam, Sistine Chapel Ceiling, 1508-12

Ignudi, or nude youths, sit in fictive architecture around these frescoes, and they are accompanied by prophets and sibyls (ancient seers who, according to tradition, foretold the coming of Christ) in the spandrels. In the four corners of the room, in the pendentives, one finds scenes depicting the Salvation of Israel.

The Deluge

Although the most famous of these frescoes is without a doubt, *The Creation of Adam*, reproductions of which have become ubiquitous in modern culture for its dramatic positioning of the two monumental figures reaching towards each other, not all of the frescoes are painted in this style. In fact, the first frescoes Michelangelo painted contain multiple figures, much smaller in size, engaged in complex narratives. This can best be exemplified by his painting of *The Deluge*.

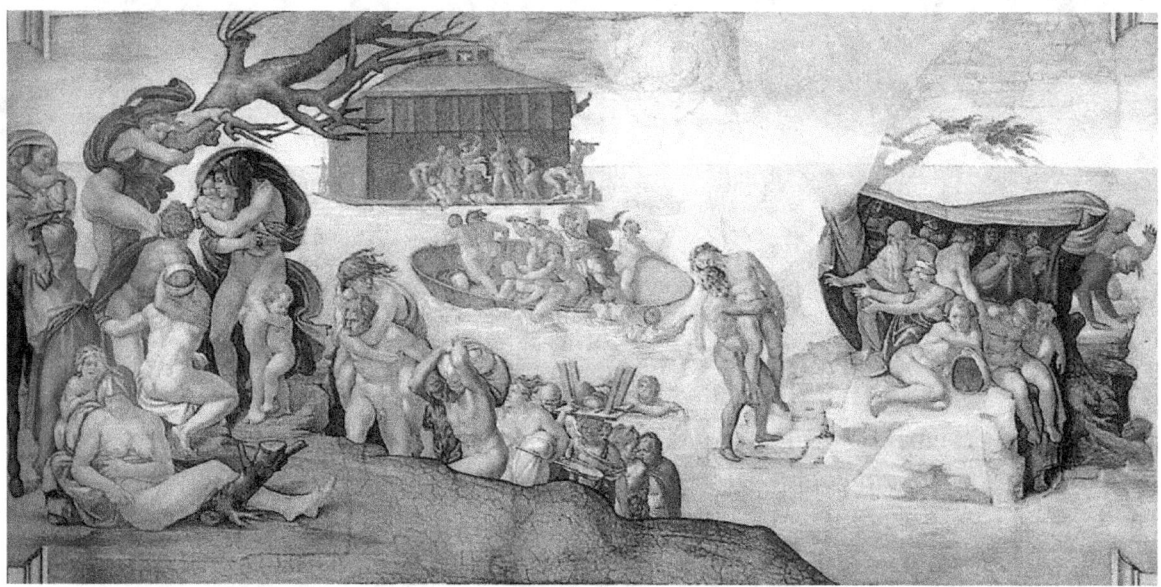

Figure 6. Michelangelo, The Deluge, Sistine Chapel ceiling, c. 1508–09

In this fresco, Michelangelo has used the physical space of the water and the sky to separate four distinct parts of the narrative.

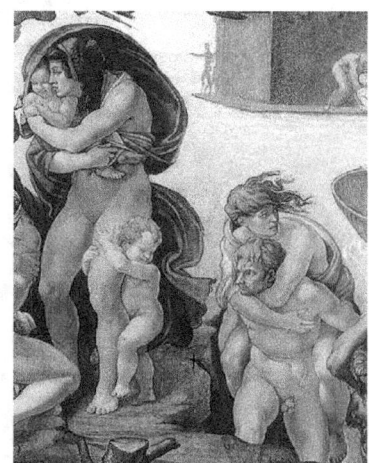

- On the right side of the painting, a cluster of people seeks sanctuary from the rain under a makeshift shelter.

- On the left, even more people climb up the side of a mountain to escape the rising water.

- Centrally, a small boat is about to capsize because of the unending downpour.

- In the background, a team of men work on building the arc—the only hope of salvation.

Figure 6. Detail of The Deluge

Up close, this painting confronts the viewer with the desperation of those about to perish in the flood and makes one question God's justice in wiping out the entire population of the earth, save Noah and his family, because of the sins of the wicked.

Unfortunately, from the floor of the chapel, the use of small, tightly grouped figures undermines the emotional content and makes the story harder to follow.

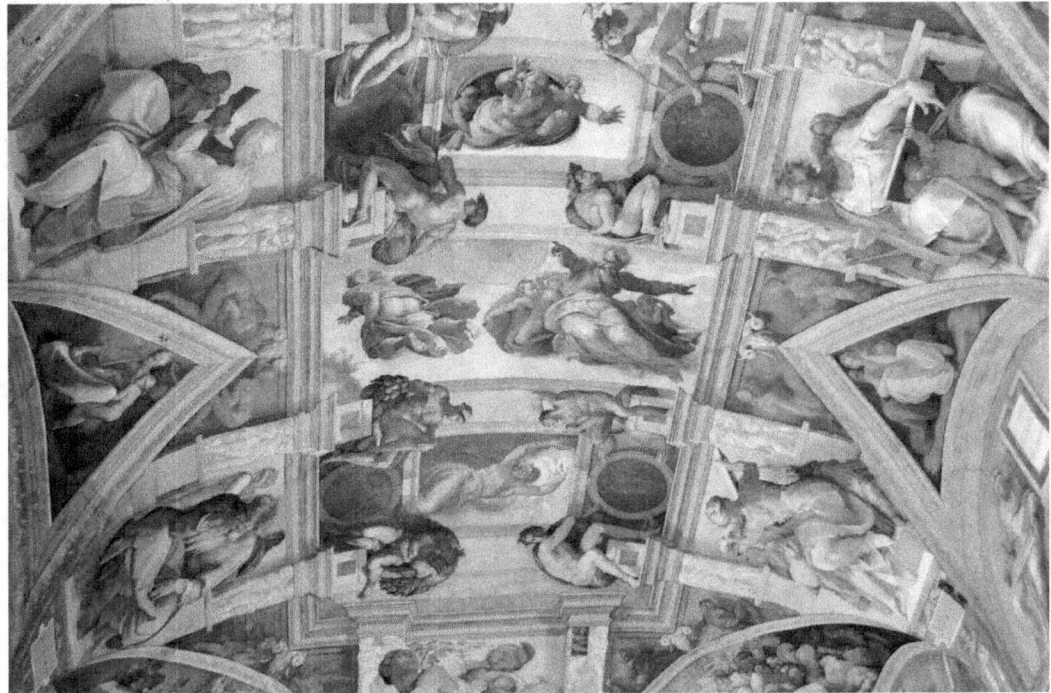

Figure 7. Michelangelo, Sistine Chapel ceiling, 1508–12, creation scenes.

A Shift in Style

In 1510, Michelangelo took a year long break from painting the Sistine Chapel. The frescoes painted after this break are characteristically different from the ones he painted before it, and are emblematic of what we think of when we envision the Sistine Chapel paintings. These are the paintings, like *The Creation of Adam*, where the narratives have been paired down to only the essential figures depicted on a monumental scale. Because of these changes, Michelangelo is able to convey a strong sense of emotionality that can be perceived from the floor of the chapel. For example, one feels the shame and despair of Eve who cowers from the angel in *The Expulsion from the Garden*. Indeed, the imposing figure of God in the three frescoes illustrating the separation of darkness from light and the creation of the heavens and the earth radiates power throughout his body, and his dramatic gesticulations help to tell the story of Genesis without the addition of extraneous detail.

The Sibyls

This new monumentality can also be felt in the figures of the sibyls and prophets in the spandrels surrounding the vault, which some believe are all based on the *Belvedere Torso*, an ancient sculpture that was then, and remains, in the Vatican's collection. One of the most celebrated of these figures is the *Delphic Sibyl* (figure 8a).

The overall circular composition of the body, which echoes the contours of her fictive architectural setting, adds to the sense of the sculptural weight of the figure.

Her arms are powerful, the heft of her body imposing, and both her left elbow and knee come into the viewer's space. At the same time, Michelangelo imbued the Delphic Sibyl with grace and harmony of proportion, and her watchful expression, as well as the position of the left arm and right hand, is reminiscent of the artist's *David*.

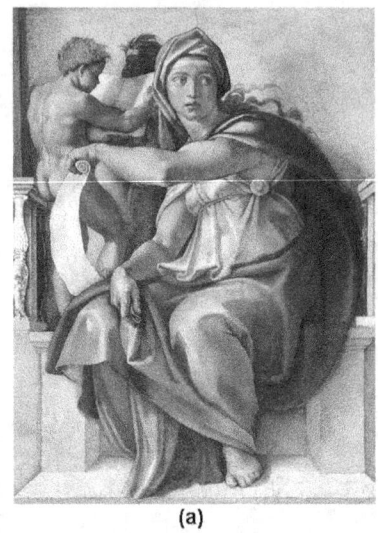
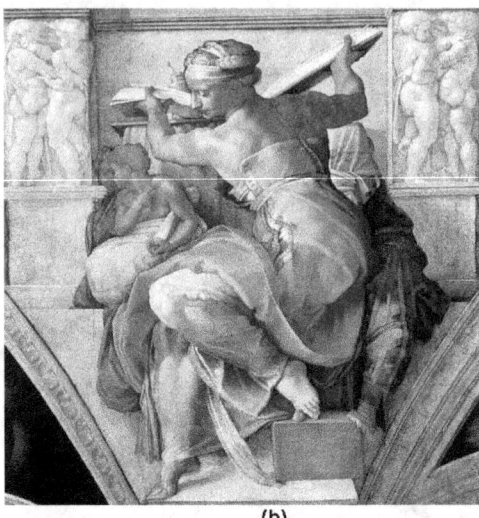

(a)   (b)

Figure 8. (a) The Delphic Sibyl; (b) The Libyan Sibyl

The Libyan Sibyl (figure 8b) is also exemplary. Although she is in a contorted position that would be nearly impossible for an actual person to hold, Michelangelo nonetheless executes her with a *sprezzatura* (a deceptive ease) that will become typical of the Mannerists who closely modeled their work on his.

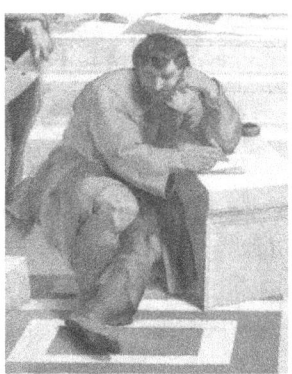

It is no wonder that Raphael, struck by the genius of the Sistine Chapel, rushed back to his *School of Athens* in the Vatican Stanze and inserted Michelangelo's weighty, monumental likeness sitting at the bottom of the steps of the school (see figure 9).

Figure 9. Raphael, School of Athens, 1509–11, Stanza della Segnatura, Vatican

Legacy

Michelangelo completed the Sistine Chapel in 1512. Its importance in the history of art cannot be overstated. It turned into a veritable academy for young painters, a position that was cemented when Michelangelo returned to the chapel twenty years later to execute the *Last Judgment* fresco on the altar wall.

The chapel recently underwent a controversial cleaning, which has once again brought to light Michelangelo's jewel-like palette, his mastery of chiaroscuro, and additional iconological details which continue to captivate modern viewers even five hundred years after the frescoes' original completion. Not bad for an artist who insisted he was not a painter.

Attributions

Sistine Chapel: Last Judgment

Dr. Beth Harris and Dr. Steven Zucker provide a description, historical perspective, and analysis of Michelangelo's *Last Judgment* in the Sistine Chapel.

- https://youtu.be/c2MuTvQM61Y

Michelangelo, *Last Judgment*, Sistine Chapel, 1534–1541, fresco, (Vatican City, Rome).

About 25 years after painting the ceiling of the Sistine Chapel and many years after the death of Pope Julius II, Michelangelo is asked to paint the wall behind the altar with a fresco of the Last Judgment by Pope Clement VII.

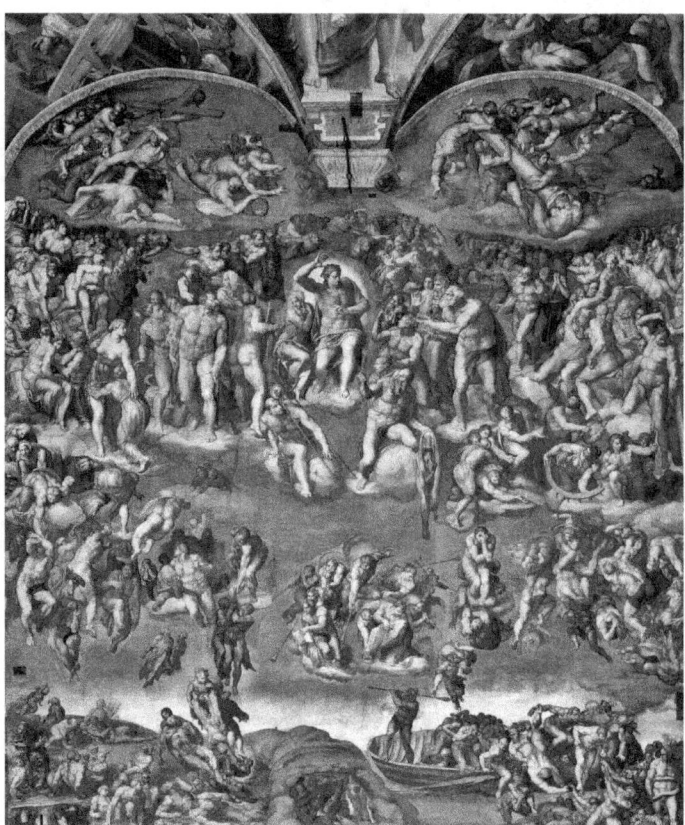

Figure 1. Michelangelo, Last Judgment

Michelangelo is not the same man he was when he painted the ceiling. His mood is more pessimistic, he is more devout and clearly concerned about the fate of his own soul. The times had changed as well. The Protestant Reformation was well under way, and the Church was beginning to turn its back on the Humanism of the High Renaissance. The Church responded to the attack by Luther by going on the offensive, bringing a powerful, energized Catholicism to the people. The subject of the Last Judgment, where we see the damned tortured in hell, needs to be seen against these historical developments.

The Last Judgment is a very old subject in art history represented by many artists. The subject is the Second Coming of Christ, where Christ returns to judge all of mankind.

Christ separates the blessed (those who will go to heaven), who he gathers on his right, from the damned (those who will go to hell), who he gathers on his left. In the ninth and tenth centuries, during the Middle Ages, this scene was often represented on the doorways of churches so that you had a frightening image of the Day of Judgment on your way in to church.

Here, Michelangelo shows us Christ in the center and below him to his (Christ's) left are the damned who are being pulled down to hell and shipped to hell where they are tortured by demons.

Below Christ to his right (careful—not our right) are the blessed who rise from their graves and float up to heaven with the aid of angels.

On either side of Christ directly are important figures, like Eve, and also Saints, many of whom died particularly painful deaths. We can identify these different Saints by what they carry. Usually Saints carry the instruments of their martyrdom, or some other identifying attribute.

Saint Catherine carries a wheel because she was martyred on the spokes of a wheel (here she is from Michelangelo's fresco). Saint Lawrence carries a grill, because he was burned to death, and Saint Sebastian carries arrows because his entire body was pierced by arrows.

Michelangelo said that these saints "sew the seeds of faith," that is, by their example of faith—a faith so firm that they were willing to undergo physical torture and death—they provide an example for us

Michelangelo also included Saint Bartholomew, who was martyred by being skinned alive. He holds the knife in one hand, and in his other he holds his skin. When we look closely at the skin of St. Bartholomew we see that Michelangelo painted his self-portrait there which appears distorted in the sagging skin.

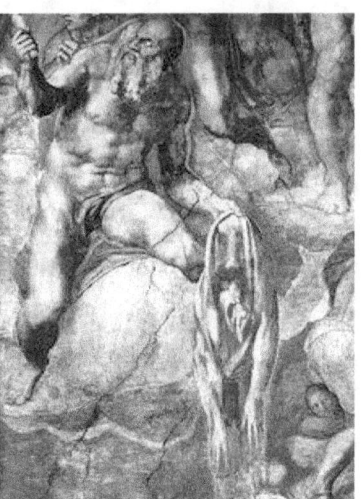

We know from Michelangelo's poetry that at this point in his life (for the 16th century he was an old man) he was feeling more devout and concerned about the fate of his own soul. He placed his self-portrait hovering precariously over hell and midway, in a diagonal line, between Christ, and the famous image of the man who has just realized that he is being pulled down toward hell.

Michelangelo certainly presents a different image of humanity in the Last Judgment than he did on the ceiling. On the ceiling Michelangelo presented us with God's plan to redeem a fallen mankind. As we saw, the figures on the ceiling are ideally beautiful, and heroic. The figures

Figure 2. Saint Bartholomew

in the Last Judgment in contrast, are ill-proportioned (their heads are too small for their bodies), and they assume ugly, awkward poses. Christ appears here not as a redeemer but as an angry judge. And Michelangelo seems to be exploring the power of ugliness to portray the terror of the Last Judgment.

Attributions

CC licensed content, Shared previously

- Michelangelo's Last Judgment (Sistine Chapel). **Authored by**: Dr. Beth Harris and Dr. Steven Zucker. **Provided by**: Khan Academy. **Located at**: https://web.archive.org/web/20140215031126/http://smarthistory.khanacademy.org/last-judgment-sistine-chapel.html. **License**: *CC BY-NC-SA: Attribution-NonCommercial-ShareAlike*

Public domain content

- The Last Judgment. **Authored by**: Michelangelo. **Located at**: https://commons.wikimedia.org/wiki/File:Michelangelo,_Giudizio_Universale_02.jpg. **License**: *Public Domain: No Known Copyright*

Marriage of the Virgin

Dr. Beth Harris and Dr. Steven Zucker provide a description, historical perspective, and analysis of Raphael's *Marriage of the Virgin*.

- https://youtu.be/H_Guv2Mk1E0

Raphael, *Marriage of the Virgin*, 1504, oil on panel, 174 × 121 cm / 69 in × 48 inches (Pinacoteca di Brera, Milan)

This canvas was commissioned from Raphael when the artists was 21 years old. It was created for the chapel of Saint Joseph in the church of San Francesco, Città di Castello in northern Umbria and paid for by the Albizzini family. In 1798, the painting was taken by the Napoleonic officer Lechi, who promptly sold it in Milan. The painting was then given to a hospital there in 1804. It has been at the Brera since 1806. Follow the link below for a brief video on the photographic documentation during the most recent conservation of the painting:

- https://vimeo.com/3019305

Attributions

Madonna of the Goldfinch

Dr. Beth Harris and Dr. Steven Zucker provide a description, historical perspective, and analysis of Raphael's *Madonna of the Goldfinch*.

- https://youtu.be/jHN0BfowL7s

Raphael, *Madonna of the Goldfinch*, 1505–6, oil on panel, 42″ × 30″ (107 × 77 cm), Uffizi, Florence

External Link

View this painting up close in the Google Art Project:

- https://www.google.com/culturalinstitute/asset-viewer/madonna-of-the-goldfinch/oAFhn-Mjj7HippQ?projectId=art-project

School of Athens

Dr. Beth Harris and Dr. Steven Zucker provide a description, historical perspective, and analysis of Raphael's *School of Athens*.

- https://youtu.be/Smd-q44ysoM

Raphael, *School of Athens*, fresco, 1509–1511 (Stanza della Segnatura, Palazzi Pontifici, Vatican)

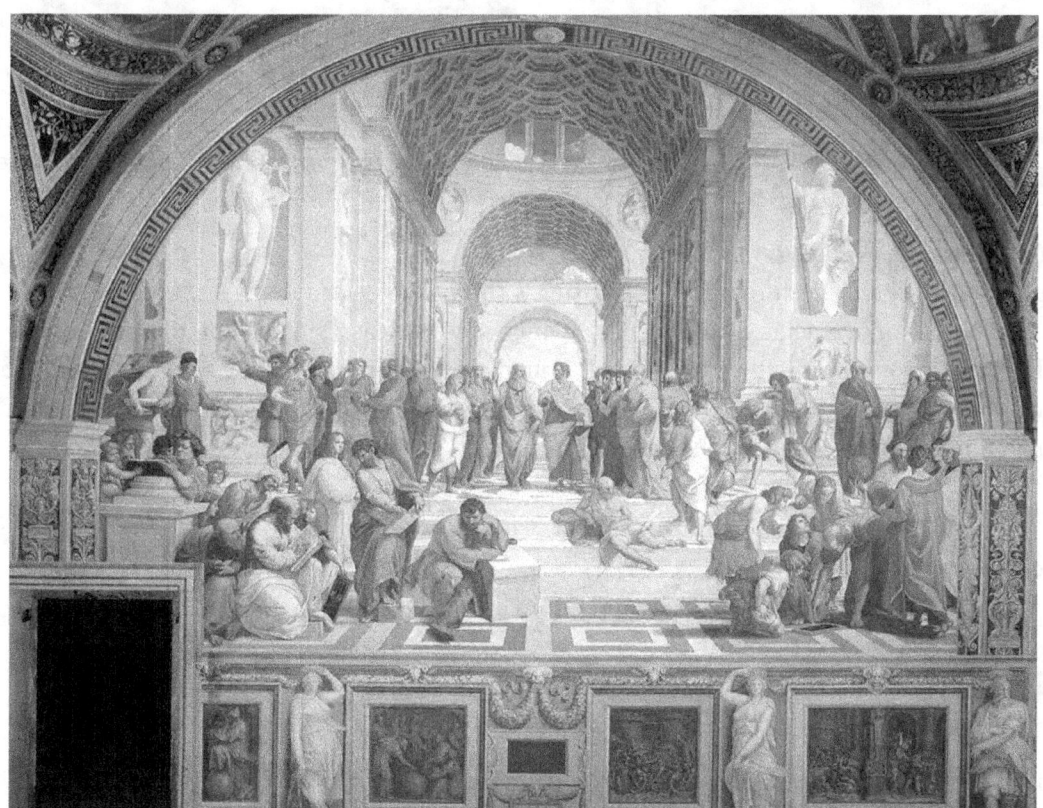

Figure 1. Raphael, School of Athens

The School of Athens represents all the greatest mathematicians, philosophers and scientists from classical antiquity gathered together sharing their ideas and learning from each other. These figures all lived at different times, but here they are gathered together under one roof.

The two thinkers in the very center, Aristotle (on the right) and Plato (on the left, pointing up) have been enormously important to Western thinking generally, and in different ways, their different philosophies were incoporated into Christianity. Plato holds his book called The Timaeus.

Plato points up because in his philosophy the changing world that we see around us is just a shadow of a higher, truer reality that is eternal and unchanging (and include things like goodness and beauty). For Plato, this otherworldly reality is the ultimate reality, and the seat of all truth, beauty, justice, and wisdom.

Aristotle holds his hand down, because in his philosophy, the only reality is the reality that we can see and experience by sight and touch (exactly the reality dismissed by Plato). Aristotle's Ethics (the book that he holds) "emphasized the relationships, justice, friendship, and government of the human world and the need to study it."

Pythagoras (lower left) believed that the world (including the movement of the planets and stars) operated according to mathematical laws. These mathematical laws were related to ideas of musical and cosmic harmony, and thus (for the Christians who interpreted him in the Renaissance) to God. Pythagoras taught that each of the planets produced a note as it moved, based on its distance from the earth. Together, the movement of all the planets was perfect harmony—"the harmony of the spheres."

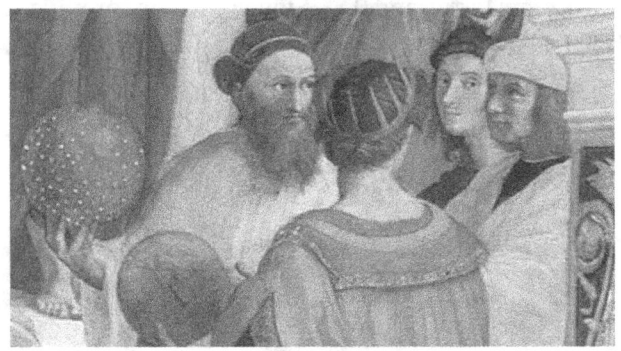

Figure 2. Raphael included a self-portrait of himself, standing next to Ptolemy. He looks right out at us.

Ptolemy (he has his back to us on the lower right), holds a sphere of the earth, next to him is Zaroaster who holds a celestial sphere. Ptolemy tried to mathematically explain the movements of the planets (which was not easy since some of them appear to move backwards!). His theory of how they all moved around the earth remained the authority until Copernicus and Kepler figured out (in the late 1500s) that the earth was not at the center of the universe, and that the planets moved in orbits the shape of ellipses not in circles.

Attributions

CC licensed content, Shared previously

- Raphael's School of Athens. **Authored by**: Dr. Steven Zucker and Dr. Beth Harris. **Provided by**: Khan Academy. **Located at**: https://web.archive.org/web/20140215031849/http://smarthistory.khanacademy.org/school-of-athens.html. **License**: *CC BY-NC-SA: Attribution-NonCommercial-ShareAlike*

Public domain content

- The School of Athens. **Authored by**: Raphael. **Located at**: https://commons.wikimedia.org/wiki/File:Sanzio_01.jpg. **License**: *Public Domain: No Known Copyright*

Saint Peter's Basilica

Dr. Beth Harris and Dr. Steven Zucker provide a description, historical perspective, and analysis of Saint Peter's Basilica.

- https://youtu.be/R5UK0dEFSoM

Numerous architects (see below), Saint Peter's Basilica (*Basilica Sancti Petri* in Latin) begun 1506 completed 1626, Vatican City.

Architectural contributors include:

- Donato Bramante whose design won Julius II's competition
- Antonio da Sangallo, a student of Bramante, designed the Pauline Chapel
- Fra Giocondo strengthened the foundation
- Raphael worked with Fra Giocondo, his redesigned building plan was not executed
- Michelangelo designed the dome, crossing, and exterior excluding the nave and facade
- Giacomo della Porta, designed the cupola
- Carlo Maderno, extended Michelangelo's plan adding a nave and grand facade
- Gian Lorenzo Bernini added the piazza, the Cathedra Petri, and the Baldacchino

External Links

Please also review these works:

- Sarcophagus of Junius Bassus
  - https://courses.candelalearning.com/zelixart101/chapter/video-sarcophagus-of-junius-bassus/
- Michelangelo's Pietà
  - https://courses.candelalearning.com/zelixart102/chapter/pieta/
- Bernini's Baldacchino, Cathedra Petri, and Piazza

○ https://www.khanacademy.org/humanities/monarchy-enlightenment/baroque-art1/
baroque-italy/v/gian-lorenzo-bernini-cathedra-petri-chair-of-st-peter-c-120-80-b-c-e

Pope Julius II commissioned Bramante to build a new basilica. This involved demolishing the Old St Peter's Basilica that had been erected by Constantine in the fourth century. The church was old, and in disrepair. But tearing it down was a bold manouever that gives us a sense of the enormous ambition of Pope Julius II, both for the papacy as well as for himself.

The site is a very holy one—it is (according to the Church) the site of the burial of St. Peter (remember he was the first Pope). Bramante did the first plan for the new church. He proposed an enormous centrally planned church in the shape of a Greek cross enclosed within a square with an enormous dome over the center, and smaller domes and half-domes radiating out. When Bramante died, Raphael took over as chief architect for St. Peter's, and when Raphael died, Michelangelo took over. Both Michelangelo and Raphael made substantial changes to Bramante's original plan. Nevertheless, the experience of being inside St. Peter's is awe-inspiring.

The two basic types of Church are the **basilica** and the **central** plan.

The basilica, with its long axis that focuses attention on the altar, has been the most popular type of church plan because of its practicality.

The other popular type of church plan is a central plan that is usually based either on the shape of a circle, or on a Greek cross (a cross with equal arms). These are called central plans because the measurements are all equidistant from a center. This type of Church, influenced by Classical architecture (think of the Pantheon), was very popular among High Renaissance architects. Besides the influence of ancient Roman architecture, the circle had spiritual associations. The circle, which has no beginning and no end, symbolized the perfection and eternal nature of God. For some thinkers in antiquity and the Renaissance the universe itself was constructed in the form of concentric circles with the sun, moon and stars moving in circular orbits around the earth.

Attributions

CC licensed content, Shared previously

Giorgione, The Tempest

Dr. Beth Harris and Dr. Steven Zucker provide a description, historical perspective, and analysis of Giorgione's *The Tempest*.

- https://youtu.be/LFA_qmGuY2A

Giorgione, *The Tempest*, c. 1506–8, oil on canvas, 83 cm × 73 cm (33 in × 29 in), (Accademia, Venice).

Attributions

CC licensed content, Shared previously

Titian, Bacchus & Ariadne

Bacchus and Ariadne is part of a mythological cycle painted by Titian and Giovanni Bellini and commissioned by Alfonso d'Este, Duke of Ferrara. The cycle also includes *The Feast of the Gods* and the *Andrians*. It was originally hung in the *studiolo* or Camerini d'Alabastro of the Duke's Ferranese castle.

Dr. Beth Harris and Dr. Steven Zucker provide a description, historical perspective, and analysis of Titian's *Bacchus and Ariadne*.

- https://youtu.be/bYyxwxEqTQo

Titian, *Bacchus and Ariadne*, 1523–24, oil on canvas now atop board, 69-1/2 × 75 inches, (National Gallery, London).

Attributions

CC licensed content, Shared previously

Titian, Venus of Urbino

Dr. Beth Harris and Dr. Steven Zucker provide a description, historical perspective, and analysis of Titian's *Venus of Urbino*.

- https://youtu.be/qD6ct0VS15c

Titian, *Venus of Urbino*, 1538, oil on canvas, 119.20 × 165.50 cm, (Galleria degli Uffizi, Florence).

Attributions

CC licensed content, Shared previously

Veronese, Feast in the House of Levi

Dr. Beth Harris and Dr. Steven Zucker provide a description, historical perspective, and analysis of Veronese's *Feast in the House of Levi*.

- https://youtu.be/9g-r2007Y8c

Paolo Veronese, *Feast in the House of Levi*, 1573, oil on canvas, 18′ 3″ × 42″, (Accademia, Venice).

The Trial of Veronese

Transcript of the trial: On Saturday, July 18, 1573, Paolo Caliari Veronese who lives in the parish of San Samuele, Venice, was summoned to appear before the Holy Tribunal by the Holy Office [the inquisition], there he stated his name when asked. When asked what he did for a living, he responded, "I paint and make figures."

Inquisition: Do you know why you are summoned here?

Veronese: No your honors.

Inquisition: Can you imagine what the reason is?

Veronese: I can.

Inquisition: Tell us.

Veronese: I was told by the priests, or rather by the Prior of SS. Giovanni e Paolo, whose's name I don't know, told me that he had visited here and that Your Great Lordships had commanded the Mary Magdalene replace the dog. I responded that that I would have happily done this and anything else for my and the sake of the painting, except that I did not believe that the figure of the Magdalene would look good there, for a variety of reasons, which I can speak to if I am given the chance.

Inquisition: What is the subject of the picture you are speaking of?

Veronese: It is a painting of the Last Supper, with Jesus Christ with his Apostles in the house of Simon.

Inquisition: Where is this picture?

Veronese: It is in the refectory of the Monastery of SS. Giovanni e Paolo.

Inquisition: Is it painted on the wall, on wood, or on canvas?

Veronese: Canvas.

Inquisition: How tall is it?

Veronese: Perhaps seventeen feet.

Inquisition: How wide is it?

Veronese: About thirty nine feet.

Inquisition: Have you painted servants at the Lord's Supper?

Veronese: Yes.

Inquisition: Tell us how many people there are, and each one's activities.

Veronese: Below the owner of the inn, Simon, I put a carver, He came, I guess, for his own amusement, to observe the goings-on at the table. There are many other figures but I cannot remember, its been a long time since I finished the painting.

Inquisition: What was your intent regarding the man whose nose is bleeding?

Veronese: I intended him to be a servant, whose nose was bloody because of some accident.

Inquisition: And what did you mean by the armed man, clothed like a German, holding a halberd?

Veronese: That will take longer to explain.

Inquisition: Tell us.

Veronese: Painters take the same poetic license that poets and madmen take, and this is how I made these two soldiers, one drinking the other eating, at the foot of the stairs, though both ready for prompt action. It seemed appropriate to me that the wealthy owner of this house, a noble I understand, would have hired security such as these men.

Inquisition: And the figure dressed as a jester with a parrot perched on his hand, why did you represent him?

Veronese: He is decorative, as is customary.

Inquisition: Who are those at the Lord's table?

Veronese: The twelve Apostles.

Inquisition: What is St. Peter doing, the first one?

Veronese: He is carving lamb, to pass it to the other side of the table.

Inquisition: And who is the other man, next to him?

Veronese: He holds a plate for St. Peter to fill.

Inquisition: What is he doing.

Veronese: He is picking his teeth with a fork.

Inquisition: Who do you believe was at the Last Supper?

Veronese: Christ was there with his Apostles. But there was more space, so I included other figures that I created.

Inquisition: Did anyone tell you to paint Germans, jesters, or buffoons in this picture?

Veronese: No. I was told to create the painting as I thought fit, it was large and could accommodate numerous figures.

Inquisition: Shouldn't painters only add figures in keeping with the subject and the most important people portrayed? Do you freely follow your imagination without restraint, without good judgment?

Veronese: My paintings are made with all the consideration I can bring to bear on them.

Inquisition: Do you think it is appropriate that the Last Supper of Our Lord includes jesters, drunks, Germans, midgets, and the like?

Veronese: No, your honor.

Inquisition: Do you not know that Germany and other places are infested with heresy and that in such place they commonly fill their paintings with sacrilegious images, that denigrate the Holy Church and spread evil to the ignorant?

Veronese: Your Honor, that would be evil. I can only repeat what I previously stated, That I have followed what others, better than me, have done.

Inquisition: What has been done by those better than you? Which things?

Veronese: In the Pope's chapel in Rome, Michelangelo rendered Our Lord, Jesus Christ, his Mother, Saint John and Saint Peter, and the court of heaven, all nude, including the Virgin Mary, in the midst movements without decorum.

Inquisition: Don't you understand that in a painting of the Last Judgment, clothing would not be worn, that there is no reason to paint clothes? Among those figures there is nothing except what befits the spiritual—there are no jesters, no dogs, no weapons, or any such silliness. Do you think this comparison, or any other that this example or any other justifies the way you painted your picture, and are you still certain that the painting appropriate to its subject?

Veronese: Your honor, I do not mean to defend it, but my intent was only good. I did not consider these issues enough, thinking that since the buffoons were outside the place where Our Lord sits, it was proper.

In the end, the judges decreed that the artist must correct his painting within three months from the day of the reprimand, in accordance with the judgment of the Holy Tribunal, and that the additional costs would be paid by Veronese.

Attributions

CC licensed content, Shared previously

- Veronese's Feast in the House of Levi. **Authored by**: Dr. Beth Harris and Dr. Steven Zucker. **Provided by**: Khan Academy. **Located at**: https://web.archive.org/web/20140215041933/http://smarthistory.khanacademy.org/veroneses-feast-in-the-house-of-levi.html. **License**: *CC BY-NC-SA: Attribution-NonCommercial-ShareAlike*

Tintoretto, The Origin of the Milky Way

Dr. Beth Harris and Dr. Steven Zucker provide a description, historical perspective, and analysis of Jacopo Tintoretto's *The Origin of the Milky Way*.

- https://youtu.be/Bgrwohxf9Ws

Jacopo Tintoretto, *The Origin of the Milky Way*, c. 1575, oil on canvas, 149.4 × 168 cm, (The National Gallery, London).

External Link

View this painting up close in the Google Art Project:

- https://www.google.com/culturalinstitute/asset-viewer/the-origin-of-the-milky-way/ZQE-exGM2Z5VjLQ?projectId=art-project

---

Introduction to Mannerism

Click on the link below to view the article "A beginner's guide to Mannerism" by Michael Clarke and Deborah Clarke, published on Khan Academy. This article will provide an introduction to the Mannerist art movement, which began in 1520 and lasted until 1580 (please note that these years are approximate).

- "A beginner's guide to Mannerism" by Michael Clarke and Deborah Clarke.:

    ◦ https://www.khanacademy.org/humanities/renaissance-reformation/mannerism1/a/a-beginners-guide-to-mannerism/

Parmigianino's Madonna of the Long Neck

Dr. Beth Harris and Dr. Steven Zucker provide a description, historical perspective, and analysis of Parmigianino's *Madonna of the Long Neck*.

- https://youtu.be/suIUUGdNyWk

Parmigianino, *Madonna of the Long Neck*, 1530–33, oil paint, 28 3/4" × 23 1/2" (73 cm × 60 cm), (Uffizi, Florence).

External Link

View this painting up close in the Google Art Project.:

- https://www.google.com/culturalinstitute/asset-viewer/madonna-with-the-long-neck/gAE-sEn4eJXVHyg?projectId=art-project

---

Attributions

El Greco's Adoration of the Shepherds

Dr. Beth Harris and Dr. Steven Zucker provide a description, historical perspective, and analysis of El Greco's *Adoration of the Shepherds*.

- https://youtu.be/3_-hYeuJTzQ

El Greco (Domenikos Theotokopoulos), *Adoration of the Shepherds*, c. 1612–1614, oil on canvas, 126 × 71 in. (319 × 180 cm), (Museo Nacional del Prado, Madrid).

Attributions

Chapter 6:
1500–1600–The Age of Reformation: Northern Renaissance Art

Chapter 6 Overview

What You'll Learn To Do: Examine Northern Renaissance art during the Reformation and its impact on art history as a whole.

In Chapter 6 we will examine Northern Renaissance art during the Reformation. We will look at how artists like Bruegel contributed to the development of Western art. It is imperative to understand Northern Renaissance art during the Reformation in order to see how it impacted later artistic developments.

Learning Activities

The learning activities for this module include:

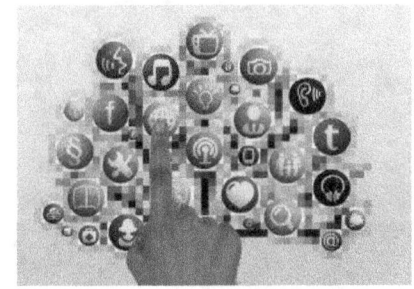

- **Review:** Key Learning Items

The Reformation

- **Watch:** Introduction to the Protestant Reformation (four videos: 8:17, 11:14, 8:15, and 9:40)

- **Watch:** Dürer's Four Apostles (5:51)

- **Watch:** Self-Portrait 1498 (2:13)

- **Watch:** Self-Portrait 1500 (3:23)

- **Read:** What Is a Print?

- **Watch:** Dürer's Prints (4:53)

- **Watch:** Bosch's Last Judgment (8:51)

- **Watch:** Altdorfer's Battle of Issus (4:43)

- **Watch:** Cranach's Adam and Eve (5:01)

- **Read:** Cranach's Wittenberg Altarpiece

- **Watch:** Holbein's The Ambassadors (7:32)

- **Watch:** Portrait of Henry the VIII (4:10)

- **Watch:** Bruegel's The Dutch Proverbs (2:20)

Attributions

CC licensed content, Original

- Art History II. **Provided by**: Extended Learning Institute of Northern Virginia Community College. **Located at**: http://eli.nvcc.edu/. **License**: *CC BY: Attribution*

Public domain content

- Image of Finger. **Authored by**: geralt. **Located at**: https://pixabay.com/en/finger-touch-hand-structure-769300/. **License**: *Public Domain: No Known Copyright*

Key Learning Items

Learning Objectives

After successful completion of this module, you will be able to:

- Understand and apply the concepts and terminology of Northern Renaissance art during the Reformation
- Investigate and apply the fundamental questions we ask when looking at art objects from this movement
- Discuss, collaborate, and generate understanding as to the meaning of Northern Renaissance art during the Reformation
- Assess and evaluate the impact of Northern Renaissance art during the Reformation on the continued evolution of Western art

Key Questions to Ask

While you are reviewing the content of this module, consider the following questions:

- How did the Protestant Reformation influence art?
- How did the Counter-Reformation influence art?
- What are the key characteristics of Northern Renaissance art?
- How does Northern Renaissance art differ from Italian Renaissance art?

Key Vocabulary Terms

- Protestant Reformation
- Counter-Reformation
- prints

- woodcut

- relief process

- line

- engraving

- intaglio process

- burin

- altarpiece

- grisaille

- anamorphic image

- memento mori

- foreshortening

Here are links to art history glossaries that will help you better understand the above key vocabulary terms.

- ArtLex: Art Dictionary

  - http://www.artlex.com/

- About.com: Art History

  - http://arthistory.about.com/od/glossary/l/bl_Art-Glossary.htm

- Artcyclopedia: A Guide to Fine Art

  - http://www.artcyclopedia.com/

Attributions

CC licensed content, Original

Introduction to the Protestant Reformation

Dr. Beth Harris and Dr. Steven Zucker provide an introduction to the Protestant Reformation in these four videos.

Setting the Stage

- https://youtu.be/qTGJMnTWrrw

Martin Luther

- https://youtu.be/dSOnLt3YVl0

Varieties of Protestantism

- https://youtu.be/F6ZsIyKHTNI

The Counter-Reformation

- https://youtu.be/C6PUlTYnxLY

mation1/v/introduction-to-the-protestant-reformation-3-of-4. **License**: *CC BY-NC-SA: Attribution-NonCommercial-ShareAlike*

- Introduction to the Protestant Reformation: The Counter-Reformation (part 4). **Authored by**: Dr. Steven Zucker and Dr. Beth Harris. **Provided by**: Khan Academy. **Located at**: https://www.khanacademy.org/humanities/renaissance-reformation/protestant-reformation1/v/introduction-to-the-protestant-reformation-the-counter-reformation-4-of-4. **License**: *CC BY-NC-SA: Attribution-NonCommercial-ShareAlike*

Dürer's Four Apostles

Dr. Beth Harris and Dr. Steven Zucker provide a description, historical perspective, and analysis of Albrecht Dürer's *The Four Apostles*.

- https://youtu.be/WyNqLrb0LRE

Albrecht Dürer, *The Four Apostles*, 1526, oil on wood, 7′ 1″ × 2′ 6″ (Alte Pinakothek, Munich)

Attributions

CC licensed content, Shared previously

Self-Portrait 1500

Dr. Beth Harris and Dr. Steven Zucker provide a description, historical perspective, and analysis of Albrecht Dürer's 1500 *Self-Portrait*.

- https://youtu.be/ZoiY6ZLEKaY

Albrecht Dürer, *Self-Portrait*, 1500 (Alte Pinakothek, Munich)

Attributions

What Is a Print?

Click on the link below to view the interactive site "What Is a Print?" developed by The Museum of Modern Art. This site defines the term *print* as it applies to art history, and it examines several different kinds of printing, including woodcuts, etchings, lithographs, and screenprints.

- "What Is a Print?"
  - http://www.moma.org/interactives/projects/2001/whatisaprint/print.html

Dürer's Prints

Dr. David Drogin and Dr. Beth Harris provide a description, historical perspective, and analysis of two of Albrecht Dürer prints.

- https://youtu.be/C3DmiEsvs6U

Prints Discussed

Albrecht Dürer, *Four Horsemen of the Apocalypse*, c. 1497–98, woodcarving.

Albrecht Dürer, St. Jerome in his Study, 1514, etching.

Attributions

CC licensed content, Shared previously

Bosch's Last Judgment

Dr. Beth Harris and Dr. Steven Zucker provide a description, historical perspective, and analysis of Hieronymus Bosch's *Last Judgment Triptych*.

- https://youtu.be/Ea6qS3nuvng

Hieronymus Bosch, *Last Judgment Triptych*, 1504–08, overall dimensions 163 × 250 cm, central panel 163× 128 cm, wings 163× 60 cm, (Akademie für bildenden Künste, Vienna).

Attributions

Cranach's Adam and Eve

Rachel Ropeik and Steven Zucker provide a description, historical perspective, and analysis of Lucus Cranach the Elder's *Adam and Eve*.

- https://youtu.be/g4XZGhnFOwM

Lucus Cranach the Elder, *Adam and Eve*, 1526, oil on panel, (Courtauld Gallery, London).

Holbein's The Ambassadors

Dr. Beth Harris and Dr. Steven Zucker provide a description, historical perspective, and analysis of Hans Holbein the Younger's *The Ambassadors*.

- https://youtu.be/PQZUIGzinZA

Hans Holbein the Younger, *The Ambassadors*, 1533, oil on oak, 207 × 209.5 cm (The National Gallery, London).

Attributions

Portrait of Henry the VIII

Dr. Beth Harris and Dr. Steven Zucker provide a description, historical perspective, and analysis of Hans Holbein the Younger's *Portrait of Henry VIII*.

- https://youtu.be/-wTI7EC-i30

Hans Holbein the Younger, *Portrait of Henry VIII*, 1540, oil on panel, (Palazzo Barberini, Rome).

> **Please note:** there have been questions raised as to whether this painting is by Holbein or his workshop, or perhaps a later copy; recent research suggests that it is an original Holbein.

Attributions

Bruegel's The Dutch Proverbs

Dr. Beth Harris and Dr. Steven Zucker provide a description, historical perspective, and analysis of Pieter Bruegel the Elder's *The Dutch Proverbs*.

- https://youtu.be/mSPumIx85l8

Pieter Bruegel the Elder, *The Dutch Proverbs*, 1559, oil on oak, 117 × 163 cm (Gemäldegalerie, Staatliche Museen zu Berlin)

External Link

View this painting up close in the Google Art Project

- https://www.google.com/culturalinstitute/asset-viewer/the-dutch-proverbs/WwG8mD89xbELbQ

Chapter 7:
1600–1700–Baroque
Art in Italy

Chapter 7 Overview

What You'll Learn To Do: Examine Italian Baroque art, its artists, and its impact on art history.

In Chapter 7 we will examine Italian Baroque art. We will look at how artists like Bernini contributed to the development of Western art. It is imperative to understand Italian Baroque art in order to see how it impacted later artistic developments.

Learning Activities

The learning activities for this module include:

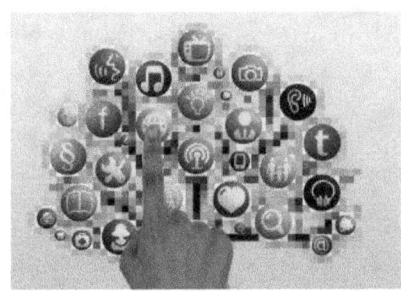

- **Review:** Key Learning Items

The Baroque

- **Read:** Introduction to the Baroque
- **Read:** Baroque Art in Italy
- **Read:** Bernini's David (includes a video: 3:54)
- **Watch:** Bernini's St. Peter's Square (2:50)
- **Read:** Bernini's Ecstasy of St. Teresa (includes a video: 7:32)
- **Watch:** Borromini's San Carlo alle Quattro Fontane (6:52)
- **Read:** Coffered Dome Explained
- **Read:** Caravaggio's Deposition
- **Read:** Caravaggio's Calling of St. Matthew (includes a video: 6:21)
- **Read:** Caravaggio and his followers
- **Watch:** Il Gesu, Rome (8:07)
- **Watch:** Gentileschi (4:00)
- **Watch:** Carracci's Ceiling of the Farnese Palace (9:37)
- **Read:** Quadro Riportato Explained

Attributions

CC licensed content, Original

- Art History II. **Provided by**: Extended Learning Institute of Northern Virginia Community College. **Located at**: http://eli.nvcc.edu/. **License**: *CC BY: Attribution*

Public domain content

- Image of Finger. **Authored by**: geralt. **Located at**: https://pixabay.com/en/finger-touch-hand-structure-769300/. **License**: *Public Domain: No Known Copyright*

Key Learning Items

Key Vocabulary Terms

- Italian Baroque
- colonnade
- piazza
- coffered dome
- cherubs
- tenebrism (tenebroso)
- chiaroscuro

- Caravaggesque/Caravaggisti

- illusionism

- quadro riportato

Here are links to art history glossaries that will help you better understand the above key vocabulary terms.

- ArtLex: Art Dictionary
    - http://www.artlex.com/

- About.com: Art History
    - http://arthistory.about.com/od/glossary/l/bl_Art-Glossary.htm

- Artcyclopedia: A Guide to Fine Art
    - http://www.artcyclopedia.com/

Attributions

CC licensed content, Original

Introduction to the Baroque

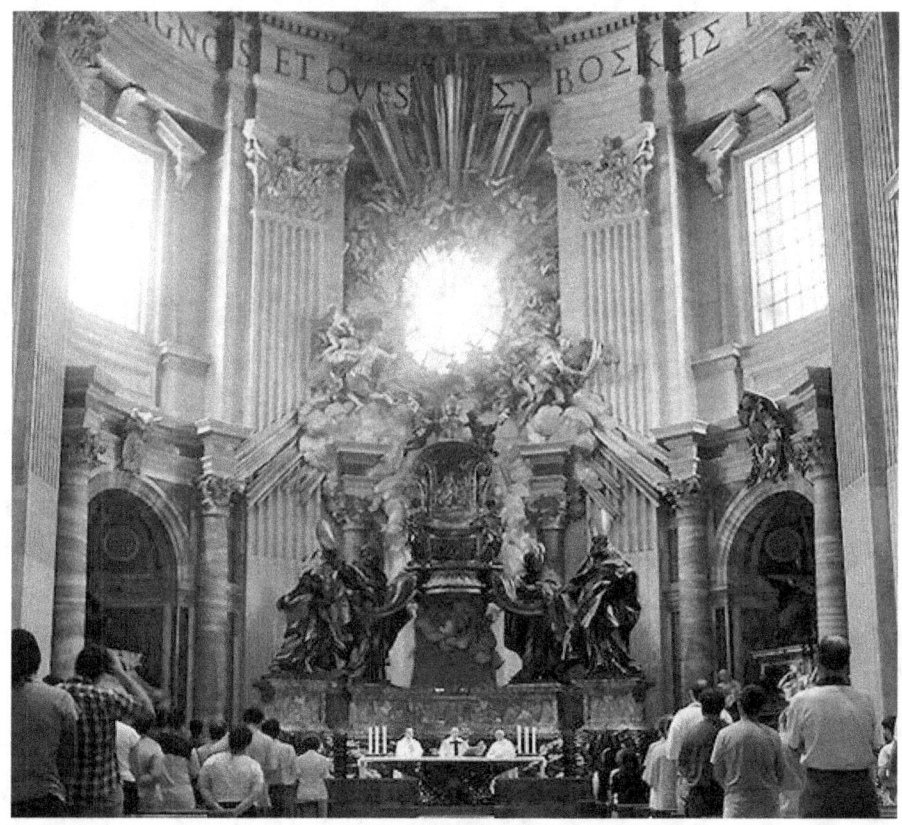

Figure 1. Gian Lorenzo Bernini, Cathedra Petri (or Chair of St. Peter), gilded bronze, gold, wood, stained glass, 1647–53 (apse of Saint Peter's Basilica, Vatican City, Rome)

Rome: From the "Whore of Babylon" to the Resplendent Bride of Christ

When Martin Luther tacked his 95 theses to the doors of Wittenburg Cathedral in 1517 protesting the Catholic Church's corruption, he initiated a movement that would transform the religious, political, and artistic landscape of Europe. For the next century, Europe would be in turmoil as new political and religious boundaries were determined, often through bloody military conflicts. Only in 1648, with the signing of the Treaty of Westphalia, did the conflicts between Protestants and Catholics subside in continental Europe.

Martin Luther focused his critique on what he saw as the Church's greed and abuse of power. He called Rome, the seat of papal power, "the whore of Babylon" decked out in finery of expensive art, grand architecture, and sumptuous banquets. The Church responded to the crisis in two ways: by internally addressing issues of corruption and by defending the doctrines rejected by the Protestants. Thus, while the first two decades of the sixteenth century were a period of lavish spending for the Papacy, the middle decades were a period of austerity. As one visitor to Rome noted in the 1560s, the entire city had become a convent. Piety and asceticism ruled the day.

By the end of the sixteenth century, the Catholic Church was once again feeling optimistic, even triumphant. It had emerged from the crisis with renewed vigor and clarity of purpose. Shepherding the faithful—instructing them on Catholic doctrines and inspiring virtuous behavior—took center stage. Keen to rebuild Rome's reputation as a holy city, the Papacy embarked on extensive building and decoration campaigns aimed at highlighting its ancient origins, its beliefs, and its divinely-sanctioned authority. In the eyes of faithful Catholics, Rome was not an unfaithful whore, but a pure bride, beautifully adorned for her union with her divine spouse.

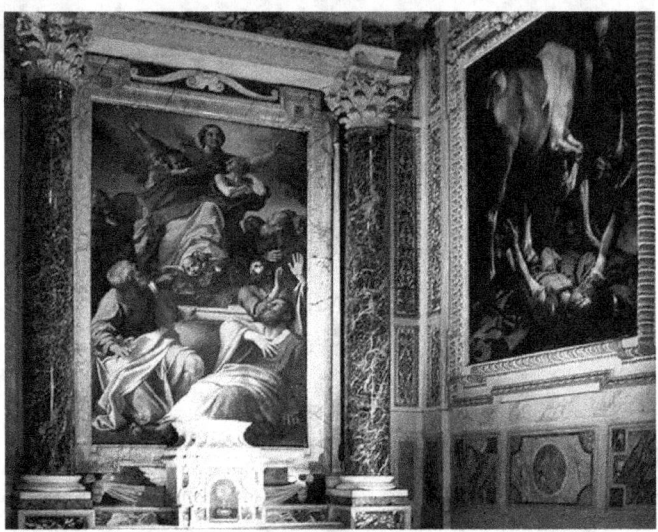

Figure 2. View of the Cerasi Chapel in Santa Maria del Popolo in Rome with Annibale Carracci's altarpiece, The Assumption of the Virgin, 1600–01, oil on canvas, 96 in × 61 inches and to the right, Caravaggio's Conversion of Saint Paul (Conversion of Saul), 1601, 91 in × 69 inches

The Art of Persuasion: To Instruct, to Delight, to Move

While the Protestants harshly criticized the cult of images, the Catholic Church ardently embraced the religious power of art. The visual arts, the Church argued, played a key role in guiding the faithful. They were certainly as important as the written and spoken word, and perhaps even more important, since they were accessible to the learned and the unlearned alike. In order to be effective in its pastoral role, religious art had to be clear, persuasive, and powerful. Not only did it have to instruct, it had to inspire. It had to move the faithful to feel the reality of Christ's sacrifice, the suffering of the martyrs, the visions of the saints.

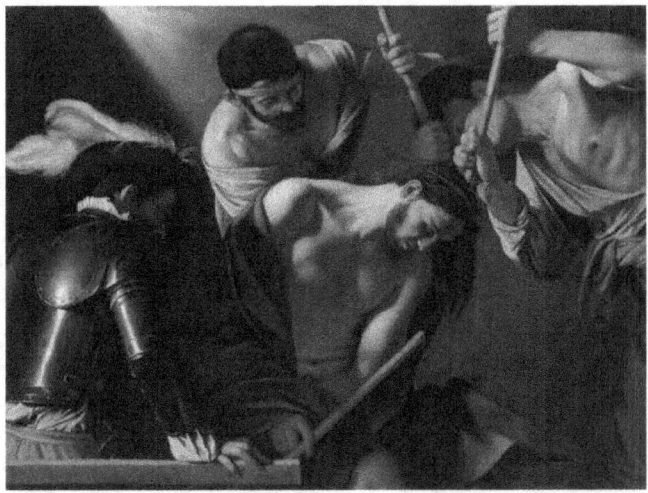

Figure 3. Caravaggio, The Crowning with Thorns, 1602–04, oil on canvas, 165.5 × 127 cm (Kunsthistorisches Museum, Vienna).

The Church's emphasis on art's pastoral role prompted artists to experiment with new and more direct means of engaging the viewer. Artists like Caravaggio turned to a powerful and dramatic realism, accentuated by bold contrasts of light and dark, and tightly-cropped compositions that enhance the physical and emotional immediacy of the depicted narrative. Other artists, like Annibale Carracci (who also experimented with realism), ultimately settled on a more classical visual language, inspired by the vibrant palette, idealized forms, and balanced compositions of the High Renaissance. Still others, like Giovanni Battista Gaulli, turned to daring feats of illusionism that blurred not only the boundaries between painting, sculpture, and architecture, but also those between the real and depicted worlds. In so doing, the divine was made physically present and palpable. Whether through shocking realism, dynamic movement, or exuberant ornamentation, seventeenth-century art is meant to impress. It aims to convince the viewer of the truth of its message by impacting the senses, awakening the emotions, and activating, even sharing the viewer's space.

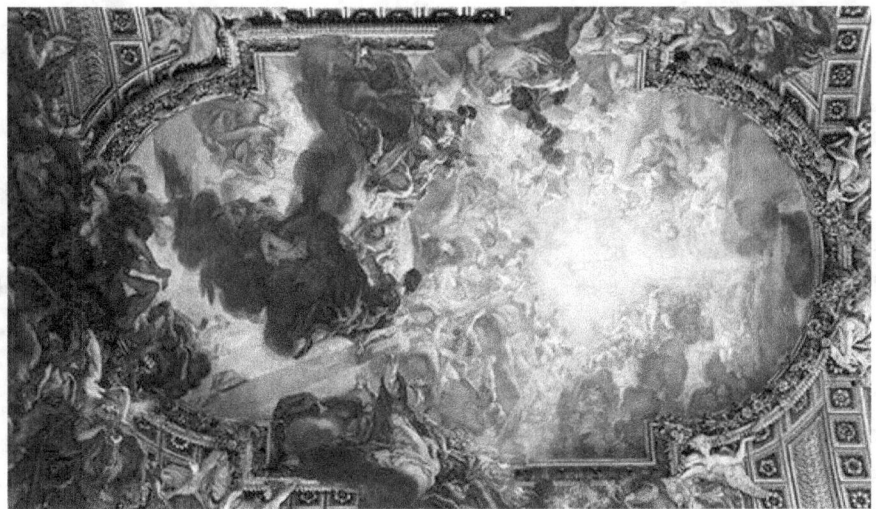

Figure 4. Giovanni Battista Gaulli, also known as il Baciccio, The Triumph of the Name of Jesus, Il Gesù ceiling fresco, 1672–1685

The Catholic Monarchs and Their Territories

The monarchs of Spain, Portugal, and France also embraced the more ornate elements of seventeenth century art to celebrate Catholicism. In Spain and its colonies, rulers invested vast resources on elaborate church facades, stunning, gold-covered chapels and tabernacles, and strikingly-realistic polychrome sculpture. In the Spanish Netherlands, where sacred art had suffered terribly as a result of the Protestant iconoclasm (the destruction of art), civic and religious leaders prioritized the adornment of churches as the region reclaimed its Catholic identity. Refurnishing the altars of Antwerp's churches kept Peter Paul Rubens' workshop busy for many years. Europe's monarchs also adopted this artistic vocabulary to proclaim their own power and status. Louis XIV, for example, commissioned the splendid buildings and gardens of Versailles as a visual expression of his divine right to rule.

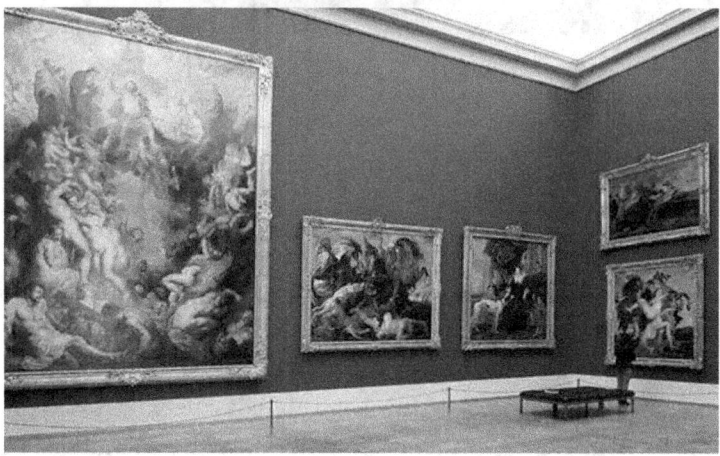

Figure 5. View of paintings by Peter Paul Rubens in the Alte Pinakothek, Munich

The Protestant North

In the Protestant countries, and especially in the newly-independent Dutch Republic (modern-day Holland), the artistic climate changed radically in the aftermath of the Reformation.

Two of the wealthiest sources of patronage—the monarchy and the Church—were now gone. In their stead arose an increasingly prosperous middle class eager to express its status, and its new sense of national pride, through the purchase of art.

By the middle of the seventeenth century a new market had emerged to meet the artistic tastes of this class. The demand was now for smaller scale paintings suitable for display in private homes. These paintings included religious subjects for private contemplation, as seen in Rembrandt's poignant paintings and prints of biblical narratives, as well as portraits documenting individual likenesses.

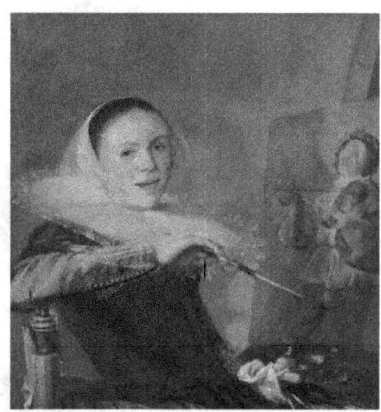

Figure 5. Judith Leyster, Self-Portrait, c. 1630, oil on canvas, 651 × 746 cm (National Gallery of Art, Washington). View this painting up close in the Google Art Project.

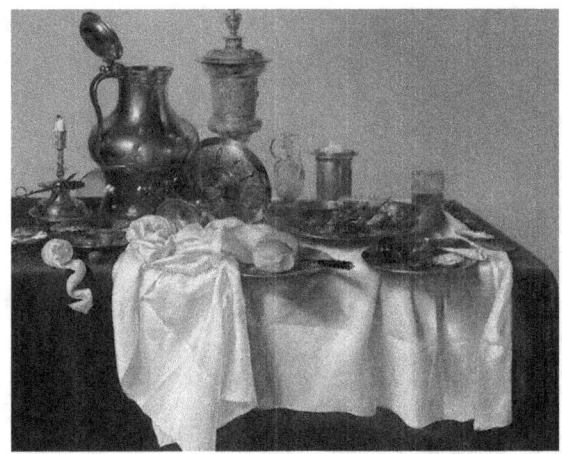

Figure 6. Willem Claesz Heda, Banquet Piece with Mince Pie, 1635, oil on canvas, 42 × 43-3/4 inches (National Gallery of Art, Washington).

But, the greatest change in the market was the dramatic increase in the popularity of landscapes, still-lifes, and scenes of everyday life (known as genre painting). Indeed, the proliferation of these subjects as independent artistic genres was one of the seventeenth century's most significant contributions to the history of Western art. In all of these genres, artists revealed a keen interest in replicating observed reality—whether it be the light on the Dutch landscape, the momentary expression on a face, or the varied textures and materials of the objects the Dutch collected as they reaped the benefits of their expanding mercantile empire. These works demonstrated as much artistic virtuosity and physical immediacy as the grand decorations of the palaces and churches of Catholic Europe.

Baroque: The Word, the Style, the Period

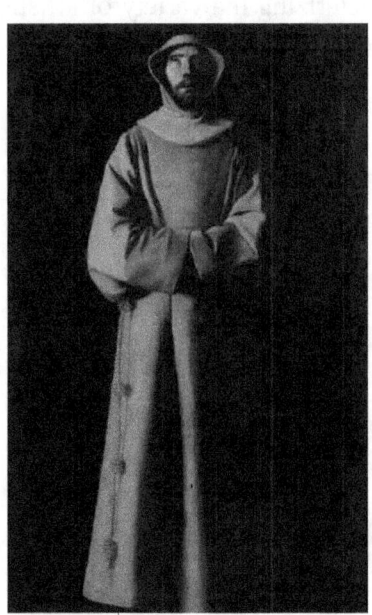

Figure 7. Francisco de Zurbarán, Saint Francis of Assisi According to Pope Nicholas V's Vision, c. 1640, oil on canvas, 110.5 × 180.5 cm (Museum Nacional d'Art de Catalunya, Barcelona).

In the context of European history, the period from c. 1585 to c. 1700/ 1730 is often called the Baroque era. The word "baroque" derives from the Portuguese and Spanish words for a large, irregularly-shaped pearl ("barroco" and "barrueco," respectively). Eighteenth century critics were the first to apply the term to the art of the seventeenth century. It was not a term of praise. To the eyes of these critics, who favored the restraint and order of Neoclassicism, the works of Bernini, Borromini, and Pietro da Cortona appeared bizarre, absurd, even diseased—in other words, misshapen, like an imperfect pearl.

By the middle of the nineteenth century, the word had lost its pejorative implications and was used to describe the ornate and complex qualities present in many examples of seventeenth-century art, music and literature. Eventually, the term came to designate the historical period as a whole. In the context of painting, for example, the stark realism of Zurbaran's altarpieces, the quiet intimacy of Vermeer's domestic interiors, and restrained classicism of Poussin's landscapes are all "Baroque" (now with a capital "B" to indicate the historical period), regardless of the absence of the stylistic traits originally associated with the term.

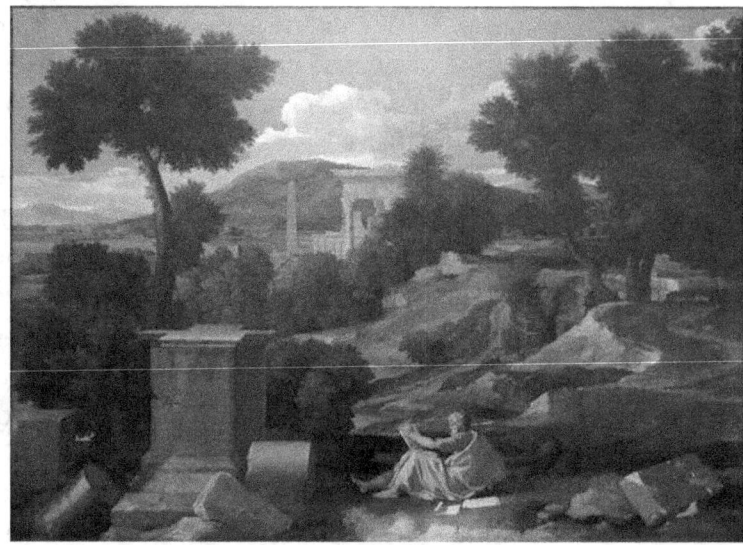

Figure 8. Nicolas Poussin, Landscape with St. John, 1640, oil on canvas, 39-1/2 × 53-5/8 inches (Art Institute of Chicago).

Scholars continue to debate the validity of this label, admitting the usefulness of having a label for this distinct historical period, while also acknowledging its limitations in characterizing the variety of artistic styles present in the seventeenth century.

Attributions

CC licensed content, Shared previously

- The Baroque: Art, Politics & Religion in 17th-century Europe. **Authored by**: Dr. Esperanca Camara. **Provided by**: Khan Academy. **Located at**: https://web.archive.org/web/20140215033011/http://smarthistory.khanacademy.org/1600-1700-the-Baroque.html. **License**: *CC BY-NC-SA: Attribution-NonCommercial-ShareAlike*

Baroque Art in Italy

Baroque art is the style of the late 1500s and 1600s. The important thing to keep in mind now is that the Baroque style in Italy is the direct result of the Counter-Reformation. The Church needs a powerful style of art to use in the fight against Martin Luther—and that's exactly what the Baroque style is—it is powerful, dramatic, muscular, sometimes frightening, and it really gets to you! Bernini, one of the greatest artists of the Baroque period, worked in Rome, often for the papacy like Michelangelo before him. To get an idea of what a great sculptor he is, and how he can make marble seem like human flesh, look at his sculpure *Pluto and Proserpina*. What about this sculpture is different than anything we've seen before? Look at her hair, how it is flying back behind her as she turns her head, and remains in mid-air.

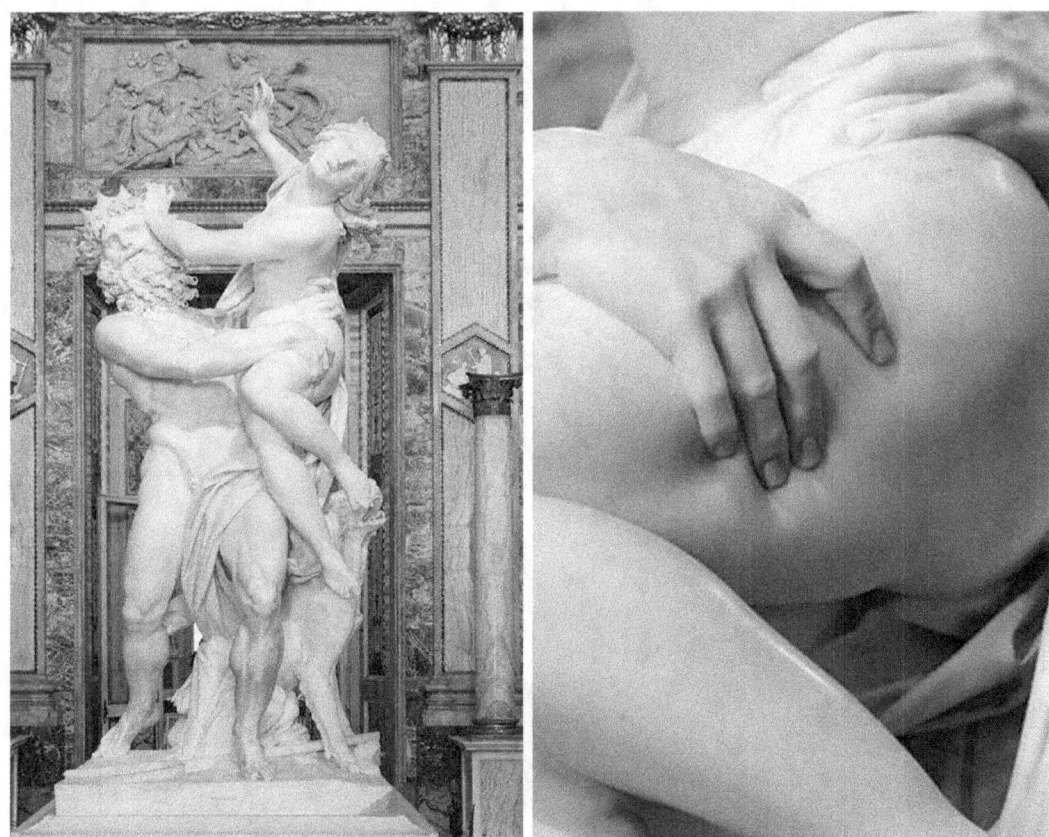

Figure 1. Gian Lorenzo Bernini, Pluto and Proserpina, marble, 1621–22 (Galleria Borghese, Rome)

Attributions

- Baroque Art in Italy. **Provided by**: Khan Academy. **Located at**: https://web.archive.org/web/20140215025925/http://smarthistory.khanacademy.org/baroque-italy.html. **License**: *CC BY-NC-SA: Attribution-NonCommercial-ShareAlike*

- Rape of Prosepina September 2015. **Authored by**: Alvesgaspar. **Located at**: https://commons.wikimedia.org/wiki/File:Rape_of_Prosepina_September_2015-3a.jpg. **License**: *CC BY-SA: Attribution-ShareAlike*

- Rape of Prosepina. **Authored by**: Alvesgaspar. **Located at**: https://commons.wikimedia.org/wiki/File:Rape_of_Prosepina_September_2015-2b.jpg. **License**: *CC BY-SA: Attribution-ShareAlike*

Bernini's David

Dr. Beth Harris and Dr. Steven Zucker provide a description, historical perspective, and analysis of Bernini's *David*.

- https://youtu.be/YKzHdQKX9RA

Gian Lorenzo Bernini, *David*, 1623–24, marble (Galleria Borghese, Rome)

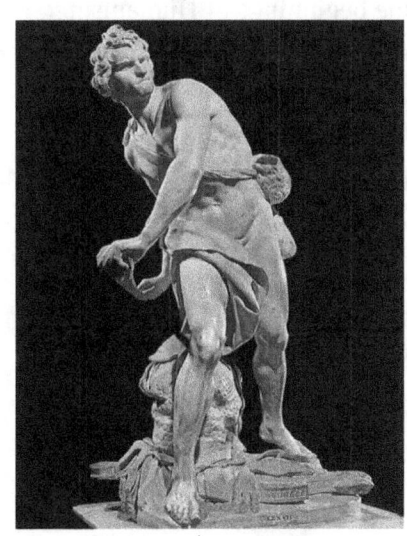

Figure 1. Gian Lorenzo Bernini, David, marble, 1623–24 (Galleria Borghese, Rome)

Bernini's *David* (figure 1) has always reminded me of a major league pitcher winding up to throw a 95 miles an hour fastball. Have you seen that? The pitcher gathers all of his strength for each pitch and puts everything he has into it. This is what Baroque art wants from us—it wants us to be able to relate to the image **in our bodies**, not just in our minds—to really feel it physically and relate to the image physically.

Think about it! Does Michelangelo's *David* (figure 3) inspire the same physical reaction in you? When looking at Bernini's *David*, don't you immediately start to feel what David is feeling? This sympathy is very important to Baroque art. Bernini's *David* really uses the space around it—reaching out into the space of the viewer—our space! (See figure 2.)

It is not content—the way Michelangelo's *David* is—to remain separate from us. Remember we talked about the pyramid composition in the High Renaissance? And pyramids are a very stable shape, right? Well, in the Baroque era we see compositions in the shape of diagonal lines, as in Bernini's *David*. The diagonal line immediately suggests movement and energy and drama—very different from the immobility of the pyramid shape!

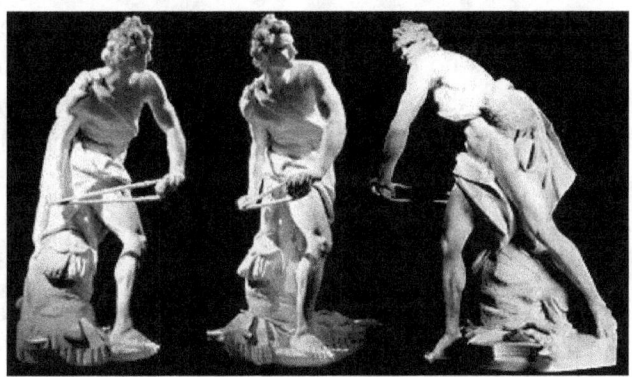

Figure 2. 360 degree view of Bernini's David

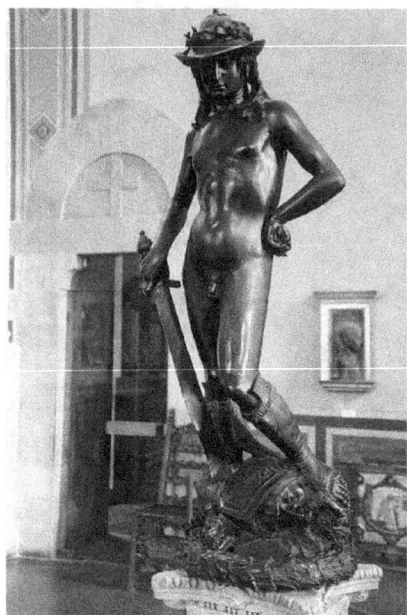 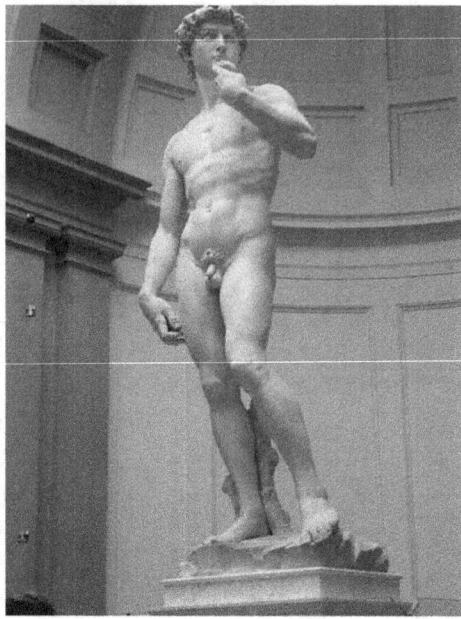

Figure 3. (left) Donatello's David; (right) Michelangelo's David

- **Donatello** shows us an early moment in the Renaissance, and the beginnings of Humanism when artists were first discovering contrapposto and the beauty of ancient Greek and Roman sculpture. His young figure of David symbolizes the Republic of Florence and its sense of being blessed by God, and so we see David victorious standing on the head of Goliath.

- **Michelangelo** shows us a figure perfectly beautiful. And so we have the full flowering of the Renaissance idea that man is created in God's image. Man is God-like. We also have the association of perfection and beauty and harmony in mathematics and God, which was so important at the height of Humanism in the High Renaissance.

- **Bernini** shows us David actively fighting Goliath—with God on his side. Perhaps the way the church itself felt as they were battling against Luther.

The Path to God in the Renaissance

I think Michelangelo is asking us to sit and contemplate the incredible beauty of David, and through contemplating beauty, and the beauty of man, God's greatest creation, we come to know God. On the other hand, there is no time for contemplation with Bernini's David, there is only time for ducking out of the way. Our reaction is in our bodies, not in our minds (the way it is with Michelangelo's). So, we could say that the path to God in the Renaissance was through the mind (this is part of Humanism as we know).

The Path to God in the Baroque Era

On the other hand, the path to God in the Baroque era is much more direct, more emotional, more bodily, and that of course relates to the embattled position of the Church, which felt as though it needed to appeal very directly to the faithful.

Attributions

Bernini's St. Peter's Square

Dr. Beth Harris and Dr. Steven Zucker provide a description, historical perspective, and analysis of Bernini's *Saint Peter's Square (Piazza San Pietro)*.

- https://www.youtube.com/watch?v=9UT43MHdTIg

Gianlorenzo Bernini, *Saint Peter's Square (Piazza San Pietro)*, Vatican City, Rome, 1656–67

Attributions

Bernini's Ecstasy of St. Teresa

Dr. Beth Harris and Dr. Steven Zucker provide a description, historical perspective, and analysis of Bernini's *Ecstasy of St. Teresa*.

- https://youtu.be/RKcJvjP9zgY

Gian Lorenzo Bernini, *Ecstasy of St. Teresa*, 1645–52, (Cornaro Chapel, Santa Maria della Vittoria, Rome).

Saint Teresa

Saint Teresa was a nun who was canonized (made a Saint by the Church) in part because of the spiritual visions she experienced. She lived during the middle of the sixteenth century in Spain—at the height of the Reformation. Saint Teresa wrote several books in which she described her visions.

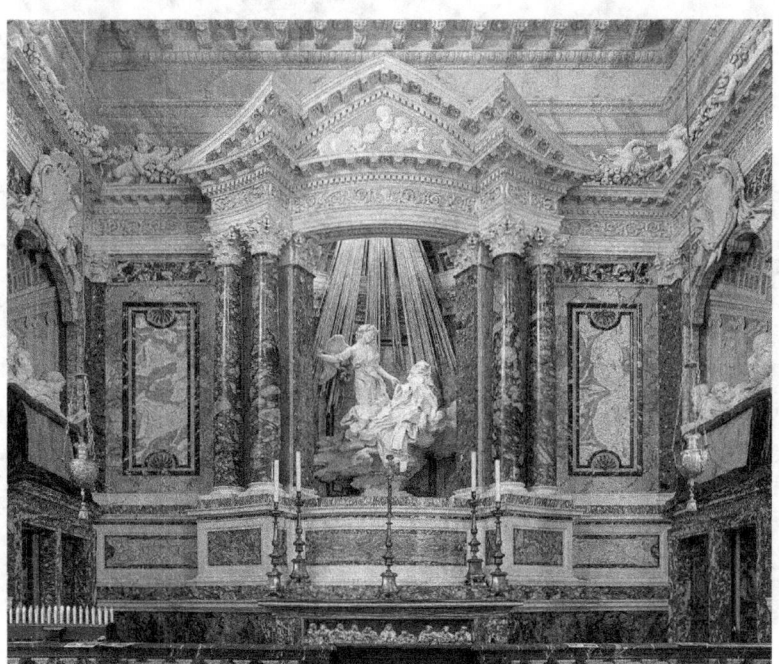

Figure 1. Gian Lorenzo Bernini, Ecstasy of St. Teresa, 1645–52 (Cornaro Chapel, Santa Maria della Vittoria, Rome)

This is her description of the event that Bernini depicts:

Beside me, on the left, appeared an angel in bodily form. . . . He was not tall but short, and very beautiful; and his face was so aflame that he appeared to be one of the highest rank of angels, who seem to be all on fire. . . . In his hands I saw a great golden spear, and at the iron tip there appeared to be a point of fire. This he plunged into my heart several times so that it penetrated to my entrails. When he pulled it out I felt that he took them with it, and left me utterly consumed by the great love of God. The pain wasso severe that it made me utter several moans. The sweetness caused by this intense pain is so extreme that one cannot possibly wish it to cease, nor is one's soul content with anything but God. This is not a physical but a spiritual pain, though the body has some share in it—even a considerable share.

Saint Teresa describes her intensely spiritual experience in very physical, even sexual terms. Why? We know that an important goal of Baroque art is to involve the viewer. Teresa is describing this in physical terms so that we can understand. After all, being visited by an angel and filled with the love of God is no small experience. How can we, with our ordinary experiences, hope to understand the intensity and passion of her experience except on our own terms?

The Cornaro Chapel

When we look at the *Ecstasy of Saint Teresa* by Bernini we have to consider the entire space of the chapel. The chapel is called the Cornaro Chapel, after the Cornaro family who controlled it and commissioned Bernini to sculpt Saint Teresa.

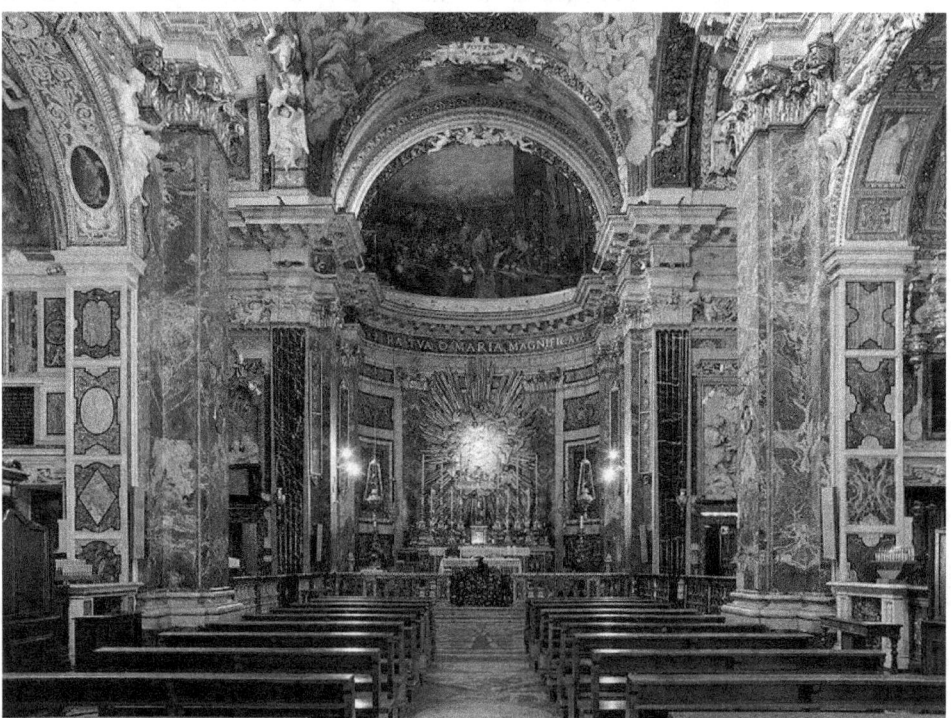

Figure 2. Bernini, Cornaro Chapel in Santa Maria della Vittoria, Rome

When we walk toward the chapel (figure 2) we see that on either side of us, on the side walls, there are what look like theater boxes. In these boxes, seated figures in appear to be talking and gesturing to each other. Perhaps they are kneeling in prayer as they watch and discuss the scene of the *Ecstasy of Saint Teresa*.

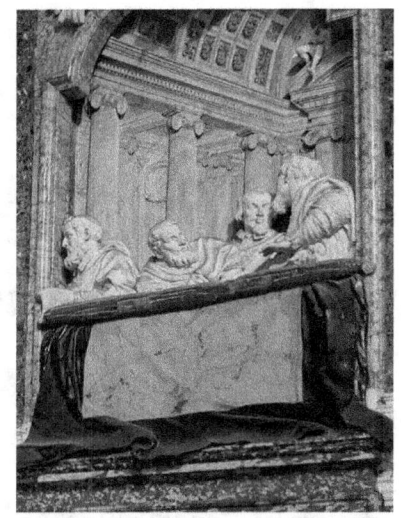

Figure 3. The patron, Federico Cornaro, is 2nd from the right

Who are these figures in the theater boxes? (See figure 3.) One is Federico Cornaro, Cadinal of Venice and the patron who paid for the Cornaro Chapel. The others are posthumous portraits of members of the Cornaro family (many of them were also Cardinals). Behind them Bernini created a fabulous illusion of architecture—a coffered barrel vault, doorway and columns. And, if we follow the metaphor of a theater, it feels as though we've got the best seats in the house! And importantly, what's happened is that we have immediately become a part of the work of art. It surrounds us, and we are literally inside of it. This is, as we have seen, a typical feature of Baroque art—breaking down the barrier between the work and the viewer, to involve us.

Attributions

Caravaggio's Deposition

With most artists we know about their lives and personalities from biographies that friends or contemporaries wrote about them. In the case of Michelangelo Merisi da Caravaggio, however, we know about his life primarily from police records! From these accounts, we learn that he had a bad temper and could be violent, and that he was frequently arrested and imprisoned for assault. He appears on the police records for mild offenses like carrying weapons without permission, as well as more serious ones where he is involved in violent fights. He was even questioned once because he "gave offense" to a woman and her daughter—one wonders what that could mean! Ultimately, he killed a man over a bet and spent the last few years of his life on the run from the police.

Deposition (or Entombment)

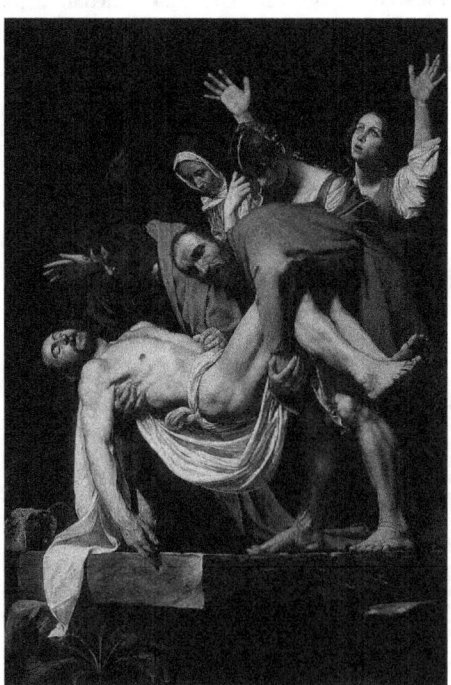

Figure 1. Caravaggio, Deposition (or Entombment), oil on canvas, c. 1600–04 (Pinocateca, Vatican)

The Subject

After the crucifixion, some on Christ's followers (Nicodemus, Joseph of Arimathea, Mary Magdalene) along with his Mother, remove Christ's body from the cross and place it in the tomb.

The Darkness (and the Light)

One of the first things you might notice about Caravaggio's style, and we see it here in his painting of *The Entombment*, is the darkness. There's actually a word for it: tenebroso, which means dark style. Caravaggio painted this scene as though it was happening in the black of night with almost a spot-light effect on the figures (doesn't it look like a dark stage that has been illuminated with a spotlight?).

There are several things that are important about this: There is no background—only darkness. No architecture, no landscape, and so as a result, we focus on the figures who are all located in the foreground of the painting. The spotlight effect of the lighting is very dramatic, and so we have very stark contrasts of light and dark. In other words, where modeling isusually a slow movement from light to dark, here we have very dark shadows *right next to* areas of bright illumination. The effect is very dramatic.

The Space

Everything is located very much in the foreground of the painting, very close to us in fact. Look at Christ's body—its so close we feel like we can touch it. And look at the ledge of the tomb, it is foreshortened and so it juts out into our space. And look at the elbow of the figure in orange carrying Christ's legs—it is foreshortened, too, and so it pops into our space. One of the main characteristics of Baroque art is the breakdown of the barrier between our space and the space of thepainting, so we feel like we're really part of it. Baroque artists use foreshortening a lot.

The Composition

Baroque artists were interested in movement. Here we see the moment when Christ is being lowered into his tomb. It's a process happening before our eyes, so once again, we have a caught moment in time. We see that the figures form a diagonal line—another very common feature of Baroque art. In the High Renaissance, we saw compositions in the shape of a pyramid—a very stable shape. Here in Baroque art we see diagonals, or sometimes interlocking diagonals in the shape of an X.

Caravaggio organized the composition so that it looks like the body of Christ is being lowered right into our space, as though we were standing in the tomb. Remember: one of the most important goals of Baroque art is to involve the viewer.

Realism

Baroque art tends to be very real—not only do the figures look "regular," but the artist is giving us a very real sense of this moment. The body of Christ looks truly dead, the figures struggle to hold the dead weight of his body and ease him down gently into his tomb.

The Figures

The figures are all very ordinary looking, they are not idealized at all, like the figures of the High Renaissance. Look at the figure holding Christ's legs. He almost looks like a homeless person. Look at his feet and legs—they are so ordinary looking—you can almost imagine the bottom of his feet being dirty. Even Christ looks rather like an ordinary man. They are figures we can relate to more —unlike the perfect figures of the High Renaissance.

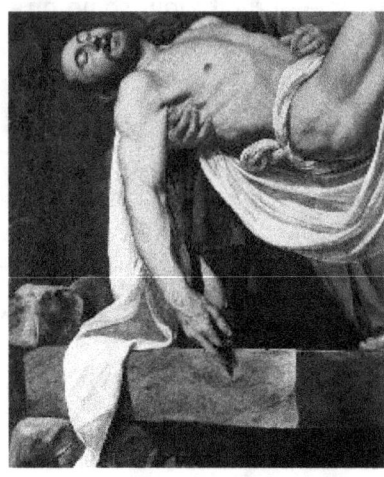

Figure 2. Details of the Deposition

One of my favorite things about this painting is the figure who carries Christ's shoulders. He has his arm under Christ's torso and his fingers, as they reached around Christ, slipped into the wound that he received when he was on the cross (Christ was stabbed by a Roman soldier in the ribs). *Ewwww! Ick!* You are probably saying to yourself. *And that is the whole idea!* Baroque art wants to get to you *in your body*—so you really feel it, and relate to it. When you know something in your mind it is one thing, but when you experience it with your body it is really different. Baroque art wants you to have an experience that's located in your body—unlike the High Renaissance, which appealed to the mind.

Attributions

CC licensed content, Shared previously

Caravaggio's Calling of St. Matthew

Dr. Beth Harris and Dr. Steven Zucker provide a description, historical perspective, and analysis of Caravaggio's *Calling of St. Matthew*.

- https://youtu.be/SZF5K8epWko

Caravaggio, *Calling of St. Matthew*, c. 1599–1600, oil on canvas, (Contarelli Chapel, San Luigi dei Francesi, Rome).

A favorite subject for Baroque artists was moments when one is going about one's everyday life, and then suddenly the divine enters into that mundane, everyday life, and everything is forever changed. As we have seen, life-changing moments, like conversion (think of St. Paul) or Spiritual visions (like St. Theresa) are also popular among Baroque artists.

The New Testament story, of Jesus calling Levi (later Matthew) to be his disciple is really a very simple one, but Caravaggio interprets it so richly. Here's the story from the gospel of Mark:

13 Then Jesus went out to the lakeshore again and taught the crowds that gathered around him.

14 As he walked along, he saw Levi son of Alphaeus sitting at his tax-collection booth. "Come, be my disciple," Jesus said to him. So Levi got up and followed him.

15 That night Levi invited Jesus and his disciples to be his dinner guests, along with his fellow tax collectors and many other notorious sinners. (There were many people of this kind among the crowds that followed Jesus.)

16 But when some of the teachers of religious law who were Pharisees saw him eating with people like that, they said to his disciples, "Why does he eat with such scum?"

17 When Jesus heard this, he told them, "Healthy people don't need a doctor—sick people do. I have come to call sinners, not those who think they are already good enough."

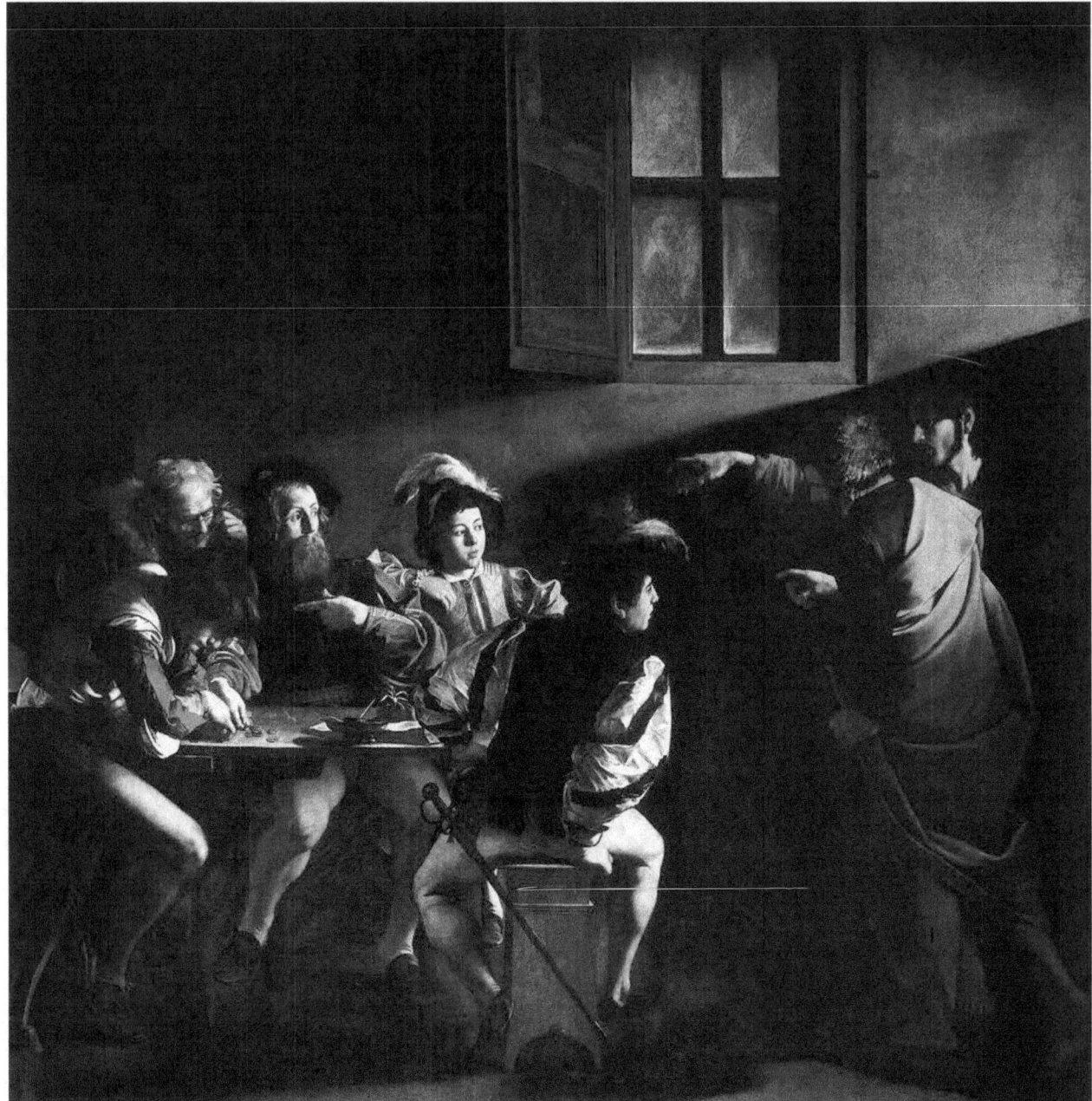

Figure 1. Caravaggio, Calling of St. Matthew

Attributions

CC licensed content, Shared previously

- Caravaggio's Calling of Saint Matthew. **Authored by**: Dr. Beth Harris and Dr. Steven Zucker. **Provided by**: Khan Academy. **Located at**: https://web.archive.org/web/20140215024035/http://smarthistory.khanacademy.org/caravaggio-matthew.html. **License**: *CC BY-NC-SA: Attribution-NonCommercial-ShareAlike*

Caravaggio and His Followers

Follwo the link below to view the page "Caravaggio and Caravaggisti in 17th-Century Europe" by Dr. Erin Benay on Khan Academy (originally developed for Oxford Art Online). Caravaggio was one of the most imitated artists, and this page takes a look at why, as well as comparing his original works to the works of artists inspired by him.

"Caravaggio and Caravaggisti in 17th-Century Europe" by Dr. Erin Benay:

- https://www.khanacademy.org/humanities/monarchy-enlightenment/baroque-art1/baroque-italy/a/caravaggio-and-caravaggisti-in-17th-century-europe

Attributions

Gentileschi

Dr. Beth Harris and Dr. Steven Zucker provide a description, historical perspective, and analysis of Artemisia Gentileschi's *Judith and Holofernes*.

- https://youtu.be/BHFuLS9NW6s

Artemisia Gentileschi, *Judith and Holofernes*, 1620–21, oil on canvas, 162.5 × 199 cm, (Uffizi Gallery, Florence).

External Link
View this painting up close in the Google Art Project.: • https://www.google.com/culturalinstitute/asset-viewer/judith-and-holofernes/oQF3gDEYNkutBA?projectId=art-project

Attributions

Carracci's Ceiling of the Farnese Palace

Dr. David Drogin and Dr. Beth Harris provide a description, historical perspective, and analysis of the ceiling of the Palazzo Farnese.

- https://youtu.be/DR9ad67Ftv0

Annibale Carracci, *Ceiling of the Palazzo Farnese*, fresco, Rome, 1597–1608

Attributions

CC licensed content, Shared previously

Chapter 8: 1600–1700–Baroque Art in Flanders, Dutch Republic, Spain and France

Chapter 8 Overview

What You'll Learn To Do: Examine Baroque art in the rest of Europe and understand its impact on later artistic developments.

In Chapter 8 we will examine Baroque art in the rest of Europe. We will look at how artists like Rembrandt contributed to the development of Western art. It is imperative to understand Baroque art in the rest of Europe in order to see how it impacted later artistic developments.

Learning Activities

The learning activities for this module include:

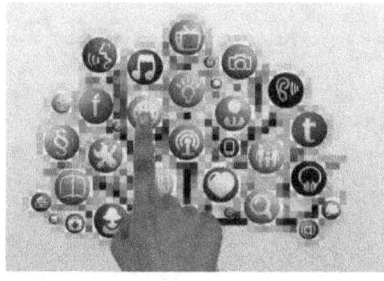

- **Review:** Key Learning Items

The Baroque

- **Read:** Baroque Terms Explained

Flanders

- **Read:** Rubens, Elevation of the Cross
- **Watch:** Rubens, Arrival of Marie de Medici (5:23)
- **Watch:** Rubens, The Consequences of War (3:54)

Dutch Republic

- **Watch:** Vermeer, Young Woman with a Water Pitcher (4:48)
- **Watch:** Vermeer, The Glass of Wine (4:16)
- **Read:** Vermeer and the Camera Obscura
- **Watch:** Rembrandt, Bathsheba at her Bath (4:02)
- **Watch:** Rembrandt, The Three Crosses (10:22)
- **Watch:** Rembrandt's Self-Portraits (10:21)

- **Watch:** Hal's Singing Boy with Flute (2:15)
- **Watch:** Hal's Malle Babbe (3:37)
- **Watch:** van Huysum, Vase with Flowers (2:56)
- **Read:** Vanitas Painting Explained
- **Read:** Dutch Genre Painting Explained

Spain

- **Watch:** Las Meninas (5:59)
- **Watch:** Los Borrachos (4:47)

France

- **Read:** Louis XIV & Versailles
- **Watch:** Poussin, Landscape with St. John (5:05)
- **Watch:** Le Nain, Peasant Family in an Interior (3:11)

Attributions

Key Learning Items

Learning Objectives

After successful completion of this module, you will be able to:

- Understand and apply the concepts and terminology of European Baroque art
- Investigate and apply the fundamental questions we ask when looking at art objects from this movement
- Discuss, collaborate, and generate understanding as to the meaning of European Baroque art
- Assess and evaluate the impact of European Baroque art on the continued evolution of Western art

Key Questions to Ask

While you are reviewing the content of this module, consider the following questions:

- How did the Baroque look different across Europe?
- What are the key characteristics of the Baroque in Flanders, Dutch Republic, Spain and France?
- What are the various genres of Baroque art in these countries?
- How did the local religious beliefs affect Baroque art in these countries?

Key Vocabulary Terms

- secular painting
- landscape
- still life
- genre painting
- portraiture

- painterly v. linear
- classicism
- etching
- drypoint
- camera obscura
- vanitas paintings
- objects d'art

Here are links to art history glossaries that will help you better understand the above key vocabulary terms.

- ArtLex: Art Dictionary
    ◦ http://www.artlex.com/
- About.com: Art History
    ◦ http://arthistory.about.com/od/glossary/l/bl_Art-Glossary.htm
- Artcyclopedia: A Guide to Fine Art
    ◦ http://www.artcyclopedia.com/

Attributions

CC licensed content, Original

Baroque Terms Explained

Click on the link below to view the website "Baroque Painting" developed by Essential Humanities. This page gives a brief introduction to Baroque painting including its general features, different stages, and examples of Baroque art. Focus on the *Key Definitions* section at the end of the page.

"Baroque Painting" by Essential Humanities

- http://www.essential-humanities.net/western-art/painting/baroque/#key-definitions

Rubens, Elevation of the Cross

Rubens in Catholic Flanders

The two most important artists of the Baroque era in Northern Europe (what we knew as Flanders in the fifteenth century)—Rubens and Rembrandt—worked under enormously different circumstances, even though they lived only a few hundred miles apart, because Flanders became divided along religious lines in the sixteenth century. The area which is today Belgium remained Catholic (where Rubens lived), while the area which is today the Netherlands, or Holland (where Rembrandt lived) broke away from Catholic Spain (which had controlled it) and established an independent Republic that was predominantly Calvinist (a form of Protestantism).

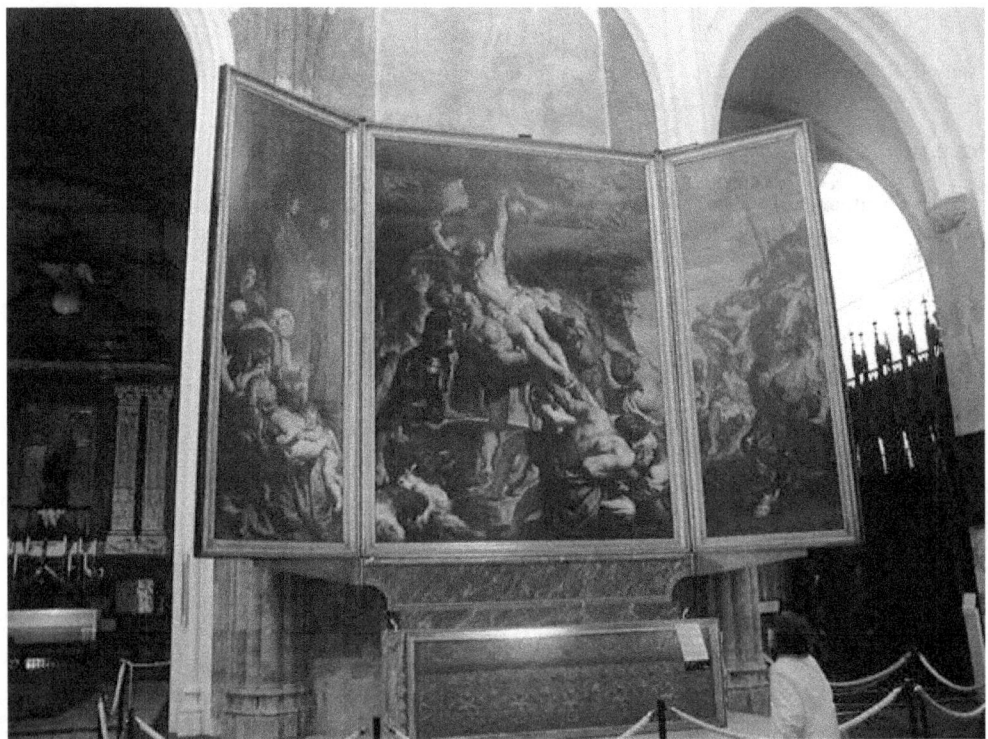

Figure 1. Peter Paul Rubens, The Elevation of the Cross, 1610, oil on wood, 15' 1 7/8" × 11' 1 1/2" (central panel), 15' 1 7/8" × 4' 11" (wings) (Now located in the transpet of the Cathedral in Antwerp, though originally intended for the main altar of Saint Walburga—a church which no longer exists)

Success in More than Just Painting

Rubens was an enormously successful artist in the first half of the 1600s. His paintings were sought after by important patrons all over Europe. A shrewd businessman, Rubens was also a devout Catholic. He is also a perfect example of the changed status of the artist: his friends and confidants were scholars, aristocrats, and even the royal families of Europe (Rubens was so trustworthy and clever that he served as a diplomat).

Travel to Italy

Rubens spent several years in Italy early in his career studying Italian Renaissance art, as well as the art of classical antiquity. He combined this with the influence of Caravaggio, the Venetian artists of the Renaissance, and the tradition of his native Flanders (think Campin and Van Eyck). Rubens was so successful that he set up a large studio in his native Antwerp (which you can still visit). There, he churned out large numbers of paintings for his royal and wealthy clients, and charged for the paintings according to how much he had personally painted. He was always responsible for the idea of a painting, but if his assistants executed most of it, the work was less expensive. In his studio Rubens had assistants working for him who specialized in different things, so they could all work on different parts of a single painting. Although Rubens perfected this system, we know that it was common practice for the "master" artist to have the idea and do much of the actual painting, but to have apprentices and assistants work on it too.

Nine Men Raise the Cross

In the central panel of the triptych of *The Elevation of the Cross* nine enormous figures with bulging muscles struggle to raise the heavy wooden cross that Christ is nailed to.

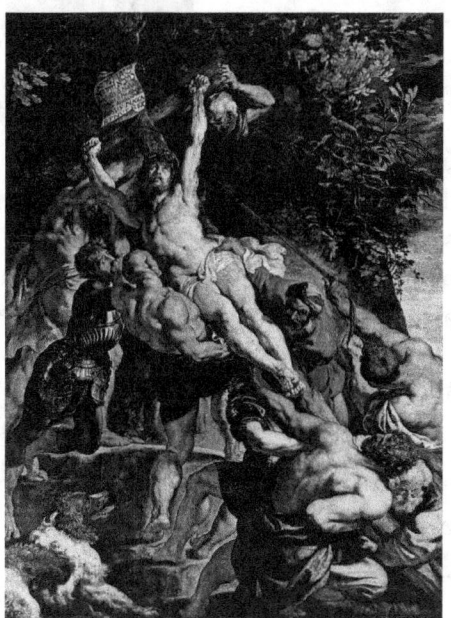

One can almost hear them grunt as they use all their strength to lift the cross. Their bodies form a compendium of different positions of the human body as it heaves a great weight: some figures at the top of the cross push forward from below, another at the center of the cross lifts straight up as he leans his body back, another figure has placed his body under the cross and uses the strength of his legs to lift it, while two others crouch at the base of the cross to pull it up and forward. Another figure helps from atop some branches and rocks, and still another pulls on rope that has been tied to the cross drawng our eye to Christ's own upward gaze and the sign attached to the cross that reads, "Jesus of Nazareth, King of the Jews." Perhaps this is the moment when Christ addresses God, and says "Father, forgive them; for they know not what they do" (Luke 23:34)?

Figure 2. The Elevation of the Cross, Central panel

It is not easy to disentangle the limbs of all of these figures—arms and legs seem to join together in one massive effort to raise the cross. Christ's body forms a diagonal line that moves back into space, and the cross is being lifted in our direction. In fact, several of the figures are so foreshortened they seem as though they will spill out into our space any second. This scene could not be closer to us. Rubens transports us to the very foot of the cross at the moment that it is lifted and its base is set into the ground. We sense the chaos of this moment. A dog barks excitedly, and it seems entirely possible that these men will fail and the cross will fall to the ground.

The Italian and Northern Traditions Come Together

Rubens combines muscled figures that remind us of Michelangelo (he had returned from a trip to Italy only two years earlier) with the descriptive realism that comes from the Northern tradition. Look for example at the way the light shines on the black armor of the figure on the left. There is also a specificity to the faces of some of the figures (the armored figure again, or the old man at the bottom) that reminds us of the Northern tradition.

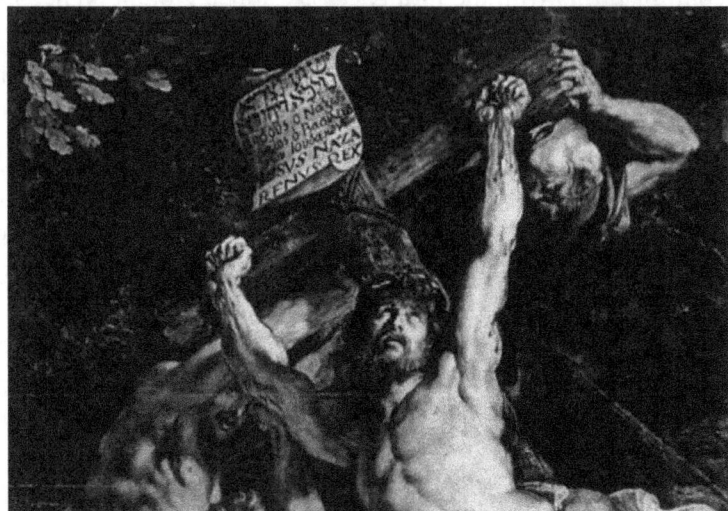

Figure 3. The Elevation of the Cross (detail)

Christ's body is simultaneously graceful and powerful as his chest lifts and pulls to his right and his head, abdomen and legs move to his left. It clearly looks back to the ideal and elegant figures of the high Renaissance, but Rubens makes the figure more dramatic on that receding diagonal and emphasizes Christ's humanity and weakness by the large nails through his hands and feet and the blood that drips down. We can also see the influence of the Italian Baroque painter Caravaggio in the strong contrasts of light and dark.

Rubens combines the physicality of classical sculpture (think of the Laocoön in the Vatican Museums), with the elegance and attention to musculature of Michelangelo, and the drama of the Baroque in what some art historians have described as his most important altarpiece.

Attributions

CC licensed content, Shared previously

- Rubens' The Elevation of the Cross. **Provided by**: Khan Academy. **Located at**: https://web.archive.org/web/20140215033902/ http://smarthistory.khanacademy.org/baroque-flanders.html. **License**: *CC BY-NC-SA: Attribution-NonCommercial-ShareAlike*

- Raising cross. **Authored by**: Alison Cassidy. **Located at**: https://commons.wikimedia.org/wiki/File:Raising_cross.jpg. **License**: *CC BY-SA: Attribution-ShareAlike*

Public domain content

- The Raising of the Cross. **Authored by**: Peter Paul Rubens. **Located at**: https://commons.wikimedia.org/wiki/ File:Peter_Paul_Rubens_068.jpg. **License**: *Public Domain: No Known Copyright*

Rubens, Arrival of Marie de Medici

The *Arrival of Marie de Medici at Marseilles* is one of 24 canvases that comprise the Medici Cycle, commissioned for the home of Marie de Medici, the Palais du Luxembourg (which now houses the French Senate and which she called the Palais Medici). The cycle loosely depicts the life of Marie de Medici. Marie was the granddaughter of the Holy Roman Emperor, the daughter of the Grand Duke of Tuscany, and the Archduchess of Austria. She married Henri IV, the King of France. In 1610, the day before the King was assassinated, she took the throne as Queen of France. She ruled as regent until her son, Louis XIII, took power.

Dr. Beth Harris and Dr. Steven Zucker provide a description, historical perspective, and analysis of Peter Paul Rubens's *Arrival (or Disembarkation) of Marie de Medici at Marseilles*.

- https://youtu.be/fbwW9mHFcgk

Peter Paul Rubens, *Arrival (or Disembarkation) of Marie de Medici at Marseilles*, 1621–25, oil on canvas, 394 × 295 cm, (Musée du Louvre, Paris).

Attributions

Rubens, The Consequences of War

Rubens, explaining his painting, *The Consequences of War*, said:

> The principal figure is Mars, who has left open the temple of Janus (which in time of peace, according to Roman custom, remained closed) and rushes forth with shield and blood-stained sword, threatening the people with great disaster. He pays little heed to Venus, his mistress, who, accompanied by Amors and Cupids, strives with caresses and emraces to hold him. From the other side, Mars is dragged forward by the Fury Alekto, with a torch in her hand. Near by are monsters personifying Pestilence and Famine, those inseparable partners of War. On the ground, turning her back, lies a woman with a broken lute, representing Harmony, which is incompatible with the discord of War. There is also a mother with her child in her arms, indicating that fecundity, procreation and charity are thwarted by War, which corrupts and destroys everything. In addition, one sees an architect thrown on his back, with his instruments in his hand, to show that which in time of peace is constructed for the use and ornamentation of the City, is hurled to the ground by the force of arms and falls to ruin. I believe, if I remember rightly, that you will find on the ground, under the feet of Mars, a book and a drawing on paper, to imply that he treads underfoot all the arts and letters. There ought also to be a bundle of darts or arrows, with the band which held them together undone; these when bound form the symbol of Concord. Beside them is the caduceus and an olive branch, attribute of Peace; these are also cast aside. That grief-stricken woman clothed in black, with torn veil, robbed of all her jewles and other ornaments, is the unfortunate Europe who, for so many years now, has suffered plunder, outrage, and misery, which are so injurious to everyone, that it is unnecessary to go into detail. Europe's attribute is the globe, borne by a small angel or genius, and surmounted by the cross, to symbolize the Christian world.
>
> —from a letter to Justus Sustermans, translated by Kristin Lohse Belin, in Rubens, Phaidon, 1998

Dr. Beth Harris and Dr. Steven Zucker provide a description, historical perspective, and analysis of Peter Paul Rubens's *The Consequences of War*.

- https://youtu.be/K9iMsmhBOjk

Peter Paul Rubens, *The Consequences of War*, 1638–39, oil on canvas, (Palatine Gallery, Palazzo Pitti, Florence).

Attributions

Vermeer, Young Woman with a Water Pitcher

Dr. Beth Harris and Dr. Steven Zucker provide a description, historical perspective, and analysis of Vermeer's *Young Woman with a Water Pitcher*.

- https://youtu.be/_38xl7p4VaM

Johannes Vermeer, *Young Woman with a Water Pitcher*, c. 1662, oil on canvas, (Metropolitan Museum of Art).

External Link

View this painting up close in the Google Art Project:

- https://www.google.com/culturalinstitute/asset-viewer/young-woman-with-a-water-pitcher/ogH-Waxey-9HBA?projectId=art-project

---

Attributions

Vermeer, The Glass of Wine

Dr. Beth Harris and Dr. Steven Zucker provide a description, historical perspective, and analysis of Vermeer's *The Glass of Wine*.

- https://youtu.be/uvA6YY4yHtM

Jan Vermeer, *The Glass of Wine*, c. 1661, oil on canvas, 67.7 × 79.6 cm, (Gemäldegalerie, Staatliche Museen zu Berlin).

<table>
<tr><td>External Link</td></tr>
</table>

View this painting up close in the Google Art Project.:

- https://www.google.com/culturalinstitute/asset-viewer/the-glass-of-wine/XQEGuvWhwW_ybg

Vermeer and the Camera Obscura

Click on the link below to view the article "Vermeer and the Camera Obscura" by the Vermeer Newsletter. This three-page article discusses evidence that Vermeer may have used some sort of camera-like device to aid him in his painting.

- "Vermeer and the Camera Obscura" by the Vermeer Newsletter
  - http://www.essentialvermeer.com/camera_obscura/co_one.html

Rembrandt, Bathsheba at her Bath

Dr. Beth Harris and Dr. Steven Zucker provide a description, historical perspective, and analysis of Rembrandt's *Bathsheba at Her Bath*.

- https://youtu.be/wsL4Uh0BrQw

Rembrandt van Rijn, *Bathsheba at Her Bath*, 1654, oil on canvas, 56 × 56 in (142 × 142 cm), (Musée du Louvre, Paris).

Attributions

CC licensed content, Shared previously

Rembrandt, The Three Crosses

Dr. David Drogin andDr. Beth Harris provide a description, historical perspective, and analysis of Rembrandt's, *The Three Crosses*.

- https://youtu.be/7PA0T4_KYC0

Rembrandt van Rijn, *The Three Crosses*, 1653, etching and drypoint.

External Link
View this painting up close in the Google Art Project.: • https://www.google.com/culturalinstitute/asset-viewer/the-three-crosses/qQEo5srrk1NJyQ?projectId=art-project

Attributions

Rembrandt's Self-Portraits

Dr. David Drogin and Dr. Beth Harris provide a description, historical perspective, and analysis of Rembrandt's Self-Portraits.

- https://youtu.be/LisBmGk1koY

Works Discussed

Studio copy, *Rembrandt with a Gorget*, oil on canvas, c. 1629 (Mauritshuis, The Hague)

Self-Portrait at the Age of 34, oil on canvas, 1640 (The National Gallery, London)

Self-Portrait, oil on canvas, 1658 (The Frick Collection)

Self-Portrait, oil on canvas, c. 1665 (Wallraf-Richartz-Museum & Fondation Corboud, Cologne)

Attributions

Hal's Malle Babbe

Dr. Beth Harris and Dr. Steven Zucker provide a description, historical perspective, and analysis of Frans Hals's *Malle Babbe*.

- https://youtu.be/9fEublFSTOg

Frans Hals, *Malle Babbe*, c. 1633, oil on canvas, 78.50 × 66.20 cm, (Gemäldegalerie, Staatliche Museen zu Berlin).

External Link
View this painting up close in the Google Art Project: • https://www.google.com/culturalinstitute/asset-viewer/malle-babbe/8gGg1YQu0B5evw

Vanitas Painting Explained

Click on the link below to view "Vanity in 17th Century Dutch Art" by the Ringling Museum Docent class 1999. This article explains how the seventeenth century Dutch art can provide a window into the culture that produced it—specifically on the things that the people were proud to have.

- "Vanity in 17th Century Dutch Art"
  - http://www.ringlingdocents.org/vanitas.htm

Dutch Genre Painting Explained

Click on the link below to view the article "Genre Painting in Northern Europe," a part of the Heilbrunn Timeline of Art History, which was developed by the Metropolitan Museum of Art. This article includes a slideshow of genre paintings as well as a discussion about the art style.

- Genre Painting in Northern Europe
    - http://www.metmuseum.org/toah/hd/gnrn/hd_gnrn.htm

Las Meninas

Dr. Beth Harris and Dr. Steven Zucker provide a description, historical perspective, and analysis of Velázquez's *Las Meninas*.

- https://youtu.be/IiTtGENiVOA

Diego Rodríguez de Silva y Velázquez, *Las Meninas*, c. 1656, oil on canvas, 125 1/4 × 108 5/8 in. (318 × 276 cm), (Museo Nacional del Prado, Madrid).

Attributions

CC licensed content, Shared previously

Louis XIV & Versailles

The Sun King

In France, Louis XIV (who reigned from 1661 to 1715), also known as the "Sun King," centralized the government around his own person and used art and architecture in the service of the monarchy. The French monarchs ruled with absolute power, meaning that there was little or no check on what they could and could not do. There was no parliament that would have balanced the power of the King (as there was in England). The King also ruled, so it was believed, by divine right. That is, that the power to rule came from God. In an effort to use art in support of the state, Louis XIV established the Royal Academy of Fine Arts to control matters of art and artistic education by imposing a classicizing style as well as other regulations and standards on art and artists.

In his portrait of Louis XIV (figure 1), Rigaud was not as interested in what the King really looked like (he is certainly idealized here). Rather, he was concerned with capturing the majesty and authority of the absolute ruler of France—as well as our own insignificance in his presence. The textures of the ermine and velvets and embroidered silk are so sumptuous that the eye focuses on them more than on the face of the Sun King.

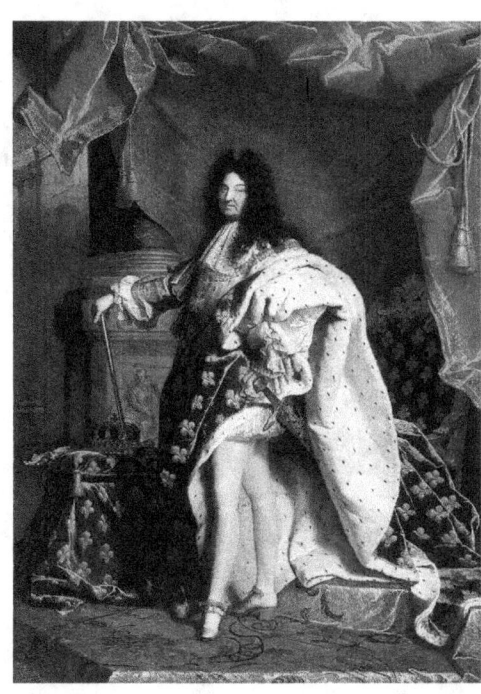

Figure 1. Hyacinthe Rigaud, Louis XIV, King of France and Navarre, oil on canvas, 1701 (Musée du Louvre, Paris)

Versailles

Louis XIV also built an opulent new palace, Versailles, which became the King's official residence in 1682. Versailles is 14 miles southwest of Paris and contains 700 rooms! It is probably impossible to get a sense of the enormity and luxury of Versailles without going there.

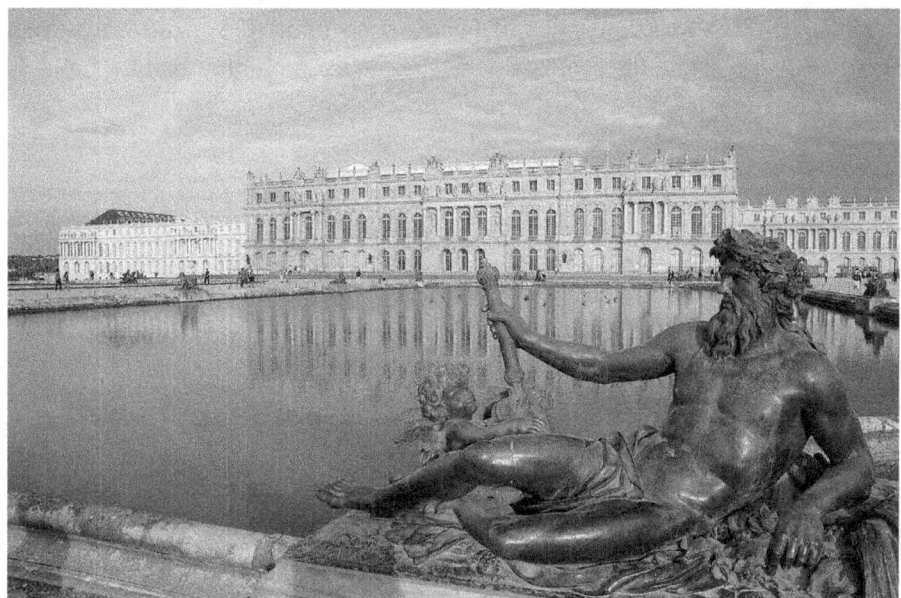

Figure 2. View of the Palace from the garden

You have probably heard of the famous *Galerie des Glaces* (or Hall of Mirrors), a room with 17 mirrors facing the windows that look out onto fabulous gardens (figure 3). The ceiling of this room is decorated with paintings extolling the virtues and achievements of Louis himself. (Here you can actually get a full, 360 degree view of this famous and extravagant hallway: http://www.panoramas.dk/fullscreen7/f30-versailles.html)

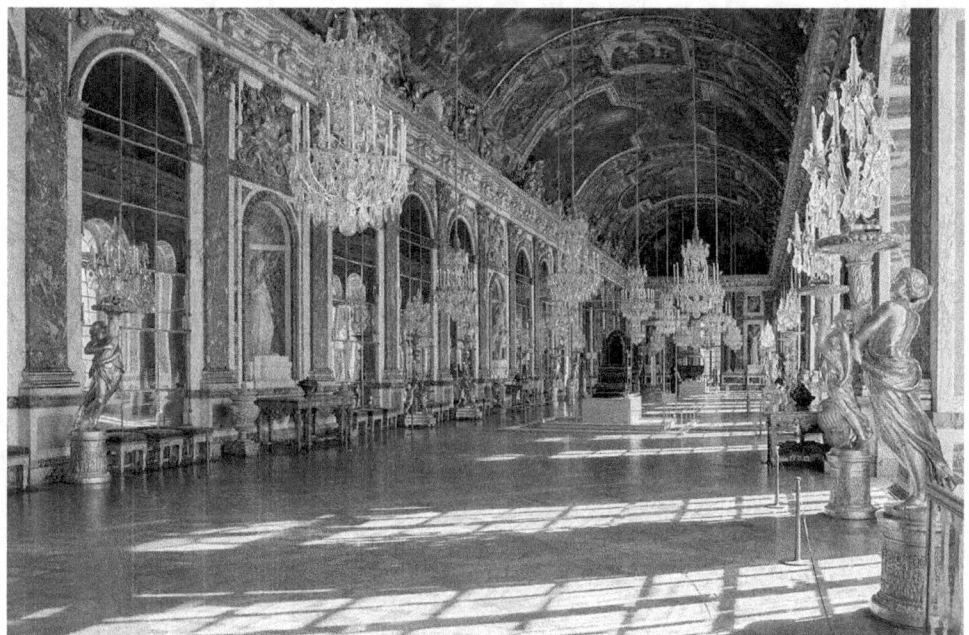

Figure 3. Hall of Mirrors, Palace of Versailles

Louis XIV eventually invited the higher French aristocrats to live at Versailles and wait upon him. And so Versailles was not just a place to live—it became the symbol of the French monarchy itself, and therefore everything about the decor had to speak of the power and accomplishments of the King. Every aspect of the King's life (waking, eating, everything!) was thoroughly ritualized, convincing everyone there of the incredible majesty of the King. The thousands of people who lived at Versailles also required entertainment, and so Versailles also became the seat of lavish spectacles including ballets, balls, hunts and receptions, all presided over by the King.

Attributions

CC licensed content, Shared previously

- France 1600-1700. **Provided by**: Khan Academy. **Located at**: https://web.archive.org/web/20130425101738/http://smarthistory.khanacademy.org/baroque-france.html. **License**: *CC BY-NC-SA: Attribution-NonCommercial-ShareAlike*

- Versailles chateau. **Authored by**: Marc Vassal. **Located at**: https://commons.wikimedia.org/wiki/File:Versailles_chateau.jpg. **License**: *CC BY-SA: Attribution-ShareAlike*

- Chateau Versailles Galerie des Glaces. **Authored by**: Myrabella. **Located at**: https://commons.wikimedia.org/wiki/File:Chateau_Versailles_Galerie_des_Glaces.jpg. **License**: *CC BY-SA: Attribution-ShareAlike*

Poussin, Landscape with St. John

Dr. Beth Harris and Dr. Steven Zucker provide a description, historical perspective, and analysis of Nicolas Poussin's *Landscape with Saint John on Patmos*.

- https://youtu.be/H3uBAVI4xC4

Nicolas Poussin, *Landscape with Saint John on Patmos*, 1640, oil on canvas, 100.3 × 136.4 cm (39-1/2 × 53-5/8 inches), (Art Institute of Chicago).

Attributions

Le Nain, Peasant Family in an Interior

Dr. Beth Harris and Dr. Steven Zucker provide a description, historical perspective, and analysis of *Peasant Family in an Interior* by one of the Le Nain brothers.

- https://youtu.be/ZSh1ksh1iO4

Antoine or Louis Le Nain, *Peasant Family in an Interior*, second quarter of the seventeenth century, oil on canvas, 1.13 × 1.59 m, (Musée du Louvre, Paris).

External Link

View this painting up close in the Google Art Project:

- https://www.google.com/culturalinstitute/asset-viewer/peasant-interior-with-an-old-flute-player/gwH2MGLHe6MUWw?projectId=art-project

Chapter 9:
1700–1800–The Age of
Enlightenment

Chapter 9 Overview

What You'll Learn To Do: Examine Rococo and Neoclassical art and understand their influence on later art movements.

In Chapter 9 we will examine Rococo and Neoclassical art. We will look at how artists like David contributed to the development of Western art. It is imperative to understand Rococo and Neoclassical art in order to see how it impacted later artistic developments.

Learning Activities

The learning activities for this module include:

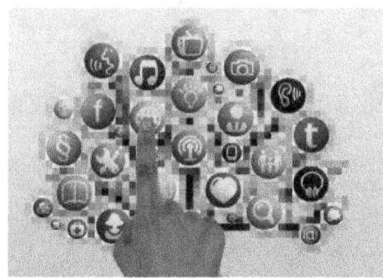

- **Review:** Key Learning Items

The 1700s and 1800s

- **Read:** Age of Enlightenment

Rococo

- **Read:** Rococo Explained
- **Read:** Fragonard's The Swing (includes a video: 3:20)
- **Watch:** Boucher's Madame de Pompadour (3:05)
- **Watch:** Vigee Le Brun's Madame Perregaux (1:43)

Neo-Classicism

- **Read:** Introduction to Neo-Classicism
- **Read:** David's Oath of the Horatii (includes a video: 6:10)
- **Read:** David's Death of Marat (includes a video: 6:22)
- **Read:** David's Napoleon Crossing the Alps
- **Read:** Antonio Canova

Britain & America in the Age of Revolution

- **Read:** Benjamin West
- **Watch:** Sir Joshua Reynolds (4:06)
- **Read:** William Hogarth
- **Read:** John Singleton Copley
- **Read:** Copley's Watson and the Shark
- **Watch:** Charles Wilson Peale (4:25)
- **Read:** Gilbert Stuart

Attributions

CC licensed content, Original

- Art History II. **Provided by**: Extended Learning Institute of Northern Virginia Community College. **Located at**: http://eli.nvcc.edu/. **License:** *CC BY: Attribution*

Public domain content

- Image of Finger. **Authored by**: geralt. **Located at**: https://pixabay.com/en/finger-touch-hand-structure-769300/. **License:** *Public Domain: No Known Copyright*

Key Learning Items

After successful completion of this module, you will be able to:

- Understand and apply the concepts and terminology of Rococo and Neoclassical art
- Investigate and apply the fundamental questions we ask when looking at art objects from this movement
- Discuss, collaborate, and generate understanding as to the meaning of Rococo and Neoclassical art
- Assess and evaluate the impact of Rococo and Neoclassical art on the continued evolution of Western art

While you are reviewing the content of this module, consider the following questions:

- What are the key characteristics of the Rococo?
- How did Neoclassicism develop?
- What are some of the key characteristics of Neoclassical art?

Key Vocabulary Terms

- Rococo
- Grand Manner
- Neoclassicism
- Enlightenment
- history painting

Here are links to art history glossaries that will help you better understand the above key vocabulary terms.

- ArtLex: Art Dictionary

    ◦ http://www.artlex.com/

- About.com: Art History

    ◦ http://arthistory.about.com/od/glossary/l/bl_Art-Glossary.htm

- Artcyclopedia: A Guide to Fine Art

    ◦ http://www.artcyclopedia.com/

Attributions

CC licensed content, Original

Age of Enlightenment

Scientific experiments like the one pictured in figure 1 were offered as fascinating shows to the public in the mid-eighteenth century. In Joseph Wright of Derby's painting *A Philosopher Giving A Lecture at the Orrery* (1765), we see the demonstration of an Orrery, a mechanical model of the solar system that was used to demonstrate the motions of the planets around the sun—making the universe seem almost like a clock.

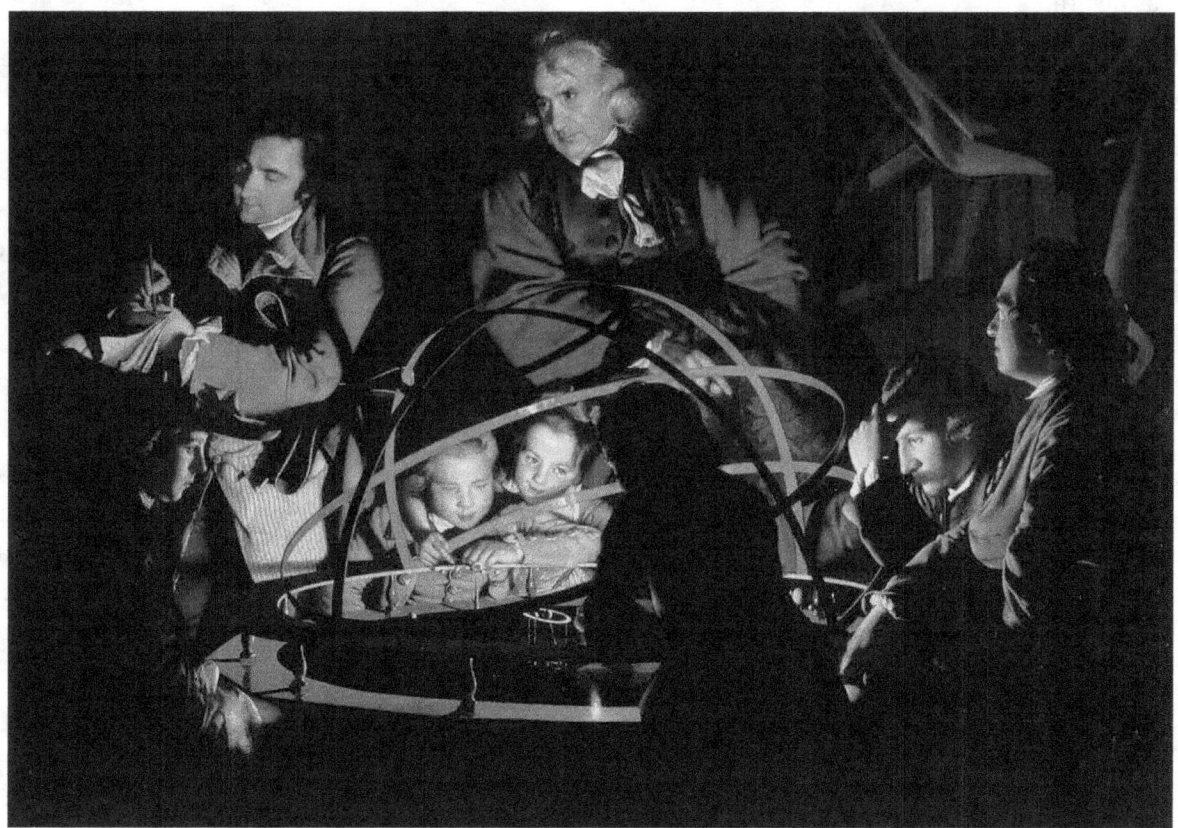

Figure 1. Joseph Wright of Derby, A Philosopher Giving that Lecture on the Orrery, c. 1766

In the center of the Orrery is a gas light, which represents the sun (though the figure who stands in the foreground with his back to us block this from our view); the arcs represent the orbits of the planets. Wright concentrates on the faces of the figures to create a compelling narrative.

With paintings like these, Wright invented a new subject: scenes of experiments and new machinery, and the beginnings of the Industrial Revolution (think cities, railroads, steam power, gas and then electric light, factories, machines, pollution). Wright's fascination with light, strange shadows, and darkness, reveals the influence of Baroque art.

Enlightenment

Toward the middle of the eighteenth century a shift in thinking occurred. This shift is known as the Enlightenment. You have probably already heard of some important Enlightenment figures, like Rousseau, Diderot and Voltaire. It is helpful I think to think about the word "enlighten" here—the idea of shedding light on something, illuminating it, making it clear.

The thinkers of the Enlightenment, influenced by the scientific revolutions of the previous century, believed in shedding the light of science and reason on the world, and in order to question traditional ideas and ways of doing things. The scientific revolution (based on empirical observation, and not on metaphysics or spirituality) gave the impression that the universe behaved according to universal and unchanging laws (think of Newton here). This provided a model for looking rationally on human institutions as well as nature.

Reason and Equality

Rousseau, for example, began to question the idea of the divine right of Kings. In *The Social Contract*, he wrote that the King does not, in fact, receive his power from God, but rather from the general will of the people. This, of course, implies that "the people" can also take away that power! The Enlightenment thinkers also discussed other ideas that are the founding principles of any democracy—the idea of the importance of the individual who can reason for himself, the idea of equality under the law, and the idea of natural rights. The Enlightenment was a period of profound optimism, a sense that with science and reason—and the consequent shedding of old superstitions—human beings and human society would improve.

You can probably tell already that the Enlightenment was anti-clerical; it was, for the most part, opposed to traditional Catholicism. Instead, the Enlightenment thinkers developed a way of understanding the universe called Deism—the idea, more or less, is that there is a God, but that this God is not the figure of the Old and New Testaments, actively involved in human affairs. He is more like a watchmaker who, once he makes the watch and winds it, has nothing more to do with it.

The Enlightenment, the Monarchy, and the Revolution

The Enlightenment encouraged criticism of the corruption of the monarchy (at this point King Louis XVI), and the aristocracy. Enloghtenment thinkers condemned Rococo art for being immoral and indecent, and called for a new kind of art that would be moral instead of immoral, and teach people right and wrong.

Denis Diderot, Enlightenment philosopher, writer and art critic, wrote that the aim of art was "to make virtue attractive, vice odious, ridicule forceful; that is the aim of every honest man who takes up the pen, the brush or the chisel' (*Essai sur la peinture*).

These new ways of thinking, combined with a financial crisis (the country was literally bankrupt) and poor harvests left many ordinary French people both angry and hungry. In 1789, the French Revolution began. In its first stage, all the revolutionaries ask for is a constitution that would limit the power of the king. Read the *Declaration of the Rights of Man*—a document produced by the revolutionaries at the beginning of the revolution: http://www.hrcr.org/docs/frenchdec.html

Ultimately the idea of a constitution failed, and the revolution entered a more radical stage. In 1792, Louis XVI and his wife Marie Antoinette, were beheaded along with thousands of other aristocrats believed to be loyal to the monarchy.

Attributions

CC licensed content, Shared previously

- 1700-1800 Age of Enlightenment. **Provided by**: Khan Academy. **Located at**: https://web.archive.org/web/20130425112940/ http://smarthistory.khanacademy.org/1700-1800-Age-of-Enlightenment.html. **License**: *CC BY-NC-SA: Attribution-NonCommercial-ShareAlike*

Public domain content

- A Philosopher Giving that Lecture on the Orrery. **Authored by**: Joseph Wright of Derby. **Located at**: https://commons.wikimedia.org/wiki/File:Wright_of_Derby,_The_Orrery.jpg. **License**: *Public Domain: No Known Copyright*

Rococo Explained

The Rococo art movement began in the eighteenth century, primarily as a response to the Baroque style. As a result the two have some marked differences. Click on the link below to view "Rococo" defined on Art Appreciation Online. This page defines Rococo as an art movement.

- **IdentifyThisArt.com**
    - http://www.identifythisart.com/art-movements-styles/pre-modern-art/rococo-art-movement/
- **Victoria and Albert Museum**
    - http://www.vam.ac.uk/content/articles/s/style-guide-rococo/
- **ArtNet News**
    - https://news.artnet.com/art-world/a-brief-history-of-rococo-art-32790
- **Encyclopædia Britannica**
    - http://www.britannica.com/art/Rococo-style-design

Fragonard's *The Swing*

The Beginnings of Rococo

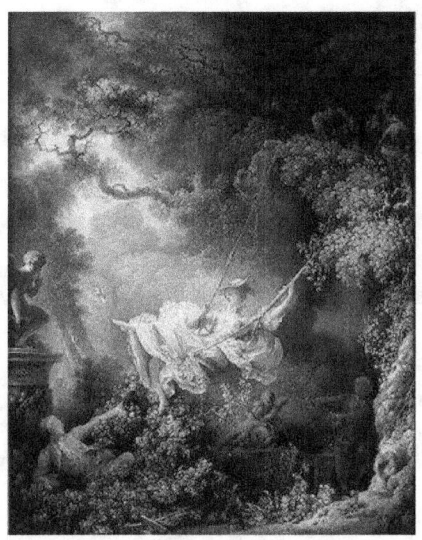

Figure 1. Jean-Honoré Fragonard, The Swing, oil on canvas, 1767 (Wallace Collection, London)

In the early years of the 1700s, at the end of the reign of Louis XIV (who dies in 1715), there was a shift away from the classicism and "Grand Manner" (based on the art of Poussin) that had governed the art of the preceding 50 years, toward a new style that we call Rococo. Versailles was abandoned by the aristocracy, who once again took up residence in Paris. A shift away from the monarchy, toward the aristocracy characterizes this period.

What kind of lifestyle did the aristocracy lead during this period? Remember that the aristocracy had enormous political power as well as enormous wealth. Many chose leisure as a pursuit and became involved themselves in romantic intrigues. Indeed, they created a culture of luxury and excess that formed a stark contrast to the lives of most people in France. The aristocracy, only a small percentage of the population of France, owned over 90% of its wealth. A small, but growing middle class does not sit still with this for long (remember the French Revolution of 1789).

Fragonard's *The Swing*

As with most Rococo paintings, the subject of Fragonard's *The Swing* is not very complicated! Two lovers have conspired to get this older fellow to push the youg lady in the swing while her lover hides in the bushes. Their idea is that as she goes up in the swing, she can part her legs, and he can get a perfect view up her skirt.

They are surrounded by a lush, over grown garden. A sculptured figure to the left puts his fingers to his mouth, as though saying "hush," while another sculpture in the background has two cupid figures cuddled together. The colors are pastel—pale pinks and greens, and although we have a sense of movement and a prominent diagonal line—the painting lacks all of the seriousness of a baroque painting.

If you look really closely you can see the loose brushstrokes in the pink silk dress, and as she opens her legs, we get a glimpse of her garter belt. It was precisely this kind of painting that the philosophers of the Enlightenment were soon to condemn. They demanded a new style of art, one that showed an example of moral behavior, of human beings at their most noble.

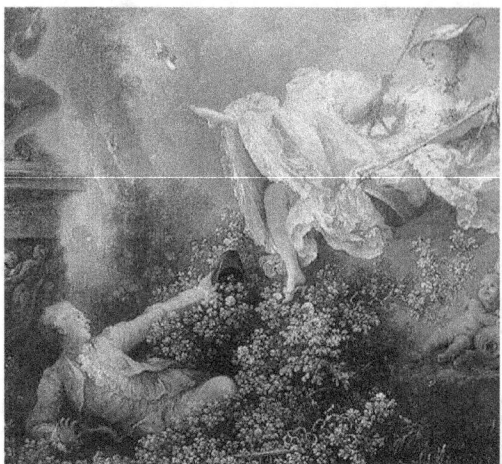

Figure 2. Detail of The Swing

- https://youtu.be/rVI5Sjm0xKI

Attributions

CC licensed content, Shared previously

- Fragonard's The Swing. **Authored by**: Dr. Beth Harris and Dr. Steven Zucker. **Provided by**: Khan Academy. **Located at**: https://web.archive.org/web/20130425140136/http://smarthistory.khanacademy.org/rococo.html. **License**: *CC BY-NC-SA: Attribution-NonCommercial-ShareAlike*

Boucher's Madame de Pompadour

Dr. Beth Harris and Dr. Steven Zucker provide a description, historical perspective, and analysis of François Boucher's *Madame de Pompadour*.

- https://youtu.be/lnJRkY0mZh4

François Boucher, *Madame de Pompadour*, oil on canvas, 1750 (extention of canvas and additional painting likely added by Boucher later), (Fogg Museum).

Attributions

Introduction to Neo-Classicism

In opposition to the frivolous sensuality of Rococo painters like Jean-Honoré Fragonard and François Boucher, the Neo-classicists looked to Nicolas Poussin for their inspiration. The decision to promote *Poussiniste* painting became an ethical consideration. They believed that strong drawing was rational, therefore morally better. They believed that art should be cerebral, not sensual.

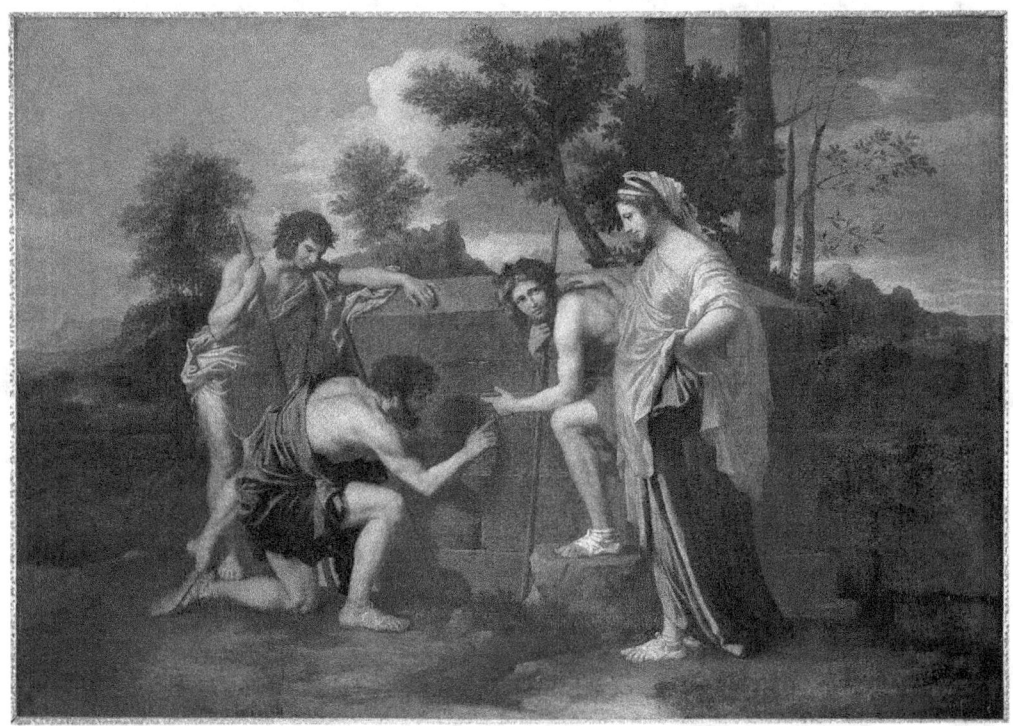

Figure 1. Nicolas Poussin, Et in Arcadia Ego, 1637–38, oil on canvas, 185 cm × 121 cm (72.8 in × 47.6 in), (Louvre).

The Neo-classicists, such as Jacques-Louis David (pronounced *Da-VEED)*, preferred the well-delineated form—clear drawing and modeling (shading). Drawing was considered more important than painting. The Neo-classical surface had to look perfectly smooth—no evidence of brush-strokes should be discernible to the naked eye.

France was on the brink of its first revolution in 1789, and the Neo-classicists wanted to express rationality and sobriety that was fitting for their times. Artists like David supported the rebels through an art that asked for clear-headed thinking, self-sacrifice to the State (as in *Oath of the Horatii*) and an austerity reminiscent of Republican Rome.

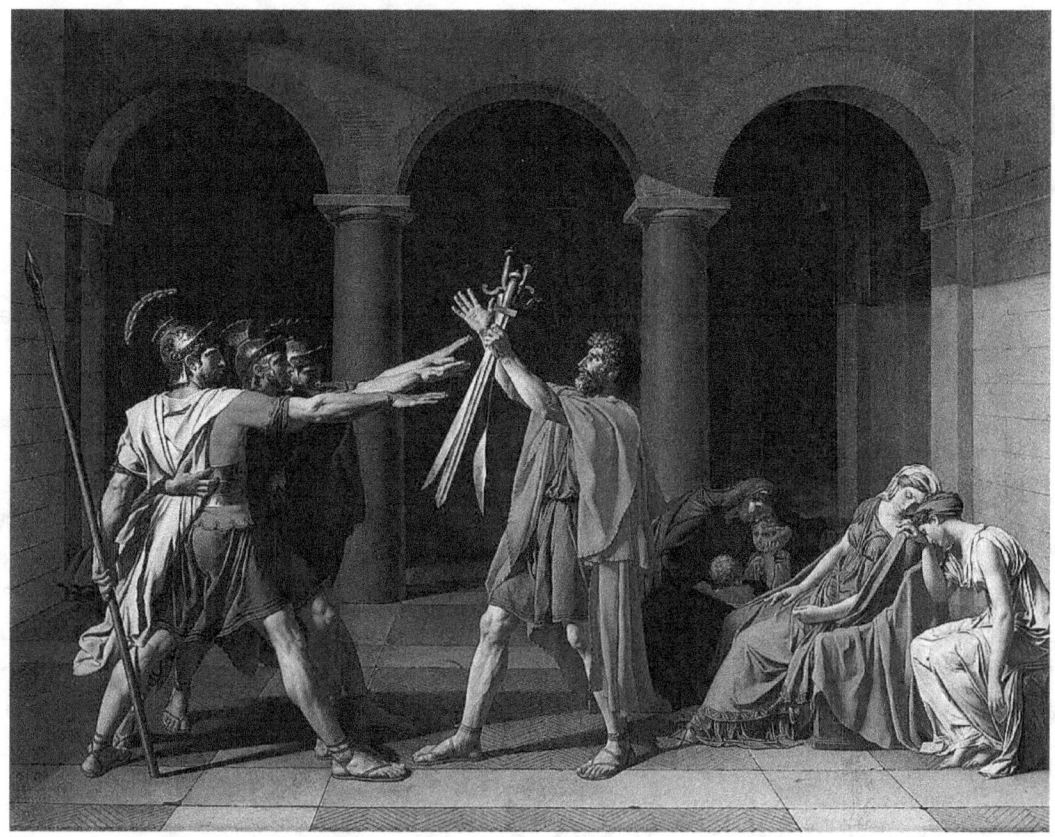

Figure 2. Jacques-Louis David, Oath of the Horatii, oil on canvas, 1784 (Musée du Louvre)

Neo-classicism was a child of the Age of Reason (the Enlightenment), when philosophers believed that we would be able to control our destinies by learning from and following the Laws of Nature (the United States was founded on Enlightenment philosophy). Scientific inquiry attracted more attention. Therefore, Neo-classicism continued the connection to the Classical tradition because it signified moderation and rational thinking but in a new and more politically-charged spirit ("neo" means "new," or in the case of art, an existing style reiterated with a new twist.)

Neo-classicism is characterized by: clarity of form; sober colors; shallow space; strong horizontal and verticals that render that subject matter timeless, instead of temporal as in the dynamic Baroque works; and, Classical subject matter—or classicizing contemporary subject matter.

Attributions

David's Oath of the Horatii

Dr. Beth Harris and Dr. Steven Zucker provide a description, historical perspective, and analysis of David's *Oath of the Horatii*.

- https://youtu.be/Mawq5PKRB6k

Jacques-Louis David, Painter to the King, the Revolution, and the Emperor

David was trained in the classicism favored by the Academy but here creates the far more severe style, Neo-Classicism. He ultimately became the painter of the Revolution and even served on the committee that voted for the beheading of the King (he would later spend time in jail for this). David was friends with Robespierre and Marat, leaders of the Reign of Terror, the revolution's most violent aspect. After the revolution, when Napoleon became Emperor of France, David served as his official painter.

David Wins the Prix de Rome: A New Style Emerges

David was raised in the wealthy and powerful family of his uncle, a minister to the King of France. The young David was at first trained in the studio of the great Rococo master François Boucher, a distant relative who also counted Fragonard amongst his students. After several failed attempts, David would win the coveted Prix de Rome, a prize given annually to one advanced art student (somewhat equivalent to a Master of Fine Arts degree student today) in each of the three beaux-arts (pronounced "bow-zart," fine arts in English), painting, sculpture and architecture.

The competition was open to the alumni of the École des Beaux-Arts (School of Fine Arts), the preeminent art school in France. The prize financed the study of art in Rome for a period of five years. Traditionally, winners took note of the works of Antiquity (ancient Greek and Roman art) and of the High Renaissance (the legacy of Raphael & Michelangelo for example) but devoted their attention primarily to selected masters of the Baroque.In contrast, David reversed this hierarchy focusing on the art of antiquity, the renaissance and the classicizing baroque artist, Nicolas Poussin (see especially Poussin's *Burial of Phocion* of 1648).

What emerged in David's painting was a sharp rejection of the Rococo style. Gone is the fluid brushwork, soft color, and the amorphous organic compositions of Boucher and Fragonard. Of equal import was the shift in subject. A telling document of the ancien regime, Fragonard's *The Swing*, celebrates the pleasures of love and of the experience of the ruling class. This is a painting intended to indulge the viewer's senses with rich, almost aromatic sights and textures.

A Story of Sacrifice

In contrast, David tells the story of three brothers that make an oath to their father that they will die in the defense of their city (this is a legend about the founding of Rome). Most Neo-Classical paintings take their subjects from Ancient Greek and Roman history and the *Oath of the Horatii* is no exception. In this painting the three Horatii brothers have been chosen to represent the city of Rome in a battle against three brothers from the neighboring city of Alba.

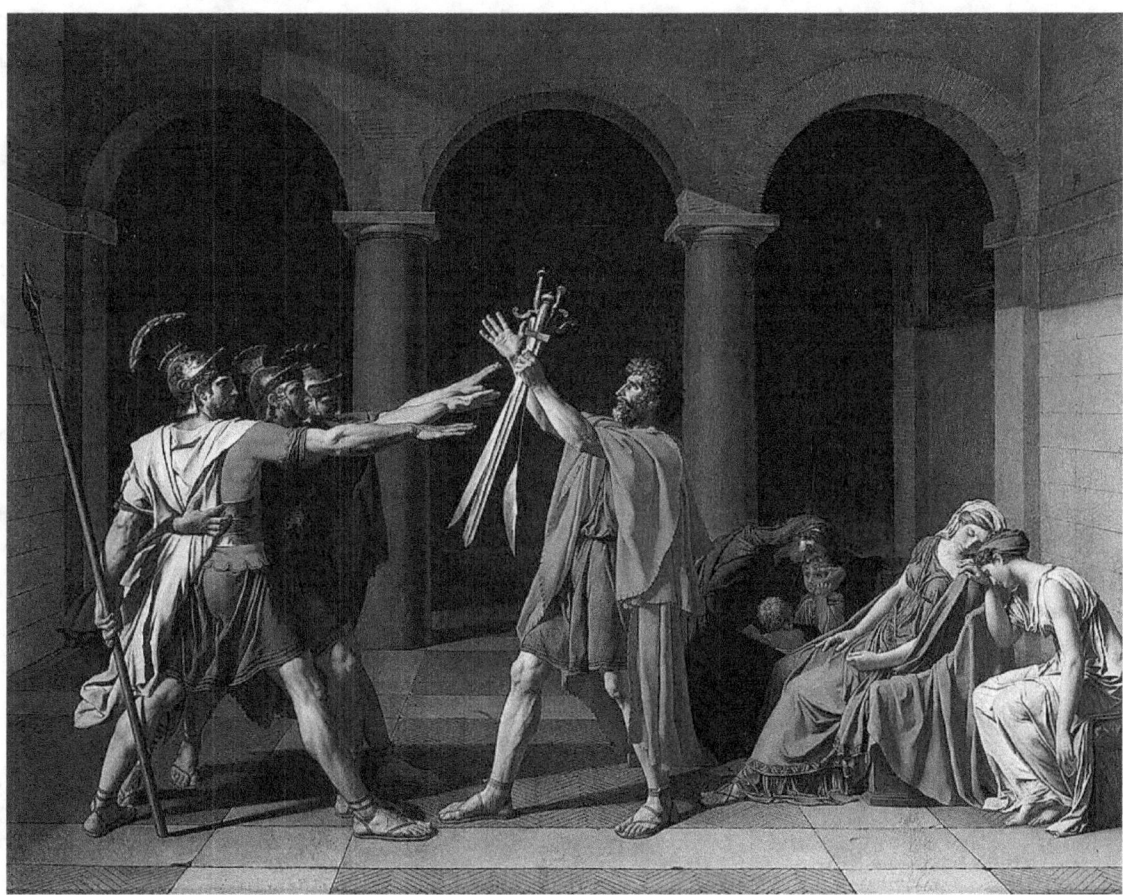

Figure 2. Jacques-Louis David, Oath of the Horatii, oil on canvas, 1784 (Musée du Louvre)

Here, the three Horatii brothers are swearing an oath on their swords which their father presents to them to fight until they die for their country.Here's the catch: one of the Horatii sisters (pictured on the right) is married to one of the men on the other side (the Curiatii). When one of the Horatii brothers returns home from the battle—the only one surviving—this sister greets him with condemnation for killing her husband and the father of her children. Because she puts herself and her family before the good of her country, her brother kills her. The idea here is that one must be willing to sacrifice—even sacrifice one's life and family members—for the state.

A Rational Style

Eschewing the Rococo style, David organizes the canvas with a geometric precision that recalls the innovation of the ancient Greeks and of the Italian Renaissance that harked back to the rationalism of antiquity. David divides the linear perspectival interior into a balanced nine-part square. This rigorous structure frames the three sets of figures as does the triple screen of doric columns and arches at the far end of the room. The angle of the light heightens the muscularity of the male figures as it rakes across the surface of their bodies. This light, which enters the room from the upper left, sharply delineates mass and volume, a kind of modified tenebrism and creates, as in the work of Caravaggio, a strong sense of physicality.

As was traditional, David's *Oath of the Horatii* was commissioned by the King as the summation of David's five years of study in Rome. Such a work was to be exhibited in an annual exhibition of new art held in a large room or salon in the monarch's palace in Paris, the Louvre (now the museum). In part because of some crafty self-promotion but primarily because of the radical style and especially because of the political implications of the painting, David's early masterpiece quickly became a sensation.

Attributions

CC licensed content, Shared previously

David's Death of Marat

By 1793, the violence of the Revolution dramatically increased until the beheadings at the Place de la Concorde became a constant, leading a certain Dr. Joseph Guillotine it invent a machine that would improve the efficiency of the ax and block and therefore make executions more humane. David was in thick of it. Early in the Revolution he had joined the Jacobins, a political club that would in time become the most rabid of the various rebel factions. Led by the ill-fated Georges Danton and the infamous Maximilien Robespierre, the Jacobins (including David) would eventually vote to execute Louis XVI and his Queen Marie Antionette who were caught attempting to escape across the border to the Austrian Empire.

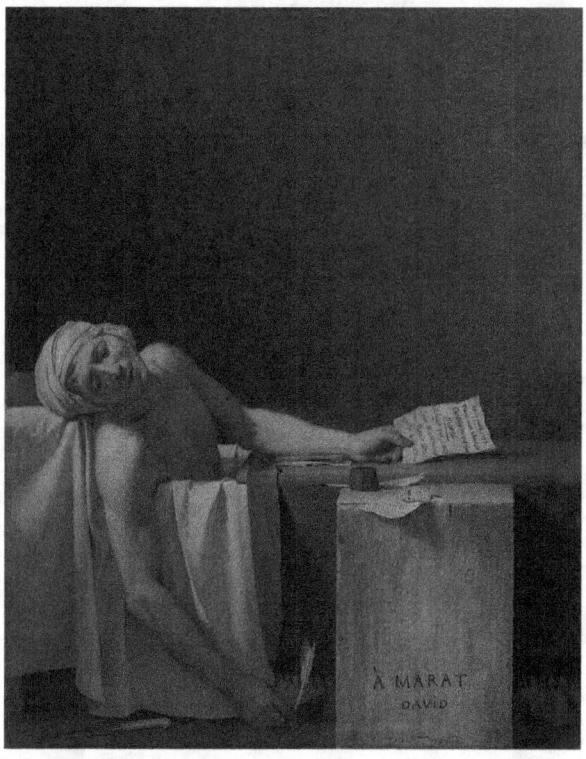

Figure 1. Jacques-Louis David, The Death of Marat, 1793, oil on canvas, 65" × 50 1/2", (Royal Museums of Fine Arts of Belgium, Brussels). View this painting up close in the Google Art Project.: https://www.google.com/ culturalinstitute/asset-viewer/marat-assassinated/ 7QGjl9R141MCBw?projectId=art-project

At the height of the Reign of Terror in 1793, David painted a memorial to his great friend, the murdered publisher, Jean Marat. As in his Death of Socrates, David substitutes the iconography (symbolic forms) of Christian art for more contemporary issues. The Death of Marat, 1793 an idealized image of David's slain friend is shown holding his murderess's (Charlotte Corday) letter of introduction. The bloodied knife lays on the floor having opened a fatal gash that functions, as does Marat's very composition, as a reference to the entombment of Christ and a sort of secularized stigmata (reference to the wounds Christ is said to have received in his hands, feet and side while on the cross). Is David attempting now to find revolutionary martyrs to replace the saints of Catholicism (which had been outlawed)?

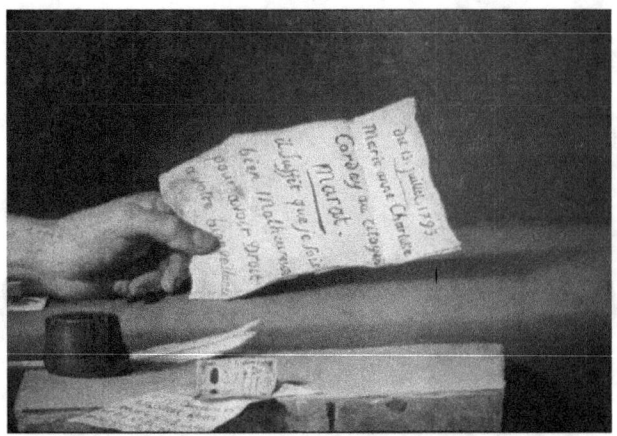

Figure 2. Detail of The Death of Marat. The English translation is: The thirteenth of July, 1793. Marie-anne Charlotte Corday to citizen Marat. Given that I am unhappy, I have a right to your help.

By 1794 the Reign of Terror had run its course. The Jacobins had begun to execute not only captured aristocrats but fellow revolutionaries as well. Eventually, Robespierre himself would die and the remaining Jacobins were likewise executed or imprisoned. David escaped death by renouncing his activities and was locked in a cell in the former palace, the Louvre, until his eventual release by France's brilliant new ruler, Napoleon Bonaparte. This diminutive Corsican had been the youngest General in the French army and during the Revolution had become a national hero by waging a seemingly endless string of victorious military campaigns against the Austrians in Belgium and Italy. Eventually, Napoleon would control most of Europe, would crown himself Emperor, and would release David in recognition that the artist's talent could serve the ruler's purposes.

Attributions

CC licensed content, Shared previously

- David's Death of Marat. **Provided by**: Khan Academy. **Located at**: https://web.archive.org/web/20130425092955/http://smarthistory.khanacademy.org/david-death-of-marat.html. **License**: *CC BY-NC-SA: Attribution-NonCommercial-ShareAlike*

- Jacques-Louis David, The Death of Marat. **Authored by**: Dr. Beth Harris and Dr. Steven Zucker. **Provided by**: Khan Academy. **Located at**: https://www.khanacademy.org/humanities/monarchy-enlightenment/neo-classicism/v/david-marat. **License**: *CC BY-NC-SA: Attribution-NonCommercial-ShareAlike*

Antonio Canova

A Beauty Queen

And the winner of "Miss Arte Italiana" is—drum roll please—Antonio Canova's Paolina Borghese as Venus Victorious! Or so, at least, is what a recent pole carried out for the Marilena Ferrari Foundation decided.

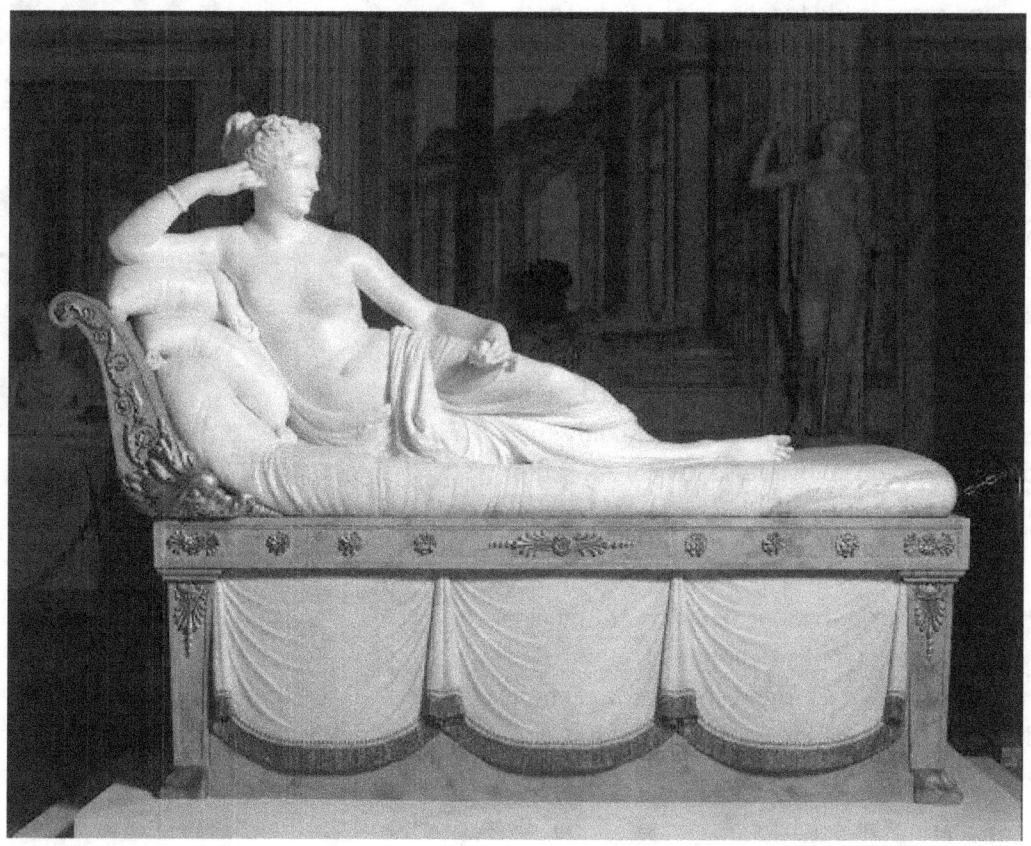

Figure 1. Antonio Canova, Paolina Borghese as Venus Victorious, 1804–08, White marble, 160 × 192 cm, Galleria Borghese, Rome

"Miss Italian Art," a cringeworthy epithet perhaps, but one which, given the strength of the competition, is nothing to sneeze at—works by Botticelli, Leonardo and Titian were also in contention.

Certainly, the semi-nude, life-size portrait of Napoleon's wayward sister is a sumptuous work of art. Four years in the making, it was commissioned by Paolina's second husband, the Italian prince, Camillo Borghese, shortly after their marriage in 1804, a union designed to help Napoleon realize his dreams of establishing a pan-European dynasty and legitimize his claims to the Kingdom of Italy.

Canova and Neoclassicism

Anotonio Canova was a leading light of the Neoclassical movement. The style, influenced by the archeological discoveries in Pompeii and Herculaneum as well as the theories of the art historian Johann Wincklemann, looked back to the artistic achievements of the Greeks and Romans with renewed interest, informed by the spirit of rational enquiry that characterized the Age of Enlightenment.

As Inspector General of Antiquities and Fine Art of the Papal States and responsible for acquiring works for the Vatican museums, Canova would have known his Phidias from his Praxiteles. However, he was no slavish imitator. Instead he wished to emulate the works of these earlier artists.

The methods he used demanded absolute precision. Working from numerous preparatory sketches he modeled the form into a life-size clay version. He then cast a plaster model of this which he marked up with points that were transferred on to the marble block. His assistants would carve the marble into shape and only then, for "the last hand", did Canova raise his chisel, sculpting the form and crucially polishing the marble, using wax, to a fine, glistening finish.

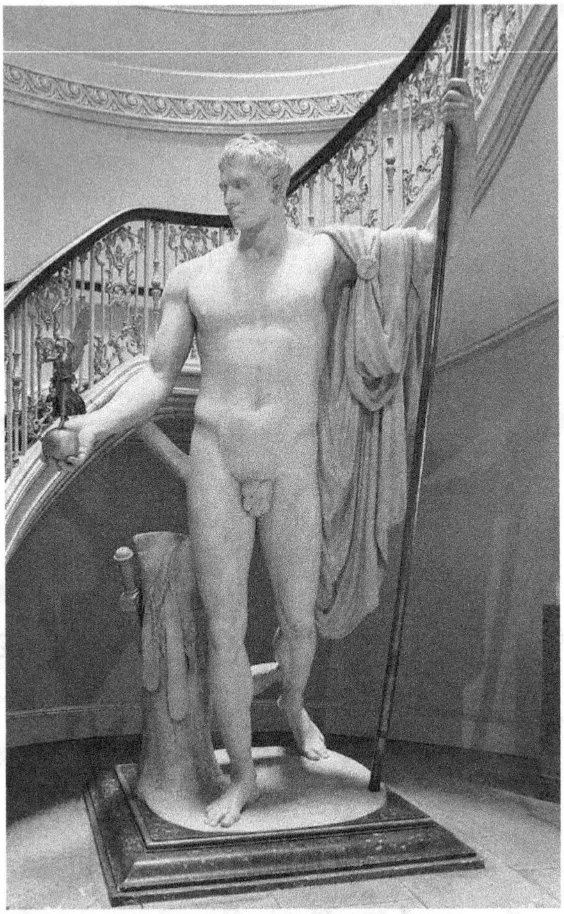

Figure 2. Antonio Canova, Napoleon as Mars the Peacemaker, Wellingtom Museum, Apsley House, London

Many of his models were great personalities of the age. Canova would portray them in antique costume. This classicizing of contemporary figures verged sometimes on the ridiculous, as in the colossal nude sculpture of *Napoleon as Mars the Peacemaker* (figure 2). His portrait of Paolina Borghese is more successful.

A Modern Day Venus

Paolina is shown reclining on a pillowed couch in a pose of studied grace, both concentrated and relaxed. The modelling of the nude body is extraordinarily lifelike, while Canova's treatment of the surface of the marble captures the soft texture of skin. The tactile quality of the piece is bought out particularly in the way the sitter's own hands are occupied, the fingers of her right connecting ever so lightly with the nape of her neck, offer a gesture charged with seductive promise. The head is raised slightly suggesting that something or someone has suddenly entered her line of vision. The apple she holds in her left hand, her fingers wrapped around it suggestive of erotic touch, identifies her as Venus Victorious, the goddess awarded the Golden Apple of Discord in perhaps the first beauty competition in the history of Western culture. The story comes from ancient Greece. Paris the Trojan prince judged Venus more beautiful than either of her rivals, Minerva and Juno. In return Venus introduced him to a Greek girl called Helen and the rest of course is the stuff of epic poetry.

Originally, Canova was to depict her as Diana, the chaste goddess of the moon and the hunt, a role that more would have require her to have been clothed. Paolina insisted on Venus, though. A bit of a loose cannon with a reputation for promiscuity, the Emperor's sister enjoyed courting controversy and posing naked would certainly have raised a few eyebrows in polite society. But there was more to it than that. Apparently, the Borghese family believed themselves to be descended from the heroic founder of Rome, Aeneas, who according to Virgil was the son of Venus. The choice then not only suited Paolina's flirtatious character, but also would have been met with approval by the Borghese family, suggesting continuity between the ancient and modern worlds.

Her hair, a mass of curls bound in a Psyche knot, serves as a visual connector between the two, being worn in imitation of ancient Greek styles as was the fashion of the day. Its careful articulation offsets the smooth shallow planes of her torso. Creating a contrast of another sort, the couch Paolina lies on is carved from a different type of marble, the base part of which is covered in rhythmically flowing drapery, much like on a catafalque, a raised platform used to bear coffins.

The allusion to mortuary art is not that surprising; in Greek and Roman art the reclining female figure is frequently found on sarcophagus lids. So conspicuous an allusion demands further explanation, though, and I suppose if one were forced to read for a meaning here it would have to be the defeat of death by beauty—as expressed through art—that is being celebrated in the image.

Reception

Canova's extraordinary capacity to breathe life into his sculptures was noted by his contemporaries. Literally animated, the sculpture would have been on a revolving mechanism, allowing the static viewer to see the work in the round. It would also have been viewed by candlelight. The finely polished waxy surface would have reflected light brilliantly, creating chiaroscuoro, a more painterly than sculptural effect, perhaps, but then Canova was a painterly sculptor. Paolina owes more to the likes of Giorgione's *Sleeping Venus* and Titian's *Venus of Urbino* and of course David's *Madame Recamier* than antique sculpture a point not lost on the Neo-classical purists of the day who condemned the work as out of keeping with their austere classical theories.

Inevitably the sculpture was going to cause a scandal. While intended for a private audience sophisticated enough to appreciate the classical allusions, given Paolina's infidelities, the sculpture also served to confirm the rumours about her.

If anything, though, Paolina enjoyed the attention. Asked if she minded having to pose nude, she replied: "Why should I? The studio was heated." Camillo refused to allow the sculpture to leave his residence. Napoleon agreed.

Impact

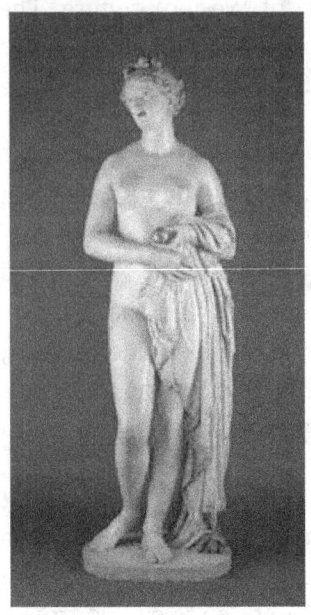

Figure 3. John Gibson, The Tinted Venus, c. 1851–56, Walker Art Gallery Liverpool

From Ingres to Renoir, from Proud'hon to Puvis de Chavannes, Paolina Borghese as Venus Victorious had an enormous impact on nineteenth century French artists. It is in the works of the English sculptor John Gibson, though, who Canova took under his wing later on in life, that we find her most faithful devotee.

Animating the figure with pools of reflected light, the glistening waxy surface of his most celebrated work *The Tinted Venus* (figure 3) owes much to *Venus Victorious*; together with his own innovative use of polychromy the sculpture provoked outrage among its Victorian audience for whom it appeared a little too real: "a naked, impudent English woman" as one review put her. Canova's own naked, impudent French woman would have been proud.

Attributions

CC licensed content, Shared previously

- Canova's Paolina Borghese as Venus Victorious. **Authored by**: Ben Pollitt. **Provided by**: Khan Academy. **Located at**: https://web.archive.org/web/20130425084334/http://smarthistory.khanacademy.org/canovas-paolina-borghese-as-venus-victorious.html. **License**: *CC BY-SA: Attribution-ShareAlike*
- Napoleon Canova London. **Authored by**: Jorg Bittner Unna. **Located at**: https://commons.wikimedia.org/wiki/File:Napoleon-Canova-London_JBU01.jpg. **License**: *CC BY-SA: Attribution-ShareAlike*

Benjamin West

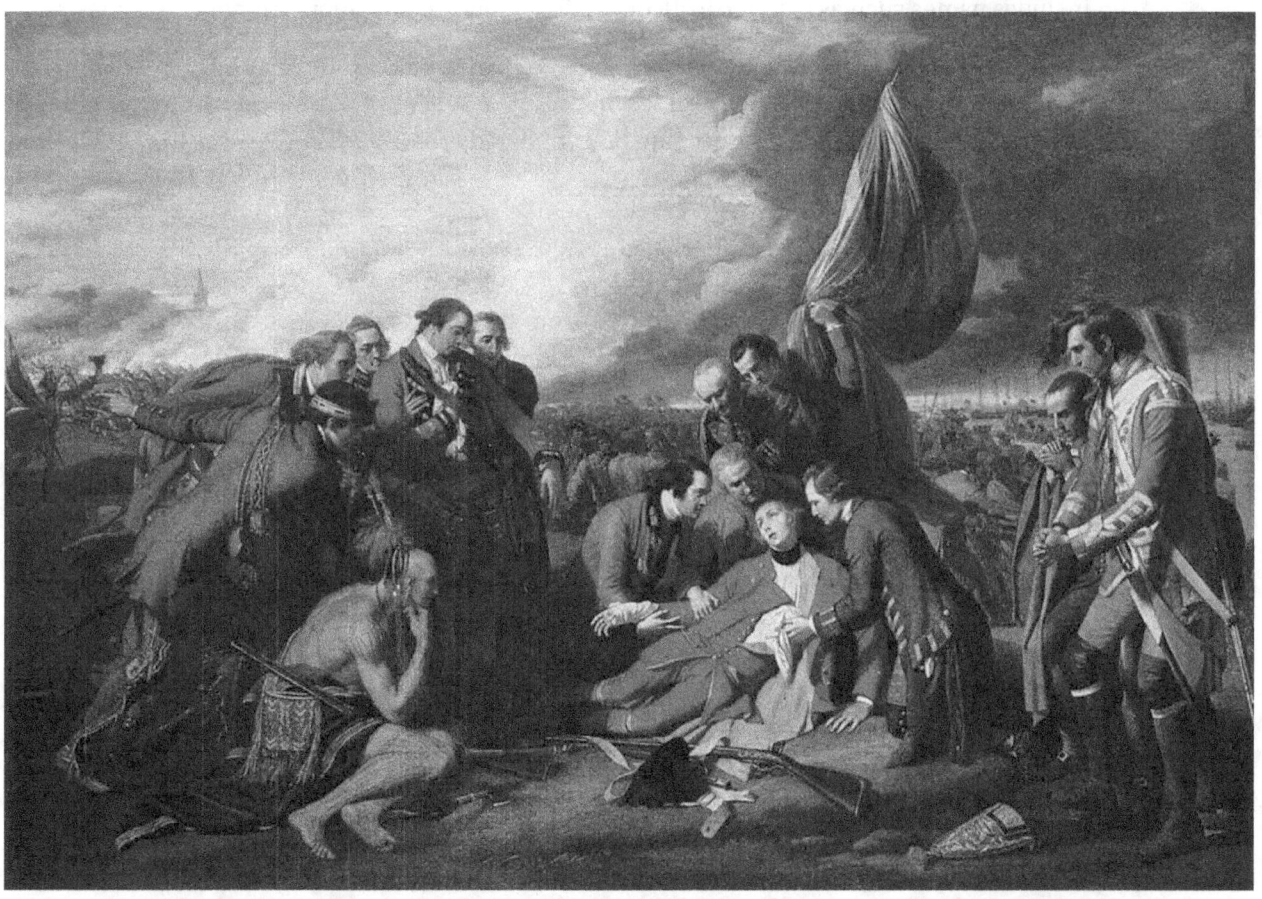

Figure 1. Benjamin West, The Death of General Wolfe, 1770, oil on canvas, 152.6 × 214.5 cm (National Gallery of Canada)

The Artist

Benjamin West (1738–1820) has always been a difficult to artist to classify. American historians generally claim him as an American artist as he was born in what would become the state of Pennsylvania. West's earliest paintings date from his fifteenth year, and if his own attempts at myth making are to believed—they should be taken with the proverbial grain of salt—he was mostly self taught.

In 1760, two wealthy Philadelphian families paid for the young artist's passage to Italy so he could learn from the great European artistic tradition. He was only 21 years old. He arrived in the port of Livorno during the middle of April and was in Rome no later than 10 July. West remained in Italy for several years and moved to London in August of 1763. He found quick success in England and was a founding member of the Royal Academy of Art when it was established in 1768. West was clearly intoxicated by the cosmopolitan London and never returned to his native Pennsylvania.

West's fame and importance today rest on two important areas.

- **West as a teacher:** West taught two successive generations of American artists. All of these men traveled to his London studio and the most returned to the United States. Indeed, a list of those who searched out his instruction comprises a "who's who" list of early American artists and includes names such as Charles Willson Peale, Gilbert Stuart, John Trumbull, Thomas Sully, and Samuel F. B. Morse.

- **West as history painter:** If his role as a teacher was the first avenue to West's fame, surely his history painting is the second. Of the many he completed, *The Death of General Wolfe* (1770) is certainly the most celebrated.

In *The Death of General Wolfe*, West departed from conventions in two important regards.

Generally, history paintings were reserved for narratives from the Bible or stories from the classical past. Instead, however, West depicted a near-contemporary event, one that occurred only seven years before. *The Death of General Wolfe* depicts an event from the Seven Years' War (known as the French and Indian War in North America), the moment when Major-General James Wolfe was mortally wounded on the Plains of Abraham outside Quebec.

Secondly, many—including Sir Joshua Reynolds and West's patron, Archbishop Drummond—strongly urged West to avoid painting Wolfe and others in modern costume, which was thought to detract from the timeless heroism of the event. They urged him to instead paint the figures wearing togas. West refused, writing, "the same truth that guides the pen of the historian should govern the pencil [paintbrush] of the artist."

Artistic License

Yet despite West's interest in "truth," there is little to be found in *The Death of General Wolfe*. Without doubt, the dying General Wolfe is the focus of the composition. West paints Wolfe lying down at the moment of his death wearing the red uniform of a British officer. A circle of identifiable men attend to their dying commander. Historians know that only one—Lieutenant Henry Browne, who holds the British flag above Wolfe—was present at the General's death.

Clearly, West took artistic license in creating a dramatic composition, from the theatrical clouds to the messenger approaching on the left side of the painting to announce the British victory over the Marquis de Montcalm and his French army in this decisive battle. Previous artists, such as James Barry, painted this same event in a more documentary, true-to-life style. In contrast, West deliberately painted this composition as a dramatic blockbuster.

This sense of spectacle is also enhanced by other elements, and West was keenly interested in giving his viewers a unique view of this North American scene. This was partly achieved through landscape and architecture. The St. Lawrence River appears on the right side of the composition and the steeple represents the cathedral in the city of Quebec. In addition to the landscape, West also depicts a tattooed Native American on the left side of the painting. Shown in what is now the universal pose of contemplation, the Native American firmly situates this as an event from the New World, making the composition all the more exciting to a largely English audience.

Wolfe as Christ

Perhaps most important is the way West portrayed the painting's protagonist as Christ-like. West was clearly influenced by the innumerable images of the dead Christ in Lamentation and Depositions paintings that he would have seen during his time in Italy. This deliberate visual association between the dying General Wolfe and the dead Christ underscores the British officer's admirable qualities. If Christ was innocent, pure, and died for a worthwhile cause—that is, the salvation of mankind—then Wolfe too was innocent, pure, and died for a worthwhile cause; the advancement of the British position in North America. Indeed, West transforms Wolfe from a simple war hero to a deified martyr for the British cause. This message was further enhance by the thousands of engravings that soon flooded the art market, both in England and abroad.

Historical Significance

Benjamin West's *The Death of General Wolfe* justifiably retains a position as a landmark painting in the history of American art. In it, West reinterprets the rules of what a history painting could be—both in regard to period depicted and the attire the figures wore—and at the same time followed a visual language that would have been familiar to its eighteenth-century audience. This composition set the stage for the many "contemporary" history paintings that John Singleton Copley and John Trumbull painted throughout the rest of the eighteenth century.

Attributions

CC licensed content, Shared previously

William Hogarth

Sex, Booze, and Eighteenth-Century Britain

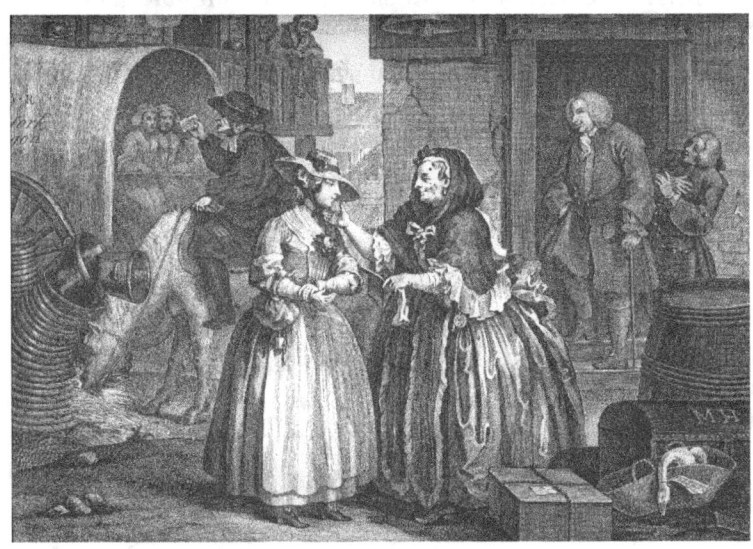

*Figure 1. William Hogarth, A Harlot's Progress, plate 1, 1732, etching
with engraving on paper, 12-3/8 × 14-15/16 inches or 31.4 × 38 cm*

If you ever needed proof that the sex, booze and a rock'n'roll lifestyle was not a twentieth century invention, you need look no further than the satirical prints of William Hogarth. He held up a moralizing mirror to eighteenth-century Britain; the harlots, the womanizers—even the clergy could not escape. Hogarth's prints play out the sins of eighteenth-century London in a kind of visual theatre that was entirely new and novel in their day.

The first example of these prints, which Hogarth himself termed "modern moral subjects," was *A Harlot's Progress* (the first panel of this series is shown in figure 1). In this series, we meet the fresh faced Moll Hackabout as she arrives for the first time in London. Moll is soon preyed upon by a brothel keeper and she descends into prostitution. The tale ends with her premature death from a sexually transmitted disease, aged just twenty-three. Despite its dark subject matter *A Harlot's Progress* was a huge success. These prints reference characters types who were well known to their contemporary London audience. For example Moll's madam was the real-life Elizabeth Needham, keeper of an exclusive London brothel and her first patron, the renowned love-rat and convicted rapist, Colonel Francis Charteris.

A Rake's Progress

These sly nods to the bad guys of the day not only made the prints hugely relevant and enjoyable to their target audience but it also made them incredibly popular. *A Rake's Progress* (1735) was Hogarth's second series and proved to be just as well loved. The main character is Tom Rakewell—a rake being a old fashioned term for a man of loose morals or a womanizer. Tom's name is intentionally general and in a modern equivalent, he might be called Mr. Immoral. Tom is not unique—he could be any number of people in eighteenth-century Britain.

The series opens with a chaotic scene: Tom's father, who was a rich merchant, has died and Tom has returned from Oxford University to collect and spend his late father's wealth. He also wastes no time in rejecting his pregnant fiancé, Sarah Young, by attempting to pay her off. Hogarth laces all his prints with clues to help us decode the scene. Here we can see Sarah sobbing into a hankie whilst holding her engagement ring in her hand. Her mother stands behind her angrily clutching the love letters Tom once wrote to her daughter and he holds out a handful of coins in an attempt to get rid of them. Sarah pops up throughout these prints representing a more wholesome life that he could have had.

A Fashionable Life

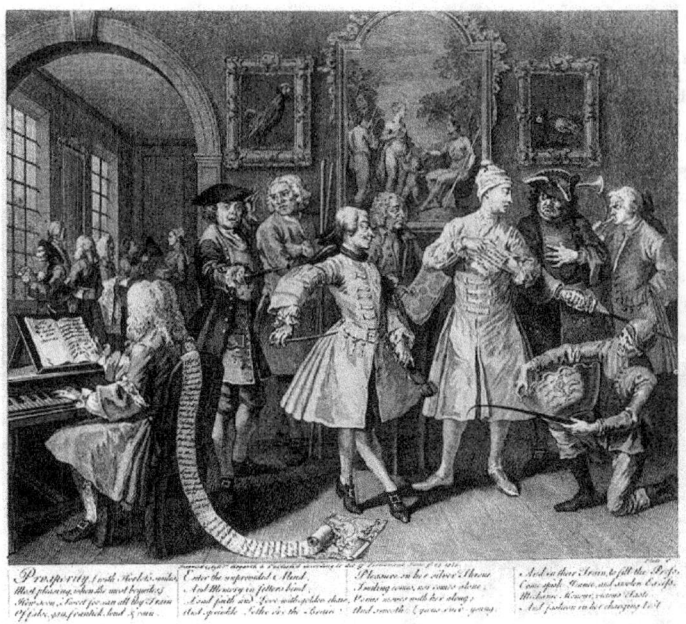

Figure 2. William Hogarth, A Rake's Progress, plate 2, "Surrounded by Artists and Professors," 1735, engraving on paper, 35.5 × 31 cm

By the next scene ("Surrounded by Artists and Professors," figure 2) Tom has already moved from his cosy, if slightly shabby family home into his new bachelor pad surrounded by a dance master, a music teacher, a poet, a tailor, a landscape gardener, a body guard and a jockey all offering their services to help Tom complete his fashionable lifestyle. He is dressed in his nightclothes indicating that he has just woken: those who wish to exploit his new found wealth are wasting no time.

Tom's fashionable life also comes with fashionable vices and soon we see him in the Rose Tavern with a group of prostitutes (see "The Tavern Scene," figure 3). He sits on the lap of one who caresses him with one hand whilst robbing him of his watch with the other. Portraits of Roman Emperors hang on the wall behind them but the only one that has not been defaced is Nero's. This is perhaps hard for a modern audience to identify but there would have been a significant number of Hogarth's classically educated audience who got the gag: Nero was a corrupt womanizer who fiercely persecuted Christians. To the very classically aware Georgians (George II was then King) the message was clear, Christian morals are not to be found here.

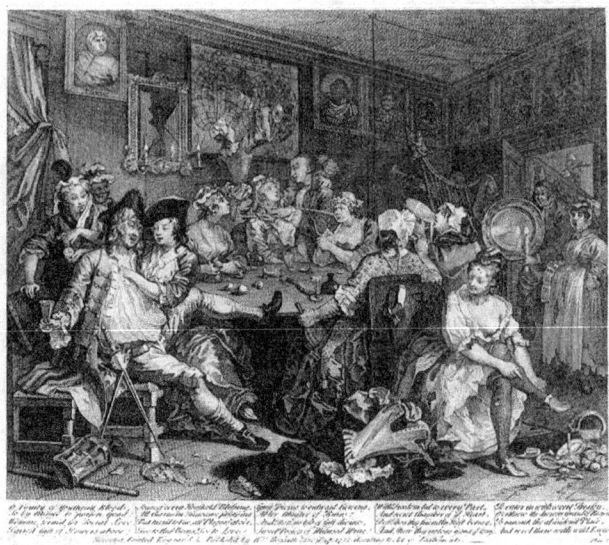

Figure 3. William Hogarth, A Rake's Progress, plate 3, "The Tavern Scene," engraving on paper, 1735 35.5 × 31 cm

A Decadent Decline

Tom's decadent lifestyle does not last for long and by the third scene his sedan chair is intercepted by bailiffs as he is en route to the Queen's birthday party. It is at this point that our heroine Sarah Young comes to the rescue. She is now working as a milliner and kindly pays Tom's bail. Although Sarah has saved Tom from the bailiffs, she cannot save him from himself. By the next scene he is marrying a wealthy old hag. The old woman's eyes lust eagerly towards the ring and Tom's towards her maid. In the background Sarah Young and her mother struggle to voice their objections but are held back by some of the guests.

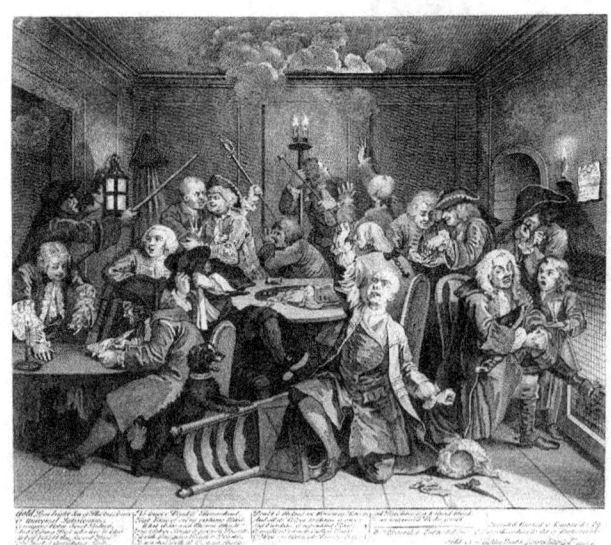

Figure 4. William Hogarth, A Rake's Progress, plate 6, "The Gaming House," 1735, engraving on paper, 35.5 × 31 cm

Tom is wealthy again but he is no better with his money now than he was last time and soon he is on his knees in a gambling den having just squandered the lot (see "The Gaming House," figure 4). Excessive gambling was a real problem in the eighteenth century and whole family fortunes could be lost in one evening. Later in the century, George III's son, who later became George IV, had to ask Parliament for money to help him pay off his gambling debts. It was given to him but it was not long before he needed even more.

Debtor's Prison

Like so many others in eighteenth-century Britain, Tom finds himself in debtor's prison, quickly coming to the end of his tether. On the one side his wife derides him for squandering their fortune, on the other the beer-boy and the jailer harass him to settle his weekly bill. Sarah Young, who has come to visit Tom with their child, has fainted on seeing him in this hopeless situation. This must have been very personally relevant for Hogarth as his father spent much of his childhood in a debtor's prison.

My favorite part of the series is played out in the background of this scene. Tom's fellow inmates are trying various schemes to get enough money to buy their freedom. However, their choice of projects cleverly illustrate just how just how impossible it was to get out of debt in Georgian Britain. One man is attempting to turn lead into gold while the other is working on solving the national debt crisis. Even Tom has written a play, thought we can clearly see a rejection letter for it lying on the table.

Bedlam

The stresses of the previous scene have proven to be more than Tom can bear and in the final scene he is found languishing in bedlam—London's notorious mental hospital (see "The Madhouse," figure 5). The mark on his chest suggests that he has stabbed himself in a failed suicide attempt. Fashionable young women, the likes of which Tom would have socialized with just a short while ago, observe the scene in amusement. All that he has left is the company and care of the faithful Sarah Young.

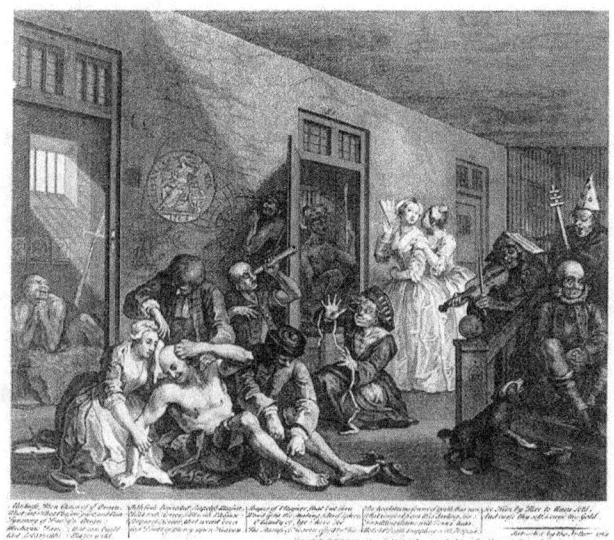

Figure 5. William Hogarth, The Rake's Progress, plate 8, "The Madhouse," 1735, engraving on paper, 35.5 x 31 cm

Popularity

Clearly Hogarth was a great story teller, but what made the prints so popular? One answer is that it appealed to the contemporary concern about people from the middle classes who tried to live like aristocrats. this was a popular issue at this time as the merchant trade was creating social mobility on a scale never seen before. However if we scratch the surface of A Rake's Progress we can see that a number of different types of people implicated. For example, Tom was on his way to the Queen's birthday party when he was stopped by bailiffs and therefore his lifestyle is actually being encouraged and supported by aristocrats. In A Rake's Progress, everyone from the Queen to the priest that performs his marriage of convenience, to common prostitutes, are part of the problem.

But it is not just Hogarth's "take no prisoners" approach to social commentary that made him so popular. Printed satire was actually already very common place and central London was full of bookshops and print sellers that displayed this kind of work. What Hogarth did do that was so completely novel was to tell a story through pictures, A Rake's Progress is like a story board for a play. In fact, Hogarth's series were adapted into plays and pantomimes during his lifetime. His visual drama offered his audience a new way to enjoy satire. It is for this reason that to find comparisons and inspirations we should be looking at authors such as Hogarth's friend and fellow moralizer, Henry Fielding or Jonathan Swift—author of Gulliver's Travels, rather than contemporary artists. The title A Rake's Progress was referencing John Bunyan's The Pilgrims Progress. We can be quite sure that most people would have gotten this reference as it is thought that, at this time, this was the most read book in Britain after the Bible. Hogarth successfully borrows from popular culture in order to express complicated ideas through an enjoyable and totally accessible story. Of course Hogarth wasn't the first to do this, but he did it so well, he is celebrated to this day.

Attributions

CC licensed content, Shared previously

John Singleton Copley

The Copley Family (figure 1) is a large work of art; it measures in at 89 by 107 inches in its frame. The figures appear roughly life-size and seem remarkably life-like; the sense of depth is so strong, that when you stand before the painting, you almost get the impression that you could walk right into the picture and join in the group portrait. It's a very sweet, charming scene: the children playfully twist out of their formal poses (as would unruly kids for any family photo), and interact with their adult family members. If you pay attention to the individual figures, you notice that each is in his or her own unique position and sports a distinctive facial expression. The tender embrace between mother and child—a personal moment revealing the sentimental bond between the two—is a detail that hints at the psychology, personality, and family dynamics of the painting's subjects. The level of intimacy in the work is not surprising when we learn that the head of the family, the man standing in the rear and looking out directly at the viewer, was also the artist: John Singleton Copley.

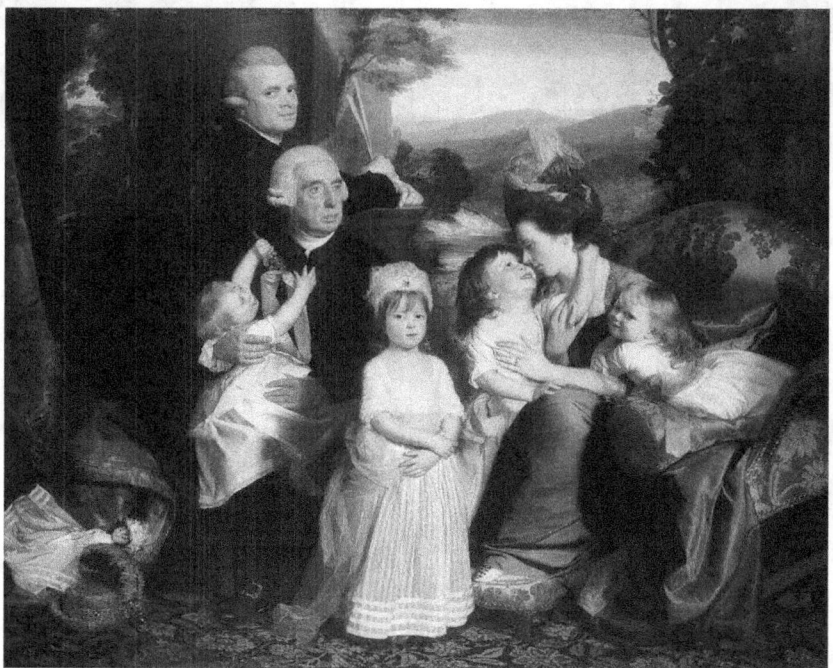

Figure 1. John Singleton Copley, *The Copley Family, 1776–77, oil on canvas (National Gallery, Washington)*

For many students new to art history, American portraiture of the colonial period can be difficult to love. When visiting museums and historic houses, viewers are often taken aback by how stiff and unnatural the subjects of these early paintings appear, how expressionless their faces, how contrived their positions. An example is John Smibert's *The Bermuda Group* (figure 2), a painting deserving of its own attention and place in history, but a work that is more somber, less legible to modern eyes, and harder for us in the twenty-first century to relate to. Copley's work stands out starkly against that of his contemporaries and predecessors: his subjects appear to inhabit a three-dimensional world instead of resting shallowly on the canvas, they seem natural, effortless, and have distinct personas. His paintings are rife with eye candy, with every illusion—the sheen of a lady's garment, the long fur of a King Charles spaniel—painstakingly rendered in incredible detail. While more "Puritan" early American paintings are also fascinating and noteworthy, it was John Singleton Copley who first truly awoke my interest and breathed life into early American art.

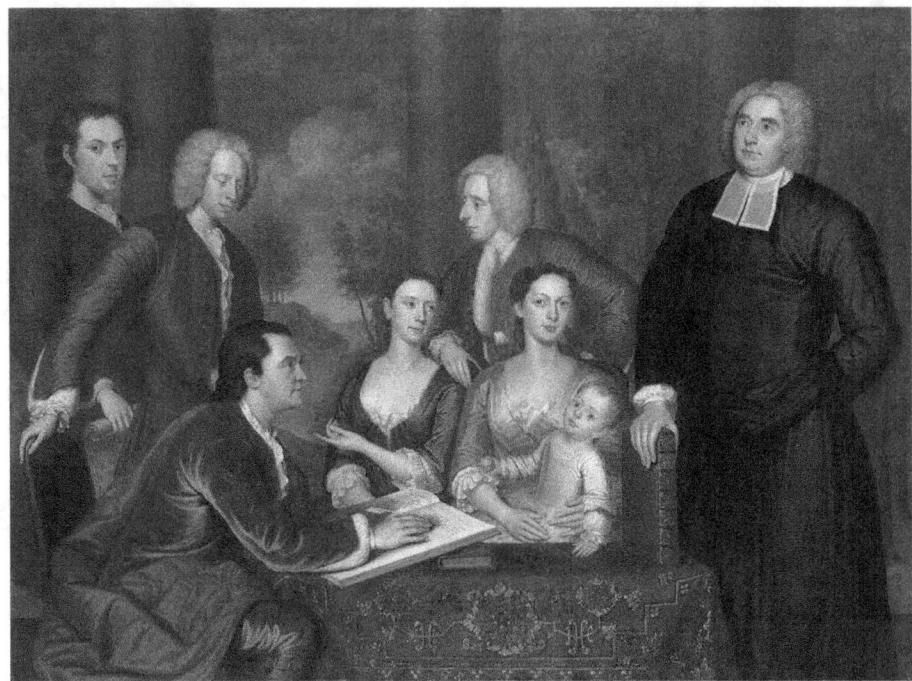

Figure 2. John Smybert, The Bermuda Group (Dean Berkely and His Entourage), 1728–39, oil on canvas, 69.5" × 93" (176.5 cm × 236.2 cm), Yale University Art Gallery

Attributions

Copley's Watson and the Shark

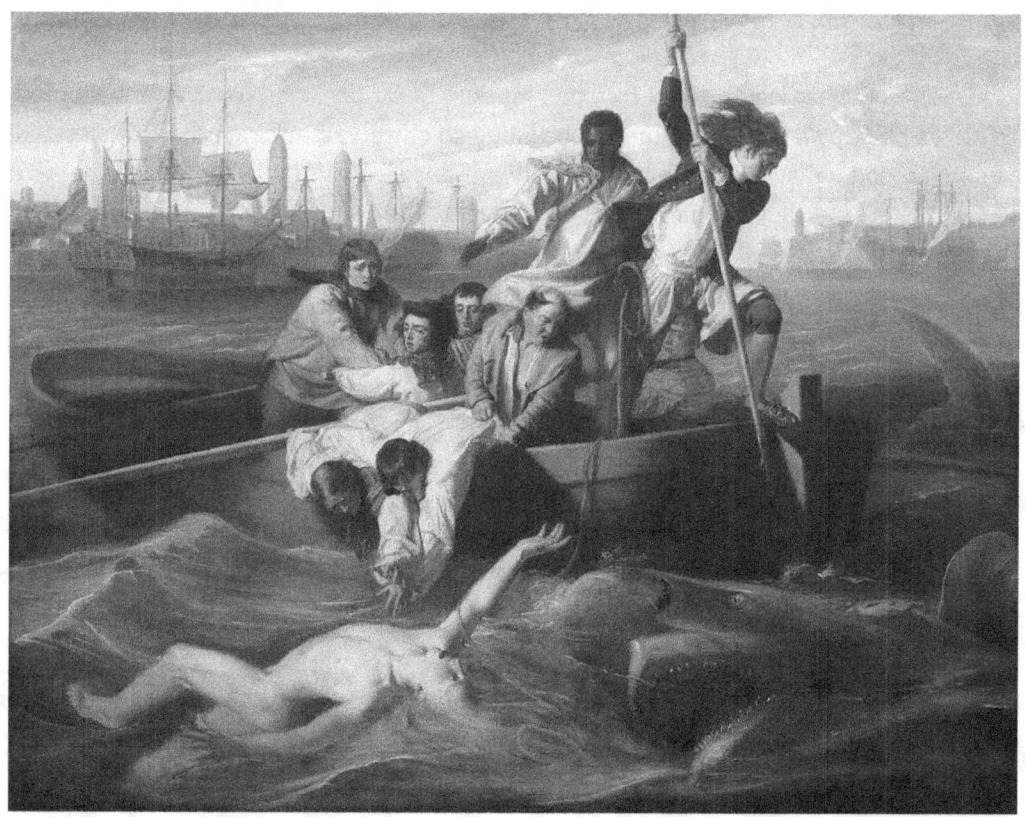

Figure 1. John Singleton Copley, Watson and the Shark, 1778, oil on canvas (National Gallery, Washington)

Copley: British or American Artist?

Eventually Copley found America's art market wanting and its political climate treacherous; after positive reception overseas, he abandoned colonial life and, after studying art in Italy, left for London in 1774, never to return to his native land. His reasons were ultimately professional, political, as well as personal: his own father-in-law, a merchant for London's East India Company, owned some of the tea shipments tossed into the harbor by the Sons of Liberty during the 1773 Boston Tea Party. Copley by no means should be labeled a Tory, however, believing that both Britain and America would emerge from the war prosperous empires redeemed through divine providence. His efforts to honor the wishes of both British and American patrons resulted in strain and criticism, with Copley in time losing the support of his colonial peers.

An example of Copley's work after his move to England, *Watson and the Shark* (figure 1) is all at once a group portrait, a portrait of the patron (London merchant Brook Watson), as well as a snapshot of a real-life event. The painting depicts Watson's trauma at age fourteen of being a victim of a shark attack off Havana, Cuba, an experience that cost the former cabin boy his leg. Copley portrays the third—and ultimately successful—rescue attempt by nearby sailors, glorifying it as a story of salvation and spiritual rebirth. Again we see Copley striving to prove his talent: he renders the choppy sea somewhat translucent to show the viewer Watson's nude and well-muscled body, a clear testimonial to Copley's study of the classical statuary of ancient Greece and Rome. The underlying messages are lofty ones as well, with Copley perhaps referencing both Christ's Resurrection as well as the renewal of the British Empire in the aftermath of the American Revolution, in the visual image of Watson emerging from the watery depths. *Watson and the Shark* solidified Copley's career in Britain and ensured his election to the Royal Academy in 1779 after its exhibition. As Watson was a British Tory, however, Copley's heroicized treatment of his patron angered many American critics and cost the artist some of his esteem back home.

Copley's relocation to Britain leaves us with some lingering questions: Can we even call Copley an American artist? With his painting style and cultural upbringing so closely mimicking the British standard, and in light of his move abroad, what—if anything—is truly American about his work? These are questions that may never be answered, but they open the door for understanding some of the complexities that characterized early American life.

Attributions

CC licensed content, Shared previously

- Copley's Watson and the Shark. **Authored by**: Meg Floryan. **Provided by**: Khan Academy. **Located at**: https://web.archive.org/web/20130425105322/http://smarthistory.khanacademy.org/copleys-watson-and-the-shark.html. **License**: *CC BY-NC-SA: Attribution-NonCommercial-ShareAlike*

Gilbert Stuart

Well Known Image

While the name Gilbert Stuart may be one unknown to most Americans, practically every American is aware of at least one of his paintings. Art historians formally call it the *Athenaeum Portrait*. Most everyone is familiar with it as the engraved image of George Washington that graces the front of the one-dollar bill. This is one of the dozens of portraits that Stuart painted of our first president.

Another, a full-length likeness, is called the *Lansdowne Portrait* (figure 1). Although not as famous as its bust-length counterpart, the *Lansdowne Portrait* retains a place of special significance within the history of American art.

Expat Education

On the brink of the American Revolutionary War, Stuart decided it was time to pursue serious artistic instruction, and so, in 1775, he sailed for London and the studio of Benjamin West, whose generosity to his colonial brethren was seemingly endless.

Stuart remained in London for almost twelve years and then relocated to Ireland. He clearly had aspirations of making American versions of European Grand Manner portraits such as the likeness Hyacinthe Rigaud painted of Louis XIV in 1701.

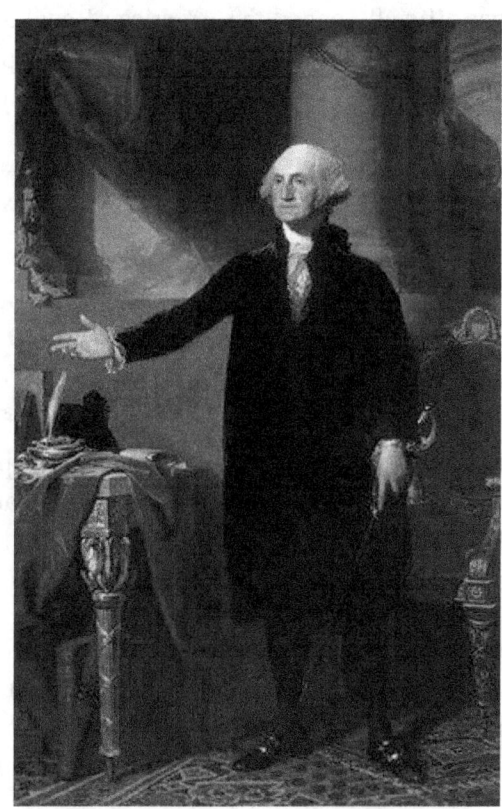

Figure 1. Gilbert Stuart, Lansdowne Portrait of George Washington, 1796, oil on canvas, 96 × 60" / 243.8 × 152.4 cm (National Portrait Gallery)

After acquiring debts sufficient to necessitate a hasty departure from the Emerald Isle, the artist told a friend about his short-term plans for Ireland and about his anticipated return to the United States:

When I can net a sum sufficient to take me to America, I shall be off to my native soil. There I expect to make a fortune by [portraits of] Washington alone. I calculate upon making a plurality of his portraits, whole lengths, what will enable me to realize; and if I should be fortunate, I will repay my English and Irish creditors. To Ireland and English I shall be adieu.

This was a task easier said than done. Stuart did not personally know the recently elected president, and the artist had been away from his homeland for 18 years.

Letter of Introduction

Rather than return to Rhode Island, the state of his birth, he instead sailed for New York City, the home of John Jay, the first Chief Justice of the Supreme Court and a close political confidant to George Washington. Stuart first met Jay in 1782 when the politician was in London negotiating the Treaty of Paris, the accord that officially ended the American Revolutionary War. Stuart arrived in New York City in early May of 1793, and a visit to Jay, one of the few people the painter could have known in Manhattan, must have been amongst Stuart's first social calls. He painted Jay several times during the months that followed and the politician provided a letter of introduction for the relatively unknown artist to meet the president. Stuart departed New York City for Philadelphia in November 1794.

Philadelphia

If painting images of George Washington was the primary reason Stuart returned to the United States, then Philadelphia was certainly the place to be. Stuart wasted little time in calling on Washington, and painted three different kinds of portraits of the president (with dozens of subsequent copies) in the years that followed. In the decades immediately preceding the invention of photography, the myriad of portraits of Washington that Stuart painted created an image Americans accepted as the portrait of their first president. The "Vaughan Type" shows Washington facing slightly to his left, the "Athenaeum Type" shows the first president facing to his right, and the "Lansdowne Type" is a full-length portrait.

Stuart painted six full-length portraits of Washington. The "Lansdowne Type" acquired its name from the owner of the first full-length portrait Stuart painted, William Petty, the first Marquis of Lansdowne. The portrait was a gift from William Bingham, a wealthy Philadelphian merchant and was intended to thank Lord Lansdowne for his financial support of the colonial cause during the American Revolutionary War.

Civilian Commander

Given his European training, Stuart was well suited to execute a Grand Manner portrait of America's first president. However, whereas previous artists such as John Trumbull and Charles Willson Peale emphasized Washington's position as an officer in the Revolutionary Army, Stuart stressed Washington's position as a civilian commander in chief. In the *Lansdowne Portrait*, Washington does not hold a scepter, wear a crown, or sit on a throne. Instead, Stuart filled the eight-foot tall composition with elements symbolic to the new republic. He wears an American made black velvet suit, one similar in fabric, cut, and color to one he frequently wore on public occasions. Washington raises his right arm in a classically inspired oratorical pose, while his left hand grasps a ceremonial sword. The President stands before a portico-like space, complete with two pairs of ionic columns and a red curtain that has been pulled aside to reveal a background of open sky.

In addition to the architectural setting and the sitter's pose, other elements within the composition transform the *Lansdowne Portrait* from a simple likeness of Washington into an official state portrait.

The Neo-Classical chair on the right side of the painting contains elements from the Great Seal of the United States. A small oval medallion on the top of the chair is divided in half. The top half contains thirteen white stars in a blue field, and thirteen alternating red and white stripes appear underneath. Two erect eagles are visible on top of the leg of the table, each of which grasps a bundle of arrows, symbols of readiness for war (figure 2). Underneath the table are several books, titled, *General Orders, American Revolution,* and *Constitution & Laws of the United States* that indicate Washington's past military and political accomplishments. More books—*Federalist* and *Journal of Congress*—stand upright on top of the table. A silver inkwell, quill, and several sheets of blank paper can be seen immediately underneath Washington's outstretched right hand.

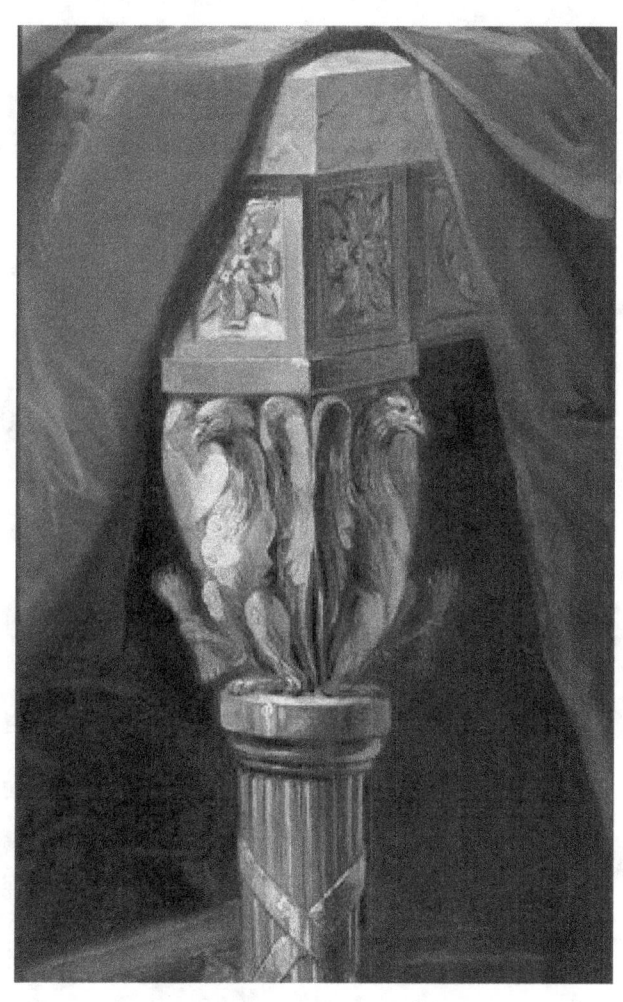

Figure 2. Detail of the table leg in the Lansdowne Portrait.

Representing the Office of the Presidency

Without question, Gilbert Stuart's Lansdowne Portrait of George Washington is far more than a portrait of the first president of the United States of America. It is instead a painting that represents not only Washington's likeness, but also the aesthetic and political trappings of the office of the presidency and of the New Republic. Utilizing all of the traditions of European Grand Manner portraiture, it became the standard full-length political likeness of Washington throughout the Federalist period.

Chapter 10: 1800–1848 – Industrial Revolution Part I

Chapter 10 Overview

What You'll Learn To Do: Examine and identify Romantic art.

In Chapter 10 we will examine Romantic art. We will look at how artists like Delacroix contributed to the development of Western art. It is imperative to understand Romantic art in order to see how it impacted later artistic developments.

Learning Activities

The learning activities for this module include:

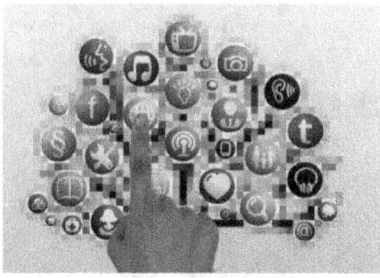

- **Review:** Key Learning Items

Romanticism

- **Read:** Introduction to Romanticism (includes a video: 8:46)

France

Delacroix

- **Read:** Liberty Leading the People (includes a video: 5:23)
- **Watch:** Scene of the Massacre at Chios (3:14)
- **Read:** Death of Sardanapalus (includes a video: 3:42)
- **Read:** Understanding Delacroix's Painterly Techniques

Gros

- **Read:** Napoleon Bonaparte Visiting the Plague-Stricken in Jaffa (includes a video: 3:37)

Gericault

- **Watch:** Raft of the Medusa (6:33)

- **Read:** Portraits of the Insane

Ingres

- **Read:** Apotheosis of Homer
- **Read:** Madame Riviere
- **Read:** Grand Odalisque (includes a video: 4:09)
- **Watch:** Princesse de Broglie (3:22)

Goya

- **Read:** Third of May, 1808
- **Read:** Sleep of Reason Produces Monsters
- **Watch:** Saturn Devouring One of His Sons (3:24)

England

- **Read:** Constable, The Haywain (includes a video: 4:28)
- **Watch:** Turner, Slave Ship (4:01)

United States

Cole

- **Read:** Hudson River School
- **Read:** The Oxbow (includes a video: 5:31)

Erastus Salisbury Field

- **Watch:** Portrait of a Young Woman (3:58)

Attributions

CC licensed content, Original

- Art History II. **Provided by**: Extended Learning Institute of Northern Virginia Community College. **Located at**: http://eli.nvcc.edu/. **License**: *CC BY: Attribution*

Public domain content

- Image of Finger. **Authored by**: geralt. **Located at**: https://pixabay.com/en/finger-touch-hand-structure-769300/. **License**: *Public Domain: No Known Copyright*

Key Learning Items

Learning Objectives

After successful completion of this module, you will be able to:

- Understand and apply the concepts and terminology of Romantic art
- Investigate and apply the fundamental questions we ask when looking at art objects from this movement
- Discuss, collaborate, and generate understanding as to the meaning of Romantic art
- Assess and evaluate the impact of Romantic art on the continued evolution of Western art

Key Questions to Ask

While you are reviewing the content of this module, consider the following questions:

- What are the key characteristics of Romantic art?
- How was Romanticism different from earlier Neoclassical art?
- How did Romantic art develop differently in the United States?

Key Vocabulary Terms

- Romanticism
- painterly
- seascape
- pastoral landscape
- sublime landscape
- Manifest Destiny

- Hudson River School

Here are links to art history glossaries that will help you better understand the above key vocabulary terms.

- ArtLex: Art Dictionary
    - http://www.artlex.com/
- About.com: Art History
    - http://arthistory.about.com/od/glossary/l/bl_Art-Glossary.htm
- Artcyclopedia: A Guide to Fine Art
    - http://www.artcyclopedia.com/

Attributions

CC licensed content, Original

- Art History II. **Provided by**: Extended Learning Institute of Northern Virginia Community College. **Located at**: http://eli.nvcc.edu/. **License**: *CC BY: Attribution*

Introduction to Romanticism

Watch this introduction to Nineteenth-Century Art, focusing on Romanticism:

- https://youtu.be/XdYgyO0RmFI

On Romanticism

Romanticism was the first major stylistic development in nineteenth-century art.

As is fairly common with stylistic rubrics, the word "Romanticism" was not developed to describe the visual arts but was first used in relation to new literary and musical schools in the beginning of the nineteenth century. Art came under this heading only later. Think of the Romantic literature and musical compositions of the early nineteenth century. The poetry of Lord Byron, Percy Shelley, and William Wordsworth and the scores of Beethoven, Richard Strauss, and Chopin (by the way, the pianist Chopin and the painter Delacroix were friends) are concerned with the spectrum and intensity of human emotion.

Even if you do not regularly listen to classical music, you've heard plenty of music by these composers. In his epic film, *2001: A Space Odyssey*, the late director Stanley Kubrick used Strauss's *Thus Spake Zarathustra* (written in 1896, Strauss based on Friedrich Nietzsche's book of the same name). Kubrick's *A Clockwork Orange* similarly uses the sweeping ecstasy and drama of Beethoven's Ninth Symphony, in this case to intensify the cinematic violence of the film.

Listen

- https://s3-us-west-2.amazonaws.com/courses-images-archive-read-only/wp-content/uploads/sites/1122/2016/03/02032459/Also_Sprach_Zarathustra.ogg

Strauss's *Thus Spake Zarathustra*

- "https://s3-us-west-2.amazonaws.com/courses-images-archive-read-only/wp-content/uploads/sites/1122/2016/03/02032459/Anthem_of_Europe.ogg"

Beethoven's Ninth Symphony (as used in the *Anthem of Europe*)

Romantic music expressed the powerful drama of human emotion: anger and passion, but also quiet passages of pleasure and joy. So too, the French painter Eugene Delacroix and the Spanish artist Francisco Goya broke with the cool, cerebral idealism of David and Ingres' Neo-Classicism. They sought instead to respond to the cataclysmic upheavals that characterized their era with line, color, and brushwork that was more physically direct, more emotionally expressive.

Attributions

CC licensed content, Shared previously

All rights reserved content

Public domain content

Liberty Leading the People

Dr. Beth Harris and Dr. Steven Zucker provide a description, historical perspective, and analysis of Delacroix's *Liberty Leading the People*.

- https://www.youtube.com/watch?v=6skizQlC-uU

Eugène Delacroix, *Liberty Leading the People*, 1830, oil on canvas, 2.6 × 3.25m, (Musée du Louvre, Paris).

The July Revolution

This painting was made in response to the political upheaval that would resulted in the overthrow of the reigning monarch, Charles X (brother of the beheaded Louis XVI). Charles X had restored the Bourbon throne after the fall of Napoleon and would himself be replaced by the restricted constitutional rule of Louis-Phillipe, the "citizen-king."

Delacroix's is a complex painting, full of historical reference, yet also full of the spectrum of human emotion—from grand heroism to angry despair—that is a central characteristic of French Romanticism. Note the complex interaction between areas that are brightly reflective and adjacent areas of dark shadow. The results are vivid contrasts which, like the rapid-fire brushwork, activates the surface and augments the painting's sense of movement and energy. Delacroix also breaks with the tradition of relying upon the painstakingly subtle modulation of color, and instead, applies brilliant and shocking traces of pure pigment. See, for example, the notes of sharp primary colors, the blues, yellows and the especially powerful reds. Again, the effect is vivid and electrifying against the broad areas of brown and gray and this fits well with the subject. Liberty rushes forward over the debris of the barricades, by then a signifier of Parisian rebellion.

A Modern Nike

Prior to the late nineteenth century, the streets of this largely medieval city were the chaotic result of organic unplanned growth. Paris was a warren of tangled streets, some little more than narrow alleys that slowed travel, trade and troops, and could be easily blocked allowing revolutionaries to fortify entire sections of the city. It is upon these very barricades that Liberty, the personification of freedom (who the French call Marianne) stands. She holds the tri-color aloft. This is the banned flag of revolution and democracy. The wind spins her drapery around her hips alluding to classical statuary.

Note that the spiraling costume of the great Hellenistic (late ancient Greek) sculpture, the *Nike (victory) of Samothrace* on view in the Musée de Louvre was found after the Delacroix was created but is a useful reference nevertheless (see figure 1).

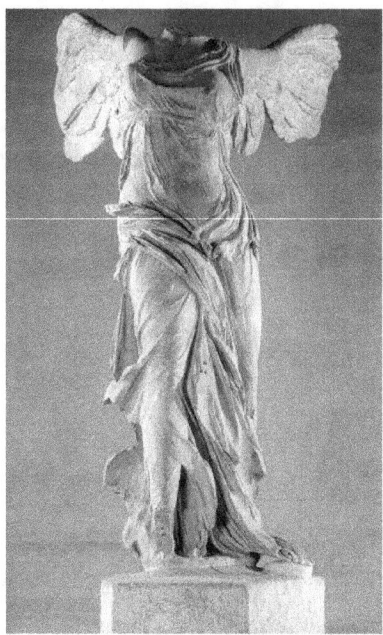

Figure 1. Winged Victory of Samothrace, c. 200–190 BCE

For what possible reason has Delacroix exposed Marianne's breasts? The answer lies in the figure not being an actual person but rather the embodiment of an idea in a human figure. Marianne is, of course, democracy. Democracy was born in Ancient Greece as Delacroix reminds us by his reference to ancient sculpture and his use of partial nudity. But there is a second reference here. During France's first revolution, the one that began in 1789, the newly created democratic state was sometimes depicted as an infant suckled by freedom, by Marianne, its mother.

Class Distinctions

Beside Marianne, we see a menacing crowd that dissolves into the smoke and the confusion of battle. But in the left middle ground, Delacroix depicts two figures with greater clarity. They stand together but represent very different social and economic positions. The man in the top hat, waistcoat and jacket is a member of the middle class. The second figure is less well off. He wears a white shirt and cap and is meant to represent a laborer, a member of the working or lower class. Delacroix's message is clear. The revolution unites these classes against the ruling aristocracy.

The Cost of Rebellion

In the foreground lay two dead bodies. The figure on the left is intended to enrage the viewer. To set the viewer firmly against the excesses of the king's troops. In this sense the painting is pure propaganda. The dead figure on the left is dressed in a long nightshirt that has been push up as his body was dragged into the street from his bedroom where, presumably, he had been shot. Delacroix is alluding to the despised practice of the royal troops who spread terror by murdering suspected revolutionary sympathizers in their beds and then dragging the bodies into the streets as a warning. The dead uniformed figure on the right is a royalist soldier. Here, Delacroix shows the enemy as vulnerable. If you look carefully at the buildings at the right you will see the battle joined and in the distance, the great Gothic cathedral, Notre Dame de Paris, a symbol of the King's power but which is now triumphantly flying the tricolor.

Attributions

CC licensed content, Shared previously

Scene of the Massacre at Chios

Dr. Beth Harris and Dr. Steven Zucker provide a description, historical perspective, and analysis of Delacroix's *Scene of the massacre at Chios*.

- https://youtu.be/CyNjK7dv-IM

Eugène Delacroix, *Scene of the massacre at Chios; Greek families awaiting death or slavery*, 1824 Salon, oil on canvas, 164″ × 139″ (419 cm × 354 cm), (Musée du Louvre, Paris).

Death of Sardanapalus

Delacroix's painting *The Death of Sardanapalus* was inspired by the great Romantic poet Lord Byron's 1821 play, *Sardanapalus.* The following is an except:

OFFICER.
The wall which skirted near the river's brink ?is thrown down by the sudden inundation
Of the Euphrates, which now rolling, swoln ?From the enormous mountains where it rises,
By the late rains of that tempestuous region,
O'erfloods its banks, and hath destroy'd the bulwark.

PANIA.
That's a black augury! it has been said
For ages, " That the city ne'er should yield "To man, until the river grew its foe."

SARDANAPALUS.
I can forgive the omen, not the ravage. ?How much is swept down of the wall?

OFFICER.
About
Some twenty stadii.

SARDANAPALUS.
And all this is left
Pervious to the assailants?

OFFICER.
For the present
The river's fury must impede the assault;
But when he shrinks into his wonted channel,
And may be cross'd by the accustom'd barks,
The palace is their own.

SARDANAPALUS.
That shall be never. Though men, and gods,- and elements, and omens,
Have risen up 'gainst one who ne'er provoked them,
My fathers' house shall never be a cave For wolves to horde and howl in....

SARDANAPALUS.
You have done your duty faithfully, and as
My worthy Pania! further ties between us
Draw near a close. I pray you take this key:
[Gives a key.It opens to a secret chamber, placed
Behind the couch in my own chamber. (Now
Press'd by a nobler weight than e'er it bore—
Though a long line of sovereigns have lain down
Along its golden frame—as bearing for
A time what late was Salemenes.) Search

The secret covert to which this will lead you;
'Tis full of treasure; take it for yourself
And your companions: there's enough to load ye,
Though ye be many. Let the slaves be freed, too;
And all the inmates of the palace, of
Whatever sex, now quit it in an hour.
Thence launch the regal barks, once form'd for pleasure,
And now to serve for safety, and embark.
The river's broad and swoln, and uncommanded
(More potent than a king) by these besiegers.
Fly! and be happy!

PANIA.
Under your protection! So you accompany your faithful guard.

SARDANAPALUS.
No, Pania! that must not be; get thee hence, ?And leave me to my fate…

SARDANAPALUS.
'Tis enough. Now order here ?Faggots, pine-nuts, and wither'd leaves, and such ?Things as catch fire and blaze with one sole spark; ?Bring cedar, too, and precious drugs, and spices, ?And mighty planks, to nourish a tall pile; ?Bring frankincense and myrrh, too, for it is ?For a great sacrifice I build the pyre; ?And heap them round yon throne.

SARDANAPALUS.
You shall know
Anon—what the whole earth shall ne'er forget.

Dr. Beth Harris and Dr. Steven Zucker provide a description, historical perspective, and analysis of Delacroix's *The Death of Sardanapalus.*

- https://youtu.be/iDBJK0y8vb0

Eugène Delacroix, *The Death of Sardanapalus*, 1827, oil on canvas, 12′ 10″ × 16′ 3″ (3.92m × 4.96m), (Musée du Louvre, Paris).

External Link

View this painting up close in the Google Art Project.:

- https://www.google.com/culturalinstitute/asset-viewer/the-death-of-sardanapalus/ GQEXB6lJVIn9wA?projectId=art-project

Attributions

CC licensed content, Shared previously

- Delacroix's The Death of Sardanapalus. **Provided by**: Khan Academy. **Located at**: https://web.archive.org/web/20141006183453/ http://smarthistory.khanacademy.org/the-death-of-sardanapalus.html. **License**: *CC BY-NC-SA: Attribution-NonCommercial-Share-Alike*

Understanding Delacroix's Painterly Techniques

A sensuous use of color subverted the neoclassical aesthetic, in which moral and intellectual messages—or, at the very least, a concept of "noble form"—were intended to dominate. In the case of Delacroix, this attention to the effects of colour is heightened by a concern with the textural qualities of paint. In order to produce a matt but bright surface, he applied thin layers of oil glaze to an initial **lay-in of distemper** (see ten-Doesschate Chu, 2001, p.102). It is thought that he was aiming to produce an effect similar to that of pastels and watercolors—many of his preliminary studies for the painting are in pastels. Indeed, Delacroix learned from various other artists. For example, he established a firm friendship with Richard Parkes Bonington, the English watercolourist. He later recalled how he and Bonington had met in around 1816, when Bonington was working on studies in the gallery of the Louvre. The two artists met again when Delacroix visited England in 1825 and later shared a studio in Paris. Delacroix admired and tried to emulate the lightness of touch and sparkle of Bonington's technique.

Check out Richard Parkes Bonington, *Rouen from the Quays:* https://s3-us-west-2.amazonaws.com/courses-images-archive-read-only/wp-content/uploads/sites/1122/2016/03/02032503/plate13-1.pdf

Whereas neoclassical work aimed to preserve a smoothed-down paint surface produced by the use of delicate, fine brushstrokes, Delacroix applied to the finished canvas of *Sardanapalus* a technique called flossing. Possibly borrowed from Constable, whose *Haywain* Delacroix had seen in the Salon of 1824, this process involves the application of short delicate strokes of color on top of the finished paint surface and enhances the impression of sparkling light. This clearly demonstrates Delacroix's adventurous approach to technique. He also borrowed from Constable, in this and earlier works, the method of applying thin color cross-hatchings to distemper in order to achieve his shadows.

Traditionally, shadows had been painted as thin, dark glazes, with no color interest at all: they had had a muddy, dirty effect, as the local (actual) color of an object had been mixed with black. Constable and Delacroix revolutionised the painting of shadow by representing it as composed of strands of colour. This was a far cry from conventional academic chiaroscuro. Chiaroscuro is the use of light and shade to model form (that is, to suggest the three-dimensional presence of objects and figures) or to create tonal effects, from the subtle to the dramatic.

Attributions

Napoleon Bonaparte Visiting the Plague-Stricken in Jaffa

Dr. Beth Harris and Dr. Steven Zucker provide a description, historical perspective, and analysis of Baron Antoine-Jean Gros's *Napoleon Bonaparte Visiting the Pest House in Jaffa*.

- https://youtu.be/Rx1HtFtc1cM

Baron Antoine-Jean Gros, *Napoleon Bonaparte Visiting the Pest House in Jaffa*, 1804, oil on canvas, 209″ × 280″, (Musée du Louvre, Paris).

Note: Gros was a student of the Neo-Classical painter David, however, this painting, sometimes also titled, *Napoleon Visiting the Pest House in Jaffa*, is a proto-Romantic painting that points to the later style of Gericault and Delacroix. Gros was trained in David's studio between 1785–1792, and is most well known for recording Napoleon's military campaigns, which proved to be ideal subjects for exploring the exotic, violent, and heroic.

In this painting, which measures more than 17 feet high and 23 feet wide, Gros depicted a legendary episode from Napoleon's campaigns in Egypt (1798–1801). On March 21, 1799, in a make-shift hospital in Jaffa, Napoleon visited his troops who were stricken with the Bubonic Plague. Gros depicts Napoleon attempting to calm the growing panic about contagion by fearlessly touching the sores of one of the plague victims. Like earlier neoclassical paintings such as David's *Death of Marat*, Gros combines Christian iconography, in this case Christ healing the sick, with a contemporary subject. He also draws on the art of classical antiquity, by depicting Napoleon in the same position as the ancient Greek sculpture, the Apollo Belvedere. In this way, he imbues Napoleon with divine qualities while simultaneously showing him as a military hero. But in contrast to David, Gros uses warm, sensual colors and focuses on the dead and dying who occupy the foreground of the painting. We see the same approach later in Delacroix's painting of *Liberty Leading the People* (1830).

Napoleon was a master at using art to manipulate his public image. In reality he had ordered the death of the prisoners who he could not afford to house or feed, and poisoned his troops who were dying from the plague as he retreated from Jaffa.

Attributions

- Gros, Napoleon Bonaparte Visiting the Plague-Stricken in Jaffa. **Authored by**: Dr. Beth Harris and Dr. Steven Zucker. **Provided by**: Khan Academy. **Located at**: https://www.khanacademy.org/humanities/becoming-modern/romanticism/romanticism-in-france/v/gros-napoleon-bonaparte-visiting-the-pest-house-in-jaffa-1804. **License**: *CC BY-NC-SA: Attribution-NonCommercial-ShareAlike*

Raft of the Medusa

Dr. Beth Harris and Dr. Steven Zucker provide a description, historical perspective, and analysis of Géricault's *Raft of the Medusa*.

- https://www.youtube.com/watch?v=jlVBaqyGKMs

Théodore Géricault, *Raft of the Medusa*, 1818–19, oil on canvas, 193 × 282 inches, (Musée du Louvre, Paris).

Attributions

CC licensed content, Shared previously

Portraits of the Insane

After *The Raft of the Medusa*

At the end of 1821 the leading Romantic painter in France, Théodore Géricault, returned from a year long stay in England where crowds had flocked to see his masterpiece *The Raft of the Medusa* displayed in the Egyptian Hall in Pall Mall, London. Despite the success of the exhibition, the French government still refused to buy the painting and his own prodigious spending meant that he was strapped for cash and in no position to embark on another ambitious and expensive large scale project like *The Raft*. His health too was soon to suffer. On his return to France, a riding accident led to complications, causing a tumor to develop on the spine that proved fatal. He died, aged 32, in January 1824.

Perhaps the greatest achievement of his last years were his portraits of the insane. There were ten of them originally. Only five have survived: *A Man Suffering from Delusions of Military Command*; *A Kleptomaniac*; *A Woman Suffering from Obsessive Envy*; *A Woman Addicted to Gambling*; and *A Child Snatcher*.

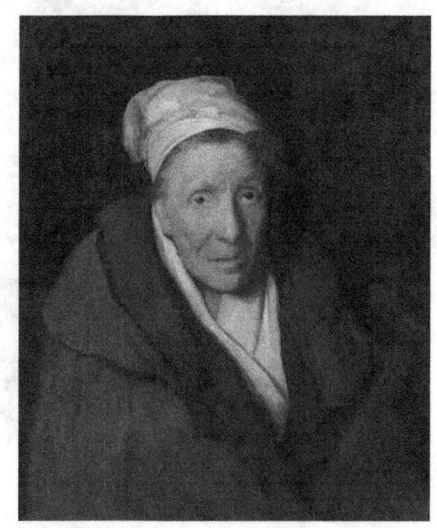

Figure 1. Théodore Géricault, A Woman Addicted to Gambling, 1822, oil on canvas, 72 × 64 cm (Musée du Louvre, Paris)

No information is available for those that have been lost. According to the artist's first biographer, Charles Clément, Géricault painted them after returning from England for Étienne-Jean Georget (1795–1828), the chief physician of the Salpêtrière, the women's asylum in Paris. The paintings were certainly in Georget's possession when he died.

Three Theories for the Commission

How the two men met is not known for sure. Possibly Georget treated Géricault as a patient, or perhaps they met in the Beaujon Hospital, from whose morgue Géricault had taken home dissected limbs to serve as studies for his figures in *The Raft*. What is more debated though, is Georget's role in the production of the paintings. There are three main theories. The first two link the portraits to the psychological toll taken out of Géricault whilst producing his great masterpiece and the nervous breakdown he is believed to have suffered in the autumn following its completion in 1819. The first theory runs that Georget helped him to recover from this episode and that the portraits were produced for and given to the doctor as a gesture of thanks; the second puts forward that Georget, as the artist's physician, encouraged Géricault to paint them as an early form of art therapy; and the third is that Géricault painted them for Georget after his return from England to assist his studies in mental illness.

It is this last that is generally held to be the most likely. Stylistically, they belong to the period after his stay in England, two years after his breakdown. Also, the unified nature of the series, in terms of their scale, composition and color scheme suggest a clearly defined commission, while the medical concept of "monomania" shapes the whole design.

Early Modern Psychiatry

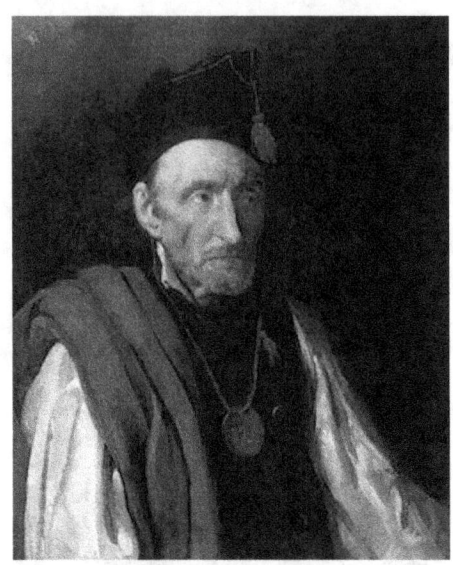

Figure 2. Théodore Géricault, Portrait of a Man Suffering from Delusions of Military Command, 1822, oil on canvas, 81 × 65 cm (Sammlung Oskar Reinhart, Winterhur)

A key figure in early modern psychiatry in France was Jean-Etienne-Dominique Esquirol (1772–1840), whose main area of interest was "monomania," a term no longer in clinical use, which described a particular fixation leading sufferers to exhibit delusional behavior, imagining themselves to be a king, for example. Esquirol, who shared a house with his friend and protégé Georget, was a great believer in the now largely discredited science of physiognomy, holding that physical appearances could be used to diagnose mental disorders. With this in mind, he had over 200 drawings made of his patients, a group of which, executed by Georges-Francoise Gabriel, were exhibited at the Salon of 1814. As an exhibitor himself that year, it seems highly likely that Géricault would have seen them there.

Georget's work developed on Esquirol's. An Enlightenment figure, he rejected moral or theological explanations for mental illness, seeing insanity, neither as the workings of the devil nor as the outcome of moral decrepitude, but as an organic affliction, one that, like any other disease, can be identified by observable physical symptoms. In his book *On Madness*, published in 1820, following Esquirol, he turns to physiognomy to support this theory,

> In general the idiot's face is stupid, without meaning; the face of the manic patient is as agitated as his spirit, often distorted and cramped; the moron's facial characteristics are dejected and without expression; the facial characteristics of the melancholic are pinched, marked by pain or extreme agitation; the monomaniacal king has a proud, inflated expression; the religious fanatic is mild, he exhorts by casting his eyes at the heavens or fixing them on the earth; the anxious patient pleads, glancing sideways, etc.

The clumsy language here—"the idiot's face is stupid"—seems a world away from Géricault's extraordinarily sensitive paintings, a point that begs the question whether Géricault was doing more than simply following the good doctor's orders in producing the series, but instead making his own independent enquiries.

Géricault had many reasons to be interested in psychiatry, starting with his own family: his grandfather and one of his uncles had died insane. His experiences while painting *The Raft* must also have left their mark. The Medusa's surgeon, J.B. Henry Savigny, at the time Géricault interviewed him, was writing an account of the psychological impact the experience had had on his fellow passengers and, of course, there was Géricault's own mental breakdown in 1819. It seems only natural then that he would be drawn to this new and exciting area of scientific study.

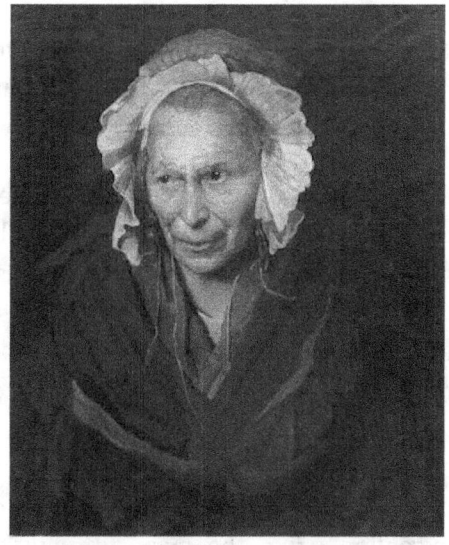

Figure 3. Théodore Géricault, Portait of a Woman Suffering from Obsessive Envy (The Hyena), 1822, oil on canvas, 72 × 58 cm (Musée des Beaux-Arts, Lyons)

Alternatively, some critics argue that Géricault's work is a propaganda exercise for Georget, designed to demonstrate the importance of psychiatrists in detecting signs of mental illness. In their very subtleties they show just how difficult this can be, requiring a trained eye such as Georget's to come to the correct diagnosis. According to Albert Boime, the paintings were also used to demonstrate the curative effects of psychiatric treatment. If the five missing paintings were ever found, he argues, they would depict the same characters—but after treatment—showing their improved state, much like 'before and after' photographs in modern day advertising.

This, of course, is impossible to prove or disprove. What is more challenging is Boime's general criticisms of early psychiatry which, he argues, by classifying, containing and observing people was effective only in silencing the voices of the mentally ill, rendering them invisible and therefore subject to abuse. The fact that the sitters of the paintings are given no names, but are defined only by their illnesses would seem to confirm this view and, for that reason, many modern viewers of the paintings do feel disconcerted when looking at them.

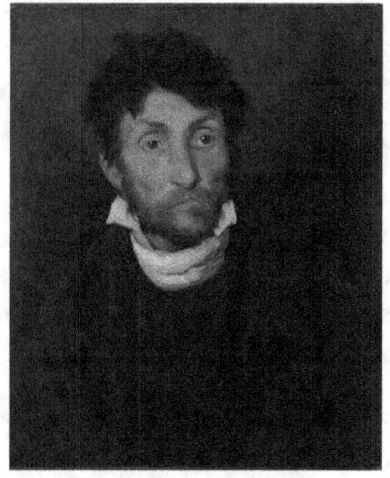

Figure 4. Théodore Géricault, Portrait of a Kleptomaniac, 1822, oil on canvas, 61 × 50 cm (Museum of Fine Arts, Ghent)

The Portraits

The five surviving portraits are bust length and in front view, without hands. The canvases vary in dimensions but the heads are all close to life-size. The viewpoint is at eye level for the three men but from above for the women, indicating that the paintings were executed in different places. It seems likely that the women were painted in the women's hospital Salpêtrière, while the men were selected from among the inmates of Charenton and Bicêtre.

None of the sitters is named; they are identified by their malady. None look directly at the viewer, contributing to an uneasy sense of distractedness in their gazes that can be read as stillness, as though they are lost in their own thoughts, or as disconnectedness from the process in which they are involved. These are not patrons and have had no say in how they are depicted.

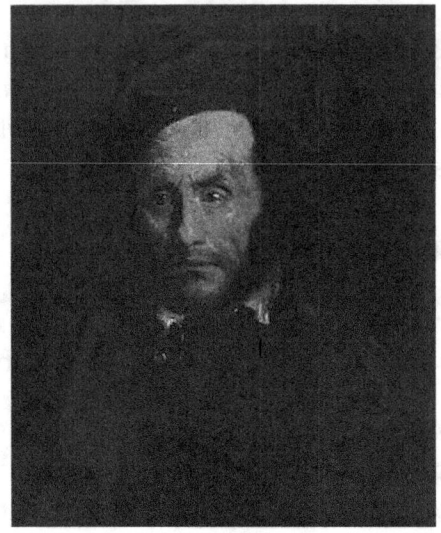

Each is shown in three-quarter profile, some to the left, some to the right. The pose is typical of formal, honorific portraits, effecting a restrained composition that does not make it apparent that they are confined in asylums. There is no evidence of the setting in the backgrounds either, which are cast in shadow, as are most of their bodies, drawing the focus largely on their faces. The dark coloring creates a sombre atmosphere, evocative of brooding introspection. Their clothing lends them a degree of personal dignity, giving no indication as to the nature of their conditions, the one exception being the man suffering from delusions of military grandeur who wears a medallion on his chest, a tasseled hat and a cloak over one shoulder, which point to his delusions. The medallion has no shine to it and the string that it hangs from looks makeshift and worn.

Figure 5. Théodore Géricault, Portait of a Child Snatcher, 1822, oil on canvas, 65 × 54 cm (Museum of Fine Arts, Springfield, Massachusets)

The paintings were executed with great speed, entirely from life and probably in one sitting. Critics often remark on the painterly quality of the work, the extraordinary fluency of brushwork, in contrast with Géricault's early more sculptural style, suggesting that the erratic brushwork is used to mirror the disordered thoughts of the patients. In places it is applied in almost translucent layers, while in others it is thicker creating highly expressive contrasts in textures.

Romantic Scientists

What perhaps strikes one most about the portraits is the extraordinary empathy we are made to feel for these poor souls, who might not strike us immediately as insane, but who certainly exhibit outward signs of inward suffering.

In bringing the sensitivity of a great artist to assist scientific enquiry Géricault was not alone among Romantic painters. John Constable's cloud studies, for example, were exactly contemporary with the portraits and provide an interesting parallel. Both artists capture brilliantly the fleeting moment, the shifting movements in Constable's cumulus, stratus, cirrus and nimbus, in Géricault the complex play of emotions on the faces of the insane. Not since

Figure 6. John Constable, Cloud Study, 1822, oil on paper laid on board, 47.6 × 57.5 cm (Tate Britain)

the Renaissance has art illustrated so beautifully the concerns of the scientific domain; in Géricault's case teaching those early psychiatrists, we might be tempted to think, to look on their patients with a more human gaze.

Attributions

CC licensed content, Shared previously

- Gericaults Portraits of the Insane. **Authored by**: Ben Pollitt. **Provided by**: Khan Academy. **Located at**: https://web.archive.org/web/20141006231220/http://smarthistory.khanacademy.org/gericaults-portraits-of-the-insane.html. **License**: *CC BY-NC-SA: Attribution-NonCommercial-ShareAlike*

Grand Odalisque

Dr. Beth Harris and Dr. Steven Zucker provide a description, historical perspective, and analysis of Ingres's *La Grande Odalisque*.

- https://youtu.be/lSV-J1JHDFY

Jean-Auguste-Dominique Ingres, *La Grande Odalisque*, 1814, oil on canvas, 36″ × 63″ (91 × 162 cm), (Musée du Louvre, Paris).

Ingres and *La Grande Odalisque*

It would be easy to characterize Ingres as a consistent defender of the Neo-Classical style from his time in David's studio into the middle of the 19th century. Remember that the *Apotheosis of Homer* dates to 1827. But the truth is more interesting than that.

Ingres actually returned to Neo-Classicism after having rejected the lessons of his teacher, David, and after having laid the foundation for the emotive expressiveness of Romanticism, the new style of Gericault and the young Delacroix that Ingres would eventually defend against. Ingres' early Romantic tendencies can be seen most famously in his painting, *La Grande Odalisque* of 1814.

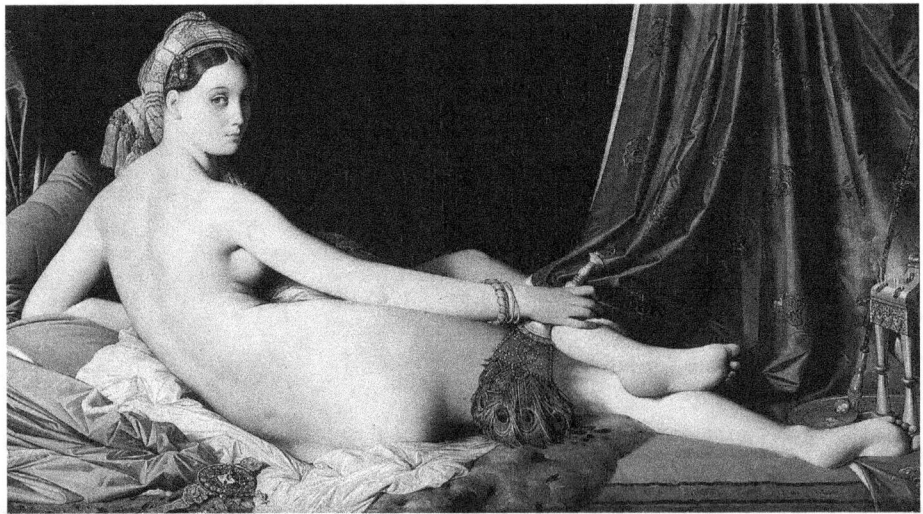

Figure 1. La Grande Odalisque

Here a languid nude is set in a sumptuous interior. At first glance this nude seems to follow in the tradition of the Great Venetian masters, see for instance, Titian's *Venus of Urbino* of 1538. But upon closer examination, it becomes clear that this is no classical setting.

Instead, Ingres has created a cool aloof eroticism accentuated by its exotic context. The peacock fan, the turban, the enormous pearls, the hookah (a pipe for hashish or perhaps opium), and of course, the title of the painting, all refer us to the French conception of the Orient. Careful—the word "Orient" does not refer here to the Far East so much as the Near East or even North Africa.

In the mind of an early 19th century French male viewer, the sort of person for whom this image was made, the odalisque would have conjured up not just a harem slave, itself a misconception, but a set of fears and desires linked to the long history of aggression between Christian Europe and Islamic Asia. Indeed, Ingres' porcelain sexuality is made acceptable even to an increasingly prudish French culture because of the subject's distance.

Where, for instance, the Renaissance painter Titan had veiled his eroticism in myth, Ingres covered his object of desire in a misty exoticism. Some art historians have suggested that colonial politics also played a role. France was at this time expanding its African and Near Eastern possessions, often brutally. Might the myth of the barbarian have served the French who could then claim a moral imperative? By the way, has anyone noticed anything "wrong" with the figure's anatomy?

Attributions

CC licensed content, Shared previously

Third of May, 1808

Napoleon Puts His Brother on the Throne of Spain

In 1807, Napoleon, bent on conquering the world, brought Spain's king, Charles IV, into alliance with him in order to conquer Portugal. Napoleon's troops poured into Spain, supposedly just passing through. But Napoleon's real intentions soon became clear: the alliance was a trick. The French were taking over. Joseph Bonaparte, Napoleon's brother, was the new king of Spain.

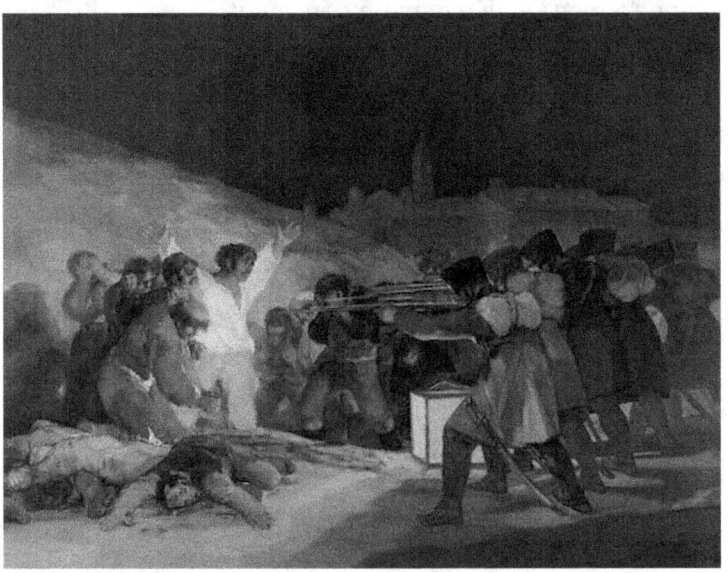

Figure 1. Francisco Goya, The Third of May 1808 in Madrid: the executions on Principe Pio hill, 1808, 1814–15, oil on canvas, 8' 9" × 13' 4" (Museo del Prado, Madrid)

The 2nd and 3rd of May, 1808

On May 2, 1808, hundreds of Spaniards rebelled. On May 3, these Spanish freedom fighters were rounded up and massacred by the French. Their blood literally ran through the streets of Madrid. Even though Goya had shown French sympathies in the past, the slaughter of his countrymen and the horrors of war made a profound impression on the artist. He commemorated both days of this gruesome uprising in paintings. Although Goya's *Second of May* (figure 2) is a tour de force of twisting bodies and charging horses reminiscent of Leonardo's *Battle of Anghiari*, his *Third of May* is acclaimed as one of the great paintings of all time, and has even been called the world's first modern painting.

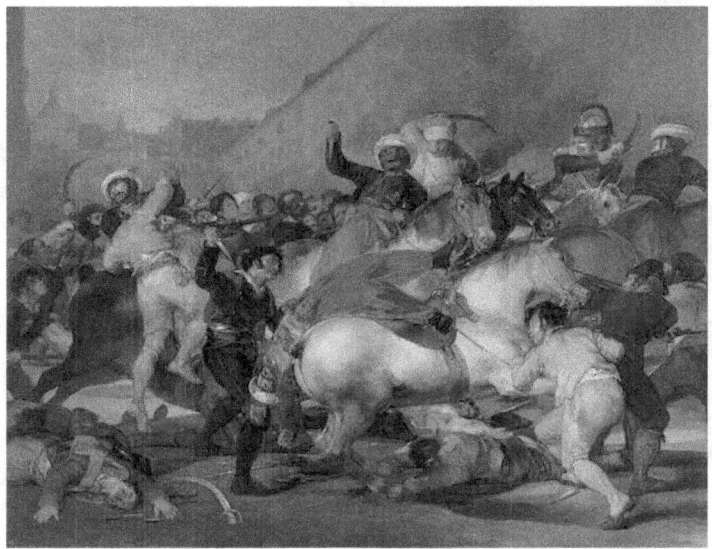

Figure 2. Francisco Goya, The Second of May, 1808, 1814, oil on canvas, 104.7 × 135.8 in. (Museo del Prado)

Death Awaits

We see row of hooded French soldiers aiming their guns at a Spanish man, who stretches out his arms in submission both to the men and to his fate. A country hill behind him takes the place of an executioner's wall. A pile of dead bodies lies at his feet, streaming blood. To his other side, a line of Spanish rebels stretches endlessly in to the landscape. They cover their eyes to avoid watching the death that they know awaits them. The city and civilization is far behind them. Even a monk, bowed in prayer, will soon be among the dead.

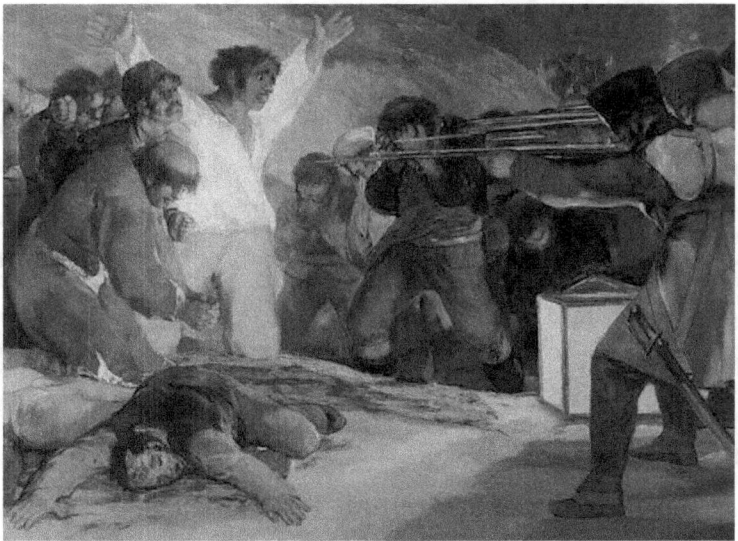

Figure 3. Francisco Goya, Third of May, 1808, 1814–15 (detail)

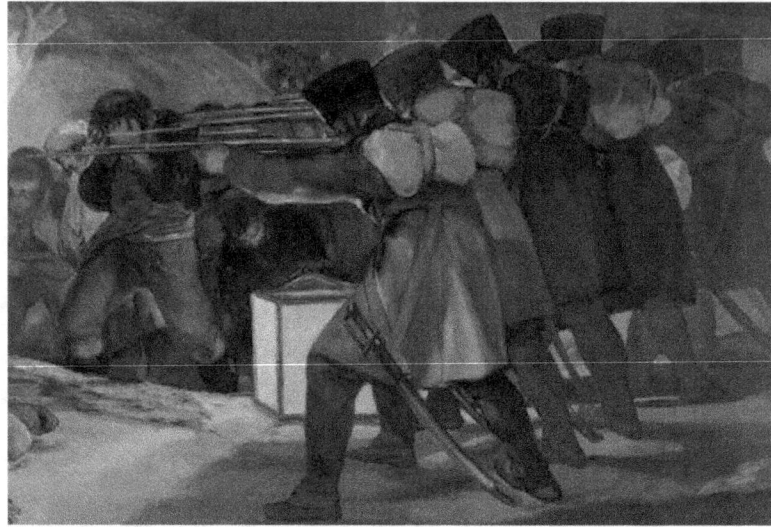

Figure 4. Figure 3. Francisco Goya, Third of May, 1808, 1814–15 (detail)

Transforming Christian Iconography

Goya's painting has been lauded for its brilliant transformation of Christian iconography and its poignant portrayal of man's inhumanity to man. The central figure of the painting, who is clearly a poor laborer, takes the place of the Crucified Christ; he is sacrificing himself for the good of his nation. The lantern that sits between him and the firing squad is the only source of light in the painting, and dazzlingly illuminates his body, bathing him in what can be perceived as spiritual light. His expressive face, which shows an emotion of anguish that is more sad than terrified, echoes Christ's prayer on the cross, "Forgive them Father, they know not what they do." Close inspection of the victim's right hand also shows stigmata, referencing the marks made on Christ's body during the Crucifixion.

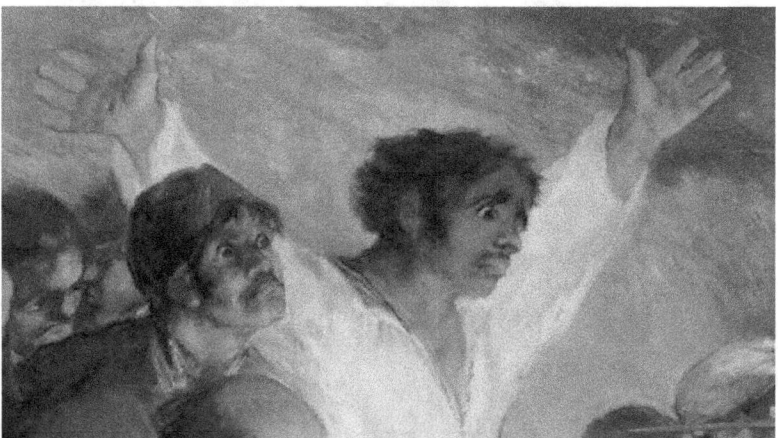

Figure 5. Francisco Goya, Third of May, 1808, 1814–15 (detail)

The man's pose not only equates him with Christ, but also acts as an assertion of his humanity. The French soldiers, by contrast, become mechanical or insect-like. They merge into one faceless, many-legged creature incapable of feeling human emotion. Nothing is going to stop them from murdering this man. The deep recession into space seems to imply that this type of brutality will never end, that it is a part of human nature itself.

Not Heroism in Battle

This depiction of warfare was a drastic departure from convention. In the eighteenth century art, battle and death was a bloodless affair with little emotional impact. Even the great French Romanticists were more concerned with producing a beautiful canvas in the tradition of history paintings, showing the hero in the heroic act, than with creating emotional impact. Goya's painting, by contrast, presents us with an anti-hero, imbued with true pathos that had not been seen since, perhaps, the ancient Roman sculpture of *The Dying Gaul*. Goya's central figure is not perishing heroically in battle, but rather being killed on the side of the road like an animal. Both the landscape and the dress of the men are nondescript, making the painting timeless. This is certainly why the work remains emotionally charged today.

Legacy

Future artists also admired *The Third of May, 1808*, and both Manet and Picasso used it for inspiration in their own portrayals of political murders (Manet's Execution of Emperor Maximillian [https://en.wikipedia.org/wiki/The_Execution_of_Emperor_Maximilian] and Picasso's Massacre in Korea [https://en.wikipedia.org/wiki/Massacre_in_Korea]). Along with Picasso's *Guernica*, Goya's *Third of May* remains one of the most chilling images ever created of the atrocities of war, and it is difficult to imagine how much more powerful it must have been in the pre-photographic era, before people were bombarded with images of warfare in the media. A powerful anti-war statement, Goya is not only criticizing the nations that wage war on one another, but is also admonishing us, the viewers, for being complicit in acts of violence, which occur not between abstract entities like "countries," but between one human being standing a few feet away from another.

Sleep of Reason Produces Monsters

A Dark Vision

In this ominous image, we see the dark vision of humanity that characterizes Goya's work for the rest of his life.

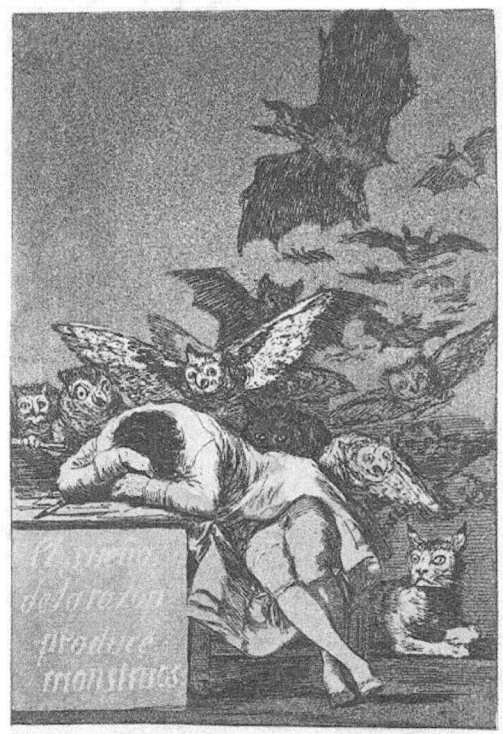

Figure 1. Francisco Goya, The Sleep of Reason
Produces Monsters, c. 1799

A man sleeps, apparently peacefully, even as bats and owls threaten from all sides and a lynx lays quiet, but wide-eyed and alert. A creature sits at the center of the composition, staring not at the sleeping figure, but at us, the viewer. Goya forces the viewer to become an active participant in the image—the monsters of his dreams even threaten us.

Los Caprichos

On 6 February 1799, Francisco Goya put an advertisement in the *Diario de Madrid*. "A Collection of Prints of Capricious Subjects," he tells the reader, "Invented and Etched by Don Francisco Goya," is available through subscription. We know this series of eighty prints as *Los Caprichos* (caprices, or folles).

Los Caprichos was a significant departure from the subjects that had occupied Goya up to that point—tapestry cartoons for the Spanish royal residences, portraits of monarchs and aristocrats, and a few commissions for church ceilings and altars.

Many of the prints in the *Caprichos* series express disdain for the pre-Enlightenment practices still popular in Spain at the end of the Eighteenth century (a powerful clergy, arranged marriages, superstition, etc.). Goya uses the series to critique contemporary Spanish society. As he explained in the advertisement, he chose subjects "from the multitude of follies and blunders common in every civil society, as well as from the vulgar prejudices and lies authorized by custom, ignorance or interest, those that he has thought most suitable matter for ridicule."

The *Caprichos* was Goya's most biting critique to date, and would eventually be censored. Of the eighty aquatints, number 43, "The Sleep of Reason Produces Monsters," can essentially be seen as Goya's manifesto and it should be noted that many observers believe he intended it as a self-portrait.

Imagination United with Reason

In the image, an artist, asleep at his drawing table, is besieged by creatures associated in Spanish folk tradition with mystery and evil. The title of the print, emblazoned on the front of the desk, is often read as a proclamation of Goya's adherence to the values of the Enlightenment—without Reason, evil and corruption prevail.

However, Goya wrote a caption for the print that complicates its message, "Imagination abandoned by reason produces impossible monsters; united with her, she is the mother of the arts and source of their wonders."

In other words, Goya believed that imagination should never be completely renounced in favor of the strictly rational. For Goya, art is the child of reason in combination with imagination.

The Beginnings of Romanticism

With this print, Goya is revealed as a transitional figure between the end of the Enlightenment and the emergence of Romanticism. The artist had spent the early part of his career working in the court of King Carlos III who adhered to many of the principles of the Enlightenment that were then spreading across Europe—social reform, the advancement of knowledge and science, and the creation of secular states. In Spain, Carlos reduced the power of the clergy and established strong support for the arts and sciences.

However, by the time Goya published the *Caprichos*, the promise of the Enlightenment had dimmed. Carlos III was dead and his less respected brother assumed the throne. Even in France, the political revolution inspired by the Enlightenment had devolved into violence during an episode known as the Reign of Terror. Soon after, Napoleon became Emperor of France.

Goya's caption for "The Sleep of Reason," warns that we should not be governed by reason alone—an idea central to Romanticism's reaction against Enlightenment doctrine. Romantic artists and writers valued nature which was closely associated with emotion and imagination in opposition to the rationalism of Enlightenment philosophy. But "The Sleep of Reason" also anticipates the dark and haunting art Goya later created in reaction to the atrocities he witnessed—and carried out by the standard-bearers of the Enlightenment—the Napoleonic Guard.

Goya brilliantly exploited the atmospheric quality of aquatint to create the fantastical look of the image. This printing process creates the grainy, dream-like tonality visible in the background of "The Sleep of Reason."

Aquatint

Although the aquatint process was invented in 17th century by the Dutch printmaker, Jan van de Velde, many consider the *Caprichos* to be the first prints to fully exploit this process.

Aquatint is a variation of etching. Like etching, it uses a metal plate (often copper or zinc) that is covered with a waxy, acid-resistant resin. The artist draws an image directly into the resin with a needle so that the wax is removed exposing the metal plate below. When the scratch drawing is complete, the plate is submerged in an acid bath. The acid eats into the metal where lines have been etched. When the acid has bitten deeply enough, the plate is removed, rinsed and heated so that the remaining resin can be wiped away.

Aquatint requires an additional process, the artist sprinkles layers of powdery resin on the surface of the plate, heats it to harden the powder and dips it in an acid bath.

The acid eats around the resin powder creating a rich and varied surface. Ink is then pressed into the pits and linear recesses created by the acid and the flat surface of the plate is once again wiped clean. Finally, a piece of paper is pressed firmly against the inked plate and then pulled away, resulting in the finished image.

Attributions

CC licensed content, Shared previously

Saturn Devouring One of His Sons

Saturn Devouring One Of His Sons is one of the "Black Paintings" that Goya painted on the walls of his house outside Madrid. This image was originally located on the lower floor of the house known as "la Quinta del Sordo." Goya painted on the walls using several materials including oil paint. The "Black Paintings" had suffered significant damage and loss in their original location and when they were removed from the walls and transferred to canvas by Baron Émile d'Erlanger shortly after he aquired the house in 1873. Please note that Saturn is also known as Cronus or Kronus.

Dr. Beth Harris and Dr. Steven Zucker provide a description, historical perspective, and analysis of Goya's *Saturn Devouring One Of His Sons*.

- https://youtu.be/3Lawz8TcPig

Francisco de Goya y Lucientes, *Saturn Devouring One Of His Sons*, 1821–23, oil paint, 143.5 cm × 81.4 cm, (Prado, Madrid).

Attributions

Constable, The Haywain

Pippa Couch and Rachel Ropeik provide a description, historical perspective, and analysis of Cimabue's Maesta of Santa Trinita.

- https://youtu.be/FKIHHeBe674

John Constable, *The Hay Wain*, 1821, oil on canvas, 51-1/4 × 73 inches (National Gallery of Art, London)

> **External Link**
>
> View this painting up close in the Google Art Project.:
>
> - https://www.google.com/culturalinstitute/asset-viewer/the-hay-wain-full-scale-study/hwE8jJqJ9SQzgA?projectId=art-project

Reviving Landscape Painting

Studying the English painter John Constable is helpful in understanding the changing meaning of nature during the industrial revolution. He is, in fact, largely responsible for reviving the importance of landscape painting in the nineteenth century. A key event, when it is remembered that landscape would become the primary subject of the Impressionists later in the century.

Landscape had had a brief moment of glory amongst the Dutch masters of the seventeenth century. Ruisdael and others had devoted large canvases to the depiction of the low countries. But in the eighteenth century hierarchy of subject matter, landscape was nearly the lowest type of painting. Only the still-life was considered less important. This would change in the first decades of the nineteenth century when Constable began to depict his father's farm on oversized six-foot long canvases. These "six-footers" as they are called, challenged the status quo. Here landscape was presented on the scale of history painting.

Why would Constable take such a bold step, and perhaps more to the point, why were his canvases celebrated (and they were, by no less important a figure than Eugene Delacroix, when Constable's *The Hay Wain* was exhibited at the Paris Salon in 1824)?

Painted in the Studio, from Sketches Done Out-of-Doors

The Hay Wain, does include an element of genre (the depiction of a common scene), that is the farm hand taking his horse and wagon (or wain) across the stream. But this action is minor and seems to offer the viewer the barest of pretenses for what is virtually a pure landscape. Unlike the later Impressionists, Constable's large polished canvases were painted in his studio. He did, however, sketch outside, directly before his subject. This was necessary for Constable as he sought a high degree of accuracy in many specifics. For instance, the wagon and tack (harness, etc.) are all clearly and specifically depicted, The trees are identifiable by species, and Constable was the first artist we know of who studied meteorology so that the clouds and the atmospheric conditions that he rendered were scientifically precise.

Constable was clearly the product of the Age of Enlightenment and its increasing confidence in science. But Constable was also deeply influenced by the social and economic impact of the industrial revolution.

From Farming to Factories, From Country to City

Prior to the nineteenth century, even the largest European cities counted their populations only in the hundreds of thousands. These were mere towns by today's standards. But this would change rapidly. The world's economies had always been based largely on agriculture. Farming was a labor intensive enterprise and the result was that the vast majority of the population lived in rural communities. The industrial revolution would reverse this ancient pattern of population distribution. Industrial efficiencies meant widespread unemployment in the country and the great migration to the cities began. The cities of London, Manchester, Paris, and New York doubled and doubled again in the nineteenth century. Imagine the stresses on a modern day New York if we had even a modest increase in population and the stresses of the nineteenth century become clear.

Industrialization remade virtually every aspect of society. Based on the political, technological and scientific advances of the Age of Enlightenment, blessed with a bountiful supply of the inexpensive albeit filthy fuel, coal, and advances in metallurgy and steam power, the northwestern nations of Europe invented the world that we now know in the West. Urban culture, expectations of leisure, and middle class affluence in general all resulted from these changes. But the transition was brutal for the poor. Housing was miserable, unventilated and often dangerously hot in the summer. Unclean water spread disease rapidly and there was minimal health care. Corruption was high, pay was low and hours inhumane.

Child Labor, Long Hours & Calls for Revolution

As is still true in too much of the world today, families would depend on the labor of even very young children. Working long days with only Sunday off was normal. The contemporaneous author Charles Dickens famously chronicled the depravity of laissez-faire or pure market capitalism that characterized this era. There were no laws to soften this harsh new world. No unemployment insurance, no health insurance, no unions, no benefits, no vacations, no retirement, few safety regulations, no child labor nor bankruptcy protections. If you couldn't pay a debt because you had been sick and lost your job, you, and sometimes your family, were sent to prison. The wealth created by the rich (the return on risked capital) was largely theirs to keep as a permanent national income tax would not become law until 1874 (UK) and 1913 (US).

Such terrible abuses were answered by both calls for reform and revolution. Radicals and bourgeois reformers slowly forced change. In 1848, Karl Marx and Frederick Engels co-authored a pamphlet that would become enormously influential, *The Communist Manifesto* while revolts raged in England, France and to a lesser extent in Germany. It is no surprise that France and England were particularly hard hit as they were amongst the most industrialized of nations.

Rural Landscape as a Lost Eden

What effect did these changes have on the ways in which the countryside was understood? Can these changes be linked to Constable's rattention to the countryside? Some art historians have suggested that Constable was indeed responding to such shifts. As the cities and their problems grew, the urban elite, those that had grown rich from an industrial economy, began to look to the countryside not as a place so wretched with poverty that thousands were fleeing for an uncertain future in the city, but rather as an idealized vision.

The rural landscape became a lost Eden, a place of one's childhood, where the good air and water, the open spaces and hard and honest work of farm labor created a moral open space that contrasted sharply with the perceived evils of modern urban life. Constable's art then functions as an expression of the increasing importance of rural life, at least from the perspective of the wealthy urban elite for whom these canvases were intended. *The Hay Wain* is a celebration of a simpler time, a precious and moral place lost to the city dweller.

Attributions

CC licensed content, Shared previously

All rights reserved content

Turner, Slave Ship

Lori Landay and Beth Harris provide a description, historical perspective, and analysis of William Turner's *Slave Ship*.

- https://youtu.be/NoCW80MEGXY

Joseph Mallord William Turner, *Slave Ship (Slavers Throwing Overboard the Dead and Dying, Typhoon Coming On)*, 1840 (Museum of Fine Arts, Boston).

Attributions

Hudson River School

Click on the link below to view the article "The Hudson River School," a part of the Heilbrunn Timeline of Art History, which was developed by the Metropolitan Museum of Art. This article includes a slideshow of paintings as well as a discussion about the school.

The Hudson River School:

- http://www.metmuseum.org/toah/hd/hurs/hd_hurs.htm

The Oxbow

Dr. Beth Harris and Dr. Steven Zucker provide a description, historical perspective, and analysis of Thomas Cole's *The Oxbow*.

- https://youtu.be/RQ0855yB2ZM

Thomas Cole, *View from Mount Holyoke, Northampton, Massachusetts, after a Thunderstorm—The Oxbow*, 1836, oil on canvas, 51 1/2″ × 76″ (130.8 cm × 193 cm), (Metropolitan Museum of Art).

An American Painter Born in England

During the nineteenth century—an expanse of time that saw the elevation of landscape painting to a point of national pride—Thomas Cole reigned supreme as the undisputed leader of the Hudson River School of landscape painters. It is ironic, however, that the person who most embodies the beauty and grandeur of the American wilderness during the first half of the nineteenth century was not originally from the United States, but was instead born and lived the first seventeen years of his life in Great Britain. Originally from Bolton-le-Moor in Lancashire (England), the Cole family immigrated to the United States in 1818, first settling in Philadelphia before eventually moving to Steubenville, Ohio, a locale then on the edge of wilderness of the American west.

Elevated Landscapes (Not History Paintings)

Cole worked briefly in Ohio as an itinerant portraitist, but returned to Philadelphia in 1823 at the age of 22 to pursue art instruction that was then unavailable in Ohio. Two years later, Cole moved to New York City where he exchanged his aspirations of painting large-scale historical compositions for the more reasonable artistic goal of completing landscapes. For instruction, Cole turned to a book, William Oram's *Precepts and Observations on the Art of Colouring in Landscaping* (1810), an instructional text that had a profound effect on Cole for the remainder of his artistic career.

Cole found quick success in New York City. In the year of his arrival, 1825, John Trumbull, the patriarch of American portraiture and history painting, and the president of the American Academy of Design 'discovered' Cole, and the older artist made it an immediate goal to promote the talented landscape painter. In the months to follow, Trumbull introduced Cole to many of the wealthy and prominent men who would become his most influential patrons in the decades to follow. One such man was Luman Reed, an affluent merchant who, in 1836, commissioned Cole to paint the five-canvas series *The Course of Empire*.

Landscapes Imbued with a Moral Message

It is in this series—and in many of the paintings to follow—that Thomas Cole found the aesthetic voice to lift the genre of landscape painting to a level that approached history painting. During the eighteenth and nineteenth centuries, great artists aspired to complete large-scale historical compositions, paintings that often had an instructive moral message. Landscape paintings, in contrast, were often though more imitative than innovative. But in *The Course of Empire*, Cole was able to take the American landscape and imbue it with a moral message, as was often found in history paintings. Indeed, the landscapes Cole began to paint in the 1830s were not entirely about the land. In these works, Cole used the land as a way to say something important about the United States.

The Oxbow: More than a Bend in the Connecticut River

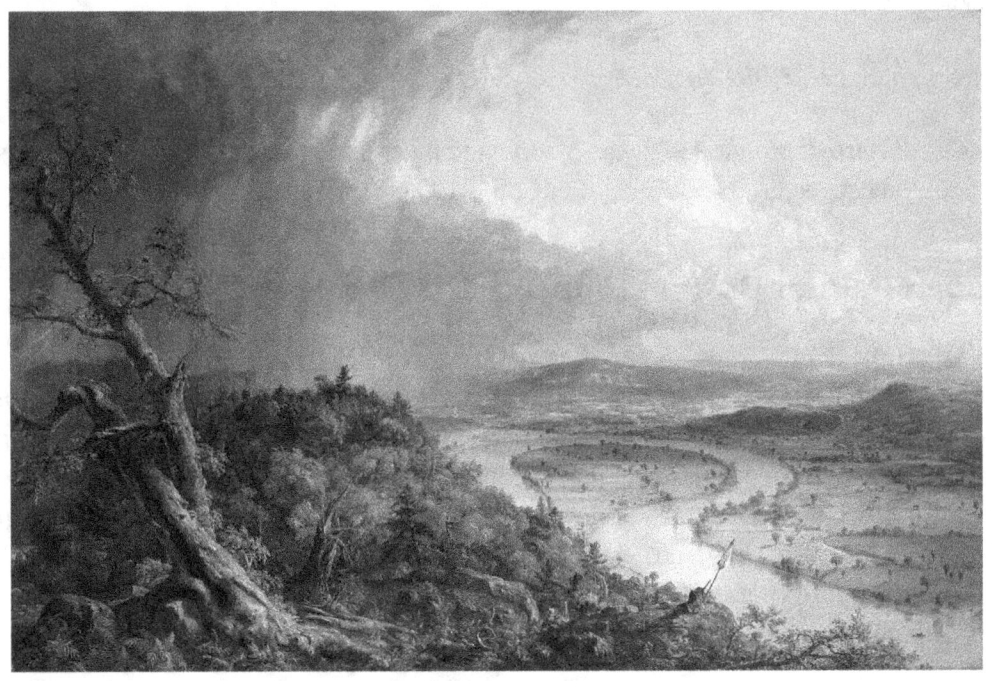

Figure 1. Thomas Cole, View from Mount Holyoke, Northampton, Massachusetts, after a Thunderstorm—The Oxbow, oil on canvas, 1836 (Metropolitan Museum of Art).

A wonderful illustration of this is Cole's 1836 masterwork, *A View from Mount Holyoke, Northampton, Massachusetts, after a Thunderstorm*, a painting that is generally (and mercifully) known as *The Oxbow*. At first glance this painting may seem to be nothing more than an interesting view of a recognizable bend in the Connecticut River. But when viewed through the lens of nineteenth-century political ideology, this painting eloquently speaks about the widely discussed topic of westward expansion.

When looking at *The Oxbow*, the viewer can clearly see that Cole used a diagonal line from the lower right to the upper left to divide the composition into two unequal halves. The left-hand side of the painting depicts a sublime view of the land, a perspective that elicits feelings of danger and even fear. This is enhanced by the gloomy storm clouds that seem to pummel the not-too-distant middle ground with rain. This part of the painting depicts a virginal landscape, nature created by God and untouched by man. It is wild, unruly, and untamed.

Within the construction of American landscape painting, American artists often visually represented the notion of the untamed wilderness through the "Blasted Tree" (figure 2), a motif Cole paints into the lower left corner. That such a formidable tree could be obliterated in such a way suggests the herculean power of Nature.

If the left side of this painting is sublime in tenor, on the right side of the composition we can observe a peaceful, pastoral landscape that humankind has subjugated to their will. The land, which was once as disorderly as that on the left side of the painting, has now been overtaken by the order and regulation of agriculture. Animals graze. Crops grow. Smoke billows from chimneys. Boats sail upon the river. What was once wild has been tamed. The thunderstorm, which threatens the left side of the painting, has left the land on the right refreshed and no worse for the wear. The sun shines brightly, filling the right side of the painting with the golden glow of a fresh afternoon.

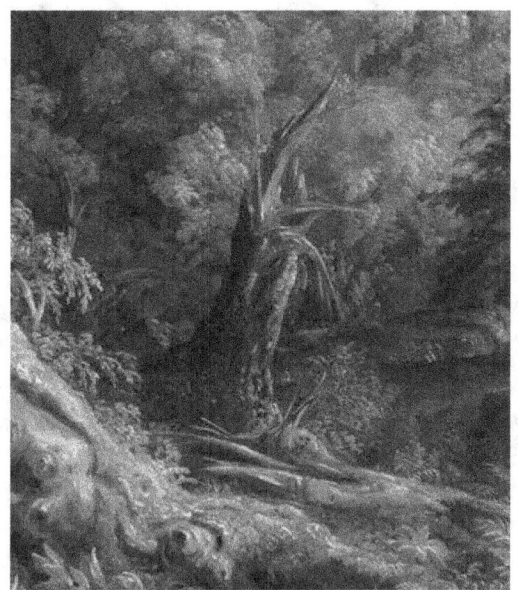

Figure 2. The Oxbow detail

Manifest Destiny

When viewed together, the right side of the painting—the view to the east—and that of the left—the west—clearly speak to the ideology of Manifest Destiny. During the nineteenth century, discussions of westward expansion dominated political discourse. The Louisiana Purchase of 1804 essentially doubled the size of the United States, and many believed that it was a divinely ordained obligation of Americans to settle this westward territory. In *The Oxbow*, Cole visually shows the benefits of this process. The land to the east is ordered, productive, and useful. In contrast, the land to the west remains unbridled. Further westward expansion—a change that is destined to happen—is shown to positively alter the land.

A Self-Portrait

Although Cole was the most influential landscape artist of the first half of the nineteenth century, he was not completely adverse to figure painting. Indeed, a close look at *The Oxbow*, reveals an easily overlooked self-portrait in the lower part of the painting (figure 3). Cole wears a coat and hat and stands before a stretched canvas placed on an easel, paintbrush in hand. The artist pauses, as if in the middle of the brushstroke, to engage the viewer. This work, then, in a kind of 'artist in his studio' self-portrait—is akin, in many ways, to

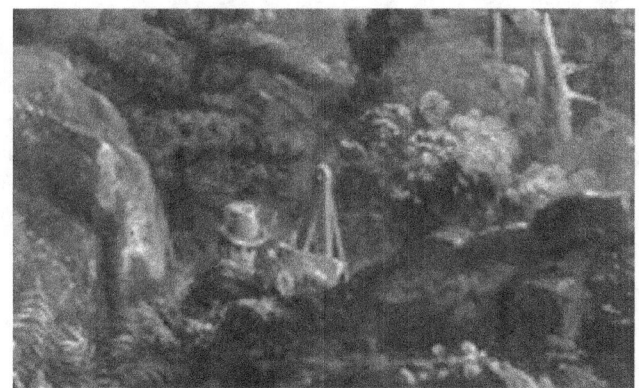

Figure 3. The Oxbow detail

Charles Willson Peale's 1822 work *The Artist in His Museum*. In each, the artist depicts himself in his own setting. For Peale, this was his natural history museum in Philadelphia. For Cole, this was the nature he is most well known for painting.

Lasting Influence

Although he only formally accepted one pupil for instruction—this was, of course, Frederic Edwin Church—Thomas Cole exerted a powerful influence on the course of landscape painting in the United States during the nineteenth century. Not content to merely paint the land, Cole elevated the landscape genre to approach the status of historical painting. The landscape painters who followed during the middle of the nineteenth century—Church, Durant, Bierstadt, and others—would often follow the trail that Cole had blazed.

Attributions

CC licensed content, Shared previously

- Cole's The Oxbow. **Authored by**: Dr. Bryan Zygmont. **Provided by**: Khan Academy. **Located at**: https://web.archive.org/web/20141007123649/http://smarthistory.khanacademy.org/romanticism-us-cole.html. **License**: *CC BY-NC-SA: Attribution-NonCommercial-ShareAlike*

All rights reserved content

- Thomas Cole, The Oxbow, 1836. **Authored by**: Smarthistory. art, history, conversation. **Located at**: https://youtu.be/RQ0855yB2ZM. **License**: *All Rights Reserved*. **License Terms**: Standard YouTube License

Chapter 11: 1848–1907 – Industrial Revolution Part II

Chapter 11 Overview

What You'll Learn To Do: Examine Nineteenth Century art and its impact on later artistic developments.

In Chapter 11 we will examine Nineteenth Century art. We will look at how artists like Monet contributed to the development of Western art. It is imperative to understand Nineteenth Century art in order to see how it impacted later artistic developments.

Learning Activities

The learning activities for this module include:

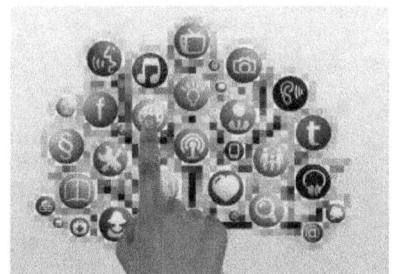

- **Review:** Key Learning Items

The Nineteenth Century

- **Read:** Becoming Modern

Early Photography

- **Read:** Introduction to Early Photography
- **Read:** Louis Daguerre
- **Read:** Timothy O'Sullivan

Realism

- **Read:** Introduction to Realism
- **Read:** Courbet, The Stone Breakers
- **Watch:** Bonheur, Plowing in the Nivernais (3:28)
- **Watch:** Millet, The Gleaners (3:48)
- **Watch:** Degas, The Dance Class (5:08)
- **Watch:** Degas, At the Races in the Countryside (3:51)

- **Watch:** Manet, Luncheon on the Grass (Le Dejeuner sur l'herbe) (6:27)
- **Watch:** Manet, Olympia (7:13)
- **Watch:** Manet, A Bar at the Folies-Bergere (10:34)

Second Empire Architecture

- **Read:** Garnier, Paris Opera (includes a video: 4:48)

Impressionism

- **Read:** Introduction to Impressionism
- **Watch:** Monet, Gare St. Lazare (5:36)
- **Watch:** Monet, Rouen Cathedral Series (4:13)
- **Watch:** Caillebotte, Paris Street; Rainy Day (4:43)
- **Watch:** Cassatt, In the Loge (4:32)
- **Watch:** Cassatt, The Child's Bath (3:05)
- **Watch:** Morisot, The Mother and Sister of the Artist (3:35)
- **Watch:** Renoir, Moulin de la Galette (5:05)

Post-Impressionism

- **Read:** Post-Impressionism Explained
- **Watch:** Seurat, La Grande Jatte (6:42)
- **Read:** Van Gogh, Self-Portrait Dedicated to Paul Gauguin (includes a video: 2:48)
- **Watch:** Van Gogh, The Bedroom (4:43)
- **Read:** Van Gogh, Self-Portrait with Bandaged Ear
- **Read:** Cezanne, Basket of Apples
- **Watch:** Cezanne, The Large Bathers (4:45)
- **Watch:** Gauguin, Vision After the Sermon (3:38)
- **Read:** Gauguin, Spirit of the Dead Watching
- **Watch:** Toulouse-Lautrec, At the Moulin Rouge (3:10)

Art Nouveau

- **Read:** Gaudi, Sagrada Familia (includes a video: 5:38)

Symbolism

- **Read:** Fin-de-siecle Explained

- **Watch:** Klimt, The Kiss (3:56)
- **Watch:** Munch, The Storm (4:00)

Modern Sculpture

- **Watch:** Rodin, Gates of Hell (4:12)

American Art Before the Civil War

- **Read:** Emanuel Leutze, Washington Crossing the Delaware

American Art After the Civil War

- **Read:** Eakins, The Gross Clinic
- **Watch:** Homer, The Life Line (4:05)

America in the Guilded Age

- **Read:** John Singer Sargent, Madame X
- **Read:** Whistler, Nocturne in Black and Gold

Attributions

Key Learning Items

Learning Objectives

After successful completion of this module, you will be able to:

- Understand and apply the concepts and terminology of Nineteenth Century art
- Investigate and apply the fundamental questions we ask when looking at art objects from this movement
- Discuss, collaborate, and generate understanding as to the meaning of Nineteenth Century art
- Assess and evaluate the impact of Nineteenth Century art on the continued evolution of Western art

Key Questions to Ask

While you are reviewing the content of this module, consider the following questions:

- How did artists of the 19-century react to developments in technology and science?
- What were the various styles created throughout the 19-century?
- What role did the emerging art market play in the creation of 19-century art?

Key Vocabulary Terms

- avante-garde
- daguerreotype
- Realism
- Impressionism
- industrialization
- en plein air

- Post-Impressionism

- complementary colors

- pointillism

- Symbolism

- Art Nouveau

- fin-de-siècle

Here are links to art history glossaries that will help you better understand the above key vocabulary terms.

- ArtLex: Art Dictionary

  ◦ http://www.artlex.com/

- About.com: Art History

  ◦ http://arthistory.about.com/od/glossary/l/bl_Art-Glossary.htm

- Artcyclopedia: A Guide to Fine Art

  ◦ http://www.artcyclopedia.com/

Attributions

CC licensed content, Original

Becoming Modern

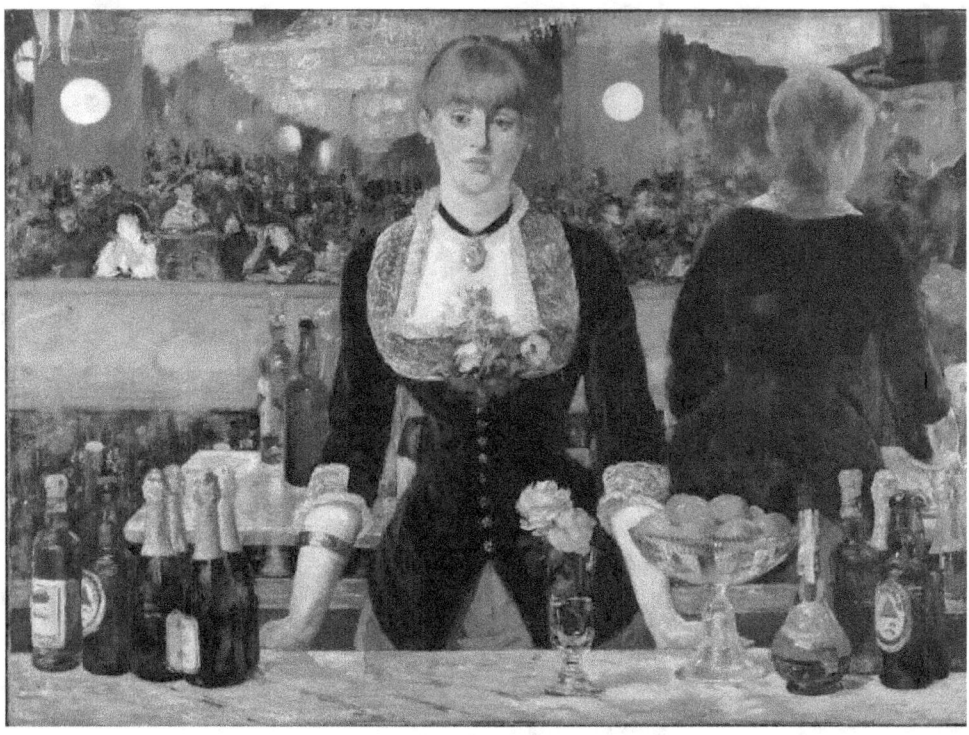

Figure 1. Édouard Manet, A Bar at the Folies-Bergère, oil on canvas, 1882 (Courtauld Gallery, London)

People use the term "modern" in a variety of ways, often very loosely, with a lot of implied associations of new, contemporary, up-to-date, and technological. We know the difference between a modern country and a third world country and it usually has less to do with art and more to do with technology and industrial progress, things like indoor plumbing, easy access to consumer goods, freedom of expression, and voting rights. In the nineteenth century, however, modernity and its connection with art had certain specific associations that people began recognizing and using as barometers to distinguish themselves and their culture from earlier nineteenth century ways and attitudes.

Chronologically, Modernism refers to the period from 1850 to 1960. It begins with the Realist Movement and ends with Abstract Expressionism. That's just a little over one hundred years. During that period the western world experienced some significant changes that transformed Europe and the United States from traditional societies that were agriculturally based into modern ones with cities and factories and mass transportation. Here are some important features that all modern societies share.

1. **Capitalism** replaced landed fortunes and became the economic system of modernity in which people exchanged labor for a fixed wage and used their wages to buy ever more consumer items rather than produce such items themselves. This economic change dramatically affected class relations because it offered opportunities for great wealth through individual initiative, industrialization and technology—somewhat like the technological and dot.com explosion of the late twentieth and early twenty-first century. The industrial revolution which began in England in the late eighteenth century and rapidly swept across Europe (hit the U.S. immediately following the Civil War) transformed economic and social relationships, offered an ever increasing number of cheaper consumer goods, and changed notions of education. Who needed the classics when a commercial/technically oriented education was the key to financial success? The industrial revolution also fostered a sense of competition and progress that continues to influence us today.

2. **Urban culture** replaced agrarian culture as industrialization and cities grew. Cities were the sites of new wealth and opportunity with their factories and manufacturing potential. People moving from small farms, towns to large cities helped to breakdown traditional culture and values. There were also new complications such as growing urban crime, prostitution, alienation, and depersonalization. In a small town you probably knew the cobbler who made your shoes and such a personal relationship often expanded into everyday economics—you might be able to barter food or labor for a new pair of shoes or delay payments. These kinds of accommodations that formed a substructure to agrarian life were swept away with urbanization. City dwellers bought shoes that were manufactured, transported by railroads, displayed in shop windows, and purchased only for cash. Assembly lines, anonymous labor, and advertising created more consumer items but also a growing sense of depersonalization. The gap between the "haves" and the "have nots" increased and were more visible in the city.

3. **Technological advances** such as industrialization, railroads, gas lighting, streetcars, factory systems, indoor plumbing, appliances, and scientific advances were rapidly made and these changes dramatically affected the way people lived and thought about themselves. One consequence was that people in industrialized areas thought of themselves as progressive and modern and considered undeveloped cultures in undeveloped countries as primitive and backward.

4. Modernity is characterized by increasing **secularism** and diminished religious authority. People did not abandon religion but they paid less attention to it. Organized religions were increasingly less able to dictate standards, values, and subject matter. Fine art moved from representing human experience and its relationship to God's creation, to a focus on personal emotions and individual spiritual experiences that were not based in any organized and institutionalized religion.

5. The modern world was extremely **optimistic**—people saw these changes as positive. They welcomed innovation and championed progress. Change became a signifier of modernity. Anything that was traditional and static signaled outmoded, old-fashioned, conservative and was to be avoided by the new modern public. Modern Europe and the U.S. internalized these positions and used modernity as a way of determining and validating their superiority. The nineteenth century was also a period of tremendous colonial growth and expansion, in the name of progress and social benefit and all of these activities were spearheaded by newly industrialized western countries.

Many artists closely identified with modernity and embraced the new techniques and innovations, the spirit of progress, invention, discovery, creativity and change. They wanted to participate in creating the modern world and they were anxious to try out new ideas rather than following the more conservative guidelines of Academic art. This is not to say that these mid-nineteenth century artists were the first to challenge an older generation or set of ideas. Many academic artists had argued over formal issues, styles and subject matter but this was much like a good natured agreement within a club; everyone in the group agreed to disagree.

By the mid-1850s, polite academic disagreements were being taken out of the Academy and onto the street. Artists were looking increasingly to the private sector for patronage, tapping into that growing group of bourgeois or middle class collectors with money to spend and houses to fill with paintings. This new middle class audience that made its money through industrialization and manufacturing had lots of "disposable income", and they wanted pictures that they could understand, that were easy to look at, fit into their homes, addressed subjects they liked. Not for them the historical cycles of gods, saints and heroes with their complex intellectual associations and references; instead, they wanted landscapes, genre scenes, and still life. They were not less educated than earlier buyers, but educated with a different focus and set of priorities. Reality was here and now, progress was inevitable, and the new hero of modern life was the modern man.

Modernity is then a composite of contexts: a time, a space, and an attitude. What makes a place or an object "modern" depends on these conditions.

The Avant-Garde

Throughout the nineteenth century there were artists who produced pictures that we do not label "modern art" generally because the techniques or subjects were associated with the conservative academic styles, techniques and approaches. On the other hand, modern artists were often called the "avant garde." This was originally a military term that described the point man (the first soldier out)—the one to take the most risk. The French socialist Henri de Saint-Simon first used the term in the early 1820's to describe an artist whose work would serve the needs of the people, of a socialist society rather than the ruling classes. The avant garde is also used to identify artists whose painting subjects and techniques were radical, marking them off from the more traditional or academic styles, but not with any particular political ideology in mind. Avant garde became a kind of generic term for a number of art movements centered on the idea of artistic autonomy and independence. In some cases the avant garde was closely associated with political activism, especially socialist or communist movements; in other cases, the avant garde was pointedly removed from politics and focused primarily on aesthetics. The avant garde was never a cohesive group of artists and what was avant garde in one nation was not necessarily the same in others.

Finally, although modern artists were working throughout many countries in Europe and the United States, most 19th art and much twentieth century modern art is centered in France and produced by French artists. Unlike England which was politically stable in the nineteenth century, France went through a variety of governments and insurrections all of which provided a unique political and cultural environment that fostered what we know as modern art.

Introduction to Early Photography

By modern standards, nineteenth-century photography can appear rather primitive. While the stark black and white landscapes and unsmiling people have their own austere beauty, these images also challenge our notions of what defines a work of art.

Photography is a controversial fine art medium, simply because it is difficult to classify—is it an art or a science? Nineteenth century photographers struggled with this distinction, trying to reconcile aesthetics with improvements in technology.

The Birth of Photography

Although the principle of the camera was known in antiquity, the actual chemistry needed to register an image was not available until the nineteenth century.

Artists from the Renaissance onwards used a camera obscura (Latin for dark chamber), or a small hole in the wall of a darkened box that would pass light through the hole and project an upside down image of whatever was outside the box. However, it was not until the invention of a light sensitive surface by Frenchman Joseph Nicéphore Niépce that the basic principle of photography was born.

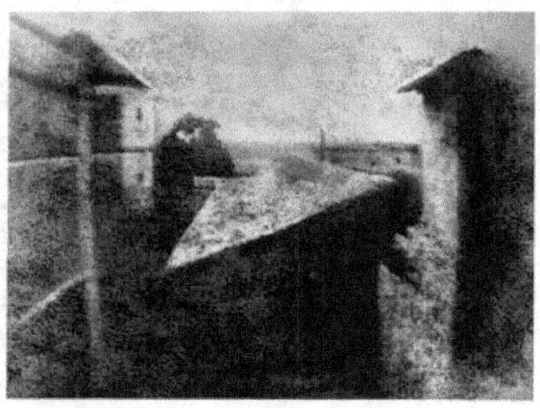

Figure 1. Joseph Nicéphore Niépce, *View from the Window at Gras, 1826*

From this point the development of photography largely related to technological improvements in three areas, speed, resolution and permanence. The first photographs, such as Niepce's famous *View from the Window at Gras* (1826) required a very slow speed (a long exposure period), in this case about 8 hours, obviously making many subjects difficult, if not impossible, to photograph. Taken using a camera obscura to expose a copper plate coated in silver and pewter, Niepce's image looks out of an upstairs window, and part of the blurry quality is due to changing conditions during the long exposure time, causing the resolution, or clarity of the image, to be grainy and hard to read. An additional challenge was the issue of permanence, or how to successfully stop any further reaction of the light sensitive surface once the desired exposure had been achieved. Many of Niepce's early images simply turned black over time due to continued exposure to light. This problem was largely solved in 1839 by the invention of hypo, a chemical that reversed the light sensitivity of paper.

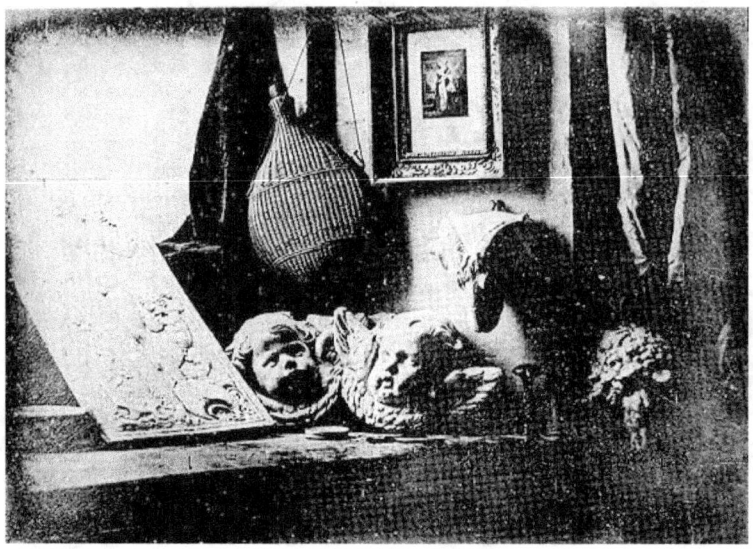

Figure 2. Louis Daguerre, The Artist's Studio, 1837, daguerreotype

Technological Improvements

Photographers after Niepce experimented with a variety of techniques. Louis Daguerre invented a new process he dubbed a daguerrotype in 1839, which significantly reduced exposure time and created a lasting result, but only produced a single image.

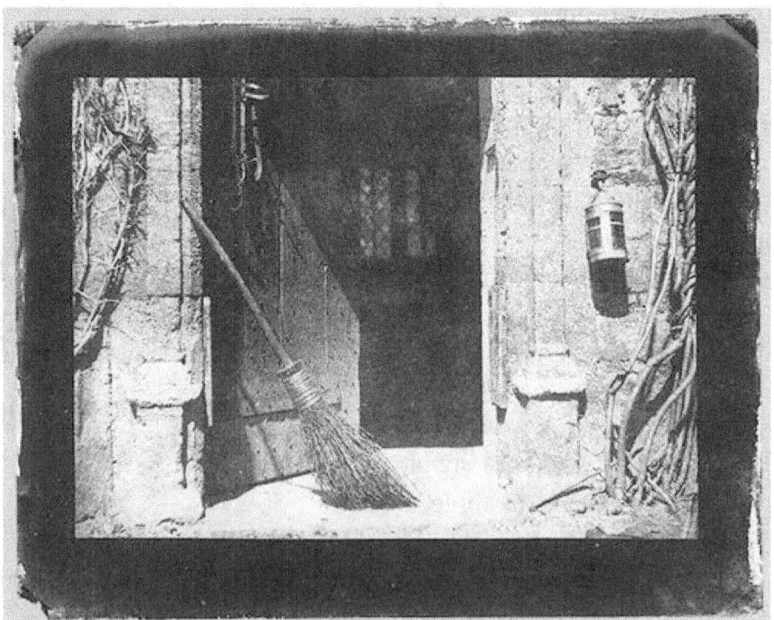

Figure 3. William Henry Fox Talbot, The Open Door, 1844, Salted paper print from paper negative

At the same time, Englishman William Henry Fox Talbot was experimenting with his what would eventually become his calotype method, patented in February 1841. Talbot's innovations included the creation of a paper negative, and new technology that involved the transformation of the negative to a positive image, allowing for more that one copy of the picture. The remarkable detail of Talbot's method can be see in his famous photograph, *The Open Door* (1844) which captures the view through a medieval-looking entrance. The texture of the rough stones surrounding the door, the vines growing up the walls and the rustic broom that leans in the doorway demonstrate the minute details captured by Talbot's photographic improvements.

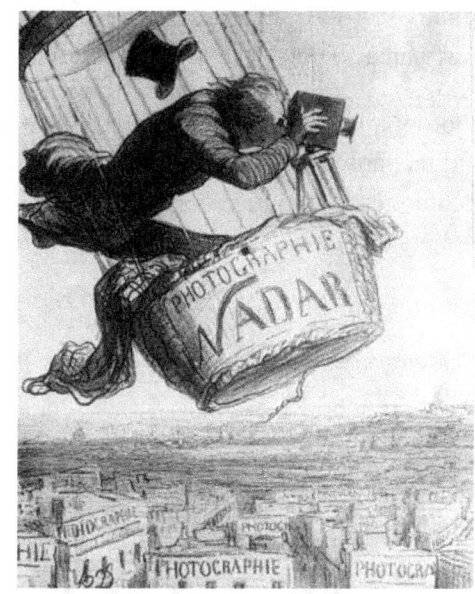

Figure 4. Honoré Daumier, Nadar élevant la Photographie à la hauteur de l'Art (Nadar elevating Photography to Art), lithograph from Le Boulevard, May 25, 1863

The collodion method was introduced in 1851. This process involved fixing a substance known as gun cotton onto a glass plate, allowing for an even shorter exposure time (3-5 minutes), as well as a clearer image.

The big disadvantage of the collodion process was that it needed to be exposed and developed while the chemical coating was still wet, meaning that photographers had to carry portable darkrooms to develop images immediately after exposure. Both the difficulties of the method and uncertain but growing status of photography were lampooned by Honore Daumier in his *Nadar Elevating Photography to the Height of Art* (1862). Nadar, one of the most prominent photographers in Paris at the time, was known for capturing the first aerial photographs from the basket of a hot air balloon. Obviously, the difficulties in developing a glass negative under these circumstances must have been considerable.

Further advances in technology continued to make photography less labor intensive. By 1867 a dry glass plate was invented, reducing the inconvenience of the wet collodion method.

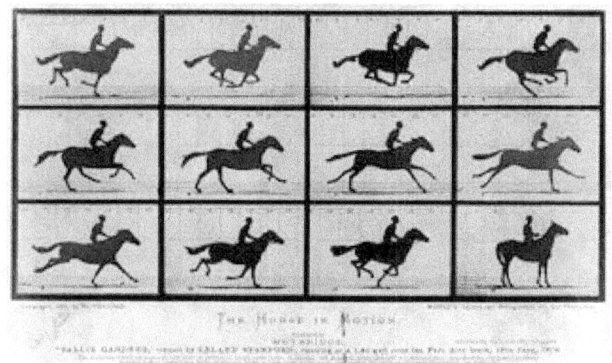

Figure 5. Eadweard Muybridge, The Horse in Motion ("Sallie Gardner," owned by Leland Stanford; running at a 1:40 gait over the Palo Alto track, 19th June 1878)

Prepared glass plates could be purchased, eliminating the need to fool with chemicals. In 1878, new advances decreased the exposure time to 1/25th of a second, allowing moving objects to be photographed and lessening the need for a tripod. This new development is celebrated in Eadweard Maybridge's sequence of photographs called Galloping Horse (1878). Designed to settle the question of whether or not a horse ever takes all four legs completely off the ground during a gallop, the series of photographs also demonstrated the new photographic methods that were capable of nearly instantaneous exposure.

Finally in 1888 George Eastman developed the dry gelatin roll film, making it easier for film to be carried. Eastman also produced the first small inexpensive cameras, allowing more people access to the technology.

Photographers in the 19th century were pioneers in a new artistic endeavor, blurring the lines between art and technology. Frequently using traditional methods of composition and marrying these with innovative techniques, photographers created a new vision of the material world. Despite the struggles early photographers must have had with the limitations of their technology, their artistry is also obvious.

Attributions

CC licensed content, Shared previously

- Early Photography. **Authored by**: Dr. Rebecca Jeffrey Easby. **Provided by**: Khan Academy. **Located at**: https://web.archive.org/web/20141007043056/http://smarthistory.khanacademy.org/early-photography.html. **License**: *CC BY-NC-SA: Attribution-NonCommercial-ShareAlike*

Louis Daguerre

The Daguerreotype

An early example of a "daguerreotype," *Paris Boulevard* is a significant step in the development of photography (figure 1). Taken in 1839 by Louis-Jacques Mande Daguerre, the photograph depicts a seemingly empty street in Paris. The elevated viewpoint emphasizes the wide avenues, tree-lined sidewalks, and charming buildings of the French capital. However, the obvious day light of the photograph begs the question—where are all the people in this normally busy city?

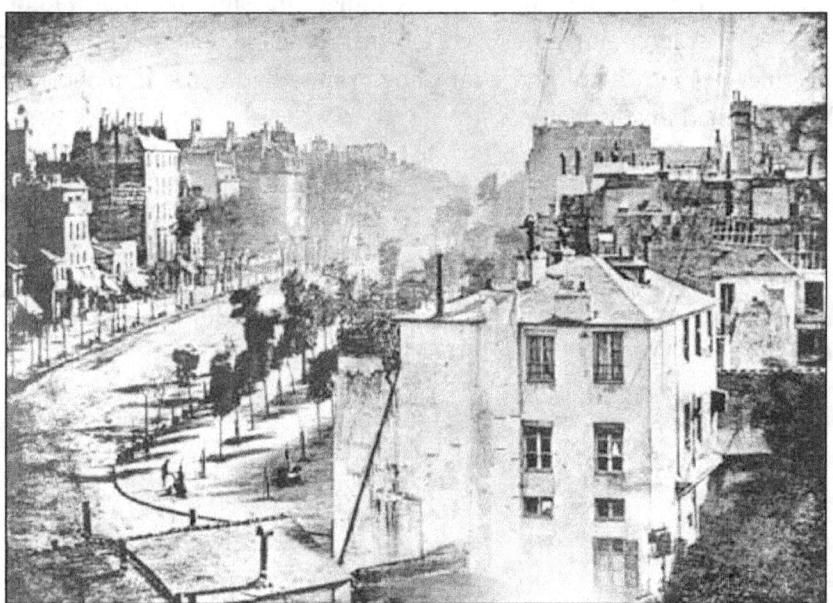

Figure 1. Louis Daguerre, Paris Boulevard, 1839, Daguerreotype

The answer to this question lies in the daguerreotype technique. The first photographs, such as Joseph Nicephore Niepce's famous *View from the Window at Gras,* took about 8 hours to expose, creating indistinct, grainy images. Daguerre was intrigued by these experiments and formed a partnership with Niepce from 1828 until the latter's death in 1833. Daguerre continued to refine the photographic method until he developed his new process.

Chemistry

His technique consisted of exposing a copper plate coated in silver and sensitized with iodine to light in a camera, and then developed it in darkness by holding it over a pan of heated vaporizing mercury. He also developed a method of creating a permanent image by using a solution of ordinary table salt. Daguerre's technique significantly reduced exposure time and created a lasting result that would not dim with further exposure to light, but only produced a single image. It would be up to others to produce the negatives that allowed for the production of multiple copies of an image.

A Shoe Shine

Daguerre's *Paris Boulevard* shows the advantages of the new technique. There is far more detail than in earlier photographs. We can clearly see the panes in the windows and the sharp corners of the building in the front of the image. The objects are no longer blurry masses of light and dark, but defined and separate structures. In fact, the only thing missing are the people, except for the small figure of a man having his shoes shined at a sidewalk stand.

The remaining problem of the daguerreotype, at least by modern standards, was the long exposure time, between 10 and 15 minutes. This meant that the people hurrying along those spacious sidewalks did not register on the photograph. The man having his shoes shined, possibly the first photographic image of a person, obviously stayed still long enough to register on the image. The haunting empty, yet evocative, image of *Parisian Boulevard* shows both how far photography had come in a short time and how much farther the technology still had to advance.

Attributions

CC licensed content, Shared previously

Timothy O'Sullivan

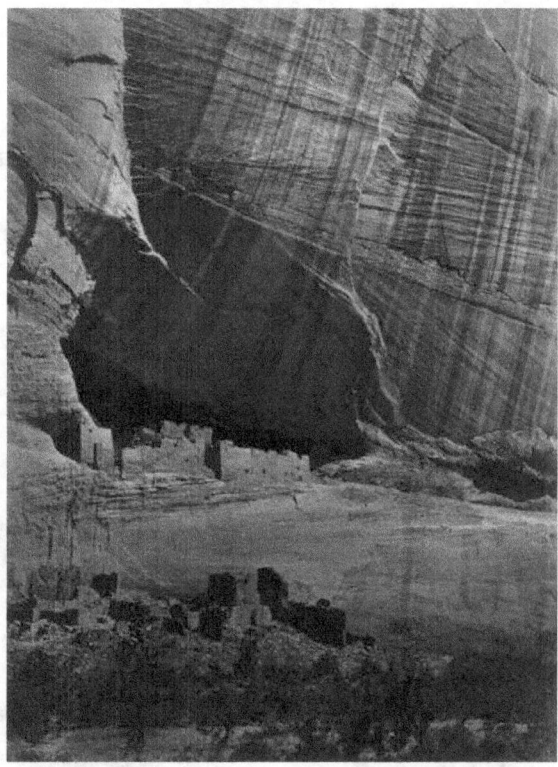

Figure 1. Timothy O'Sullivan, Ancient Ruins in the Cañon de Chelle, N.M. In a niche 50 feet above present cañon bed, 1873, photographic albumen print, 27.5 x 20.2 cm (note: Canyon de Chelly is in Arizona close the New Mexico border)

The impressive natural landscape of Timothy O'Sullivan's photograph *Ancient Ruins in the Canyon de Chelly* (1873) immediately commands attention (figure 1). The yawning black hole in the center is emphasized by the dramatic striations in the rocks, the black and white contrast of the photograph making the layers of sediment far more obvious than they would be in reality. In fact, the drama of the surrounding landscape makes it possible to almost overlook the ancient ruins at the mouth of a black cave.

Borrowing from Landscape Painting

Although clearly a documentary image of the scene, the photograph also employs many of the artistic conventions of landscape painting. The narrowly focused composition does not allow the viewer's eye to wander through the landscape. In fact, our vision in confined solely to the rock and the ruins, without the standard light source found in most landscape painting. However, light plays an obvious role in the play of light and dark on the rock walls. The ruins themselves, which suggest the passage of time, are so small as to emphasize the traditional Romantic interest in man's insignificance when confronted with the immensity of nature.

The Realities of War

Timothy O'Sullivan began his photographic career as an apprentice in the studio of Mathew Brady. At the start of the Civil War, he became part of Brady's team assigned to document the conflict, although O'Sullivan resigned after an argument with Brady over who was to receive credit for authorship of his photos. Many of O'Sullivan's war images have a haunting quality, for example, *A Harvest of Death* (1863), which captures a misty landscape in Gettysburg, Pennsylvania littered with corpses. At a time when standard war images consisted of portraits of soldiers in uniform and camp life, O'Sullivan's photograph is a stark reminder of the realities of the conflict.

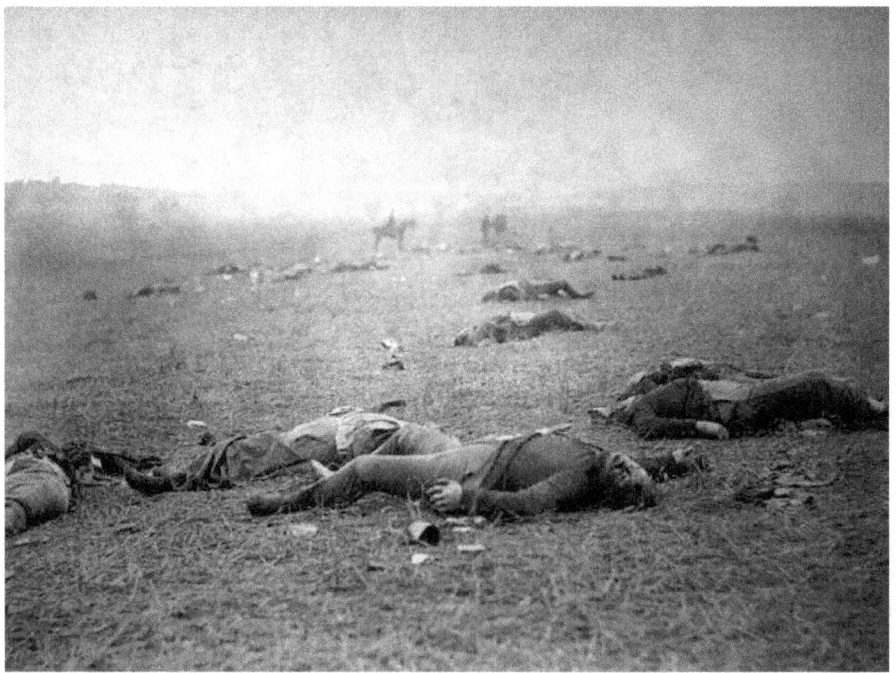

Figure 2. The Harvest of Death. Union dead on the battlefield at Gettysburg, Pennsylvania, photographed July 5–6, 1863

Geological Expeditions

During the late 1860s and 70s O'Sullivan traveled west several times photographing as part of various geological survey teams. The difficulties of these trips must have been huge, carrying men and equipment through the wilderness in wagons and small boats. O'Sullivan himself nearly drowned on an early expedition when he was thrown from a boat and carried down stream by rapids before finally making his way to shore. Managing his personal equipment must have also been a challenge. Photographs at the time were exposed on large glass plates, and understandably, many of O'Sullivan's images simply didn't make it home.

In 1873 O'Sullivan himself led a group to explore the rock formations and long abandoned archaeological remains found in Arizona around the Canyon de Chelly. The ancient pueblos in the photograph were built by the Anasazi or Navajo for "ancient ones." Although O'Sullivan was one of the first to capture this impressive scene, many others have followed in his footsteps, including the legendary twentieth-century landscape photographer Ansel Adams. The Canyon de Chelly became a National Monument in 1931 and is today jointly managed by the National Park Service and the Navajo Nation.

Attributions

CC licensed content, Shared previously

Introduction to Realism

Realism and the Painting of Modern Life

The Royal Academy supported the age-old belief that art should be instructive, morally uplifting, refined, inspired by the Classical tradition, a good reflection of the national culture, and, above all, about beauty.

But trying to keep young nineteenth-century artists' eyes on the past became an issue!

The world was changing rapidly and some artists wanted their work to be about their contemporary environment—about themselves and their own perceptions of life. In short, they believed that the modern era deserved to have a modern art.

The Modern Era begins with the Industrial Revolution in the late eighteenth century. Clothing, food, heat, light and sanitation are a few of the basic areas that "modernized" the nineteenth century. Transportation was faster, getting things done got easier, shopping in the new department stores became an adventure, and people developed a sense of "leisure time"—thus the entertainment businesses grew.

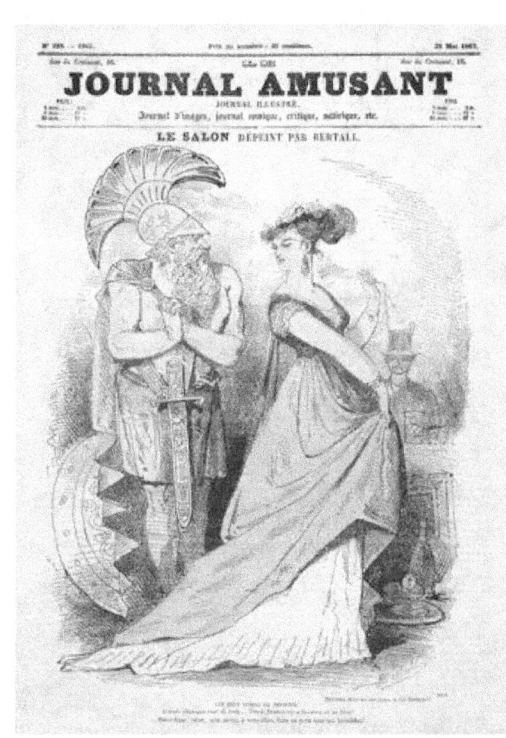

Figure 1. Charles Albert d'Arnoux Bertall, in Le Journal Amusant, no. 595 (May 25, 1867) (The Research Library, The Getty Research Institute)

Paris Transformed

In Paris, the city was transformed from a medieval warren of streets to a grand urban center with wide boulevards, parks, shopping districts and multi-class dwellings (so that the division of class might be from floor to floor—the rich on the lower floors and the poor on the upper floors in one building—instead by neighborhood).

Therefore, modern life was about social mixing, social mobility, frequent journeys from the city to the country and back, and a generally faster pace which has accelerated ever since.

How could paintings and sculptures about Classical gods and biblical stories relate to a population enchanted with this progress?

In the middle of the nineteenth century, the young artists decided that it couldn't and shouldn't. In 1863 the poet and art critic Charles Baudelaire published an essay entitled "The Painter of Modern Life," which declared that the artist must be of his/her own time.

Courbet

Gustave Courbet, a young fellow from the Franche-Comté, a province outside of Paris, came to the "big city" with a large ego and a sense of mission. He met Baudelaire and other progressive thinkers within the first years of making Paris his home. Then, he set himself up as the leader for a new art: Realism—"history painting" about real life. He believed that if he could not see something, he should not paint it. He also decided that his art should have a social consciousness that would awaken the self-involved Parisian to contemporary concerns: the good, the bad and the ugly.

Attributions

CC licensed content, Shared previously

- Realism. **Authored by**: Beth Gersh-Nesic. **Provided by**: Khan Academy. **Located at**: https://web.archive.org/web/20141007000912/http://smarthistory.khanacademy.org/realism.html. **License**: *CC BY-NC-SA: Attribution-NonCommercial-ShareAlike*

Courbet, The Stone Breakers

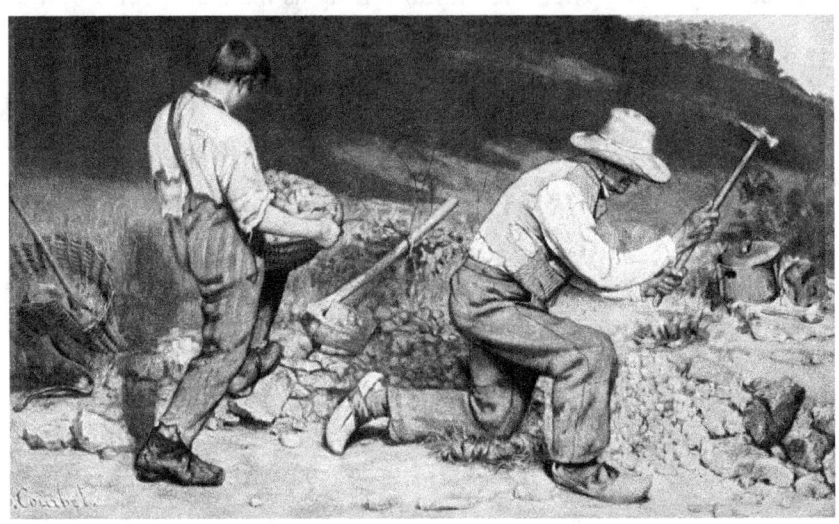

Figure 1. Gustave Courbet, The Stone Breakers, 1849, Oil on canvas, 165 × 257 cm (Gemäldegalerie, Dresden (destroyed))

Realism and Reality

If we look closely at Courbet's painting *The Stone Breakers* of 1849 (painted only one year after Karl Marx and Friedrich Engels wrote their influential pamphlet, *The Communist Manifesto*) the artist'sconcern for the plight of the poor is evident. Here, two figures labor to break and remove stone from a road that is being built. In our age ofpowerful jackhammers and bulldozers, such work is reserved as punishment for chain-gangs.

Unlike Millet (figure 2), who was known for depicting idealized, hale and hearty rural folk, Courbet depicts figures who wear ripped and tattered clothing. None of Millet's mythologized farm workers appear here. Courbet wants to show what is "real," and so he has depicted a man that seems far too old and a boy that seems still too young for such back-breaking labors.

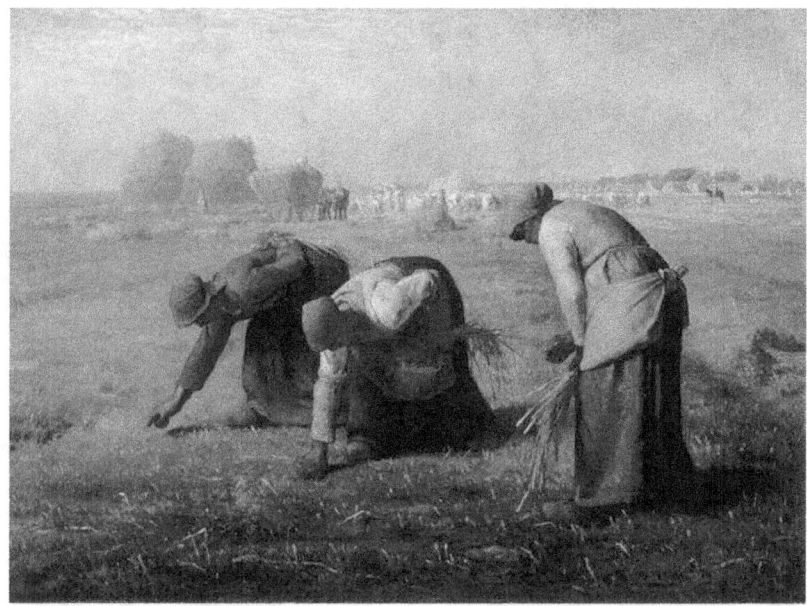

Figure 2. Jean-François Millet, The Gleaners, 1857 (Musée d'Orsay, Paris)

But this is not meant to be heroic: it is meant to be an accurate account of the abuse and deprivation that was a common feature of mid-century French rural life. And as with so many great works of art, there is a close affiliation between the narrative (story)and the formal choices made by the painter, meaning elements such as brushwork, composition, line, and color.

The two stone breakers in Courbet's painting are set against a low hill of the sort common in the rural French town of Ornan, where the artist had been raised and continued to spend a much of his time. The hill reaches to the top of the canvas everywhere but the upper right corner, where a tiny patch of bright blue sky appears. The effect is to isolate these laborers, and to suggest that they are physically and socio-economically trapped by their work.

Like the stones themselves, Courbet's brushwork is rough—more so than might be expected during the mid-nineteenth century. This suggests that the way the artist painted his canvas was in part a conscious rejection of the highly polished, refined Neoclassicist style that still dominatedFrench art in 1848.

Perhaps most characteristic of Courbet's style is his refusal to focus on the parts of the image that would usually receive the most attention. Traditionally, an artist would spent the most time on the hands, faces, and foregrounds. Not Courbet. If you look carefully, you will notice that he attempts to be even-handed, attending to faces and rock equally. So what, then, is Courbet's Realism?

Attributions

Bonheur, Plowing in the Nivernais

Dr. Beth Harris and Dr. Steven Zucker provide a description, historical perspective, and analysis of Rosa Bonheur's *Plowing in the Nivernais*.

- https://youtu.be/kOnzZHJYzb4

Rosa Bonheur, *Plowing in the Nivernais (or The First Dressing)*, 1849, oil on canvas, (Musée d'Orsay, Paris).

External Link

View this painting up close in the Google Art Project.:

- https://www.google.com/culturalinstitute/asset-viewer/ploughing-in-nevers/PgFNI-UZGQrkBDQ?projectId=art-project

---

Millet, The Gleaners

Dr. Beth Harris and Dr. Steven Zucker provide a description, historical perspective, and analysis of Jean-François Millet's *The Gleaners*.

- https://youtu.be/Dk1nuM5JKqQ

Jean-François Millet (French), *The Gleaners*, 1857, oil on canvas, 33″ × 43″ (83.5 cm × 110 cm), (Musée d'Orsay, Paris).

External Link
View this painting up close in the Google Art Project.: • https://www.google.com/culturalinstitute/asset-viewer/gleaners/GgHsT2RumWxbtw?projectId=art-project

Attributions

Degas, The Dance Class

Dr. Beth Harris and Dr. Steven Zucker provide a description, historical perspective, and analysis of Degas's *The Dance Class*.

- https://youtu.be/NigP3DjV3NY

Edgar Degas, *The Dance Class*, 1874, oil on canvas, (Metropolitan Museum of Art).

Hilaire-Germain-Edgar De Gas—who will later contract his name to Degas—is one of the most beloved artists of all time. When there is a Degas exhibition, it becomes a major event. Visitors crowd the galleries and the gift shops do a brisk business selling scarves, umbrellas, and notebooks printed with details from the artist's paintings and drawings of ballerinas. And that's the subject that people want. Yes, of course his bathers and race horses are popular, still it is his dancers that have captured the public's imagination. By the way, Degas hated the fact that he was known as the "painter of dancers" Still, he did return to this theme throughout his career. I find it remarkable that while people see his extraordinary use of line, light, and composition they so often miss the less savory aspects of these images.

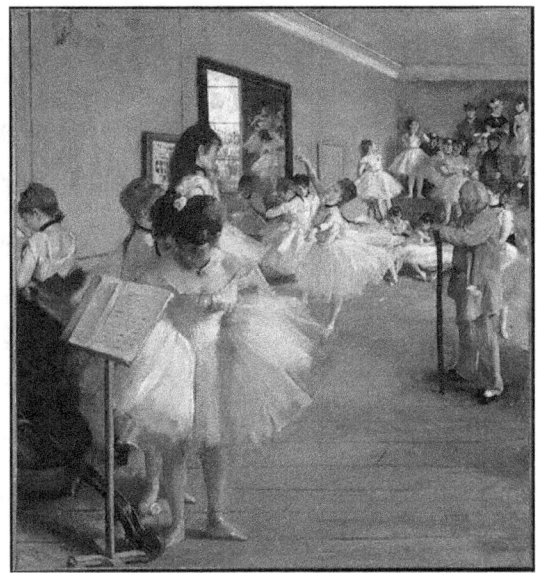

Figure 1. Edgar Degas, The Dance Class, oil on canvas, 1874 (Metropolitan Museum of Art)

Degas, At the Races in the Countryside

Dr. Beth Harris and Dr. Steven Zucker provide a description, historical perspective, and analysis of Degas's *At the Races in the Countryside*.

- https://youtu.be/6HTBjvqn9uw

Edgar Degas, *At the Races in the Countryside*, 1869, oil on canvas, 36.5 × 55.9 cm (14-3/8 × 22 inches), (Museum of Fine Arts, Boston).

External Resources

View this painting up close in the Google Art Project:

- https://www.google.com/culturalinstitute/asset-viewer/at-the-races-in-the-countryside/fAG5E-YLY4Q57g?projectId=art-project

Attributions

Manet, Luncheon on the Grass (Le Dejeuner sur l'herbe)

Dr. Beth Harris and Dr. Steven Zucker provide a description, historical perspective, and analysis of Manet's *Le déjeuner sur l'herbe.*

- https://www.youtube.com/watch?v=3xBGF8H3bQ4

Édouard Manet, *Le déjeuner sur l'herbe (Luncheon on the Grass)*, 1863, oil on canvas, 208 cm × 265.5 cm (81.9 in × 104.5 in), (Musée d'Orsay, Paris).

External Link

View this painting up close in the Google Art Project:

- https://www.google.com/culturalinstitute/asset-viewer/luncheon-on-the-grass/twEL-HYoc3ID_VA?projectId=art-project

Manet, Olympia

Dr. Beth Harris and Dr. Steven Zucker provide a description, historical perspective, and analysis of Manet's *Olympia*.

- https://youtu.be/bihBbqzL96Y

Édouard Manet, *Olympia*, 1863, oil on canvas, 130.5 cm × 190 cm (51.4 in × 74.8 in), (Musée d'Orsay, Paris).

Édouard Manet brought to Realism his curiosity about social mores. However, he was not interested in mirroring polite parlor conversations and middle class promenades in the Bois de Boulogne (Paris' Central Park). Rather, Manet invented subjects that set the Parisians' teeth on edge.

In 1865, Manet submitted his risqué painting of a courtesan greeting her client (in this case, you), *Olympia*, of 1863, to the French Salon. The jury for the 1865 Salon accepted this painting despite their disapproval of the subject matter, because two years earlier, Manet's Luncheon on the Grass created such a stir when it was rejected from the Salon. (It was instead exhibited in Emperor Napoleon III's conciliatory exhibition—the *Salon des Réfusés*, or the Exhibition of the Refused. Crowds came to the Salon des Réfusés specifically to laugh and jeer at what they considered Manet's folly.)

Somehow they were afraid another rejection would seem like a personal attack on Manet himself. The reasoning was odd, but the result was the same—Olympia became infamous and the painting had to be hung very high to protect it from physical attacks.

Manet was a Realist, but sometimes his "real" situations shocked and rocked the Parisian art world to its foundations. His later work was much tamer.

Attributions

Manet, A Bar at the Folies-Bergere

Dr. Beth Harris and Dr. Steven Zucker provide a description, historical perspective, and analysis of Manet's *A Bar at the Folies-Bergère*.

- https://youtu.be/kMACjCg9r4E

Édouard Manet, *A Bar at the Folies-Bergère*, 1882, 3′ 2″ x 4′ 3″, (Courtauld Gallery, London).

Attributions

CC licensed content, Shared previously

Garnier, Paris Opera

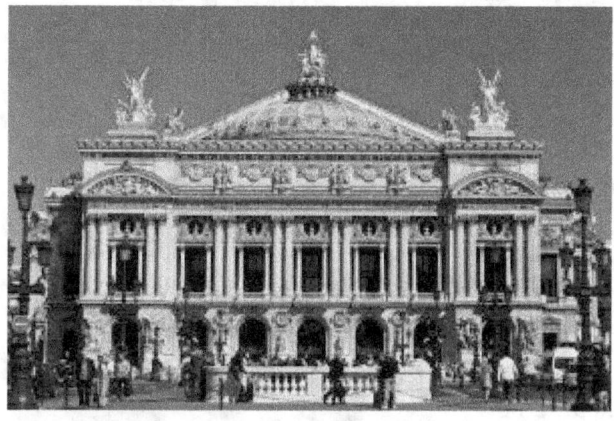

The Paris Opéra (1860–75), designed by Charles Garnier, is one of the jewels of Napoleon III's newly reconstructed city. Frequented by Degas and the source for much of his ballet imagery, the Paris Opéra is key to understanding the somewhat perverse culture of voyeurism and spectacle among the prosperous classes of the Second Empire.

- https://youtu.be/EtTGyLsR7lk

Marvin Trachtenberg & Isabel Hyman have called the huge Opéra house, "the new cathedral of bourgeois [middle, really upper-middle class] Paris. . . . The glittering centerpiece of the new Paris . . . was meant to be much more than a theater in the ordinary sense.

For Charles Garnier, an architect of the Ecole des beaux-arts, it was a setting for a ritual in which the spectators were also actors, participants in the rite of social encounter, seeing and being seen." The division of the structure supports his vision.

Look at the cross-section in figure 2. The dome sits above the audience and orchestra, the high roof over the stage. Behind the stage are the rehearsal rooms where Degas often sketched.

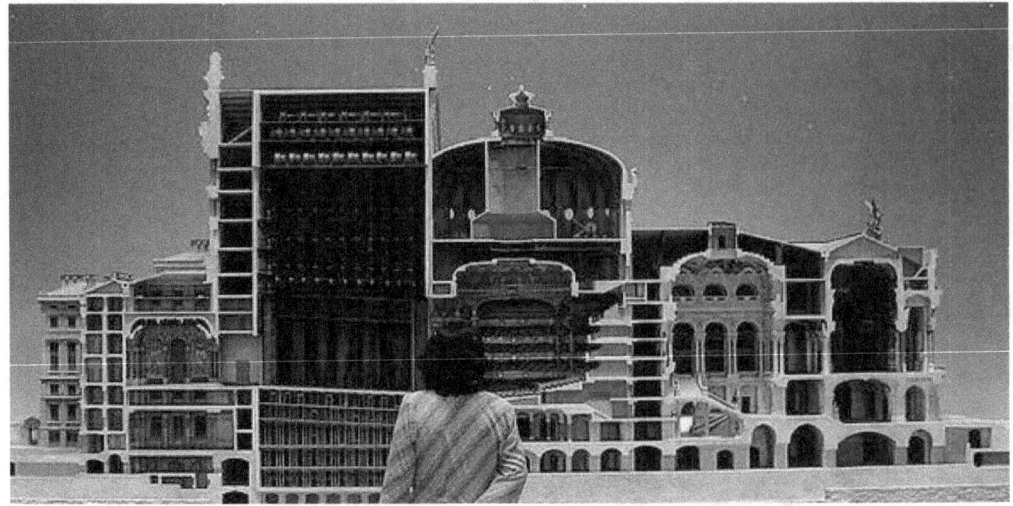

Figure 2. A cross-section of the Paris Opéra

But the single largest area, from the front facade to the seats below the dome, is reserved for the foyers and the grand stair hall. This area was, in essence, a second stage. Far more ornate then the performance stage, the lobbies of the Paris Opéra was where the social dramas of the rich were enacted.

Strolling along the new boulevards or posing in the opera's grand foyers, the ruling classes paraded their wealth. The *flâneur,* a new denizen of the city, was a man of leisure (itself a by-product of the capital generated by industrialization). Walking the streets not for work or need, but for the pleasures of observation, the *flâneur* was at home in the Opéra.

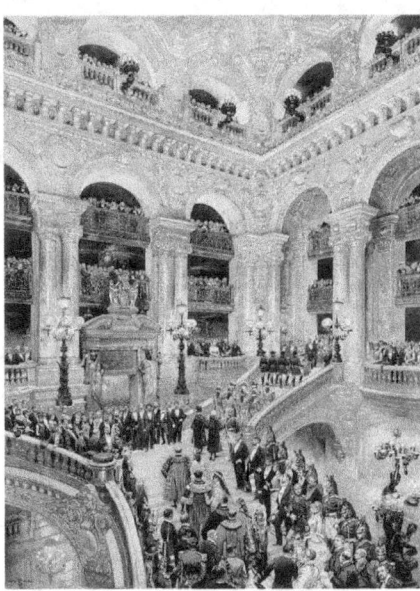

Figure 3. Inauguration of the Paris Opera in 1875 (Édouard Detaille, 1878)

Attributions

Introduction to Impressionism

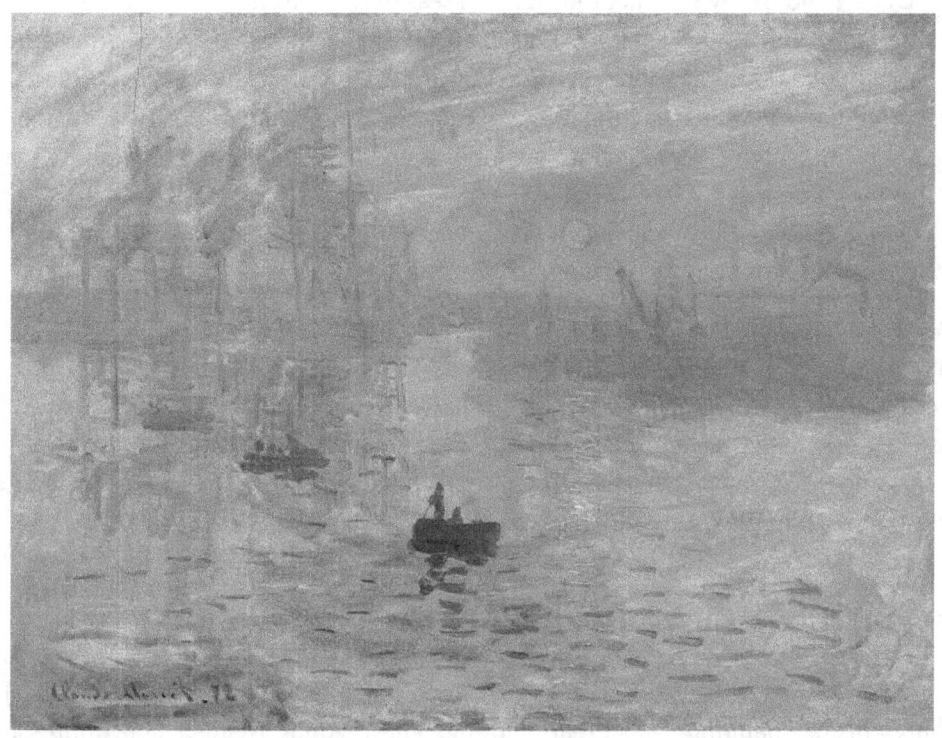

Figure 1. Claude Monet, Impression Sunrise, 1872 (exhibited at the first Impressionist exhibition in 1874)

Establishing their Own Exhibitions—Apart from the Salon

The group of artists who became known as the Impressionists did something ground-breaking, in addition to their sketchy, light-filled paintings. They established their own exhibition—apart from the annual salon. At that time, the salon was really the only way to exhibit your work (the work was chosen by a jury). Claude Monet, August Renoir, Edgar Degas, Berthe Morisot, Alfred Sisley, and several other artists could not afford to wait for France to accept their work. They all had experienced rejection by the Salon jury in recent years and knew waiting a whole year in between each exhibition was no longer tenable. They needed to show their work and they wanted to sell it.

So, in an attempt to get recognized outside of the official channel of the salon, these artists banded together and held their own exhibition. They pooled their money, rented a studio that belonged to the famous photographer Nadar and set a date for their first exhibition together. They called themselves the Anonymous Society of Painters, Sculptors, and Printmakers. The show opened at about the same time as the annual Salon, May 1874. The Impressionists held eight exhibitions from 1874 through 1886.

The decision was based on their frustration and their ambition to show the world their new, light-filled images.

The impressionists regarded Manet as their inspiration and leader in their spirit of revolution, but Manet had no desire to join their cooperative venture into independent exhibitions. Manet had set up his own pavilion during the 1867 World's Fair, but he was not interested in giving up on the Salon jury. He wanted Paris to come to him and accept him—even if he had to endure their ridicule in the process.

Monet, Renoir, Degas, and Sisley had met through classes. Berthe Morisot was a friend of both Degas and Manet (she would marry Édouard Manet's brother Eugène by the end of 1874). She had been accepted to the Salon, but her work had become more experimental since then. Degas invited Berthe to join their risky effort. The first exhibition did not repay them monetarily but it drew the critics who decided their art was abominable. It wasn't finished. They called it "just impressions." (And not in a complimentary way.)

The Lack of "Finish"

Remember that the look of a J.A.D. Ingres or even a surly Delacroix had a "finished" surface. These younger artists' completed works looked like sketches. And not even detailed sketches but the fast, preliminary "impressions" that artists would dash off to preserve an idea of what to paint later. Normally, an artist's "impressions" were not meant to be sold, but were meant to be aids for the memory—to take these ideas back to the studio for the masterpiece on canvas. The critics thought it was insane to sell paintings that looked like slap-dash impressions and consider these paintings works "finished."

Landscape and Contemporary Life (not History Painting!)

Also—Courbet, Manet and the Impressionists challenged the Academy's category codes. The Academy deemed that only "history painting" was great painting. These young Realists and Impressionists opened the door to dismantling this hierarchy of subject matter. They believed that landscapes and genres scenes were worthy and important.

Color

In their landscapes and genre scenes of contemporary life, the Impressionist artists tried to arrest a moment in their fast-paced lives by pinpointing specific atmospheric conditions—light flickering on water, moving clouds, a burst of rain. Their technique tried to capture what they saw. They painted small commas of pure color one next to another. The viewer would stand at a reasonable distance so that the eye would mix the individual marks, thus blending the colors together optically. This method created more vibrant colors than those colors mixed on a palette. Becoming a team dedicated to this new, non-Academic painting gave them the courage to pursue the independent exhibition format—a revolutionary idea of its own.

Light

An important aspect of the Impressionist painting was the appearance of quickly shifting light on the surface. This sense of moving rapidly or quickly changing atmospheric conditions or living in a world that moves faster was also part of the Impressionist's criteria. They wanted to create an art that seemed modern: about contemporary life, about the fast pace of contemporary life, and about the sensation of seeing light change incessantly in the landscape. They painted outdoors (en plein air) to capture the appearance of the light as it really flickered and faded while they worked.

Mary Cassatt was an American who met Edgar Degas and was invited to join the group as they continued to mount independent exhibitions. By the 1880s, the Impressionist accepted the name the critics gave them. The American Mary Cassatt began to exhibition with the Impressionists in 1877.

For a very long time, the French refused to find the work worthy of praise. The Americans and other non-French collectors did. For this reason, the US and other foreign collections own most of the Impressionist art. (The Metropolitan Museum of Art owns a good portion of the Havermayer Collection. Louisine Havermayer knew Mary Cassatt, who advised Louisine when she visited Paris.)

Attributions

CC licensed content, Shared previously

- Impressionism. **Authored by**: Beth Gersh-Nesic. **Provided by**: Khan Academy. **Located at**: https://web.archive.org/web/20141007161132/http://smarthistory.khanacademy.org/impressionism-france.html. **License**: *CC BY-NC-SA: Attribution-NonCommercial-ShareAlike*

Monet, Gare St. Lazare

Dr. Beth Harris and Dr. Steven Zucker provide a description, historical perspective, and analysis of Monet's *Gare St. Lazare*.

- https://youtu.be/sYQ5CSyACpc

Claude Monet, *Gare St. Lazare*, 1877, oil on canvas, 75 cm × 104 cm, (Musee d'Orsay).

Attributions

Monet, Rouen Cathedral Series

Claude Monet painted more than 30 canvases depicting Rouen cathedral between 1892 and 1893. Dr. Beth Harris and Dr. Steven Zucker provide a description, historical perspective, and analysis of four paintings of these paintings in the collection of the Musée d'Orsay in Paris:

- https://youtu.be/LnPKrSVMLnQ

Works Discussed

Claude Monet, *Rouen Cathedral, the Portal, gray weather*, 1892

Claude Monet, *Rouen Cathedral, The Portal Seen from the Front*, 1892

Claude Monet, *Rouen Cathedral, The Portal and Tower, sunlight*, 1893

Claude Monet, *Rouen Cathedral The Portal, morning sun*, 1893

Claude Monet, *Rouen Cathedral, The Portal and Tower, morning effect*, 1893

Caillebotte, Paris Street; Rainy Day

Dr. Beth Harris and Dr. Steven Zucker provide a description, historical perspective, and analysis of Gustave Caillebotte's *Paris Street; Rainy Day*.

- https://youtu.be/U8d45ETt78o

Gustave Caillebotte, *Paris Street; Rainy Day*, 1877, oil on canvas 83-1/2 × 108-3/4 inches (212.2 × 276.2 cm), (The Art Institute of Chicago).

External Link
View this work up close in the Google Art Project: • https://www.google.com/culturalinstitute/asset-viewer/paris-street-rainy-day/5wEUCOlEf-EaVQ?projectId=art-project

Attributions

Cassatt, In the Loge

Dr. Beth Harris and Dr. Steven Zucker provide a description, historical perspective, and analysis of Mary Cassatt's *In the Loge*.

- https://youtu.be/HVuyK_vIMfc

Mary Cassatt, *In the Loge*, 1878, oil on canvas, 81.28 × 66.04 cm (32 × 26 inches), (Museum of Fine Arts, Boston).

At the Opera

In nineteenth century France, the gaze of the observer—whether on Napoleon's grand new boulevards or in the opera—was very much structured by issues of economic status. Mary Cassatt's remarkable painting *In the Loge* (c. 1878–79) clearly shows the complex relationship between the gaze, public spectacle, gender, and class privilege.

Cassatt was a wealthy American artist who had adopted the style of the Impressionists while living in Paris. Here she depicts a fashionable upper-class woman in a box seat at the Paris opera (as it happens, the sitter is Cassatt's sister, Lydia). Lydia is shown holding opera glasses up to her eyes; but instead of tilting them down, as she would if she were watching the performance below, her gaze is level. She peers straight across the chamber perhaps at another member of the audience. Look closely and you will notice that, in turn, and in one of the boxes across the room, a gentleman is gazing at her. Lydia is then, in a sense, caught between his gaze and ours even as she spies another.

Attributions

- Cassatt, In the Loge. **Authored by**: Dr. Beth Harris and Dr. Steven Zucker. **Provided by**: Khan Academy. **Located at**: https://www.khanacademy.org/humanities/becoming-modern/avant-garde-france/impressionism/v/mary-cassatt-in-the-loge-1878. **License**: *CC BY-NC-SA: Attribution-NonCommercial-ShareAlike*

Cassatt, The Child's Bath

Dr. Beth Harris and Dr. Steven Zucker provide a description, historical perspective, and analysis of Mary Cassatt's *The Child's Bath*.

- https://youtu.be/O4St29B7cmU

Mary Cassatt, *The Child's Bath*, 1893, oil on canvas, 100.3 × 66.1 cm (39 1/2 × 26 inches), (Art Institute of Chicago).

External Link
View this painting up close in the Google Art Project: • https://www.google.com/culturalinstitute/asset-viewer/the-child-s-bath/FQGpjnFFEcrMyw?projectId=art-project

Morisot, The Mother and Sister of the Artist

Dr. Beth Harris and Dr. Steven Zucker provide a description, historical perspective, and analysis of Berthe Morisot's *The Mother and Sister of the Artist*.

- https://youtu.be/BSQr7Ii_vbY

Berthe Morisot, *The Mother and Sister of the Artist*, c. 1869/1870, oil on canvas 39 3/4″ × 32 3/16″ (101 cm × 81.8 cm), (National Gallery of Art).

Attributions

CC licensed content, Shared previously

Renoir, Moulin de la Galette

Dr. Beth Harris and Dr. Steven Zucker provide a description, historical perspective, and analysis of Renoir's *Moulin de la Galette*.

- https://youtu.be/x6rAFt5FW_Q

Pierre-Auguste Renoir, *Moulin de la Galette,* 1876, oil on canvas, 51 1/2 × 68 7/8 in. (131 × 175 cm), (Musée d'Orsay, Paris).

External Link
View this painting up close in the Google Art Project: • https://www.google.com/culturalinstitute/asset-viewer/dance-at-le-moulin-de-la-galette/rQEx7CtGiKE3yg?projectId=art-project

Attributions

CC licensed content, Shared previously

Post-Impressionism Explained

Click on the link below to view the website "Post-Impressionism" developed by Saint Michael's College. This website gives an overview of Post-Impressionism in the 1800s and 1900s and includes analyses of some notable paintings.

"Post-Impressionism" developed by Saint Michael's College

- http://academics.smcvt.edu/awerbel/Survey%20of%20Art%20History%20II/PostImpression-ism.htm

Seurat, La Grande Jatte

Dr. Beth Harris and Dr. Steven Zucker provide a description, historical perspective, and analysis of Georges Seurat's *A Sunday on La Grande Jatte—1884*.

- https://youtu.be/wNB9Vm6MoDQ

Georges Seurat, *A Sunday on La Grande Jatte—1884*, 1884–86, oil on canvas, 81-3/4 × 121-1/4 inches (207.5 × 308.1 cm), (The Art Institute of Chicago).

External Link
View this painting up close in the Google Art Project: • https://www.google.com/culturalinstitute/asset-viewer/a-sunday-on-la-grande-jatte-1884/twGyqq52R-lYpA?projectId=art-project

Attributions

Van Gogh, Self-Portrait Dedicated to Paul Gauguin

Dr. Beth Harris and Dr. Steven Zucker provide a description, historical perspective, and analysis of Vincent van Gogh's *Self-Portrait Dedicated to Paul Gauguin.*

- https://youtu.be/gqSpWPONekE

Vincent van Gogh, *Self-Portrait Dedicated to Paul Gauguin*, 1888, oil on canvas, 24 × 19-11/16 inches, (Fogg, Harvard Art Museums).

This self portrait, where the artist represents himself with monastic severity was painted for Paul Gauguin as part of swap between the artists. The other painting shown in the video above is Paul Gauguin's *Self-Portrait Dedicated to Vincent van Gogh (Les Misérables)*, 1888, oil on canvas. The title is a reference to the heroic fugitive, Jean Valjean, in Victor Hugo's novel *Les Misérables*. Gauguin's painting also contains a portrait of Emile Bernard that was painted not by Gauguin but by Bernard within Gauguin's painting.

The following is a letter by Van Gogh to his brother Theo about the painting exchange with Gauguin dated October 7, 1888:

> My dear Theo,
>
> Many thanks for your letter. How glad I am for Gauguin; I shall not try to find words to tell you – let's be of good heart.
>
> I have just received the portrait of Gauguin by himself and the portrait of Bernard by Bernard and in the background of the portrait of Gauguin there is Bernard's on the wall, and vice versa.
>
> The Gauguin is of course remarkable, but I very much like Bernard's picture. It is just the inner vision of a painter, a few abrupt tones, a few dark lines, but it has the distinction of a real, real Manet.
>
> The Gauguin is more studied, carried further. That, along with what he says in his letter, gave me absolutely the impression of its representing a prisoner. Not a shadow of gaiety. Absolutely nothing of the flesh, but one can confidently put that down to his determination to make a melancholy effect, the flesh in the shadows has gone a dismal blue.

So now at last I have a chance to compare my painting with what the comrades are doing. My portrait, which I am sending to Gauguin in exchange, holds its own, I am sure of that. I have written to Gauguin in reply to his letter that if I might be allowed to stress my own personality in a portrait, I had done so in trying to convey in my portrait not only myself but an impressionist in general, had conceived it as the portrait of a bonze, a simple worshiper of the eternal Buddha.

And when I put Gauguin's conception and my own side by side, mine is as grave, but less despairing. What Gauguin's portrait says to me before all things is that he must not go on like this, he must become again the richer Gauguin of the "Negresses."

I am very glad to have these two portraits, for they finally represent the comrades at this stage; they will not remain like that, they will come back to a more serene life.

And I see clearly that the duty laid upon me is to do everything I can to lessen our poverty.

No good comes the way in this painter's job. I feel that he is more Millet than I, but I am more Diaz then he, and like Diaz I am going to try to please the public, so that a few pennies may come into our community. I have spent more than they, but I do not care a bit now that I see their painting—they have worked in too much poverty to succeed.

Mind you, I have better and more saleable stuff than what I have sent you, and I feel that I can go on doing it. I have confidence in it at last. I know that it will do some people's hearts good to find poetic subjects again, "The Starry Sky," "The Vines in Leaf," "The Furrows," the "Poet's Garden."

So then I believe that it is your duty and mine to demand comparative wealth just because we have very great artists to keep alive. But at the moment you are as fortunate, or at least fortunate in the same way, as Sensier if you have Gauguin and I hope he will be with us heart and soul. There is no hurry, but in any case I think that he will like the house so much as a studio that he will agree to being its head. Give us half a year and see what that will mean.

Bernard has again sent me a collection of ten drawings with a daring poem – the whole is called At the Brothel.

You will soon see these things, but I shall send you the portraits when I have had them to look at for some time.

I hope you will write soon, I am very hard up because of the stretchers and frames that I ordered.

What you told me of Freret gave me pleasure, but I venture to think that I shall do things which will please him better, and you too.

Yesterday I painted a sunset.

Gauguin looks ill and tormented in his portrait!! You wait, that will not last, and it will be very interesting to compare this portrait with the one he will do of himself in six months' time.

Someday you will also see my self-portrait, which I am sending to Gauguin, because he will keep it, I hope.

It is all ashen gray against pale veronese (no yellow). The clothes are this brown coat with a blue border, but I have exaggerated the brown into purple, and the width of the blue borders.

The head is modeled in light colours painted in a thick impasto against the light background with hardly any shadows. Only I have made the eyes *slightly* slanting like the Japanese.

Write me soon and the best of luck. How happy old Gauguin will be.

A good handshake, and thank Freret for the pleasure he has given me. Good-by for now.

Ever yours,

Vincent.

Attributions

CC licensed content, Shared previously

- Van Gogh, Self-Portrait Dedicated to Paul Gauguin. **Authored by**: Dr. Beth Harris and Dr. Steven Zucker. **Provided by**: Khan Academy. **Located at**: https://web.archive.org/web/20141007060250/http://smarthistory.khanacademy.org/van-gogh-self-portrait-dedicated-to-paul-gauguin.html. **License**: *CC BY-NC-SA: Attribution-NonCommercial-ShareAlike*
- Letter from Vincent van Gogh to Theo van Gogh Arles, 7 October 1888. **Authored by**: Vincent Van Gogh. **Provided by**: WebExhibits. **Located at**: http://www.webexhibits.org/vangogh/letter/18/545.htm. **Project**: Van Gogh's Letters: Unabridged and Annotated. **License**: *CC BY-SA: Attribution-ShareAlike*

Van Gogh, The Bedroom

Dr. Beth Harris and Dr. Steven Zucker provide a description, historical perspective, and analysis of Vincent van Gogh's *The Bedroom.*

- https://youtu.be/E1tA9-ypx0g

Vincent van Gogh, *The Bedroom*, 1889, oil on canvas, 29 × 36-5/8 inches (73.6 × 92.3 cm), (Art Institute of Chicago).

External Link
View this painting up close in the Google Art Project: • https://www.google.com/culturalinstitute/asset-viewer/the-bedroom/KwF-AdF1REQl6w?projectId=art-project

Attributions

Van Gogh, Self-Portrait with Bandaged Ear

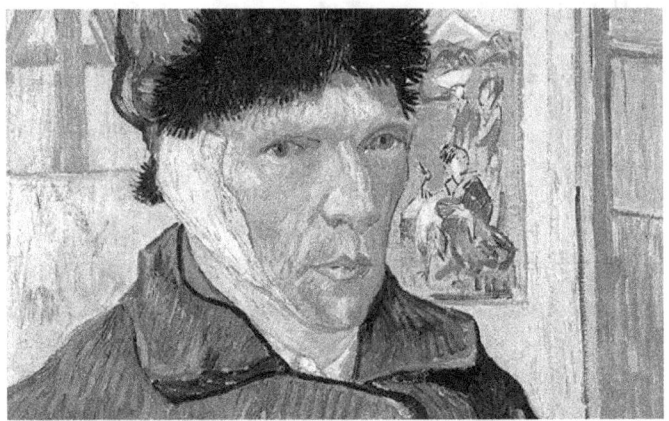

Figure 1. Vincent van Gogh, Self-Portrait with Bandaged Ear (detail), 1889, oil on canvas, 60 × 49cm (Courtauld Galleries, London)

The Unfortunate Man

The following report appeared in the Arles journal *Le Forum Republicain* on December 30, 1888:

> Last Sunday, at 11:30 in the evening, Vincent Vaugogh [sic], a painter of Dutch origin, called at the Brothel No. 1, asked for a woman called Rachel and handed her . . . his ear, saying: "Guard this object with your life." Then he disappeared. When informed of the action, which could only be that of a pitiful madman, the police went the next day to his house and discovered him lying on his bed apparently at the point of death. The unfortunate man has been rushed to hospital.

Accounts of what took place that night vary. Whatever the exact circumstances, though, whatever underlying motivations could have compelled van Gogh to do it, the episode effectively put an end to one of the most famous working relationships in the history of art, as Paul Gauguin boarded the train to Paris the next day.

For nine weeks they had lived together sharing lodgings in the Yellow House, just outside the old town walls of Arles in the South of France, spurring each other on as collaborators and as rivals too. The dream had been to set up "a studio in the South," as van Gogh put it, a community of artists, with himself and Gauguin, the founding fathers, all working in harmony with nature and, as he hoped, with each other.

A Brave Face?

The painting, completed two weeks after the event, is often read as a farewell to that dream. For Steven Naifeh and Gregory White Smith, the most recent biographers of the artist, however, the portrait was first and foremost a plea to van Gogh's doctors.

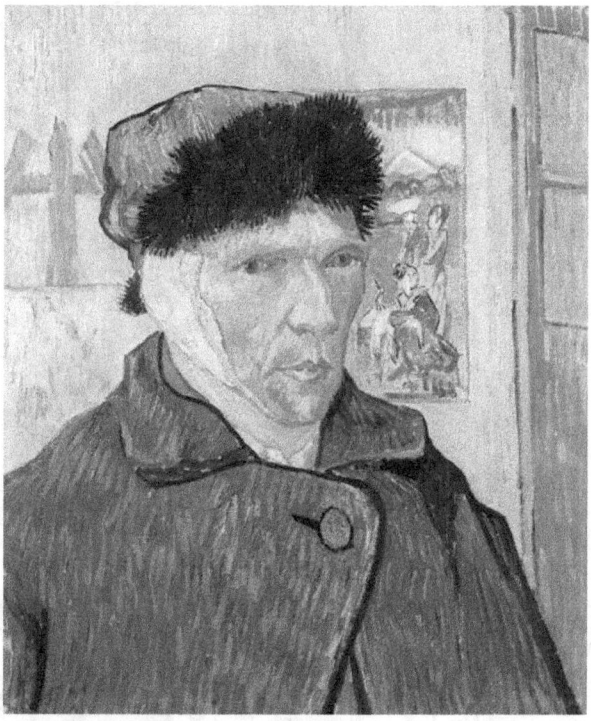

Figure 2. Vincent van Gogh, Self-Portrait with Bandaged Ear, 1889, oil on canvas, 60 × 49cm (Courtauld Galleries, London)

It shows the artist in three-quarter profile standing in a room in the Yellow House wearing a closed coat and a fur cap. His right ear is bandaged. It was in fact his left ear that was bandaged, the painting being a mirror image. To his right is an easel with a canvas on it. Barely visible, a faint outline underneath reveals what looks to be a still-life which appears to have been painted over. The top of the easel has been cropped by the edge of the canvas and the sitter's hat so as to form a fork-like shape. To his left is a blue framed window, and partly obscured by the gaunt ridge of his cheek, a Japanese woodblock print shows two geishas in a landscape with Mount Fuji in the background.

Naifeh and White Smith argue that van Gogh, following his release from hospital, was anxious to persuade his doctors that he was indeed perfectly fit and able to take care of himself and that, despite his momentary lapse, it would not be necessary for them to have him committed, as had been suggested, to one of the local insane asylums; hence the winter coat and hat, to keep warm as they had advised, and with the window ajar still getting that much-needed fresh air into his system. The bandage too, which would have been soaked in camphor, suggests that he both accepts what has happened and is happy, literally, to take his medicine. The same note of stoic optimism, if one wishes to read the painting this way, is also found in the letters to his brother Theo, in which van Gogh, far from abandoning his dream of a "studio in the South," talks of continuing the project, expressing the desire for more artists to come to Arles, even proposing that Gauguin and he could "start afresh."

Yet, of course, whether or not van Gogh was willing to admit to it, the project had most definitely reached its end. And though for a short time he did get to carry on living in the Yellow House, within a few weeks, acting on a petition handed in to the local authorities and signed by 30 of his neighbors, he was forcefully removed and taken to Arles Hospital where he was locked in an isolation cell. In May van Gogh committed himself to the private asylum in Saint-Remy a small town north of Arles and in a little over a year he was dead.

An Obsession with Japanese Art

Though Naifeh and White Smith's argument is convincing, how the artist accounts for himself in his letters and how he expresses himself in paint, are different things. For my own part, what is most interesting about the image is what it reveals about van Gogh's artistic practice and particularly his obsession with Japanese art: "All my work to some extent is based on Japanese art," he wrote in July, 1888.

Three years earlier, while in the port city of Antwerp in Belgium, he would wander through the markets there where woodblock prints of the Ukiyo-e school, the so-called "artists of the floating world" were readily available and could be bought for just a few centimes. These first glimpses into the art of Japan came at a pivotal moment in the artist's career: half way between his native Holland where he had schooled himself in the Realist tradition of artists such as Jozef Israëls, with his dark, earthy palette and sympathy for the rural poor, and Paris where he would encounter the colorful urbanity of the Impressionists.

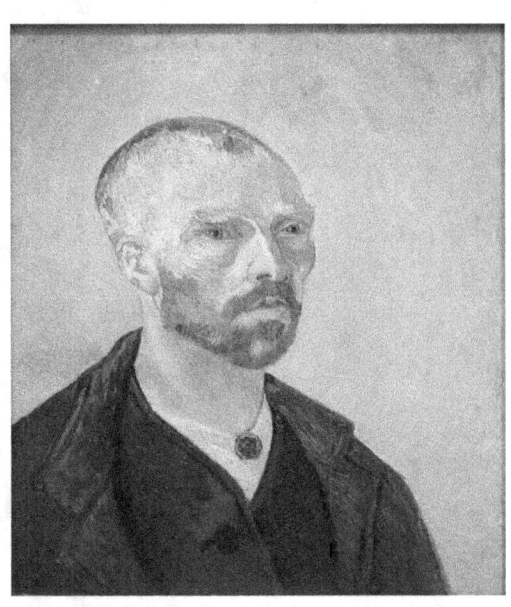

Figure 3. Vincent van Gogh, Self-Portrait (Dedicated to Gauguin), 1888, 65 × 52 cm (Fogg Art Museum, Cambridge)

For van Gogh, the artists of Japan offered the perfect meeting-point of theory and practice. The most famous of them was Hokusai, "the Dickens of Japan," who shared the Dutchman's passion for depicting the lives of the poor. It was this compassionate dimension of Japanese art that van Gogh hoped to bring to Impressionism, a movement that—by the time he arrived in Paris in 1886—had already absorbed the visual inventiveness of the Ukiyo-e school.

As time went on, the links went still further. In his two-year sojourn in Paris, the city of strangers, it was fellowship above all else that he yearned for, and so he came to imagine the Impressionists, among whose ranks he claimed to belong, to be as he imagined the Japanese, a united body of artists, sharing the same goals and ideals. It was this that prompted the journey south. On arriving in Arles he wrote to his brother, declaring his hope that "other artists will rise up in this lively country and do for it what the Japanese have done for theirs." And again, while decorating his new house with paintings of sunflowers, he wrote to Theo: "Come now, isn't it almost a true religion which the simple Japanese teach us, who live in nature as though they themselves were flowers."

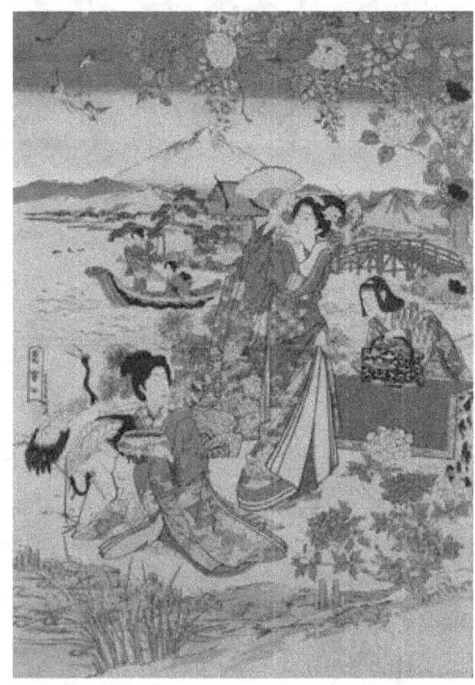

Figure 4. Sato Torakiyo (publisher), Geishas in a Landscape, c 1870–80, Coloured woodblock print, 60 × 43cm, Courtauld Museum, London

It was in Arles that he read Pierre Loti's novel *Madame Chrysanthème*, best known today as the literary source for Puccini's opera *Madame Butterfly*. While its self-sacrificing heroine worked her graceful way into van Gogh Orientalist fantasies, Loti's description of Buddhist priests inspired his own *Self-Portrait (Dedicated to Paul Gauguin)*, a painting that draws out the direction he hoped the two artists would follow.

How very different *Self-Portrait with Bandaged Ear* is to this earlier portrait. With its formal setting; the repeated triangles, for example, in the form of his coat, the top of the easel and the view offered of Mount Fuji itself, lending the painting it's aspirational quality, its upward thrust. And yet the dominant feeling is surely conveyed by the internal frames: the window, the canvas and print, each of which appears condensed and somewhat forced into the painting, as though hemming the sitter in.

The Japanese print as van Gogh painted it in *Self-Portrait with Bandaged Ear* differs from the original. Comparing them we see how van Gogh shifted the composition to the right, deliberately discarding one of the figures in favour of the heron, whose razor-sharp beak rears up as if to stab at the artist's ear. Opposite it, the canvas squeezed in to the left with its ghostly imprint of flowers surmounted by the fork of the easel sets up a formally satisfying but psychologically unsettling parallel. Is there a hint in all this, albeit unconsciously expressed, that the dream of an artist's community in Arles has turned against him?

Perhaps, but then of course there is always van Gogh's color—the joyous application of pigment onto canvas, the glorious use of impasto, thick and swift; that fabulous hatching technique, in places evoking the textures it depicts, the weave of the coat, the threads of the bandage, the fur of the hat. And note the tonal array of strokes that make up the face: violet, green, red, brown, orange, straw yellow; the blacks centred in those piercing pupils.

A yearning to be proved sane or a heartfelt cry of anguish, whatever we may read in the image about van Gogh the man, from a purely art historical point of view, it is here in his brushwork and in his palette that one discovers the source of André Derain's "deliberate disharmonies." How fitting then that it was while on holiday in the South of France, a favourite haunt of that early Modernist movement to which he belonged—the Fauves—that Derain painted his friend and fellow artist Matisse; enough perhaps to say that Van Gogh's hope and prediction that "other artists will rise up in this lively country" was not so wildly off the mark after all.

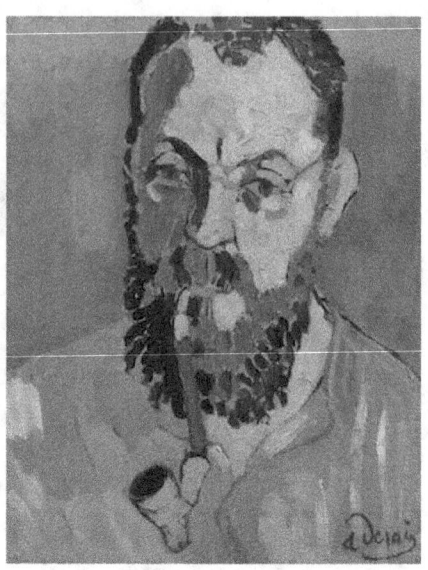

Figure 5. André Derain, Henri Matisse, 1905, oil on canvas, 71 × 60cm (Tate Modern, London)

Attributions

CC licensed content, Shared previously

- Van Gogh's Self-Portrait with Bandaged Ear. **Authored by**: Ben Pollitt. **Provided by**: Khan Academy. **Located at**: https://web.archive.org/web/20141007161958/http://smarthistory.khanacademy.org/van-goghs-self-portrait-with-bandaged-ear.html. **License**: *CC BY-NC-SA: Attribution-NonCommercial-ShareAlike*

Cezanne, Basket of Apples

In David's era, still life was considered the least important subject. Only the most minor artists bothered with what was then seen as the most purely decorative and trivial type of painting. The hierarchy of subjects went roughly like this: most important—historical & religious themes (often very large scale); important—portraiture (usually of moderate scale), less important—landscape & genre (themes of common life, usually of modest scale); least important—still life (small).

There had been one significant historical exception. In the seventeenth century in Northern Europe and particularly in the Netherlands, still life blossomed. But this period was brief and had little impact in France other than in the work of Chardin. So why would Cézanne turn so often to this discredited subject? Actually, it was the very fact that still life was so neglected that seems to have attracted Cézanne to it. So outmoded was the iconography (symbolic forms and references) in still life that this rather hopeless subject was freed of virtually all convention. Here was a subject that offered extraordinary freedom, a blank slate that gave Cézanne the opportunity to invent meaning unfettered by tradition. By the way, Cézanne would almost single-handedly revive the subject of still life and he made it an important subject for Picasso, Matisse, and others in the twentieth century.

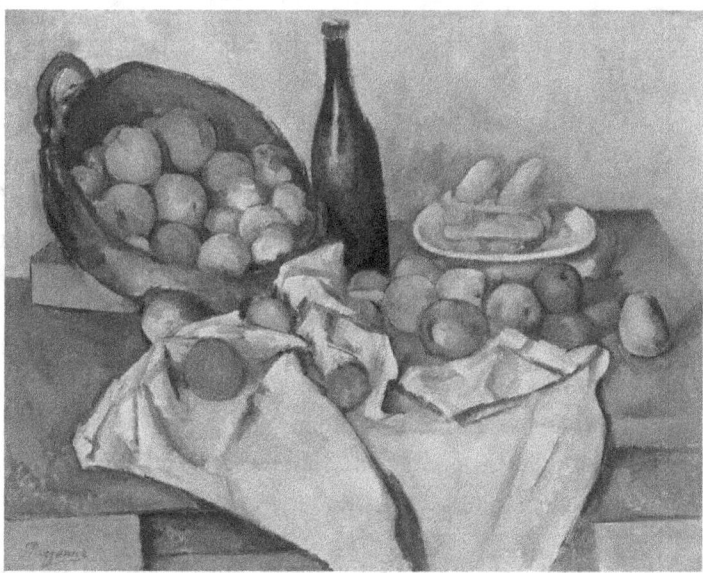

Figure 1. Paul Cézanne, The Basket of Apples, oil on canvas, 1893
(Art Institute of Chicago)

The image above looks simple enough, a wine bottle, a basket of fruit tipped up to expose a bounty of fruit inside, a plate of what are perhaps stacked cookies or rolls, and a tablecloth both gathered and draped. Nothing remarkable, at least not until one begins to notice the odd errors in drawing. Look, for instance, at the lines that represent the close and far edge of the table. I remember an old student of mine, in a class several years back, looking at this a shouting out, "I would never hire him as a carpenter!" What she had noticed was the odd stepping of a line that we expect to be straight.

But that is not all that is wrong. The table seems to be too steeply tipped at the left, so much so that the fruit is in danger of rolling off it. Also, the bottle looks tipsy and the cookies are very odd indeed. The cookies stacked below the top layer seem as if they are viewed from the side, but at the same moment, the two on top seem to pop upward as if we were looking down at them. This is a key to understanding the questions that we've raised about Cézanne's pictures so far.

Like Edouard Manet, from whom he borrowed so much, Cézanne was prompted to rethink the value of the various illusionistic techniques that he had inherited from the masters of the Renaissance and Baroque eras. This was due in part to the growing impact of photography and its transformation of modern representation. While Claude Monet borrowed from the camera the fragmenting of time, Cézanne, ever at odds with Monet, saw this mechanized segmenting of time as artificial and at odds with the preception of the human eye. By Cézanne's era, the camera did shatter time into tiny fragments as do modern cameras that can easily be set so that the shutter is open to light for only 1/1000 of a second.

Cézanne pushed this distinction between the vision of the camera and of human vision even further. He reasoned that the same issues applied to the illusionism of the old masters, of Raphael, Leonardo, Caravaggio, etc. For instance, think about how linear perspective works. Since the Early Renaissance, constructing the illusion of space required that the artist remain frozen in a single point in space in order maintain consistent recession among all receding orthogonals. This frozen vantage point belongs to both the artist and then the viewer. But is it a full description of the the experience of human sight? Cézanne's still life suggests that it is not.

If a Renaissance painter set out to render Cézanne's still life objects (not that they would, mind you), that artist would have placed himself in a specific point before the table and taken great pains to render the collection of tabletop objects only from that original perspective. Every orthoganol line would remain consistant (and straight). But this is clearly not what Cézanne had in mind. His perspectives seems jumbled. When we first look carefully, it may appear as if he was simply unable to draw, but if you spend more time, it may occur to you that Cézanne is, in fact, drawing carefully, although according to a new set of rules.

Seemingly simple, Cézanne's concern with representing the true experience of sight had enormous implications for twentieth century visual culture. Cézanne realized that unlike the fairly simple and static Renaissance vision of space, people actually see in a fashion that is more complex, we see through both time and space. In other words, we move as we see. In contemporary terms, one might say that human vision is less like the frozen vision of a still camera and more like the continuous vision of a video camera. Also, Cézanne faced an additional problem, the static nature of the canvas.

So very tentatively, he began the purposeful destruction of the unified image. Let me give you an example. Look again at the cookies, or whatever they are, stacked upon the plate in the upper right. Is it possible that the gentle disagreements that we have noted result from the representation of two slightly different view points? These are not large ruptures, but rather, they suggest careful and tentative discovery. It is as if Cézanne had simply depicted the bottom cookies as he looked across at them and then as he looked more slightly down at the top cookies after shifting his weight to his forward leg. Furthermore, I'm not sure that he was all that proud of these breaks that allow for more than a single perspective. Look, for instance, at the points where the table must break to express these multiple perspectives and you will notice that they are each hidden from view. Nevertheless, in doing this, Cézanne changed the direction of painting.

Cézanne pushes these issues even further in his painting of 1895, *Still Life with Plaster Cupid* (at the Courtauld Gallery, London). Here Cézanne's discoveries enter into the realm of Cartesian philosophy.

- http://www.wikiart.org/en/paul-cezanne/still-life-with-plaster-cupid-1895

Attributions

CC licensed content, Shared previously

- Cezanne, The Basket of Apples. **Provided by**: Khan Academy. **Located at**: https://web.archive.org/web/20141006205940/ http://smarthistory.khanacademy.org/still-life-with-basket-of-apples.html. **License**: *CC BY-NC-SA: Attribution-NonCommercial-ShareAlike*

Cezanne, The Large Bathers

Dr. Beth Harris and Dr. Steven Zucker provide a description, historical perspective, and analysis of Cézanne's *The Large Bathers*.

- https://youtu.be/YFtf-xA7_oM

Paul Cézanne, *The Large Bathers*, 1906, oil on canvas, 82-7/8 × 98-3/4 inches (210.5 × 250.8 cm), (Philadelphia Museum of Art).

Attributions

CC licensed content, Shared previously

Gauguin, Vision After the Sermon

Dr. Beth Harris and Dr. Steven Zucker provide a description, historical perspective, and analysis of Paul Gauguin's *Vision after the Sermon*, or *Jacob Wrestling with the Angel*.

- https://youtu.be/y5lhKvKvWPg

Paul Gauguin, *Vision after the Sermon*, or *Jacob Wrestling with the Angel*, 1888, oil on canvas, 2′ 4 3/4″ × 3′ 1/2″ (National Gallery of Scotland, Edinburgh)

Attributions

CC licensed content, Shared previously

Gauguin, Spirit of the Dead Watching

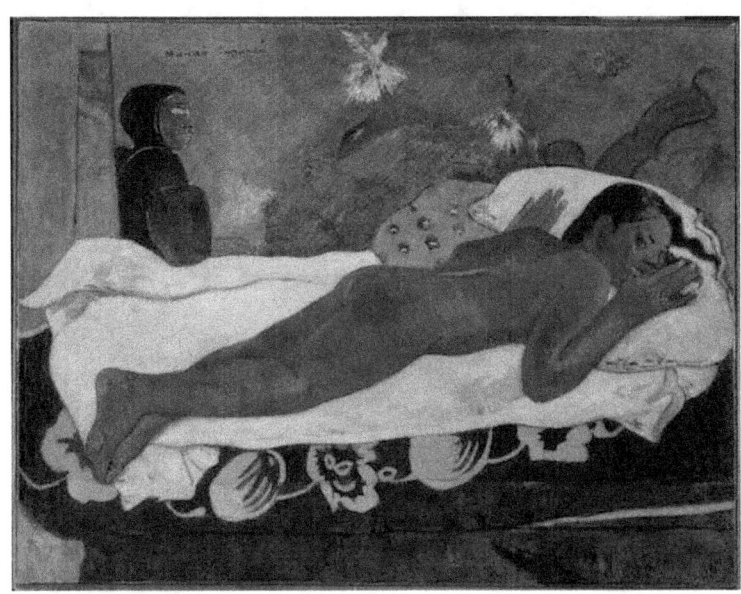

Figure 1. Paul Gauguin, Spirit of the Dead Watching, 1892, oil on burlap mounted on canvas, 45 11/16 × 53 × 5 1/4 inches 116.05 × 134.62 × 13.34 cm (Albright-Knox Art Gallery)

Be Mysterious

"Soyez mysterieuses"—be mysterious—Gauguin said. Perhaps he had this command in mind when he produced the most significant painting—by his own reckoning—to come out of his first stay in Tahiti, *The Spirit of the Dead Watching*. Few critics would doubt the importance of this work. Its mysteriousness and openness to interpretation has secured for it a position among Gauguin's key works.

Gauguin made his first visit to Tahiti (a French colony) in March 1891, returning to Paris in May 1893. It was a hugely productive period in Gauguin's career. "In the two years I have spent here," he wrote, "with only a few months lost, I have produced sixty-six more or less fine canvases and a number of ultra-primitive sculptures. That is enough for any one man."

A Background of Terror

To herald his return to Europe and also to rescue his family from penury, with the help of his Danish wife, Mette, Gauguin organized an exhibition of his work in Copenhagen. Among the nine canvases he sent from Tahiti was *The Spirit of the Dead Watching*, carrying with it an asking price—the most expensive in the sale—of between 1,500 and 2,000 francs. Clearly highly prized by Gauguin, the best of two years' worth of "fine" canvases, the painting depicts an adolescent girl (the model was Gauguin's Tahitian girlfriend Tehura, who was only fourteen years old), lying belly down on a bed, her face staring out at the viewer with a fearful expression. The bed is covered with a blue pareo (a wraparound skirt worn by Tahitians) and a light chrome-yellow sheet. Behind the bed, silhouetted and in profile, a woman watches over the child.

Gauguin created a haunting, supernatural quality by exploiting what he considered to be the emotional potential of color. When describing the painting to Mette, he points out how the shades of purple on the wall create "a background of terror" and how the sheet "must be yellow, because, in this colour, it arouses something unexpected for the spectator." Using colors to arouse feelings was very much in line with the work of other Post-Impressionist artists, such as Gauguin's contemporary and friend, Vincent van Gogh.

The Spirit of the Dead

Aside from color, the composition is itself unsettling, particularly the relationship between the girl and the old woman behind her whose simplified form and disproportionate scale suggest Tahitian statuary or tiki. If she is a carved statue of wood, though, what or who does it signify? If not, then is she real or otherworldly? Is this the spirit of the dead watching that the title refers to? And if she is imagined, then by whom? Is all that surrounds the girl the conjurings of her own haunted imagination? Or is it what she looks out at—the space we ourselves inhabit—that is the source of her terror? Could it be, then, that we are the spirit of the dead watching? The Tahitian language certainly allows for such ambiguities. The expression, manoa tupapau means either watching the spirit of the dead or the spirit of the dead watching.

Other formal features of the painting seem to enhance this ambivalence. Notice, for example, the complex vantage point we hold. Our gaze is level with the luminous eyes of the old woman, while at the same time, we look down at the figure of the young woman.

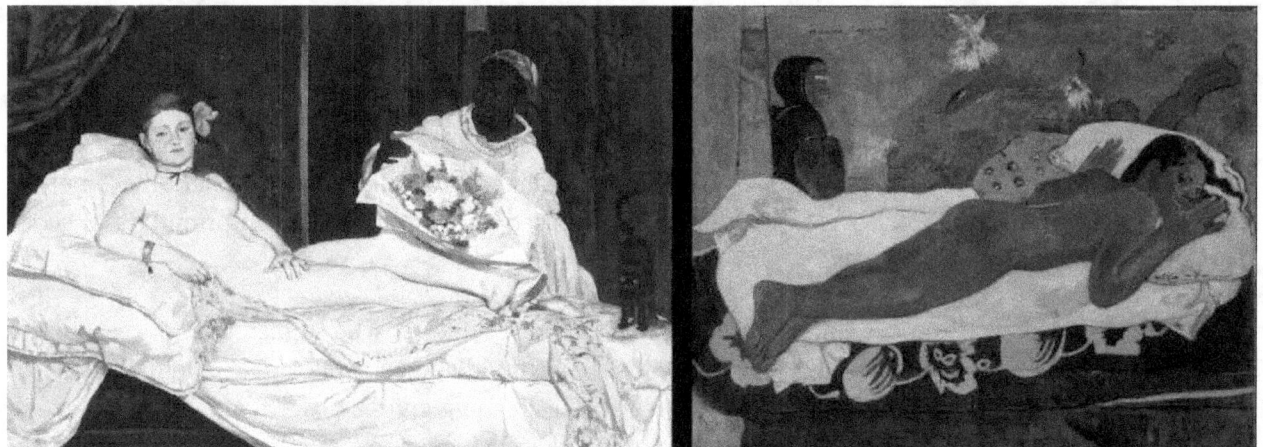

Figure 2. Manet, Olympia, 1863 (left) and Gauguin, Spirit of the Dead Watching, 1892 (right). Click for a larger view.

A Slightly Indecent Study of a Nude

We can also consider this painting within the tradition of the female nude and recall Manet's *Olympia* (1865). Manet's work provided a template for younger artists, one that rejected long-established conventions in the representation of the nude and challenged the moral values of the bourgeoisie. Gauguin, for one, admired *Olympia* enough to have produced a copy of it in 1891.

He was keen to shock the bourgeoisie and certainly his own nude in *The Spirit of the Dead Watching*—"a slightly indecent study" as he described it—is in many ways as radical as Manet's. The body is awkwardly positioned and disproportionate. The feet overhang the bed and the hands are larger than the feet. And most shocking of all, is the age of the model.

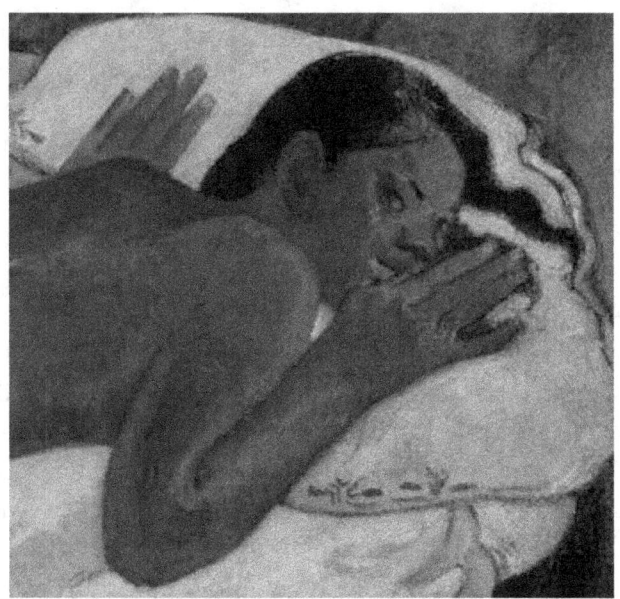

Figure 3. Spirit of the Dead Watching, 1892 (detail)

Equally disturbing is the fear she exhibits. Gauguin described this in letters to his wife, Mette. Having walked that day to a neighboring village, Gauguin didn't return to his house until the early morning. On entering, he found Tehura naked on the bed staring at him in terror. The reason for her fear, according to Gauguin, was that Tehura believed in tupapaus, the spirits of the dead who in Tahitian mythology inhabit the interior of the island and whose presence illuminates the forest at night.

Gauguin was skeptical about this belief, holding that these phosphorescent night glows that Tahitians took for spirits were in fact a type of fungus that grows on dead trees. Either way, for Tehura, to walk through the interior after sundown risked disturbing the tupapaus with potentially disastrous consequences; hence her fear and so too those glimmering spectral forms that feature in the background of the painting and that Gauguin stated stood for the tupapaus themselves.

Critical Readings

Given his construction of Tahitian culture as "primitive," Gauguin's version of these events has been scrutinized by art historians who have cast doubt on whether Tehura would have actually held these beliefs (since she was a practicing Christian). Gauguin is thus accused of projecting his own primitivist preconceptions onto his subject.

Another critique comes from the art historian, Nancy Mowll Mathews, who argues that it was not the spirits that Tehura was frightened of, but Gauguin himself, the middle-aged, white, male colonialist against whom, as a sexual predator, she had little power to resist. This reading gives a disturbing twist to the image with Gauguin taking sadistic pleasure in depicting the fear that he himself caused. It's worth noting that in Gauguin's account, seeing her in this state moved him to declare that she never looked so beautiful, and that he was drawn to comfort her, promising never to leave her again.

The critic Stephen Eisenman takes a different line of argument, describing the painting as "an assault upon the tradition of the European nude." Of particular interest for Eisenman is the viewer's uncertainty regarding the sex of the figure, the large hands and narrow hips suggesting a male rather than a female form. "The posture and anatomy of Tehura, which emphasizes her boyishness, is derived from various androgynous and hermaphroditic prototypes," Eisenman argues, citing the Borghese Hermaphrodite as one of them. Seen in this light, the painting, far from being an image of patriarchal dominion over the colonized body, is instead a subversive attack on that patriarchy and all the gendered values that it maintains.

However we choose to look at the painting, it provokes endless questioning, in which we are forced to encounter the other, whether that be in terms of age, faith, gender, spirituality, ethnicity, sexuality, culture, whatever you will, it is a painting that explores the heterogeneous nature of identity, asking profound questions as to who and what we are.

Attributions

Toulouse-Lautrec, At the Moulin Rouge

Dr. Beth Harris and Dr. Steven Zucker provide a description, historical perspective, and analysis of Henri de Toulouse-Lautrec's *At the Moulin Rouge*.

- https://youtu.be/XLcbGHNFcpM

Henri de Toulouse-Lautrec, *At the Moulin Rouge*, 1893-95, oil on canvas, 48-1/2 × 55-1/2 inches (123 × 141 cm), (Art Institute of Chicago).

External Link

View this painting up close in the Google Art Project:

- https://www.google.com/culturalinstitute/asset-viewer/at-the-moulin-rouge/pAGg8GwiH-leSkA?projectId=art-project

---

Attributions

Gaudi, Sagrada Familia

Dr. Beth Harris and Dr. Steven Zucker provide a description, historical perspective, and analysis of the Church of the Sagrada Família.

- https://youtu.be/SMqERP-J2tQ

Antoni Gaudí, Church of the Sagrada Família or Basílica i Temple Expiatori de la Sagrada Família Basilica, 1882– (consecrated 2010, but still under construction), Barcelona, Spain

Although Gaudí was influenced by John Ruskin's analysis of the Gothic early in his career, he sought an authentic Catalan style at a time, the late 19th century, when this region was experiencing a resurgence of cultural and political pride. Ruskin, an English critic, rejected ancient classical forms in favor of the Gothic's expressive, even grotesesque qualities. This interest in the value of medieval architecture resulted in Gaudi being put in charge of the design of Sagrada Família (Sacred Family) shortly after construction had begun.

Gaudí was a deeply religious Catholic whose ecstatic and brilliantly complex fantasies of organic geometry are given concrete form throughout the church. Historians have identified numerous influences especially within the northeast façade, the only part of the church he directly supervised (the remainder of the church, including three of the southwest trancept's four spires are based on his design but were completed after Gaudí's death in 1926), these include African mud architecture, Gothic, Expressionist, of course a varient of Art Nouveau that emphasizes marine forms.

The iconographic and structural programs of the church are complex but its plan is based on the traditional basilica cruciform found in nearly all medieval cathedrals. However, unlike many these churches, Sagrada Familia is not built on an east-west axis. Instead, the church follows the diagonal orientation that defines so much of Barcelona, placing the church on a southeast-nothwest axis.

- **The Glory Façade (southeast):** This will eventually be church's main façade and entrance. As with the transcept entrances, it holds a triple portal dedicated to charity, faith, and hope. The façade itself is dedicated to mankind in relation to the divine order.

- **The Passion Façade (southwest):** Dedicated to the Passion of Christ, its four existing belltowers are between 98 and 112 meters tall and are dedicated to the apostles James the Lesser, Bartholomew, Thomas and Philip (left to right). Josep Maria Subirachs is responsible for the façade sculpture.

- **The Nativity Façade (northeast):** Depicts the birth of Christ and is the only façade to be completed during Gaudi's lifetime. Its four existing belltowers are between 98 and 112 meters tall and are dedicated to the saints Barnabas, Jude, Simon and Matthew (left to right).

Ten additional belltowers (98–112 meters high) are planned though these will be overwhelmed by six towers that will be significantly taller. Four of these towers will be dedicated to the Evangelists, one to the Virgin Mary, and the grandest, rising to 170 meters, to Jesus Christ.

Attributions

CC licensed content, Shared previously

- Gaudi, Sagrada Familia. **Provided by**: Khan Academy. **Located at**: https://web.archive.org/web/20141006065628/http://smarthistory.khanacademy.org/gaudi-sagrada-familia.html. **License**: *CC BY-NC-SA: Attribution-NonCommercial-ShareAlike*

Fin-de-siecle Explained

Click on the link below to view the article "Fin de siècle" from the Art History portion of About.com. This page will help you to define the term *fin de siècle*—a phrase borrowed into English from French—and understand it in the context of art history.

- "Fin de siècle":
    - http://arthistory.about.com/od/glossary/g/findesiecle.htm

Klimt, The Kiss

Dr. Beth Harris and Dr. Steven Zucker provide a description, historical perspective, and analysis of Gustav Klimt's *The Kiss*.

- https://youtu.be/BRUOACBkFRg

Gustav Klimt, *The Kiss*, 1907–8, oil and gold leaf on canvas, 180 × 180 cm, (Österreichische Galerie Belvedere, Vienna).

External Link
View this painting up close in the Google Art Project: • https://www.google.com/culturalinstitute/asset-viewer/the-kiss/HQGxUutM_F6ZGg?projectId=art-project

Munch, The Storm

Dr. Beth Harris and Dr. Steven Zucker provide a description, historical perspective, and analysis of Edvard Munch's *The Storm*.

- https://youtu.be/653ZKHd_PYo

Edvard Munch, *The Storm*, 1893, oil on canvas, 36 1/8 × 51 1/2″ (91.8 × 130.8 cm), (MoMA).

Attributions

CC licensed content, Shared previously

Rodin, Gates of Hell

When the building that was earlier on what is now the site of the Musée d'Orsay in Paris, was destroyed by fire during the Commune in 1871, plans were drawn up to replace it with a museum of decorative arts. Rodin won the competition to design a great set of doors for its entry way. Although the museum was never built, Rodin continued to work on the doors. They became an ongoing project; a grand stage for his sculptural ideas. It's fitting that the plaster of this great unfinished sculpture, *The Gates of Hell*, is now on display at the d'Orsay, the former railway terminal that was built on this site instead of the museum of decorative arts and that, by lovely coincidence, was converted into one of the world's great art museums.

Dr. Beth Harris and Dr. Steven Zucker provide a description, historical perspective, and analysis of Rodin's *The Gates of Hell*.

- https://youtu.be/TgLTzYXg530

Auguste Rodin, *The Gates of Hell*, 1880–1917, plaster (Musée d'Orsay, Paris)

Attributions

CC licensed content, Shared previously

Emanuel Leutze, Washington Crossing the Delaware

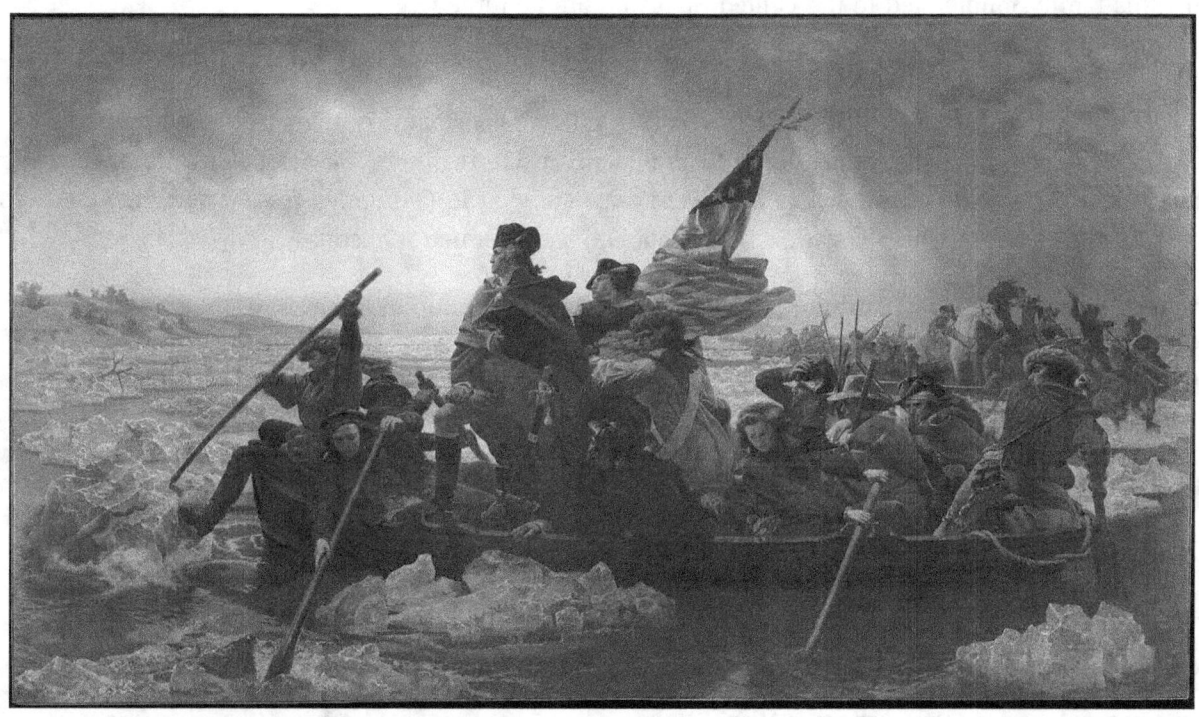

Figure 1. Emanuel Leutze, Washington Crossing the Delaware, 1851, oil on canvas, 149 × 255 inches / 378.5 × 647.7 cm (Metropolitan Museum of Art)

An American Icon (Made in Germany)

Washington Crossing the Delaware is one of the most recoginizable images in the history of American art. You might be surprised, however, to learn that it was not painted by an American artist at work in the United States, but was instead completed by Emanuel Leutze, an artist born in Germany, and that it was painted in Düsseldorf during the middle of the nineteenth century.

Leutze painted two versions of this painting. He began the first in 1849 immediately following the failure of Germany's own revolution. This initial canvas was eventually destroyed during an Allied bombing raid in World War II. The artist began the second version of *Washington Crossing the Delaware* in 1850. This later painting was transported to New York where it was exhibited in a gallery in October 1851. Two years later, Marshall O. Roberts, a wealthy capitalist, purchased the work for the then-staggering price of $10,000. It was donated to the Metropolitan Museum of Art in 1897. It remained there until 1950 when long held curatorial concerns about its bombastic, crowd-pleasing qualities led the museum to send it to Dallas and eventually to a site near the actual river crossing. The painting returned to New York in 1970.

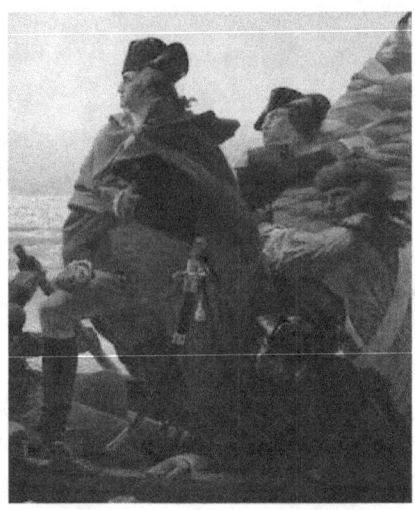

Figure 2. *Washington Crossing the Delaware (detail)*

Although Emanuel Leutze was born in Schwäbisch Gmünd, Germany, his family immigrated to the United States before he turned ten years of age. His first art instruction came in 1834 when he studied drawing and portraiture with John Rubens Smith, a London-born artist who worked in the United States during the first half of the 19th Century. Wealthy Philadelphian patrons recognized Leutze's talent and sponsored the young artist to study at the Königliche Kunstacademie in Düsseldorf. While there, Leutze came to know many American artists who were then studying in Germany. These artists included Worthington Whittredge, Albert Bierstadt, Charles Wilmar, and Eastman Johnson.

Although he was active in portraiture, Leutze's fame today rests upon his history paintings, and among these, *Washington Crossing the Delaware* is the most recognizable and ambitious. It is, in one word, *colossal*, both in scale and patriotic zeal.

Brilliance and Desperation on a Vast Scale

Little can prepare a viewer for the experience of standing before a painting that measures more than 12 × 21 feet. The monumental scale of the composition is matched by the importance of the historical event Leutze painted. Without doubt, Leutze took his subject from one of the turning points in the American Revolutionary War.

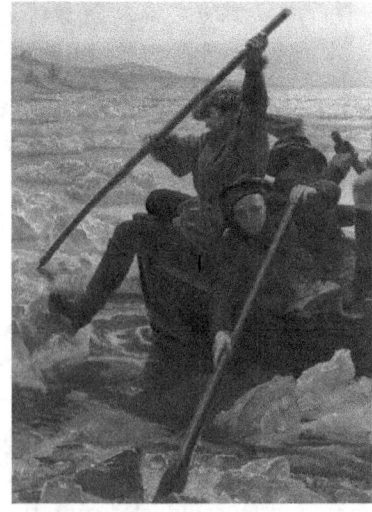

The Colonial cause appeared exceptionally bleak as the year 1776 came to a close. In a military move that navigated the fine line between brilliance and desperation, George Washington led the Colonial army across the Delaware River shortly after nightfall on 25 December in order to attack the Hessian encampment outside Trenton, New Jersey. Washington and his army achieved an unprecedented tactical surprise and delivered a much-needed military and moral victory. Washington's army killed 22 Hessian soldiers, wounded 98 more, and captured more than 1,000 (Hessians were Germans soldiers hired by the

Figure 3. *Washington Crossing the Delaware (detail)*

British Empire). The Colonial Army had less than ten combined dead and wounded soldiers. After many military setbacks in the North, Washington's bold move on Christmas night 1776 helped provide a sense of hope for the Colonial cause.

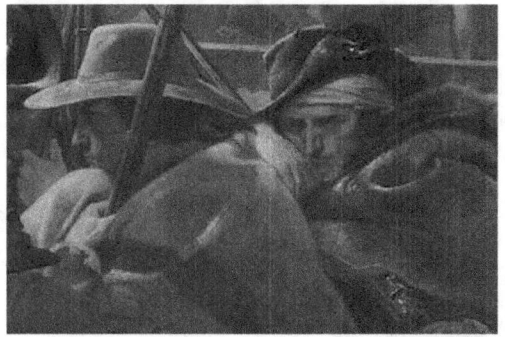

Figure 4. Washington Crossing the Delaware (detail)

In addition to General Washington, Leutze has filled the boat with a variety of 'types' of soldiers. Washington and his two officers are distinguished by their blue coats, the trademark attire of a Continental officer.

The remaining nine men appear to be members of the militia. Three men row at the bow of the boat. One is an African American, another wears the checkerboard bonnet of a Scotsman, and the third wears a coonskin cap.

Two farmers, distinguished by their broad-brimmed hats, huddle against the frigid cold in the middle of the boat, while the man at the stern wears the moccasins, pants, and hat of a Native American. This collection of people suggests the all-inclusive nature of the Colonial cause in the American Revolutionary War.

Poetic License

Despite Leutze's interest in history, there is little historical accuracy to be found within the painting. First, the "Stars and Stripes" flag shown in the painting was not in use until September 1777, and the size of the boat is far too small to accommodate the twelve men who occupy it.

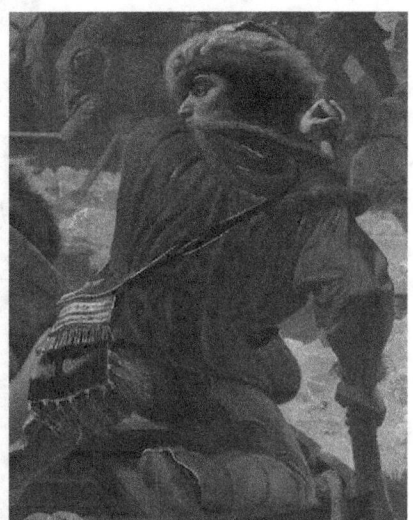

Figure 5. Washington Crossing the Delaware (detail)

And although this event happened in the middle of the night, Leutze shows the crossing occurring at the break of dawn. Rather than depict the Delaware River, a waterway that was rather narrow where Washington and the Continental Army crossed, Leutze paints what appears to be a river with the breadth and ice formation of the Rhine. Finally, and perhaps most interestingly, Leuzte paints Washington standing upright, an unlikely and precarious posture for anyone in a short-walled rowboat.

It is clear then that *Washington Crossing the Delaware*'s strength is not in the correct rendering of an historical event. Leutze's primary goal was to create a work of art that deliberately glorified General Washington, the Colonial-American cause, and commemorated a military action of particular significance. In doing so, Leutze created one of the most iconic images in the history of American art.

Eakins, The Gross Clinic

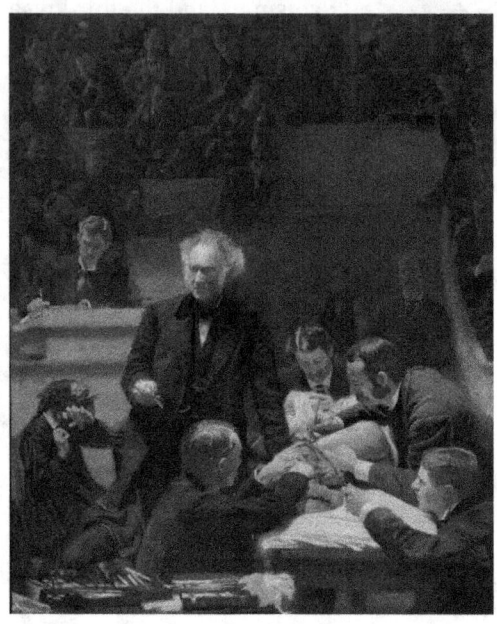

Figure 1. Thomas Eakins, The Gross Clinic, 1875, oil on canvas (Philadelphia Museum of Art & the Pennsylvania Academy of Fine Arts).

Thomas Eakins's deep connection to his birthplace remained a theme throughout his career. Perhaps his most well-known and ambitious work for the city of Philadelphia was *The Gross Clinic;* a painting completed in 1875, that spotlights the local physician Samuel David Gross. The scene depicts Gross overseeing a surgery and lecturing to a class of medical students—evoking Rembrandt's art historical precedent *The Anatomy Lesson of Dr. Tulp* (1636). Much like Rembrandt's version, *The Gross Clinic* documents medical sanitary procedures of its time, but the painting's real focus are living figures. Always a portraitist, Eakins calculated the work as a visual record of all the individuals present in the medical amphitheater. It is not solely a portrait of Dr. Gross; in addition to including the students and the assistants, Eakins inserted his own likeness among the audience (one might consider Eakins the Alfred Hitchcock of nineteenth-century American painting). The core of the work is still Dr. Gross, however, as light and composition conspire to attract the eye to the esteemed lecturer.

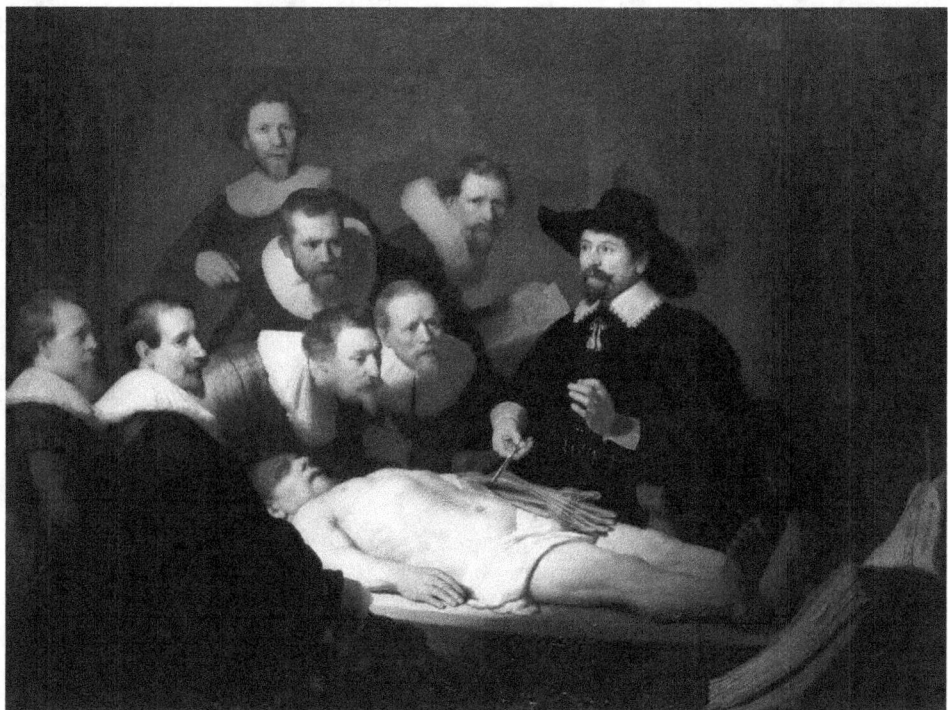

Figure 2. Rembrandt, The Anatomy Lesson of Dr. Tulp, 1636

Completed for the Centennial Exposition, Eakins intended *The Gross Clinic* as a statement of his artistic skill and as a way in which to affirm himself as a hero of Philadelphia. Though the work was rejected, the tactic was overall a success. While some critics lashed out against its gruesome subject matter, seemingly vulgar treatment, and inherent melodrama (note the near-swooning, hysterical woman in the left middle ground), viewers were nonetheless captivated by the work's theatricality. Through his mastery of rendering convincing volume, individual representation, and psychological intensity, Eakins showcases his academic training and—in a style that has been dubbed "scientific realism"—reveals an uncompromising desire to portray honest details of form, depth, and proportion. He was obsessed with accuracy, and was known to project photographs onto canvases in order to laboriously trace figures though also to shift objects for a more harmoniously composed scene.

After *The Gross Clinic's* exhibition at the U.S. Army Post Hospital—in a first-aid room meant to introduce viewers to modern medical paraphernalia—the Jefferson Medical College (where Eakins himself had taken anatomy classes) purchased the painting. A reproduction now hangs in the school, which was forced to sell the original in 2006. The work was considered so central to the history of Philadelphia, however, that the city's two major art museums successfully rallied support to keep the tour de force in town with an ambitious fundraising effort that proved the work's enduring value and underscored the fact that cultural artifacts can ignite complex debates.

In closing, it should be noted that *The Gross Clinic* is not the only such medical scene Eakins produced. He later returned to the same popular formula to honor the surgeon David Hayes Agnew in a similarly composed (and equally controversial) work entitled *The Agnew Clinic*(1889), also on display at the Philadelphia Museum of Art.

Attributions

- Eakins's The Gross Clinic. **Authored by:** Meg Floryan. **Provided by:** Khan Academy. **Located at:** https://web.archive.org/web/20141007052145/http://smarthistory.khanacademy.org/eakins-the-gross-clinic.html. **License:** *CC BY-NC-SA: Attribution-NonCommercial-ShareAlike*

Homer, The Life Line

Dr. Beth Harris and Dr. Steven Zucker provide a description, historical perspective, and analysis of Winslow Homer's The Life Line.

- https://youtu.be/WV3MXLAfIi4

Winslow Homer, *The Life Line*, 1884, oil on canvas, 28-5/8 × 44-3/4 inches (72.7 × 113.7 cm), (Philadelphia Museum of Art).

External Link

View this painting up close in the Google Art Project:

- https://www.google.com/culturalinstitute/asset-viewer/the-life-line/xQE9eAXWkRGPUQ?projectId=art-project

---

Attributions

John Singer Sargent, Madame X

A Controversial Beauty

Madame X is perhaps Sargent's most infamous painting. When it debuted at the Paris Salon of 1884, critics lashed out at the artist for what they deemed a scandalous, immoral image. While the title omitted the sitter's name, the public immediately recognized her as the notorious Parisian beauty Virginie Gautreau. The gown's plunging neckline was considered too provocative for the times, and its right strap—which originally was shown to have slipped off the shoulder—ultimately led to Sargent repainting it in its proper position to appease outraged viewers and Gautreau's own family.

Madame X mixes the Gilded Age penchant for portraying status and wealth in portraiture with a daring seductive aesthetic. For all that it shocked onlookers, however, much of its details were based in older classical traditions: Madame Gautreau's hairstyle is based on one of ancient Greece, and she wears a diamond crescent that is the symbol of the huntress Diana.

John Singer Sargent intended the portrait to establish his reputation, and despite the notoriety it attracted, the work did succeed: *Madame X* advertized his ability to paint his sitters in the most flattering and fashionable manner possible, and led to a healthy career in Britain and great esteem in America from the late 1880s onward. Though he was born oversees, traveled worldwide, and spent much of his life abroad, Sargent's career truly matured in his family's native land, and he always considered himself an American artist. He toiled for nearly three decades on a mural commission for the Boston Public Library,

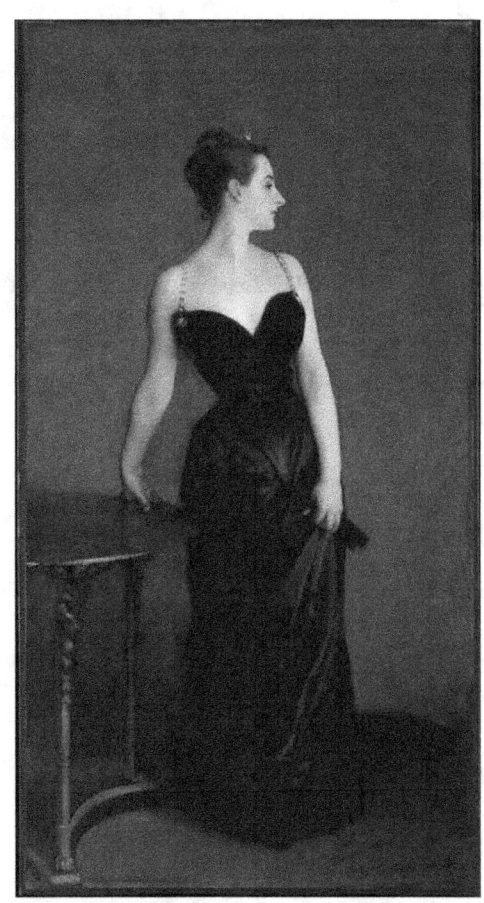

Figure 1. Madame X (Madame Pierre Gautreau), 1883–1884, oil on canvas (Metropolitan Museum of Art, New York)

he frequently painted fellow American expatriates, and in 1906 he was appointed full academician of the National Academy of Design in New York. In 1916 the Metropolitan Museum of Art bought Madame X, which Sargent considered "the best thing I have done."

The painting—which debuted to severe disparagement but is today treasured as a masterpiece beloved in the history of Western art—is but one example of an artwork that gradually evolved from epitomizing the condemned to the celebrated. Much of a work's initial reception is based upon society's tastes, standards of etiquette, and values of the era, and as these attitudes shift over the decades, the public may begin to look at older paintings with new eyes. Sargent's *Madame X* is perhaps a more dramatic example of this trend, yet it poses intriguing questions about what really defines an artwork's popularity, legacy, and fame.

External Link

View this painting up close in the Google Art Project:

- https://www.google.com/culturalinstitute/asset-viewer/madame-x-madame-pierre-gautreau/4QGaPNGLuGOBCw?projectId=art-project

---

Attributions

Whistler, Nocturne in Black and Gold

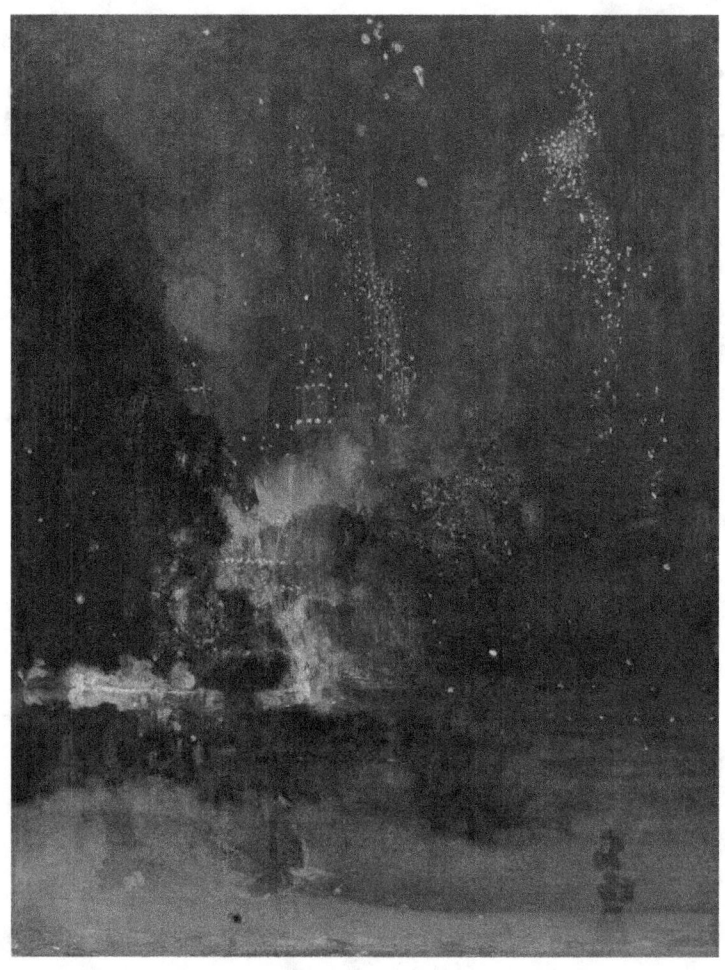

Figure 1. James Abbott McNeill Whistler, Nocturne in Black and Gold: The Falling Rocket, 1875, oil on panel, Detroit Institute of the Arts, Detroit

A Personal Interpretation

One might say that for some artworks, seeing beyond the artist's intention to form a more indefinite, personal interpretation is, ironically, the creator's ultimate objective after all. Much like Alice stepping tentatively through the two-dimensional plane of the looking glass into the possibilities beyond, the viewer is invited to deduce his own meaning, to form his own associations, thus essentially taking part in the creative process itself. While ambiguity is standard in the conceptual contemporary pieces of today, what mattered most in early American art was what could be read on the surface: narrative clarity, illusionistic detail, realism, and straightforward moral instruction. When did things change? Perhaps, it seems, around the time avant-garde artists began to pursue abstraction, flirt with modernism, and challenge the aesthetic standards of the past.

Consider *Nocturne in Black and Gold: The Falling Rocket* of 1875. In the mass of shadowy dark hues, vague wandering figures, and splashes of brilliant color, museum-goers might construe myriad meanings from the same scene: perhaps sparks from a blazing campfire, flickering Japanese lanterns, or visions of far-off galaxies mystically appearing on a clear summer night. Indeed, while the Massachusetts-born artist James Abbott McNeill Whistler (1834-1903) was inspired by a specific event (a fireworks display over London's Cremorne Gardens) the intangibility, both in appearance and theme, of the oil on panel was deliberate. The questions it conjures, the emotions it evokes, may differ from one viewer to another, and frankly, that's the point.

"Flinging a pot of paint in the public's face"

The Falling Rocket resonates with many 21st-century beholders, yet when it was first exhibited at a London gallery in 1877, detractors deemed the paintin too slapdash, incomprehensible, even insulting. Art critic John Ruskin dismissed Whistler's effort as "flinging a pot of paint in the public's face," as in his opinion it contained no social value. In response, Whistler—cheeky man that he was—sued Ruskin for libel, and though he won the case in court, he was awarded only a farthing in damages. During the highly publicized trial, the artist defended his series of atmospheric "noctures" as artistic arrangements whose worth lay not in any imitative aspects but in their basis in transcendent ideals of harmony and beauty.

Music

Whistler saw his paintings as musical compositions illustrated visually, and delineated this idea is his famed "Ten O'Clock" lecture of 1885:

> Nature contains the elements, in colour and form, of all pictures, as the keyboard contains the notes of all music. But the artist is born to pick and choose . . . that the result may be beautiful—as the musician gathers his notes, and forms his chords, until he brings forth from chaos glorious harmony.

Many of his titles incorporate allusions to music: "nocturnes," "symphonies," "arrangements," and "harmonies." The immaterial, the spiritual—these principles are subtly interwoven throughout Whistler's oeuvre, and he preached his ideas on the new religion of art throughout his career.

Attributions

Chapter 12: 1907–1960–Age of Global Conflict Part I

Chapter 12 Overview

What You'll Learn To Do: Examine Modern art and how its artists contributed to the development of Western art.

In Chapter 12 we will examine Modern art. We will look at how artists like Matisse contributed to the development of Western art. It is imperative to understand Modern art in order to see how it impacted later artistic developments.

Learning Activities

The learning activities for this module include:

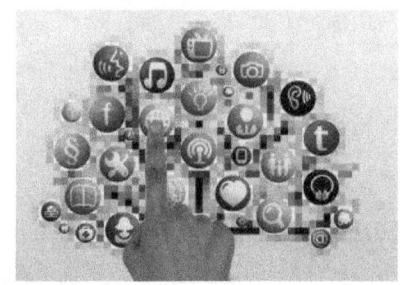

- **Review:** Key Learning Items

Fauvism

- **Read:** Introduction to Fauvism
- **Read:** Matisse, Bonheur de Vivre
- **Read:** Matisse, The Red Studio (includes a video: 9:10)
- **Read:** Matisse, The Piano Lesson (includes a video: 4:06)

Expressionism

- **Watch:** Kirchner, Street, Dresden (9:55)
- **Watch:** Kandinsky, Composition VII (11:19)
- **Watch:** Schiele, Seated Male Nude (2:59)

Cubism

- **Read:** Picasso, Still Life with Chair Caning (includes a video: 13:36)
- **Read:** Picasso's Early Works
- **Read:** Picasso, Portrait of Gertrude Stein

- **Read:** Picasso, Les Demoiselles d'Avignon (includes a video: 7:44)
- **Watch:** Picasso, The Reservoir (4:15)
- **Watch:** Picasso, Guitar (4:16)
- **Watch:** Picasso, Guernica (?)
- **Read:** Braque, The Portuguese
- **Read:** Braque, The Viaduct at L'Estaque (includes a video: 3:50)

Dada

- **Watch:** Duchamp and the Ready-Mades (10:12)
- **Watch:** Duchamp, In Advance of the Broken Arm (10:07)
- **Watch:** Duchamp, Fountain (3:11)
- **Watch:** Duchamp, The Red Box (4:59)
- **Watch:** Arp, Untitled (3:34)
- **Watch:** Hoch, Cut with the Kitchen Knife (12:00)
- **Watch:** Klee, Twittering Machine (4:10)

Futurism

- **Read:** An Introduction to Futurism (includes a video: 0:19)
- **Watch:** Three Futurists (11:25)

Suprematism

- **Watch:** Malevich (10:26)

DeStijl

- **Watch:** Mondrian, Composition No. II (6:02)

School of Paris

- **Watch:** Modigliani, Young Woman in a Shirt (4:36)

Neue Sachlichkeit

- **Watch:** Otto Dix (7:57)

Bauhaus

- **Watch:** Feininger, Cathedral (6:10)

- **Watch:** Maholy-Nagy (4:14)

Attributions

Key Learning Items

After successful completion of this module, you will be able to:

- Understand and apply the concepts and terminology of Modern art
- Investigate and apply the fundamental questions we ask when looking at art objects from this movement
- Discuss, collaborate, and generate understanding as to the meaning of Modern Century art
- Assess and evaluate the impact of Modern art on the continued evolution of Western art

Key Questions to Ask

While you are reviewing the content of this module, consider the following questions:

- How did Modern art develop?
- What were its precursors?
- What was the influence of WWI on art?
- How did Modern art reflect societal changes?

Key Vocabulary Terms

- Fauvism
- Expressionism
- avant-garde
- optical effect
- pure hue

- undulating lines

- Primitivism

- abstractionism

- Cubism

- Analytic Cubism

- Synthetic Cubism

- collage

- Dada

- ready-made sculpture

- found object

- Futurism

- Suprematism

- De Stijl

- nonobjective art/ nonobjective forms

- School of Paris

- Neue Sachlichkeit

- Bauhaus

Here are links to art history glossaries that will help you better understand the above key vocabulary terms.

- ArtLex: Art Dictionary

  ◦ http://www.artlex.com/

- About.com: Art History

  ◦ http://arthistory.about.com/od/glossary/l/bl_Art-Glossary.htm

- Artcyclopedia: A Guide to Fine Art

  ◦ http://www.artcyclopedia.com/

Attributions

CC licensed content, Original

Introduction to Fauvism

Fauvism developed in France to become the first new artistic style of the twentieth century. In contrast to the dark, vaguely disturbing nature of much fin-de-siècle, or turn-of-the-century, Symbolist art, the Fauves produced bright cheery landscapes and figure paintings, characterized by pure vivid color and bold distinctive brushwork.

When shown at the 1905 Salon d'Automne (an exhibition organized by artists in response to the conservative policies of the official exhibitions, or salons) in Paris, the contrast to traditional art was so striking it led critic Louis Vauxcelles to describe the artists as "Les Fauves" or "wild beasts," and thus the name was born.

One of several Expressionist movements to emerge in the early twentieth century, Fauvism was short lived, and by 1910, artists in the group had diverged toward more individual interests. Nevertheless, Fauvism remains signficant for it demonstrated modern art's ability to evoke intensely emotional reactions through radical visual form.

The best known Fauve artists include Henri Matisse, André Derain, and Maurice Vlaminck who pioneered its distinctive style. Their early works reveal the influence of Post-Impressionist artists, especially Neo-Impressionists like Paul Signac, whose interest in color's optical effects had led to a divisionist method of juxtaposing pure hues on canvas. The Fauves, however, lacked such scientific intent. They emphasized the expressive potential of color, employing it arbitrarily, not based on an object's natural appearance.

In *Luxe, calm et volupté* (1904), for example, Matisse employed a pointillist style by applying paint in small dabs and dashes. Instead of the subtle blending of complimentary colors typical of Neo-Impressionism Seurat, for example), the combination of firey oranges, yellows, greens and purple is almost overpowering in its vibrant impact.

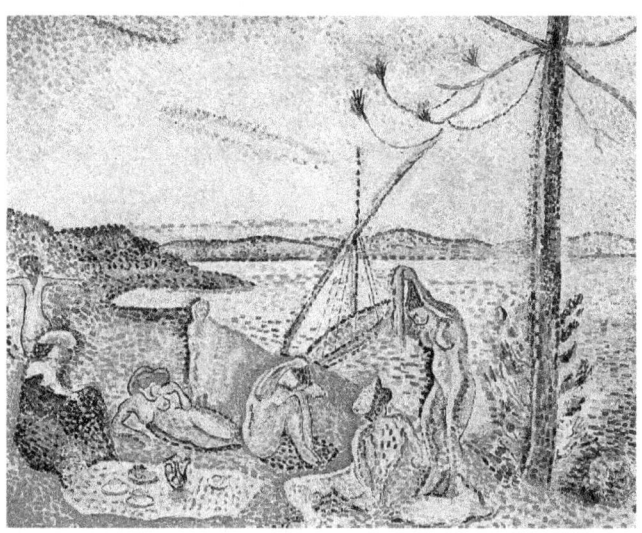

Figure 1. Henri Matisse, Luxe, calme et volupté, 1904, oil on canvas, 37 × 46 inches (Museé d'Orsay, Paris)

Similarly, while paintings such as Vlaminck's *The River Seine at Chantou* (1906) appear to mimic the spontaneous, active brushwork of Impressionism, the Fauves adopted a painterly approach to enhance their work's emotional power, not to capture fleeting effects of color, light or atmosphere on their subjects. Their preference for landscapes, carefree figures and lighthearted subject matter reflects their desire to create an art that would appeal primarily to the viewers' senses.

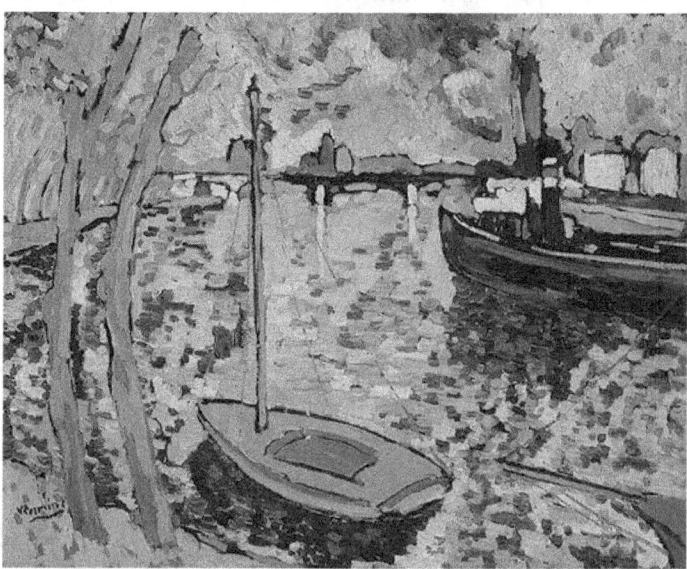

Figure 2. Maurice de Vlaminck, The River Seine at Chatou, 1906, Oil on canvas, 32 1/2 × 40 1/8 in./ 82.6 × 101.9 cm (The Metropolitan Museum of Art)

Paintings such as Matisse's *Bonheur de Vivre* (1905–06) epitomize this goal. Bright colors and undulating lines pull our eye gently through the ideallic scene, encouraging us to imagine feeling the warmth of the sun, the cool of the grass, the soft touch of a caress, and the passion of a kiss.

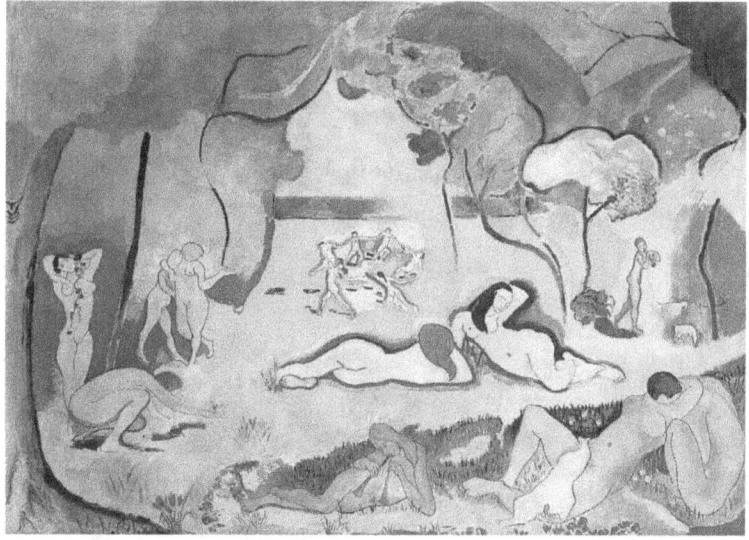

Figure 3. Henri Matisse, Bonheur de Vivre (Joy of Life), oil on canvas, 1905–06 (Barnes Foundation)

Like many modern artists, the Fauves also found inspiration in objects from Africa and other non-western cultures. Seen through a Colonialist lens, the formal distinctions of African art reflected current notions of Primitivism—the belief that, lacking the corrupting influence of European civilization, non-western peoples were more in tune with the primal elements of nature.

Blue Nude (Souvenir of Biskra) of 1907 shows how Matisse combined his traditional subject of the female nude with the influence of primitive sources. The woman's face appears mask-like in the use of strong outlines and harsh contrasts of light and dark, and the hard lines of her body recall the angled planar surfaces common to African sculpture. This distorted effect, further heightened by her contorted pose, clearly distinguishes the figure from the idealized odalisques of Ingres and painters of the past.

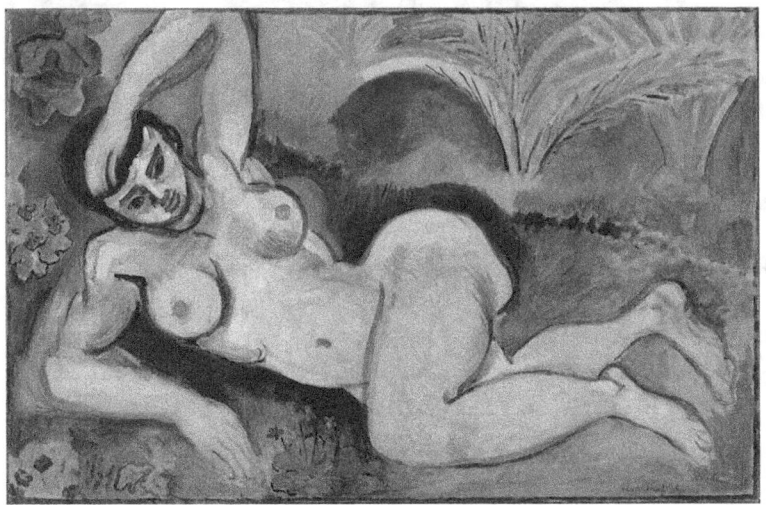

Figure 6. Henri Matisse, The Blue Nude (Souvenir de Biskra), oil on canvas, 1907 (Baltimore Museum of Art)

The Fauves interest in Primitivism reinforced their reputation as "wild beasts" who sought new possibilities for art through their exploration of direct expression, impactful visual forms and instinctual appeal.

Attributions

CC licensed content, Shared previously

- Fauvism. **Authored by**: Dr. Virginia B. Spivey. **Provided by**: Khan Academy. **Located at**: https://web.archive.org/web/20141006183442/http://smarthistory.khanacademy.org/fauvism.html. **License**: *CC BY-NC-SA: Attribution-NonCommercial-Share-Alike*

Matisse, Bonheur de Vivre

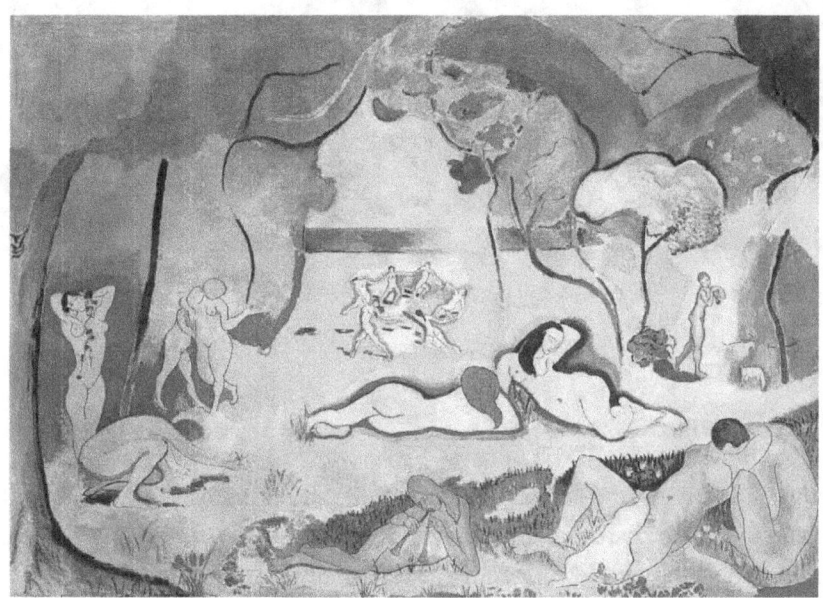

Figure 1. Henri Matisse, Bonheur de Vivre (Joy of Life), oil on canvas, 1905–06 (Barnes Foundation)

The *Joy of Life*

In 1906, Henri Matisse finished what is often considered his greatest Fauve painting, the *Bonheur de vivre*, or the "Joy of Life." It is a large-scale painting (nearly 6 feet in height, 8 feet in width), depicting an Arcadian landscape filled with brilliantly colored forest, meadow, sea, and sky and populated by nude figures both at rest and in motion. As with the earlier Fauve canvases, color is responsive only to emotional expression and the formal needs of the canvas, not the realities of nature. The references are many, but in form and date, *Bonheur de Vivre* is closest to Cézanne's last great image of bathers.

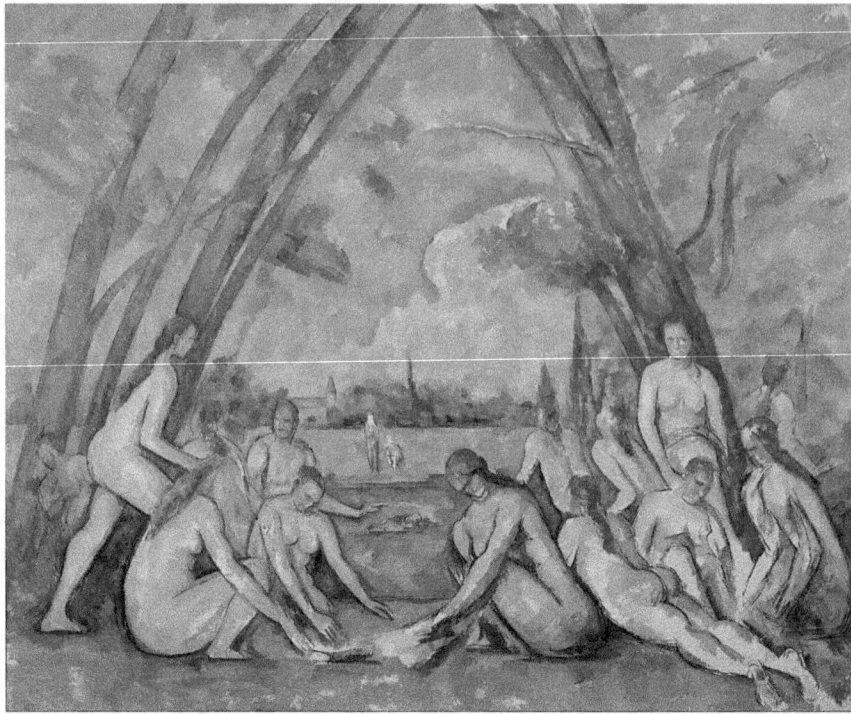

Figure 2. Paul Cézanne, The Large Bathers, oil on canvas, 1906 (Philadelphia Museum of Art)

Matisse and His Sources

Like Cézanne, Matisse constructs the landscape so that it functions as a stage. In both works trees are planted at the sides and in the far distance, and their upper boughs are spread apart like curtains, highlighting the figures lounging beneath. And like Cézanne, Matisse unifies the figures and the landscape. Cézanne does this by stiffening and tilting his trunk-like figures. In Matisse's work, the serpentine arabesques that define the contours of the women are heavily emphasized, and then reiterated in the curvilinear lines of the trees.

Matisse creates wildly sensual figures in *Bonheur de Vivre,* which show how he was clearly informed by Ingres's odalisques and harem fantasies.

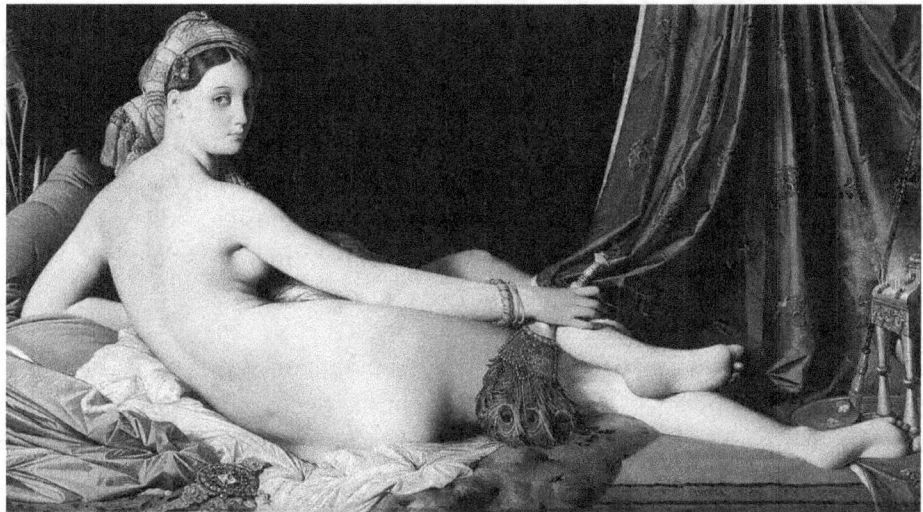

Figure 3. Jean-Auguste-Dominique Ingres, La Grande Odalisque, oil on canvas, 1814 (Louvre)

Additionally, Matisse references Titian. For like Titian's *Bacchanal of the Andrians,* the scene depicted in *Bonheur de Vivre* is an expression of pure pleasure. Here is a place full of life and love and free from want or fear. Instead of a contemporary scene in a park, on the banks of the Seine, or other recognizable places in nature, Matisse has returned to mythic paradise.

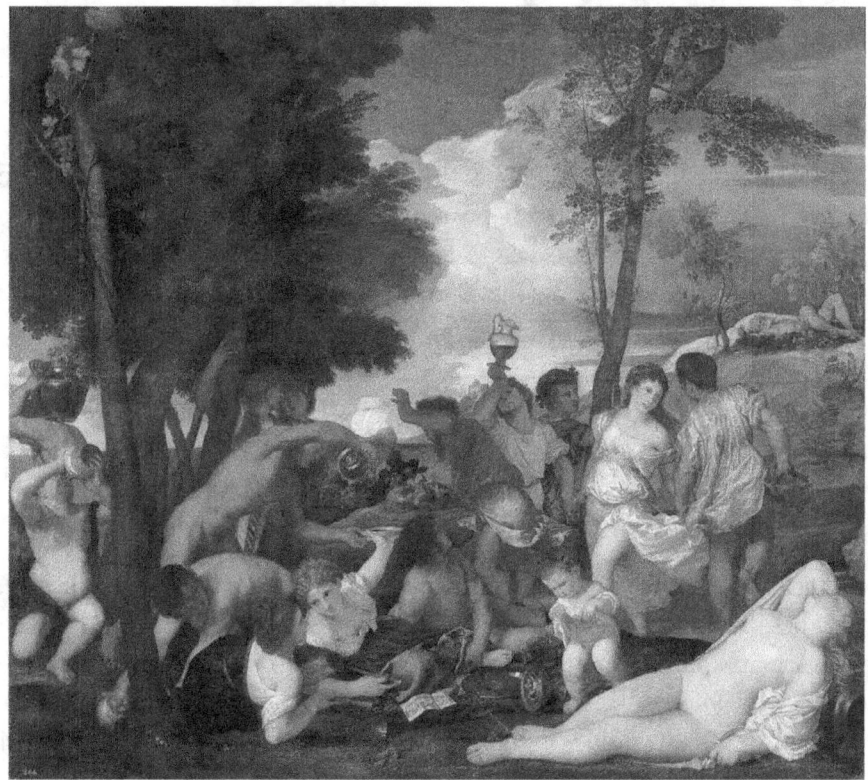

Figure 4. Titian, Bacchananal of the Andrians, oil on canvas, 1523–25 (Prado)

Radicalism, or How to Color Outside the Lines

But do not be misled by his interest in myth—Matisse is not joining in with Bouguereau or any other Salon artist. This is the epitome of Fauvism, a radical new approach that incorporate purely expressive, bright, clear colors and wildly sensual forms. Matisse's painting s perhaps the first canvas to clearly understand Cézanne's great formal challenge, and to actually further the elder master's ideas. In fact, despite its languid poses, *Bonheur de Vivre* was regarded as the most radical painting of its day. Because of this, Matisse became known, briefly, as the most daring painter in Paris.

So what was daring about this canvas? Here is one key issue: unlike the paintings by Cézanne, Ingres, or Titian, Matisse's work does not depict forms that recede in the background and diminish in scale. If you study the figures in the foreground and the middle ground of *Bonheur de Vivre*, you will notice that their scale is badly skewed. The shift of scale between the player of the double flute (bottom center) and the smooching couple (bottom right) is plausible, if we take the musician to be a child, but what of the giants just behind them? Compared to the figures standing in the wings, who are obviously mature women (middle ground left), these center women are of enormous proportion. They are simply too big to make sense of within the traditional conventions of Western painting.

Perspective, Patronage, and Picasso

So why has Matisse done this? How could these shifts of scale make sense? Have we seen anything like this before? Well, in a sense we have. Cézanne's painting ruptured forms in order to accurately explore vision as experienced through time and space—in other words, forms look different depending on where we are in relation to them.

In fact, this exploration of vision through space is the key to understanding Matisse's work. By incorporating shifting perspectives, he brought this idea to a grand scale. Put simply, Matisse's shifting scale is actually the result of our changing position vis-à-vis the figures. As a result of his experimentation with perspective, the viewer relates differently to the painting and is required to "enter" the scene. It is only from the varied perspectives within this landscape that the abrupt ruptures of scale make sense.

The painting was purchased by a wealthy expatriate American writer-poet named Gertrude Stein and her brother, Leo Stein, who shared a home filled with modern art at 27 Rue de Fleurus, in Paris. This was also the location for Gertrude Stein's weekly salon. Here, Matisse, Apollinaire, the young and largely unknown Picasso and other members of the avant-garde came together to exchange ideas.

Stein was able to attract such a crowd not only because of her literary skills but because she often provided financial support to these nearly destitute artists. In fact, the Steins bought Matisse's *Bonheur de Vivre* soon after its completion and hung it in their dining room for all to see. One person who saw it there was Picasso. By all accounts the painting's fame was too much for the terribly competitive young Spaniard. He determined to out do Matisse, and he did with his 1907 canvas, *Demoiselles d'Avignon* (MoMA).

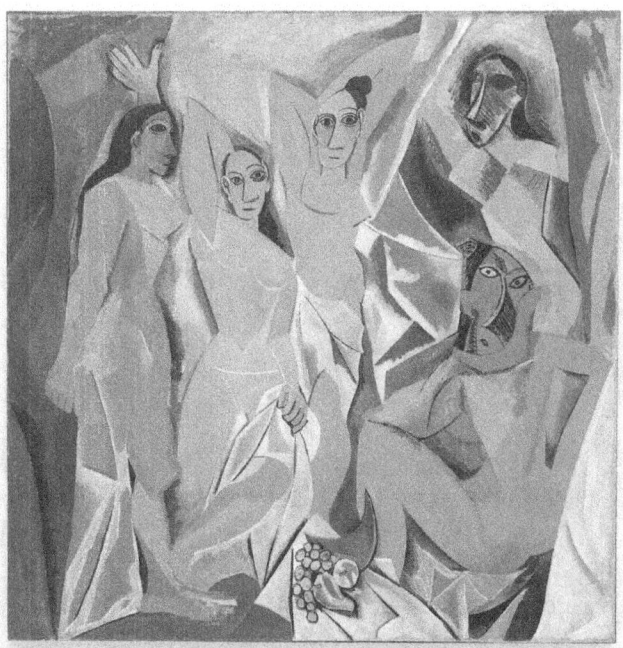

Figure 5. Pablo Picasso, Les Demoiselles d'Avignon, oil on canvas, 1907 (MoMA)

Picasso turned Matisse's sensuality into violent pornography. Matisse in turn responds to the challenge of what was then called "primitivism" with his own brand of aggression in his *Blue Nude.*

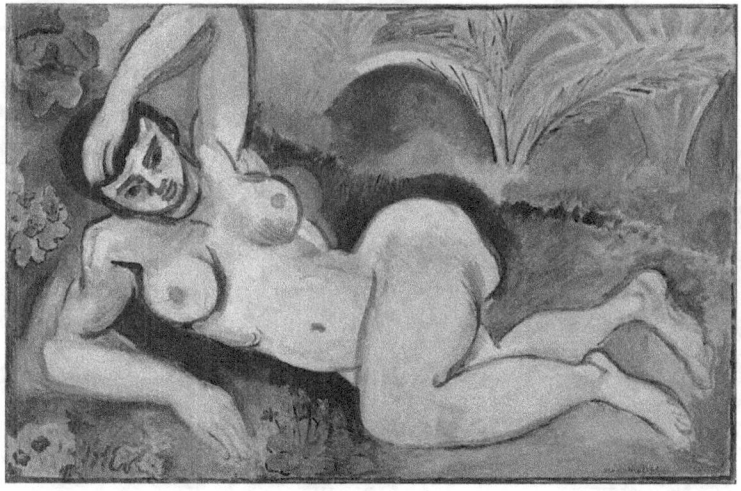

Figure 6. Henri Matisse, The Blue Nude (Souvenir de Biskra), oil on canvas, 1907 (Baltimore Museum of Art)

Attributions

CC licensed content, Shared previously

Matisse, The Red Studio

Dr. Beth Harris and Dr. Steven Zucker provide a description, historical perspective, and analysis of Matisse's *The Red Studio*.

- https://www.youtube.com/watch?v=nz_zwsgjRbw

Henri Matisse, *The Red Studio*, 1911, oil on canvas, 5′ 4″ x 4′ 3″, (MoMA).

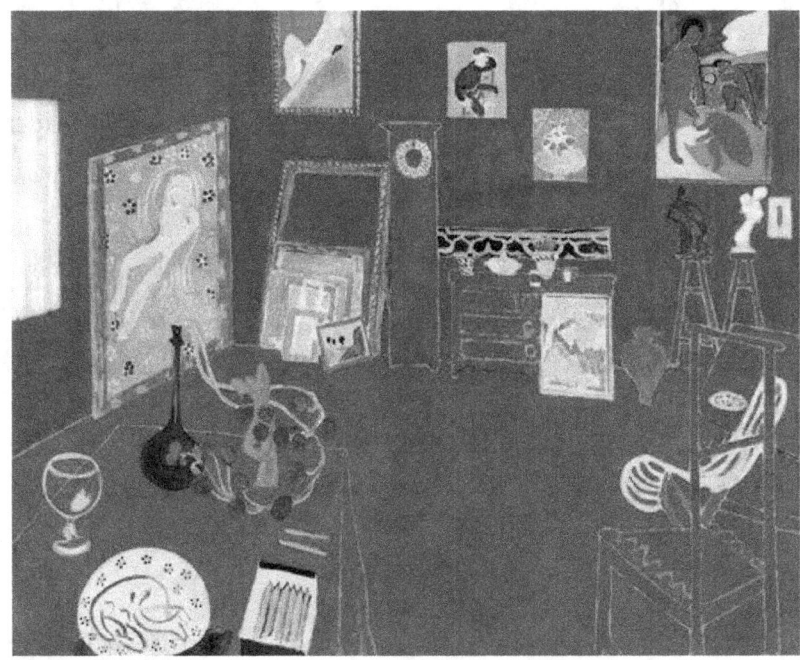

Figure 1. Henri Matisse, The Red Studio, oil on canvas, 1911 (MoMA)

Dismantling Spatial Illusion

Since Manet (and Degas, Monet, and Cezanne), artists have sought to undermine the illusion of space that had ruled painting since about 1425. Spatial illusion was increasingly seen as a defect that reduced the integrity of painting. But as the earlier painters of the avant-garde have shown, ridding a painting of illusion is almost impossible. The audience is trained to expect three dimensional space and sees it given the opportunity. This is Matisse's challenge. He meets this challenge–the destruction of spatial illusion, in three stages.

The Color Red

Red is often thought of as the most aggressive color. It has the most punch, and that's what Matisse needed here. This canvas was a part of a series, there is, for instance, a Pink Studio too. But that canvas was concerned with different issues. Here, the red is an attempt to find a color that is forceful enough to resist the illusion of deep space by pushing to the surface. The red is, of course painted onto the flat canvas but actually fails to remain there visually. Instead, the red becomes the walls and furnishing of the room seen in space. Illusion triumphs–Matisse is thwarted.

Illusionism

This triumph of illusion is due in part to the linear perspective that defines the table, chairs, and the walls and floor of the studio. But look! Matisse has constructed some of the worst linear perspective ever seen. Receding lines should converge, but look at the chair on the lower right. The lines widen as they go back. And look to rear left corner of the room. The corner is defined by the edge of the pink canvas but above that painting, the line that must define the corner is missing! Matisse is literally dismantling the perspective of the room but it makes no difference, we still see the room as an inhabitable space. Illusion still triumphs.

Figure-Ground Relationship

Although it is very difficult to see in reproduction, if seen in person at MoMA, it is clear that the whitish lines that define form in the red field are not painted on top of the red. Instead, they are reserve lines. In other words, the white lines are actually the canvas below. Matisse painted the red planes up to the line on either side, leaving a narrow gap of white canvas in between. This is really **important**. Stay with me on this. The white line is actually emerging from below the red. It is beneath. The red is of course painted on top of the white canvas.

Okay, now pay attention. Matisse has realized that illusion is almost certain to triumph no matter how aggressively he tries to undermine it. We, as the audience, will see space if given the slightest opportunity. So if we see illusion at such a basic level, what hope does Matisse have of destroying it? In fact, his reserve line are his really brilliant solution. The chairs, the dresser, the clock, each object, or figure in the Red Studio is constructed out of the canvas below. At the same time, the ground which supports those figures, is constructed out of a plane of red that is physically above the canvas. What Matisse has done then is reverse the figure ground relationship. He has made the figure out of the ground (the canvas) and made the ground out of the figure (the red paint on top). When seen in person, the recognition of this does finally destroy illusion, Matisse triumphs! Yeah!

Kirchner, Street, Dresden

Dr. Juliana Kreinik, Dr. Beth Harris, and Dr. Steven Zucker provide a description, historical perspective, and analysis of Ernst Ludwig's *Kirchner, Street, Dresden*.

- https://youtu.be/zfZu–psur8

Ernst Ludwig, *Kirchner, Street, Dresden*, 1908, oil on canvas, 4′ 11″ x 6′ 7″, (MoMA).

Attributions

CC licensed content, Shared previously

Kandinsky, Composition VII

Dr. Beth Harris, Dr. Juliana Kreinik, and Dr. Steven Zucker provide a description, historical perspective, and analysis of Kandinsky's *Composition VII*.

- https://youtu.be/i16sGRY7SZ4

Wassily Kandinsky, *Composition VII*, 1913, oil on canvas, 79 × 119 in (200.7 × 302.3 cm), (State Tretyakov Gallery, Moscow).

Attributions

All rights reserved content

Schiele, Seated Male Nude

Dr. Beth Harris and Dr. Steven Zucker provide a description, historical perspective, and analysis of Egon Schiele's *Seated Male Nude (Self-Portrait)*.

- https://youtu.be/croM4PvOdbM

Egon Schiele, *Seated Male Nude (Self-Portrait)*, 1910, oil and gouache on canvas, 152.5 × 150 cm, (Leopold Museum, Vienna).

External Link
View this painting up close in the Google Art Project: • https://www.google.com/culturalinstitute/asset-viewer/seated-male-nude-self-portrait/2QEjbgnQo_ZsVQ?projectId=art-project

Attributions

CC licensed content, Shared previously

Picasso, Still Life with Chair Caning

Dr. Beth Harris, Dr. Steven Zucker, and Sal Khan provide a description, historical perspective, and analysis of Picasso's *Still Life with Chair Caning*.

- https://youtu.be/286FiUvOeFs

The Evolution of Cubism

Beginning in 1908, and continuing through the first few months of 1912, Braque and Picasso co-invent the first phase of Cubism. Since it is dominated by the analysis of form, this first stage is usually referred to as Analytic Cubism. But then during the summer of 1912, Braque leaves Paris to take a holiday in Provence. During his time there, he wanders into a hardware store, and there he finds a roll of oil cloth. Oil cloth is an early version of contact paper, the vinyl adhesive used to line the shelves or drawers in a cupboard. Then, as now, these materials come in a variety of pre-printed patterns.

Braque purchased some oil cloth printed with a fake wood grain. That particular pattern drew his attention because he was at work on a Cubist drawing of a guitar, and he was about to render the grain of the wood in pencil. Instead, he cut the oil cloth and pasted a piece of the factory-printed grain pattern right into his drawing. With this collage, Braque changed the direction of art for the next ninety years.

Collage

As you might expect, Picasso was not far behind Braque. Picasso immediately begins to create collage with oil cloth as well—and adds other elements to the mix (but remember, it was really Braque who introduced collage—he never gets enough credit). So what is the big deal? Oil cloth, collage, wood grain patterns—what does this have to do with art and Cubism? One of the keys to understanding the importance of Cubism, of Picasso and Braque, is to consider their actions and how unusual they were for the time. When Braque, and then Picasso placed industrially-produced objects ("low" commercial culture) into the realm of fine art ("high" culture) they acted as artistic iconoclasts (icon=image/clast=destroyer).

Moreover, they questioned the elitism of the art world, which had always dictated the separation of common, everyday experience from the rarefied, contemplative realm of artistic creation. Of equal importance, their work highlighted—and separated—the role of technical skill from art-making. Braque and Picasso introduced a "fake" element on purpose, not to mislead or fool their audience, but rather to force a discussion of art and craft, of high and low, of unique and mass-produced objects. They ask: "Can this object still be art if I don't actually render its forms myself, if the quality of the art is no longer directly tied to my technical skills or level of craftsmanship?"

Still-Life with Chair Caning

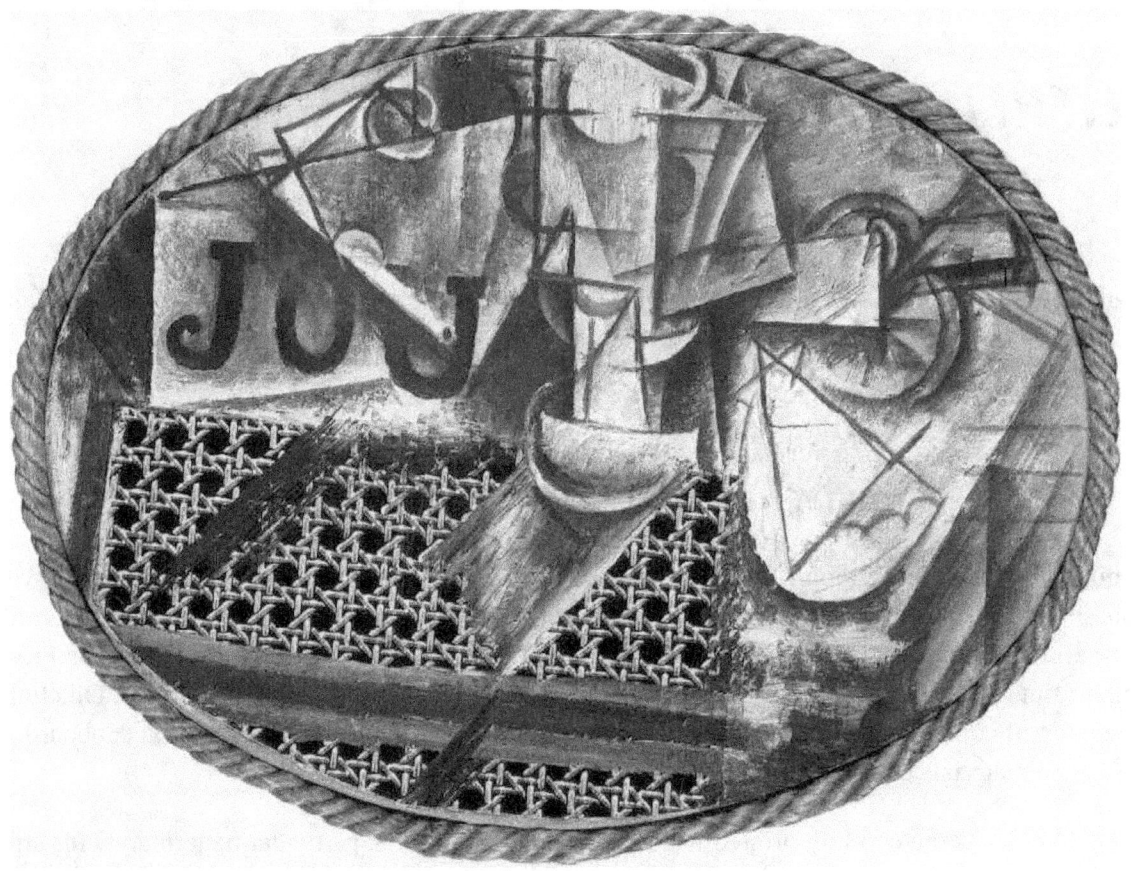

Picasso, Still-Life with Chair Caning, 1912 (Musée Picasso)

Virtually all avant-garde art of the second half of the twentieth century is indebted to this brave renunciation. But that doesn't make this kind of Cubism, often called Synthetic Cubism (piecing together, or synthesis of form), any easier to interpret. At first glance, Picasso's *Still-Life with Chair Caning* of 1912 might seem a mish-mash of forms instead of clear picture. But we can understand the image—and other like it—by breaking down Cubist pictorial language into parts. Let's start at the upper right: almost at the edge of the canvas (at two o'clock) there is the handle of a knife. Follow it to the left to find the blade. The knife cuts a piece of citrus fruit. You can make out the rind and the segments of the slice at the bottom right corner of the blade.

Below the fruit, which is probably a lemon, is the white, scalloped edge of a napkin. To the left of these things and standing vertically in the top center of the canvas (twelve o'clock) is a wine glass. It's hard to see at first, so look carefully. Just at the top edge of the chair caning is the glass's base, above it is the stem (thicker than you might expect), and then the bowl of the glass. It is difficult to find the forms you would expect because Picasso depicts the glass from more than one angle. At eleven o'clock is the famous "JOU," which means "game" in French, but also the first three letters of the French word for newspaper (or more literally, "daily"; journal=daily). In fact, you can make out the bulk of the folded paper quite clearly. Don't be confused by the pipe that lays across the newspaper. Do you see its stem and bowl?

Looking Down and Looking Through

But there are still big questions: why the chair caning, what is the gray diagonal at the bottom of the glass, and why the rope frame? (Think of a ship's port hole. The port hole reference is an important clue.) Also, why don't the letters sit better on the newspaper? Finally, why is the canvas oval? It has already been determined that this still life is composed of a sliced lemon, a glass, newspaper, and a pipe. Perhaps this is a breakfast setting, with a citron pressé (French lemonade). In any case, these items are arranged upon a glass tabletop. You can see the reflection of the glass. In fact, the glass allows us to see below the table's surface, which is how we see the chair caning—which represents the seat tucked in below the table.

Okay, so far so good. But why is the table elliptical in shape? This appears to be a café table, which are round or square but never oval. Yet, when we look at a circular table, we never see it from directly above. Instead, we see it at an angle, and it appears elliptical in shape as we approach the table to sit down. But what about the rope, which was not mass-produced, nor made by Picasso, but rather something made especially for this painting? We can view it as the bumper of a table, as it was used in some cafés, or as the frame of a ship's port hole, which we can look "through," to see the objects represented. The rope's simultaneous horizontal and vertical orientation creates a way for the viewer (us) to read the image in two ways—looking down and looking through/across. Put simply, Picasso wants us to remember that the painting is something different from that which it represents. Or as Gertrude Stein said, "A rose is a rose is a rose."

Attributions

CC licensed content, Shared previously

Picasso's Early Works

Age Twenty and Looking Rather Goth

When I'm in the galleries at The Museum of Modern Art in New York, I obviously spend a good deal of time looking at the art. But I also watch people look at the art and listen to what they have to say. The comments that people make can be quite thoughtful and visitor comments and questions have added enormously to my appreciation of the art over the years. Still, there are many comments that are born of pure befuddlement. And many of these target Picasso.

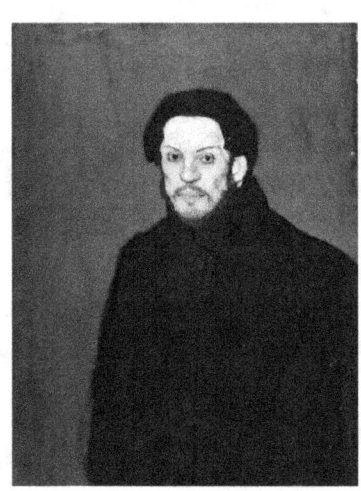

Many people seem to believe that Picasso's abstraction of the human figure, his penchant for reconfiguring the body by mis-aligning a nose or an eye, for instance, is the result of his inability to draw. Nothing could be farther from the truth. There is an old anecdote that tells of Picasso, who, upon emerging from an exhibition of drawings by young children, says, "When I was their age I could draw like Raphael, but it took me a lifetime to learn to draw like them."

Figure 1. Pablo Picasso, Self Portrait, 1901 (Musée Picasso)

Perhaps this quote is apocryphal, but it points to something undeniably true: Picasso was an extraordinary craftsman, even when measured against the old masters. That he chose to struggle to overcome his visual heritage in order to find a language more responsive to the modern world is an important triumph that has had a vast effect upon our world. Picasso's art has transformed and inspired not only artists, but also architects, designers, writers, mathematicians, and even philosophers. We may look at Picasso's art in museums, but his art—via these translators—has therefore had a profound influence on what we see in our everyday life. Just think of the advertisements for products we buy, buildings in which we live and work, books we read, and even the way we conceive of reality.

"My kid could make that"

There is no question that Picasso's art has had a most profound impact on the twentieth century. While Picasso suggests the value of unlearning the academic tradition, it is important to remember that he had mastered its techniques by a very early age. His father, Don José Ruiz Blasco, was a drawing teacher and curator at a small museum. The young Picasso began drawing and painting by age seven or eight. By age ten, Picasso assisted his father, sometimes painting the minor elements of the elder's canvases. Soon after his father became a professor at the art academy in Barcelona, the young Picasso completed the entrance examinations (in record time) and was advanced to the school's upper-level program. He repeated this feat when he applied to the Royal Academy in Madrid.

Picasso in Paris

Like Van Gogh had done before him, Picasso arrived in Paris determined to work through the avant-garde's techniques and subjects to better understand such art. An example of his explorations of the achievements of contemporary art in Paris can be seen by comparing a painting by Degas to one by Picasso.

Figure 2. Pablo Picasso, Study of a Torso, After a Plaster Cast, 1893–94 (Musée Picasso), age 12 or 13

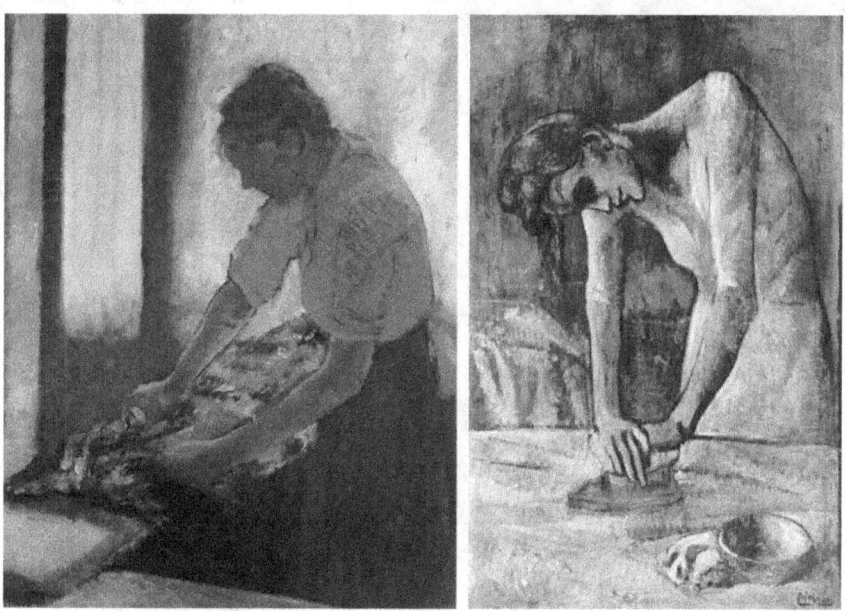

Figure 3. (left) Edgar Degas, Woman Ironing, oil on canvas, ca. 1890 (Walker Art Gallery, Liverpool); (right) Pablo Picasso, Woman Ironing, oil on canvas, 1904 (Guggenheim Museum, New York)

It is not surprising that Picasso, the great draftsman, would be interested in the work of the "odd man out" Degas, who nearly alone among the Impressionists retained the primacy of line. In the example above, Picasso has infused a somewhat maudlin weariness to his attenuated and curiously sensual laborer. Still, Picasso understands Degas's experimentation with abstraction. Note how in Degas's image, the luminous negative space defined between the arms refuses to recede beyond the figure, remaining trapped instead.

Likewise, Picasso defines and centers an almost identical form. Notice, too, the bowl that Picasso places in the lower right corner. Like everything in this canvas, it is roughly formed with a dry brush. Still, the simple strokes of white and dark gray that define the volume speak to the magical pleasure of rendering space, a love that Picasso carries with him through out his career.

Family of Saltimbanques

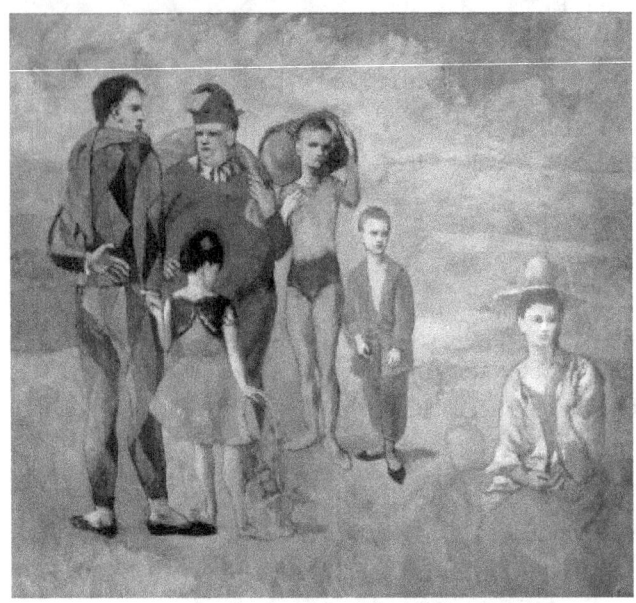

Figure 4. Pablo Picasso, Family of Saltimbanques, oil on canvas, 1905 (National Gallery of Art, Washington, D.C.)

This great, early painting by Picasso portrays a family of saltimbanques. These are wandering circus performers that move from town to town—never truly welcome, and only briefly tolerated for their ability to entertain.

Like so many of Picasso's early subjects during his so-called Blue and Rose periods in the first years of the twentieth century, here is a group of disenfranchised, alienated people that live on the fringes of society. This particular group includes characters from the sixteenth-century Italian performing tradition of *commedia dell'arte*. One such figure is the rogue wit known as the Harlequin, who wears a suit of multicolored triangles. Picasso seems to have identified with such characters at this time. As he often reminded people, he was very poor at this point in his career. A Spaniard in France who did not yet speak the language, and still an unknown artist only in his mid-twenties, Picasso might well have felt an affinity with itinerant outsiders such as the saltimbanques.

Attributions

Picasso, Les Demoiselles d'Avignon

Dr. Beth Harris and Dr. Steven Zucker provide a description, historical perspective, and analysis of Picasso's *Les Demoiselles d'Avignon.*

- https://youtu.be/fy2TlYnYIzA

Pablo Picasso, *Les Demoiselles d'Avignon*, 1907, oil on canvas, 243.9 cm × 233.7 cm (96 in × 92 in), (Museum of Modern Art).

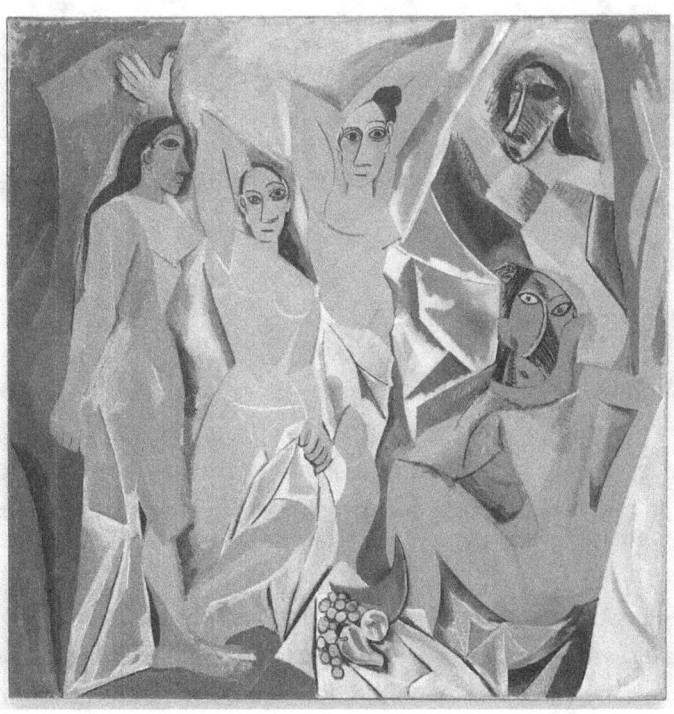

Figure 1. Pablo Picasso, Les Demoiselles d'Avignon, oil on canvas, 1907 (MoMA)

Cézanne's Ghost, Matisse's *Bonheur de Vivre*, and Picasso's Ego

One of the most important canvases of the twentieth century, Picasso's great breakthrough painting *Les Demoiselles d'Avignon* was constructed in response to several significant sources. First amongst these was his confrontation with Cézanne's great achievement at the posthumous retrospective mounted in Paris a year after the artist's death in 1907. The retrospective exhibition forced the young Picasso, Matisse and many other artists to contend with the implications of Cézanne's art. Matisse's *Bonheur de Vivre* of 1906 was one of the first of many attempts to do so, and the newly completed work was quickly purchased by Leo & Gertrude Stein and hung in their living room so that all of their circle of avant-garde writers and artists could see and praise it. And praise it they did. Here was the promise of Cézanne fulfilled—and one which incorporated lessons learned from Seurat and Van Gogh, no less! This was just too much for the young Spaniard.

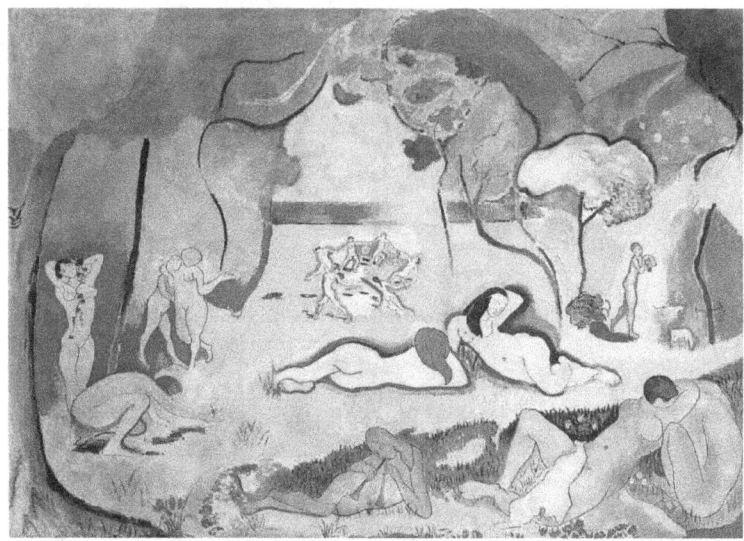

Figure 2. Henri Matisse, Bonheur de Vivre (Joy of Life), oil on canvas, 1905–06 (Barnes Foundation)

Pablo Becomes Picasso

By all accounts, Picasso's intensely competitive nature literally forced him to out do his great rival.*Les Demoiselles D'Avignon* is the result of this effort. Let's compare canvases: Matisse's landscape is a broad open field with a deep recessionary vista. The figures are uncrowded. They describe flowing arabesques that in turn relate to the forms of nature that surround them. Here is languid sensuality set in the mythic past of Greece's golden age.

In very sharp contrast, Picasso, intent of making a name for himself (rather like the young Manet and David), has radically compressed the space of his canvas and replaced sensual eroticism with a kind of aggressively crude pornography (note, for example, the squatting figure at the lower right). His space is interior, closed, and almost claustrophobic. Like Matisse's later*Blue Nude* (itself a response to *Les Demoiselles d'Avignon*), the women fill the entire space and seem trapped within it. No longer set in a classical past, Picasso's image is clearly of our time. Here are five prostitutes from an actual brothel, located on a street named Avignon in the red-light district in Barcelona, the capital of Catalonia in northern Spain—a street, by the way, which Picasso had frequented.

Picasso has also dispensed with Matisse's clear, bright pigments. Instead, the artist chooses deeper tones befitting urban interior light. Gone too, is the sensuality that Matisse created. Picasso has replaced the graceful curves of *Bonheur de Vivre* with sharp, jagged, almost shattered forms. The bodies of Picasso's women look dangerous as if they were formed of shards of broken glass. Matisse's pleasure becomes Picasso's apprehension. But while Picasso clearly aims to "out do" Matisse, to take over as the most radical artist in Paris, he also acknowledges his debts. Compare the woman standing in the center of Picasso's composition to the woman who stands with elbows raised at the extreme left of Matisse's canvas: like a scholar citing a borrowed quotation, Picasso footnotes.

The Creative Vacuum Cleaner

Picasso draws on many other sources to construct *Les Demoiselles D'Avignon*. In fact, a number of artists stopped inviting him to their studio because he would so freely and successfully incorporate their ideas into his own work, often more successfully than the original artist. Indeed, Picasso has been likened to a "creative vacuum cleaner," sucking up every new idea that he came across. While that analogy might be a little coarse, it is fair to say that he had an enormous creative appetite. One of several historical sources that Picasso pillaged is archaic art, demonstrated very clearly by the left-most figure of the painting, who stands stiffly on legs that look awkwardly locked at the knee. Her right arm juts down while her left arm seems dislocated (this arm is actually a vestige of a male figure that Picasso eventually removed). Her head is shown in perfect profile with large

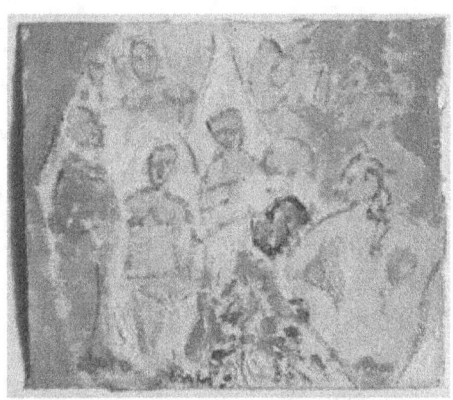

Figure 3. Pablo Picasso, Study for Les Demoiselles d'Avignon, o/c, 1907 (MoMA)

almond shaped eyes and a flat abstracted face. She almost looks Egyptian. In fact, Picasso has recently seen an exhibition of archaic (an ancient pre-classical style) Iberian (from Iberia–the land mass that makes up Spain and Portugal) sculpture at the Louvre. Instead of going back to the sensual myths of ancient Greece, Picasso is drawing on the real thing and doing so directly. By the way, Picasso purchased, from Apollinaire's secretary, two archaic Iberian heads that she had stolen from the Louvre! Some have suggested that they were taken at Picasso's request. Years later Picasso would anonymously return them.

Spontaneity, Carefully Choreographed

Because the canvas is roughly handled, it is often thought to be a spontaneous creation, conceived directly. This is not the case. It was preceded by nearly one hundred sketches. These studies depict different configurations. In some there are two men in addition to the women. One is a sailor. He sits in uniform in the center of the composition before a small table laden with fruit, a traditional symbol of sexuality. Another man originally entered from the left. He wore a brown suit and carried a textbook, he was meant to be a medical student.

The (Male) Artist's Gaze

Each of these male figures was meant to symbolize an aspect of Picasso. Or, more exactly, how Picasso viewed these women. The sailor is easy to figure out. The fictive sailor has been at sea for months, he is an obvious reference to pure sexual desire. The medical student is trickier. He is not there to look after the women's health but he does see them with different eyes. While the sailor represents pure lust, the student sees the women from a more analytic perspective. He understands how their bodies are constructed, etc. Could it be that Picasso was expressing the ways that he saw these women? As objects of desire, yes, but also, with a knowledge of anatomy probably superior to many doctors. What is important is that Picasso decides to remove the men. Why? Well, to begin, we might imagine where the women focused their attention in the original composition. If men are present, the prostitutes attend to them. By removing these men, the image is no longer self-contained. The women now peer outward, beyond the confines of the picture plane that ordinarily protect the viewer's anonymity. If the women peer at us, like in Manet's *Olympia* of 1863, we, as viewers, have become the customers. But this is the twentieth century, not the nineteenth, and Picasso is attempting a vulgar directness that would make even Manet cringe.

Picasso's Perception of Space

So far, we have examined the middle figure which relates to Matisse's canvas; the two masked figures on the right side who refer, by their aggression, to Picasso's fear of disease; and, we have linked the left-most figure to archaic Iberian sculpture and Picasso's attempt to elicit a sort of crude primitive directness. That leaves only one woman unaccounted for. This is the woman with her right elbow raised and her left hand on a sheet pulled across her left thigh. The table with fruit that had originally been placed at the groin of the sailor is no longer round, it has lengthened, sharpened, and has been lowered to the edge of the canvas. This table/phallus points to this last woman. Picasso's meaning is clear, the still life of fruit on a table, this ancient symbol of sexuality, is the viewer's erect penis and it points to the woman of our choice. Picasso was no feminist. In his vision, the viewer is male.

Although explicit, this imagery only points to the key issue. The woman that has been chosen is handled distinctly in terms of her relation to the surrounding space. Yes, more about space. Throughout the canvas, the women and the drapery (made of both curtains and sheets) are fractured and splintered. Here is Picasso's response to Cezanne and Matisse. The women are neither before nor behind. As in Matisse's *Red Studio*, which will be painted four years later, Picasso has begun to try to dissolve the figure/ground relationship. Now look at the woman that Picasso tells us we have chosen. Her legs are crossed and her hand rests behind her head, but although she seems to stand among the others, her position is really that of a figure that lies on her back. The problem is, we see her body perpendicular to our line of sight. Like Matisse and Cezanne before him, Picasso here renders two moments in time: as you may have figured out, we first look across at the row of women, and then we look down on to the prostitute of our/Picasso's choice.

African Masks, Women Colonized

The two figures at the right are the most aggressively abstracted with faces rendered as if they wear African masks. By 1907, when this painting was produced, Picasso had begun to collect such work. Even the striations that represent scarification is evident. Matisse and Derain had a longer standing interest in such art, but Picasso said that it was only after wandering into the Palais du Trocadero, Paris's ethnographic museum, that he understood the value of such art. Remember, France was a major colonial power in Africa in the nineteenth and twentieth centuries. Much African art was ripped from its original geographic and artistic context and sold in Paris. Although Picasso would eventually become more sophisticated regarding the original uses and meaning of the non-Western art that he collected, in 1907 his interest was largely based on what he perceived as its alien and aggressive qualities.

William Rubin, once the senior curator of the department of painting and sculpture at The Museum of Modern Art, and a leading Picasso scholar, has written extensively about this painting. He has suggested that while the painting is clearly about desire (Picasso's own), it is also an expression of his fear. We have already established that Picasso frequented brothels at this time so his desire isn't in question, but Rubin makes the case that this is only half the story.*Les Demoiselles D'Avignon* is also about Picasso's intense fear…his dread of these women or more to the point, the disease that he feared they would transmit to him. In the era before antibiotics, contracting syphilis was a well founded fear. Of course, the plight of the women seems not to enter Picasso's story.

Attributions

CC licensed content, Shared previously

Picasso, Guitar

I have seen what no man has seen before. When Pablo Picasso, leaving aside painting for a moment, was constructing this immense guitar out of sheet metal whose plans could be dispatched to any ignoramus in the universe who could put it together as well as him, I saw Picasso's studio, and this studio, more incredible than Faust's laboratory, this studio which, according to some, contained no works of art, in the old sense, was furnished with the newest of objects. . . . Some witnesses, already shocked by the things that they saw covering the walls, and that they refused to call paintings because they were made of oilcloth, wrapping paper, and newspaper, said, pointing a haughty finger at the object of Picasso's clever pains: "What is it? Does it rest on a pedestal? Does it hang on a wall? What is it, painting or sculpture?" Picasso, dressed in the blue of Parisian artisans, responded in his finest Andalusian voice: "It's nothing, it's el guitare!"; And there you are! The watertight compartments are demolished. We are delivered from painting and sculpture, which already have been liberated from the idiotic tyranny of genres. It is neither this nor that. It is nothing. It's el guitare!

—André Salmon, New French Painting, August 9, 1919

A conversation between Salman Khan and Steven Zucker about Pablo Picasso's sculpture, *Guitar* and related work:

- https://youtu.be/bfy6IxsN_lg

Pablo Picasso, *Guitar*, 1912–14, ferrous sheet metal and wire, 30 1/2 x 13 3/4 x 7 5/8″ (77.5 x 35 x 19.3 cm), (The Museum of Modern Art).

Attributions

CC licensed content, Shared previously

Picasso, Guernica

- https://youtu.be/PbLTE-ERzY0

- https://youtu.be/nf3Q7gS_YSA

Picasso, *Guernica*, oil on canvas, 1937 (Museo Reina Sofia, Madrid)

Braque, The Portuguese

Cold Coffee and Analytic Cubism

To understand Cubism it helps to go back to Cézanne's still life paintings or even further, to the Renaissance. Let me use an example that worked nicely in the classroom. I was lecturing, trying to untangle Cubism while drinking incresingly cold coffee from a paper cup. I set the cup on the desk in the front of the room and began.

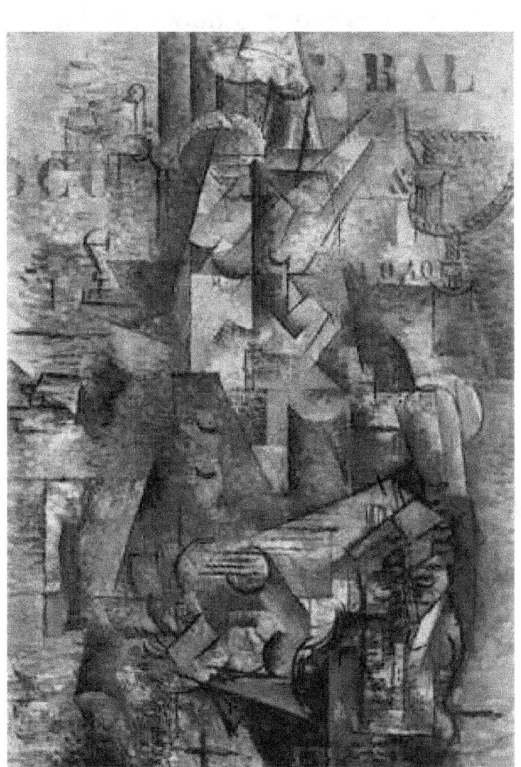

Figure 1. Georges Braque, The Portuguese, o/c, 1911 (Basel)

If I were a Renaissance artist in mid-fifteenth century Italy painting that cup on that table, I would position myself at particular point in space and construct the surrounding objects and space frozen in that spot and from that single perspective. On the other hand, if this was the late nineteenth century and I was Cézanne, I might allow myself to open this view up quite a bit. Perhaps I would focus on, and record, the perceptual changes of shape and line that result when I shift my weight from one leg to the other or when I lean in toward the cup to get a closer look. I might even allow myself to render slightly around the far side of the paper cup since, as Cézanne, I am interested in vision and memory working together. Finally, if I were Braque or Picasso in the early twentieth century, I would want to express even more on the canvas. I would not be satisfied with the limiting conventions of Renaissance perspective nor even with the initial explorations of the master Cézanne.

As a Cubist, I want to express my total visual understanding of the paper coffee cup. I want more than the Renaissance painter or even Cézanne, I want to express the entire cup simultaneously on the static surface of the canvas since I can hold all that visual information in my memory. I want to render the cup's front, its sides, its back, and its inner walls, its bottom from both inside and out, and I want to do this on a flat canvas. How can this be done? The answer is provided by *The Portuguese*. In this canvas, everything was fractured. The guitar player and the dock was just so many pieces of broken form, almost broken glass. By breaking these objects into smaller elements, Braque and Picasso are able to overcome the unified singularity of an object and instead transform it into an object of vision.

At this point the class began to look a little confused, so I turned back to the paper cup and began to tear it into pieces (I had finished the coffee). I concluded by saying, "If I want to be able to show you both the back and front and inside and outside simultaneously, I can fragment the object. Basically, this is the strategy of the Cubists."

Attributions

CC licensed content, Shared previously

- Braque, The Portuguese. **Provided by**: Khan Academy. **Located at**: https://web.archive.org/web/20141007010342/http://smarthistory.khanacademy.org/braque-the-portuguese.html. **License**: *CC BY-NC-SA: Attribution-NonCommercial-ShareAlike*

Braque, The Viaduct at L'Estaque

Dr. Beth Harris and Dr. Steven Zucker provide a description, historical perspective, and analysis of Georges Braque's *Le Viaduc à L'Estaque.*

- https://youtu.be/j2-95i4pq9g

Georges Braque, *Le Viaduc à L'Estaque, (The Viaduct at L'Estaque)*, 1908, oil on canvas, 28-5/8 x 23-1/4 inches (72.5 x 59 cm), (Musée national d'art moderne, Centre Pompidou, Paris).

Inventing Cubism

During the summer of 1908, Braque returned to Cézanne's old haunt for a second summer in a row. Previously he had painted this small port just south of Aix-en-Provence with the brilliant irreverent colors of a Fauve (Braque along with Matisse, Derain, and others defined this style from about 1904 to 1907). But now, after Cézanne's death and after having met Picasso, Braque set out on a very different tack, the invention of Cubism.

Cubism is a terrible name. Except for a very brief moment, the style has nothing to do with cubes. Instead, it is an extension of the formal ideas developed by Cézanne and broader perceptual ideas that became increasingly important in the late nineteenth and early twentieth centuries. These were the ideas that inspired Matisse as early as 1904 and Picasso perhaps a year or two later. We certainly saw such issues asserted in *Les Demoiselles d'Avi-*

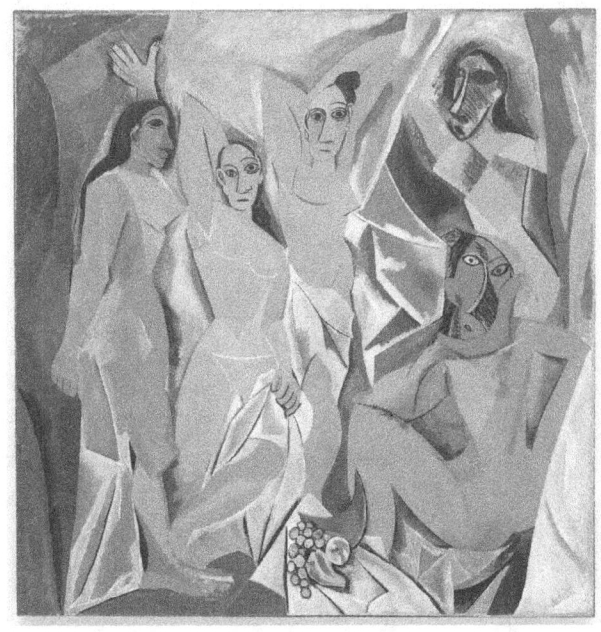

Figure 1. Pablo Picasso, Les Demoiselles d'Avignon, oil on canvas, 1907 (MoMA)

gnon. But Picasso's great 1907 canvas is not yet Cubism. It is more accurate to say that it is the foundation upon which Cubism is constructed. If we want to really see the origin of the style, we need to look beyond Picasso to his new friend Georges Braque.

A New Perspective

The young French Fauvist, Georges Braque that had been struck by both the posthumous Cézanne retrospective exhibition held in Paris in 1907 and his first sight of Picasso's radical new canvas, *Les Demoiselles d'Avignon.* Like so many people that saw it, Braque is reported to have hated it—Matisse, for example, predicted that Picasso would be found hanged behind the work, so great was his mistake. Nevertheless, Braque stated that it haunted him through the winter of 1908. Like every good Parisian, Braque fled Paris in the summer and decided to return to the part of Provance in which Cézanne had lived and worked. Braque spent the summer of 1908 shedding the colors of Fauvism and exploring the structural issues that had consumed Cézanne and now Picasso. He wrote: "It [Cézanne's impact] was more than an influence, it was an invitation. Cézanne was the first to have broken away from erudite, mechanized perspective…" (quoted in William Rubin's *Picasso and Braque: Pioneering Cubism,* New York: The Museum of Modern Art, 1989, p.353). Like Cézanne, Braque sought to undermine the illusion of depth by forcing the viewer to recognize the canvas not as a window but as it truly is, a vertical curtain that hangs before us.

Brothers of Invention

In canvases such as *Houses at L'Estaque and The Viaduct at L'Estaque* (from the video above), Braque simplifies the form of the houses, here are the so called cubes, but he nullifies the obvious recessionary overlapping with the trees that force forward even the most distant building. When Braque returned to Paris in late August, he found Picasso an eager audience. Almost immediately, Picasso began to exploit Braque's investigations. But far from being the end of their working relationship, this exchange becomes the first in a series of collaborations that lasts six years and creates an intimate creative bound between these two artists that is unique in the history of art. Between the years 1908 and the beginning of the First World War in 1914, Braque and Picasso work together so closely that even experts can have difficulty telling the work of one artist from the other. For months on end they would visit each others studio on an almost daily basis sharing ideas and challenging each other as they went. Still, a pattern did emerge and it tended to be to Picasso's benefit. When a radical new idea was introduced, more then likely, it was Braque that recognized

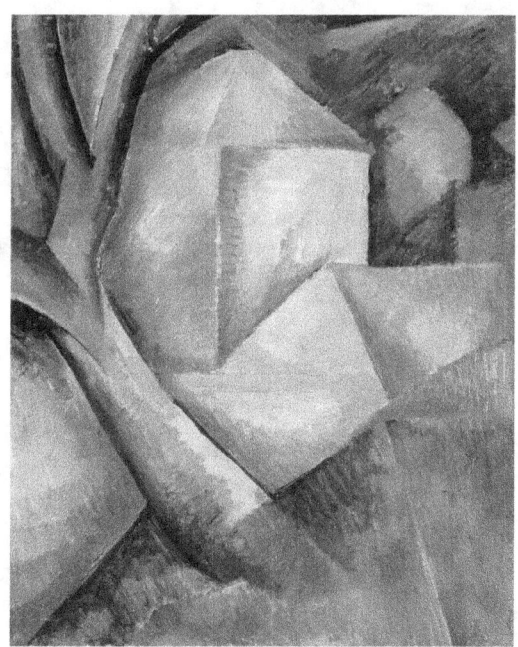

Figure 2. Georges Braque, Houses at l'Estaque, o/ c, 1908 (Bern)

its value. But it was inevitably Picasso who realized its potential and was able to fully exploit it.

Tough Art

By 1910, Cubism had matured into a complex system that is seemingly so esoteric that it appears to have rejected all esthetic concerns. The average museum visitor, when confronted by a 1910 or 1911 canvas by Braque or Picasso, the period known as Analytic Cubism, often looks somewhat put upon even while they may acknowledge the importance of such work. I suspect that the difficulty, is, well . . . the difficulty of the work. Cubism is an analysis of vision and of its representation and it is challenging. As a society we seem to believe that all art ought to be easily understandable or at least beautiful. That's the part I find confusing.

Attributions

Duchamp, Fountain

Dr. Beth Harris and Dr. Steven Zucker provide a description, historical perspective, and analysis of Marcel Duchamp's *Fountain*.

- https://youtu.be/FmjSUyyc-3M

Marcel Duchamp, *Fountain*, 1917/1964, porcelain urinal, paint, (San Francisco Museum of Modern Art).

Attributions

CC licensed content, Shared previously

Arp, Untitled

Dr. Beth Harris and Dr. Steven Zucker provide a description, historical perspective, and analysis of Jean (Hans) Arp's *Untitled.*

- https://youtu.be/3wm0589mLbM

Jean (Hans) Arp, *Untitled (Collage with Squares Arranged According to the Laws of Chance),* 1916-17, mixed media, (MoMA).

Klee, Twittering Machine

Dr. Juliana Kreinik and Dr. Steven Zucker provide a description, historical perspective, and analysis of Paul Klee's *Twittering Machine (Die Zwitscher-Maschine)*.

- https://youtu.be/M7yd8F3eay4

Paul Klee, *Twittering Machine (Die Zwitscher-Maschine)*, 1922, watercolor, ink, and gouache on paper, 25 1/4″ × 19″, (MoMA).

Attributions

An Introduction to Futurism

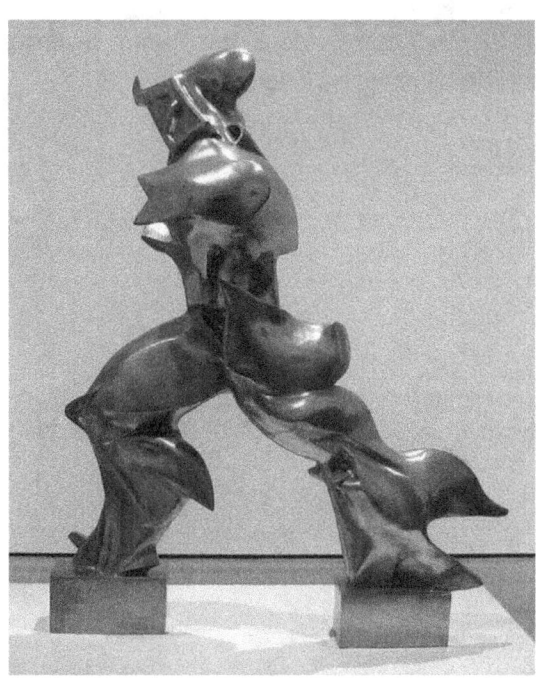

Figure 1. Umberto Boccioni, Unique Forms of Continuity in Space, 1913 (cast 1931), bronze, 43 7/8 × 34 7/8 × 15 3/4" (MoMA)

Can you imagine being so enthusiastic about technology that you name your daughter Propeller? Today we take most technological advances for granted, but at the turn of the last century, innovations like electricity, x-rays, radio waves, automobiles and airplanes were novel and extremely exciting. Italy lagged Britain, France, Germany, and the United States in the pace of its industrial development. Culturally speaking, the country's artistic reputation was grounded in Ancient, Renaissance and Baroque art and culture. Simply put, Italy represented the past.

In the early 1900s, a group of young and rebellious Italian writers and artists emerged determined to celebrate industrialization. They were frustrated by Italy's declining status and believed that the "Machine Age" would result in an entirely new world order and even a renewed consciousness. Filippo Tommaso Marinetti, the ringleader of this group, called the movement Futurism. Its members sought to capture the idea of modernity, the sensations and aesthetics of speed, movement, and industrial development.

A Manifesto

Marinetti launched Futurism in 1909 with the publication his "Futurist manifesto" on the front page of the French newspaper *Le Figaro*. The manifesto set a fiery tone. In it Marinetti lashed out against cultural tradition (*passatismo*, in Italian) and called for the destruction of museums, libraries, and feminism. Futurism quickly grew into an international movement and its participants issued additional manifestos for nearly every type of art: painting, sculpture, architecture, music, photography, cinema—even clothing. The Futurist painters—Umberto Boccioni, Carlo Carrà, Luigi Russolo, Gino Severini, and Giacomo Balla—signed their first manifesto in 1910 (the last named his daughter Elica—Propeller!). Futurist painting had first looked to the color and the optical experiments of the late 19th century, but in the fall of 1911, Marinetti and the Futurist painters visited the Salon d'Automne in Paris and saw Cubism in person for the first time. Cubism had an immediate impact that can be seen in Boccioni's *Materia* of 1912 for example. Nevertheless, the Futurists declared their work to be completely original.

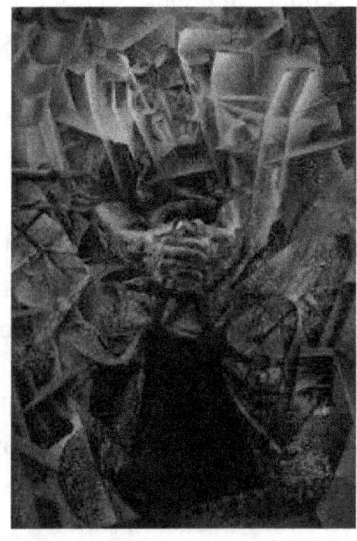

Figure 2. Umberto Boccioni, Materia, 1912 (reworked 1913), oil on canvas, 226 × 150 cm (Mattioli Collection loaned to Peggy Guggenheim Collection, Venice)

Dynamism of Bodies in Motion

The Futurists were particularly excited by the works of late nineteenth-century scientist and photographer Étienne-Jules Marey, whose chronophotographic (time-based) studies depicted the mechanics of animal and human movement.

- https://youtu.be/kMh7GI9pEIY

A precursor to cinema, Marey's innovative experiments with time-lapse photography were especially influential for Balla. In his painting *Dynamism of a Dog on a Leash* (figure 3), the artist playfully renders the dog's (and dog walker's) feet as continuous movements through space over time.

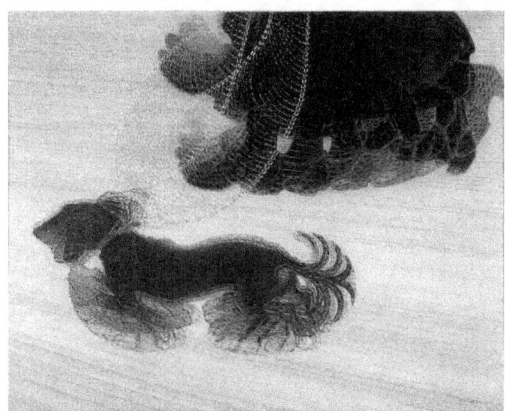

Figure 3. Giacomo Balla, Dynamism of a Dog on a Leash, 1912, oil on canvas, 35 1/2 × 43 1/4 " (Albright-Knox Art Gallery, Buffalo)

The choice of shiny bronze lends a mechanized quality to Boccioni's sculpture, so here is the Futurists' ideal combination of human and machine. The figure's pose is at once graceful and forceful, and despite their adamant rejection of classical arts, it is also very similar to the *Nike of Samothrace* (figure 4).

Politics and War

Futurism was one of the most politicized art movements of the twentieth century. It merged artistic and political agendas in order to propel change in Italy and across Europe. The Futurists would hold what they called *serate futuriste*, or Futurist evenings, where they would recite poems and display art, while also shouting politically charged rhetoric at the audience in the hope of inciting riot. They believed that agitation and destruction would end the status quo and allow for the regeneration of a stronger, energized Italy.

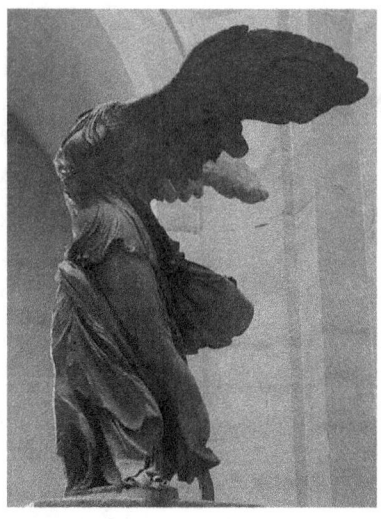

Figure 4. Nike of Samothrace, marble, c. 190 BCE, (Louvre, Paris)

These positions led the Futurists to support the coming war, and like most of the group's members, leading painter Boccioni enlisted in the army during World War I. He was trampled to death after falling from a horse during training. After the war, the members' intense nationalism led to an alliance with Benito Mussolini and his National Fascist Party. Although Futurism continued to develop new areas of focus (*aeropittura*, for example) and attracted new members—the so-called "second generation" of Futurist artists—the movement's strong ties to Fascism has complicated the study of this historically significant art.

Attributions

CC licensed content, Shared previously

- Italian Futurism: An Introduction. **Authored by**: Emily Casden. **Provided by**: Khan Academy. **Located at**: https://web.archive.org/web/20140713183155/http://smarthistory.khanacademy.org/futurism.html. **License**: *CC BY-NC-SA: Attribution-NonCommercial-ShareAlike*

- Nike of Samothrace. **Authored by**: Jorg Bittner Unna. **Located at**: https://commons.wikimedia.org/wiki/File:Nike_JBU03.JPG. **License**: *CC BY: Attribution*

All rights reserved content

- Etienne Jules Marey - L Homme Machine. **Authored by**: meisenstrasse. **Located at**: https://youtu.be/kMh7GI9pEIY. **License**: *All Rights Reserved*. **License Terms**: Standard YouTube License

Three Futurists

Dr. Beth Harris and an anonymous professional provide a description, historical perspective, and analysis of three futurist paintings: *Dynamism of a Dog on a Leash, Dynamic Hieroglyph of the Bal Tabarin,* and *Unique Forms of Continuity in Space.*

- https://youtu.be/JHul281Kmtk

Works Discussed

Giacoma Balla, *Dynamism of a Dog on a Leash*, oil, 1912 (Albright-Knox, Buffalo)

Gino Severini, *Dynamic Hieroglyph of the Bal Tabarin*, oil, 1912 (MoMA)

Umberto Boccioni, *Unique Forms of Continuity in Space*, bronze, 1913 (MoMA)

Malevich

Sal Khan, Steven Zucker, and Beth Harris discuss art and its context using Monet's *Cliff Walk at Pourville* and Malevich's *Suprematist Composition: White on White* to illustrate their points.

- https://youtu.be/2aUFB9hQncQ

Works Discussed

Claude Monet, *Cliff Walk at Pourville*, 1882, oil on canvas, 66.5 cm × 82.3 cm (26 1⁄8 in × 32 7⁄16 in), (Art Institute of Chicago).

Kazmir Malevich, *Suprematist Composition: White on White*, 1918, oil on canvas, 79.4 cm × 79.4 cm (31 1/4 in × 31 1/4 in), (Museum of Modern Art, New York City).

Attributions

Mondrian, Composition No. II

Dr. Beth Harris and Dr. Steven Zucker provide a description, historical perspective, and analysis of Mondrian's *Composition No. II, with Red and Blue.*

- https://youtu.be/NpWxl4C0OWU

Piet Mondrian, *Composition No. II, with Red and Blue*, oil on canvas, 1929 (original date partly obliterated; mistakenly repainted 1925 by Mondrian). Oil on canvas, 15 7/8 × 12 5/8″ (40.3 × 32.1 cm), (The Museum of Modern Art)

Attributions

Modigliani, Young Woman in a Shirt

Dr. Beth Harris and Dr. Steven Zucker provide a description, historical perspective, and analysis of Amedeo Modigliani's *Young Woman in a Shirt*.

- https://youtu.be/3sCB3udmu1Y

Amedeo Modigliani, *Young Woman in a Shirt*, 1918, oil on canvas, (Albertina, Vienna).

External Link

View this painting up close in the Google Art Project:

- https://www.google.com/culturalinstitute/asset-viewer/young-woman-in-a-shirt-1918/CwGG-pJkW2nrjpQ?projectId=art-project

---

Attributions

Maholy-Nagy

Dr. Beth Harris and Dr. Steven Zucker provide a description, historical perspective, and analysis of László Moholy-Nagy's *Composition A.XX*.

- https://youtu.be/YeBe-yDGVnU

László Moholy-Nagy, *Composition A.XX*, 1924, oil on canvas, 135.5 × 115 cm, (Musée national d'art moderne, Centre Georges Pompidou, Paris).

Attributions

Chapter 13:
1907–1960–Age of
Global Conflict Part II

Chapter 13 Overview

What You'll Learn To Do: Examine Modern art and its influence on art history as a whole.

In Chapter 13 we will continue to examine Modern art. We will look at how artists like Pollock contributed to the development of Western art. It is imperative to understand Modern art in order to see how it impacted later artistic developments.

Learning Activities

The learning activities for this module include:

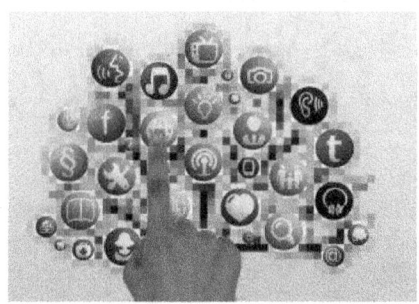

- **Read:** Key Learning Items

Surrealism

- **Read:** Man Ray, The Gift
- **Watch:** Giacometti, The Palace at 4 a.m. (2:20)
- **Watch:** Giacometti, The City Square (7:26)
- **Watch:** Magritte, The Treachery of Images (3:40)
- **Watch:** Dali, The Persistence of Memory (6:27)
- **Read:** Dali, Metamorphosis of Narcissus (includes a video: 4:07)

Art in Nazi Germany

- **Read:** House of Art (includes a video: 7:21)

Ashcan School

- **Watch:** George Bellows (3:35)

American Regionalism

- **Watch:** Grant Wood, American Gothic (6:19)

American Abstraction

- **Watch:** Georgia O'Keeffe (2:35)

American Realism

- **Read:** Edward Hopper, Nighthawks (includes a video: 4:47)

Latin American Modernism

- **Watch:** Frida Kahlo and Diego Rivera (3:48)

Abstract Expressionism

- **Read:** Origins of Abstract Expressionism
- **Read:** Impact of Abstract Expressionism
- **Watch:** Pollock, One: Number 31, 1950 (7:34)
- **Watch:** Pollock's Painting Techniques (12:17)
- **Watch:** Rothko, No. 3/No. 13 (5:11)
- **Watch:** Rothko's Painting Technique (3:28)
- **Watch:** Newman, Onement 1 (4:52)
- **Watch:** Newman's Painting Technique (3:44)
- **Watch:** de Kooning, Woman I (3:39)
- **Read:** Robert Motherwell (includes a video: 4:00)

New York School

- **Watch:** Jasper Johns (6:04)
- **Watch:** Rauschenberg (4:47)
- **Watch:** Reinhardt (4:34)

Photography

- **Read:** Introduction to Photography
- **Watch:** Cartier-Bresson (4:02)

Sculpture

- **Watch:** Brancusi, Bird in Space (2:38)

Architecture

- **Read:** Gilbert, Woolworth Building
- **Watch:** Frank Lloyd Wright, Guggenheim Museum (7:12)
- **Watch:** Mies van der Rohe, Seagram Building (9:08)

Attributions

CC licensed content, Original

- Art History II. **Provided by**: Extended Learning Institute of Northern Virginia Community College. **Located at**: http://eli.nvcc.edu/. **License**: *CC BY: Attribution*

Public domain content

- Image of Finger. **Authored by**: geralt. **Located at**: https://pixabay.com/en/finger-touch-hand-structure-769300/. **License**: *Public Domain: No Known Copyright*

Key Learning Items

Key Vocabulary Terms

- Surrealism
- Ashcan School
- American Regionalism
- American Abstraction
- American Realism
- Latin American Modernism

- Abstract Expressionism

- Action Painting

- drip technique

- Color Field Painting

- New York School

- combine

Here are links to art history glossaries that will help you better understand the above key vocabulary terms.

- ArtLex: Art Dictionary

  - http://www.artlex.com/

- About.com: Art History

  - http://arthistory.about.com/od/glossary/l/bl_Art-Glossary.htm

- Artcyclopedia: A Guide to Fine Art

  - http://www.artcyclopedia.com/

Attributions

CC licensed content, Original

Man Ray, The Gift

Man Ray and *The Gift*

The American artist Man Ray (born Emanuel Radnitzky in 1890; d. 1976) arrived in Paris in 1921. Within a year, the artist had his first solo show at a Parisian gallery. Among the works he exhibited was one unlisted sculpture: the object, which he called *The Gift*, was an everyday flatiron with brass tacks glued in a column down its center. According to Man Ray in his autobiography *Self-Portrait*, the object was made quickly, in a bout of inspiration, the day of the gallery opening.

What do we make of Man Ray's relatively simple, yet subversive act of presenting a modified household appliance as a work of art? The flatiron—intended to smooth wrinkles from fabric—has been rendered useless with the addition of a row of brass tacks. We are perhaps expected to react the way the store owner supposedly did when Man Ray purchased these items, by exclaiming, "But you'll ruin the shirt if you put tacks there!"

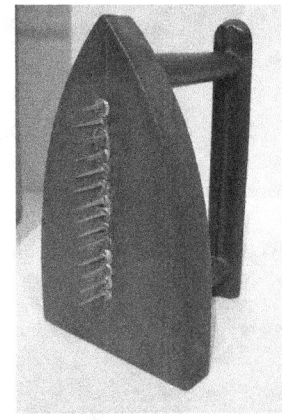

Figure 1. Man Ray, Cadeau (Gift), flatiron with brass tacks, 1921 (remade in 1963)

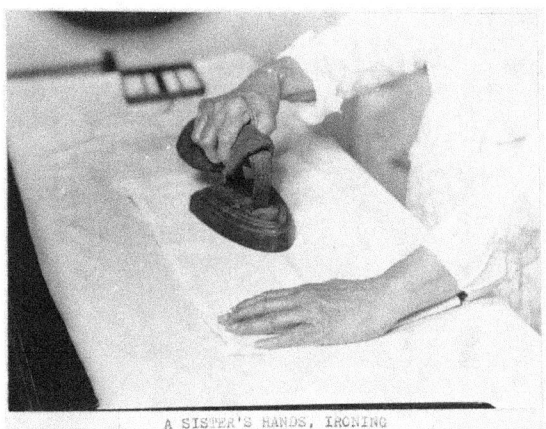

Figure 2. A flatiron in use, 1930s, photograph by Samuel Kravitt, "A Sister's Hands Ironing," Hancock Shaker Village, Massachusetts, c. 1931–36 (Library of Congress)

Dada, or the Nonsense of the Everyday

Before arriving in Paris, May Ray was associated with the New York Dada group, which included the artist Marcel Duchamp. As a loosely-affiliated group of like-minded artists, they were particularly interested in using humor and antagonism to question the definition of a work of art. Re-defining art was prevalent in Duchamp's Readymades, such as his *Bicycle Wheel*, a sculpture made by conjoining a bicycle wheel and a stool, two utilitarian objects.

The Surrealist Object

Although made in the spirit of Dada, Man Ray's Gift prefigured by several years a key artistic practice that would develop within the Surrealist movement: the "Surrealist object," a type of three-dimensional art work that included found objects, modified objects, and sculpted objects.

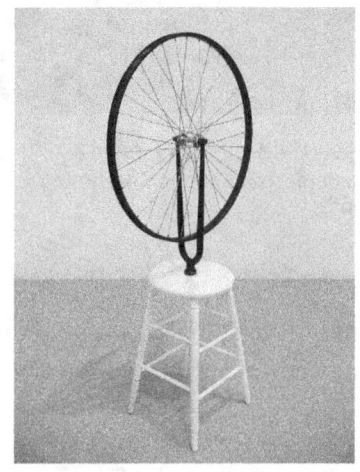

The Surrealist object—one of many literary and visual practices in the movement—became prominent beginning in 1936, after its association with a series of extravagant international expositions organized in London and Paris. Surrealism had been first publicly announced in 1924, with the publication of André Breton's first "Manifesto of Surrealism." Stridently activist, Surrealists sought to release society from cultural constraints and the need to conform to social norms, which they felt curtailed people's desires to live as they wished.

Figure 3. Marcel Duchamp, Bicycle Wheel, 1913

Function/Dysfunction

Of the many types of Surrealist objects that were produced, two important features are present in Man Ray's *The Gift*. First, an everyday object has been changed so that its original function is denied. Indeed, the artist's relatively simple addition of tacks transforms a useful device into a destructive one.

Second, Man Ray's alteration gives a common object a symbolic function. The flatiron, associated with social expectations of propriety and middle-class values, becomes a subversive attack on social expectations. Even if Man Ray's tack-lined iron is no longer used for pressing clothes, the object resonates with ruinous, violent possibilities.

Denial and Destruction

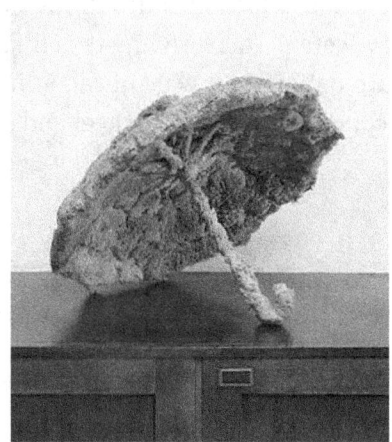

Figure 4. Wolfgang Paalen,
Articulated Cloud, umbrella in foam,
1938

While denial and destruction are qualities are not intrinsic to all Surrealist art, there are striking examples, like *The Gift*, that show Surrealists working with banal objects to question the viewer's expectations, and force us to re-evaluate the function of those objects in our lives.

Wolfgang Paalen's work from 1938, *Articulated Cloud* (figure 4), an umbrella crafted from spongy foam, denies the object's intended function by causing water to be absorbed rather than repelled. It also makes the umbrella rather useless for anyone seeking shelter from rain.

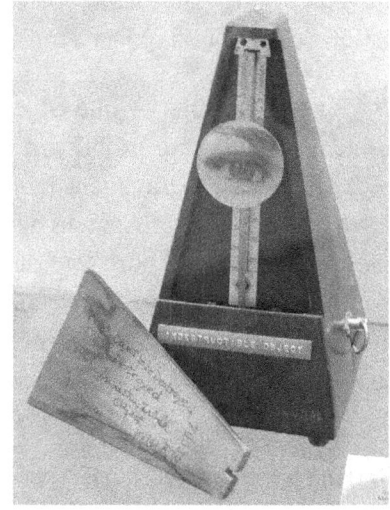

Figure 5. Man Ray, Object to Be
Destroyed (Renamed Indestructible
Object), 1923 (1964 replica)

Another object by Man Ray—a metronome with a photograph of a woman's open eye clipped to it—adds an ominous sense of relentless observation to an ordinary musician's timing instrument. Man Ray's title of the piece, *Object to Be Destroyed*, seems mysterious at first.

But when we consider the psychological effects of such obsessive observation—and think about what kind of impulses such regulations might evoke—the artist's title becomes easier to understand.

No longer a simple time-keeping device, *Object To Be Destroyed* summons feelings of irritation over being watched, and powerlessness in the face of endless time. There is no means to stop the cycle, except to destroy the object itself.

Don't Touch the Art!

The violent implications of *The Gift* and other Surrealist objects by Man Ray came to fruition in 1957 when *Object to Be Destroyed* was lost during a Man Ray retrospective. Varying stories exist as to the fate of the sculpture. In his autobiography, Man Ray recounts that a group of students visited the exhibition and caused a scene, during which one of them walked off with the sculpture, and it was never seen again. Numerous historians, however, state that during the exhibition one of the students took the title literally and smashed it with a hammer.

Whether stolen or smashed, *Object to Be Destroyed* no longer existed. This compelled Man Ray to remake the sculpture, but he pointedly changed the title to *Indestructible Object*.

Attributions

cial-ShareAlike

- Man Ray: Cadeau (Gift), 1963. **Authored by**: Tom Ipri. **Located at**: https://flic.kr/p/aerxW2. **License**: *CC BY-SA: Attribution-ShareAlike*

- Bicycle Wheel. **Authored by**: spDuchamp. **Located at**: https://flic.kr/p/3wMXs. **License**: *CC BY: Attribution*

- W. Paalen, Nuage articule II. **Authored by**: Andreas Neufert. **Located at**: https://commons.wikimedia.org/wiki/File:W.Paalen,_Nuage_articul%C3%A9_II_small.jpg. **License**: *CC BY-SA: Attribution-ShareAlike*

- Man Ray, Indestructible Object, 1923 / 1963. **Authored by**: Andrew Russeth. **Located at**: https://flic.kr/p/7agxav. **License**: *CC BY-SA: Attribution-ShareAlike*

Public domain content

- A sister's hands, ironing. **Authored by**: Samuel Kravitt. **Provided by**: Library of Congress. **Located at**: http://www.loc.gov/pictures/item/2005680454/. **License**: *Public Domain: No Known Copyright*

Giacometti, The Palace at 4 a.m.

Dr. Beth Harris and Dr. Steven Zucker provide a description, historical perspective, and analysis of Alberto Giacometti's *Palace at 4am.*

- https://youtu.be/3zU90x0OZ0Y

Alberto Giacometti, *Palace at 4am*, 1932, wood, glass, wire and string, (MoMA).

Attributions

CC licensed content, Shared previously

Giacometti, The City Square

Dr. Beth Harris and Dr. Steven Zucker provide a description, historical perspective, and analysis of Alberto Giacometti's *City Square*.

- https://youtu.be/6pSOOgJz44o

Alberto Giacometti, *City Square*, 1948, bronze, (MoMA).

Attributions

Magritte, The Treachery of Images

Dr. Beth Harris and Dr. Steven Zucker provide a description, historical perspective, and analysis of René Magritte's *The Treachery of Images*.

- https://youtu.be/w702yvnip_w

René Magritte, *The Treachery of Images* (Ceci n'est pas une pipe), 1929 (LACMA)

Dali, The Persistence of Memory

Sal Khan and Dr. Steven Zucker provide a description, historical perspective, and analysis of Salvador Dalí's *The Persistence of Memory*.

- https://youtu.be/6mp-fBJNQmU

Salvador Dalí, *The Persistence of Memory*, 1931 (The Museum of Modern Art).

Attributions

Dali, Metamorphosis of Narcissus

Dr. Beth Harris and Dr. Steven Zucker provide a description, historical perspective, and analysis of Salvador Dalí's *Metamorphosis of Narcissus.*

- https://youtu.be/HUZDPWLTZ0g

Salvador Dalí, *Metamorphosis of Narcissus*, 1937, oil on canvas, 51.1 × 78.1 cm (Tate Modern, London).

The ancient source of this subject is Ovid's *Metamorphosis* (Book 3, lines 339–507), which tells of Narcissus who upon seeing his own image reflected in a pool so falls in love that he could not look away, eventually he vanishes and in his place is a "sweet flower, gold and white, the white around the gold."

Dalí's poem, below, accompanied the painting when it was initially exhibited:

> Narcissus,
> in his immobility,
> absorbed by his reflection with the digestive slowness of carnivorous plants,
> becomes invisible.
> There remains of him only the hallucinatingly white oval of his head,
> his head again more tender,
> his head, chrysalis of hidden biological designs,
> his head held up by the tips of the water's fingers,
> at the tips of the fingers
> of the insensate hand,
> of the terrible hand,
> of the mortal hand
> of his own reflection.
> When that head slits
> when that head splits
> when that head bursts,
> it will be the flower,
> the new Narcissus,
> Gala—my Narcissus

Attributions

CC licensed content, Shared previously

- Dali, Metamorphosis of Narcissus. **Authored by**: Dr. Beth Harris and Dr. Steven Zucker. **Provided by**: Khan Academy. **Located at**: https://www.khanacademy.org/humanities/art-1010/art-between-wars/surrealism1/v/dal-metamorphosis-of-narcissus-1937. **License**: *CC BY-NC-SA: Attribution-NonCommercial-ShareAlike*

House of Art

Dr. Beth Harris and Dr. Steven Zucker provide a historical discussion on the House of (German) Art (1933–37) in relation to the *Great Exhibition of German Art* and the *Entartete Kunst (Degenerate Art)* Exhibitions of 1937 in Munich. The House of German Art now exhibits international contemporary art in direct opposition to original National Socialist intent.

- https://youtu.be/hpY22uSAPAA

Nazi Art Policy

How do you destroy an artwork? You can hide it, scratch it, tear it, put a slogan over it, burn it, or, as the Nazis did in 1937, simply show it to millions of people.

If you visited Munich in the summer of that year, you could see two spectacular exhibitions that were held only a few hundred meters apart. One was the Great German Art Exhibition, showcasing recent leading examples of *Aryan* art. The other was the Degenerate Art Exhibition, which offered a tour through the art that the National Socialist Party had rejected on ideological grounds. It was made up of art that was not considered *Aryan* and offered a last glimpse before these works of art disappeared.

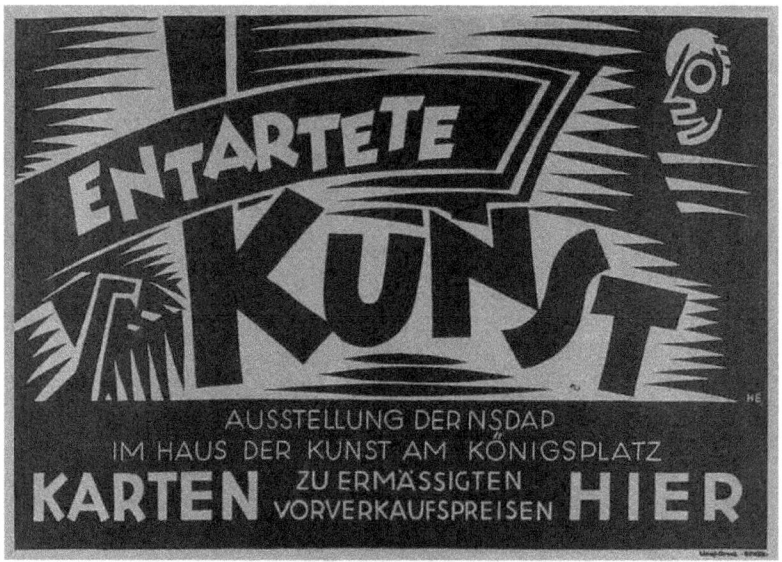

Figure 1. Entartete Kunst poster, Berlin, 1938

The Degenerate Art Exhibition cleverly manipulated visitors to loathe and ridicule the art on exhibit, in part by erasing their original meaning. Until shortly before the exhibition, these paintings and sculptures had been displayed at the nation's greatest museums, but now they were the principal performers in a freak show. The shock-value was enhanced by only allowing over-18s into the exhibition. The lines for the Degenerate Art Exhibition went around the block. Inside, many pictures had been taken out of their frames, and were attached to walls that were emblazoned with outraged slogans. Rather than whispering respectfully, people pointed and snickered. The paintings and sculptures had lost their status as artworks, and were now reduced to dangerous and outrageous rubbish.

Visual symbolism was important to the Nazis, and Hitler himself had been a painter, so it is not surprising that they dedicated significant resources promoting their ideals through art. So how was the decision made? How were "degenerate" and "Aryan" artworks selected? If you look at the works of art that were glorified and compare them to those that were attacked by the Nazis, the differences usually seem clear enough; experimental, personal, non-representational art was rejected, whilst conventionally 'beautiful,' stereotypically heroic art was revered. This seems like an obvious line to be taken by a totalitarian regime: everyone will find these artworks beautiful, and everyone will feel and think the same thing about them, without the risk of unwanted, random, personal, or unclear interpretations.

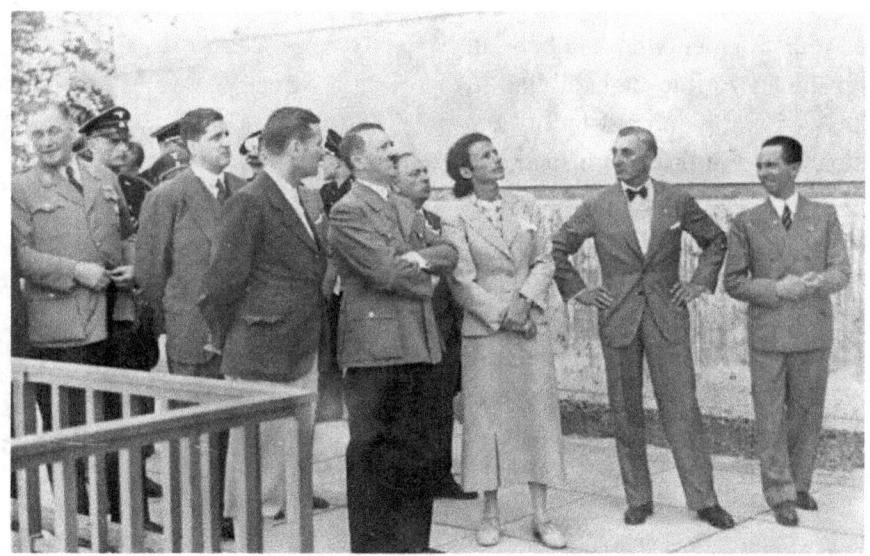

Figure 2. Tour of the House of German Art by Adolf Hitler on 05/05/37. In addition, Prof. Troost, president of the Academy of Fine Arts Ziegler and Dr. Goebbels were in attendance.

A Very Simple Decision

And the Nazis presented it as a very simple decision, any true German would immediately be able to tell the difference. But in reality, a four-year battle was fought all the way to the top echelons of the Nazi hierarchy over what 'Aryan' art was supposed to be, exactly. The opinions on this could not have been more contradictory, and top Nazi officials such as Heinrich Himmler, Joseph Goebbels and Alfred Rosenberg championed the art they each preferred.

Surprisingly, before 1937, Goebbels–and many other Nazis–collected modern art. Goebbels had works of modern art in his study, his living room and was a fan of many artists that eventually ended up in the

Degenerate Art Exhibition. Heinrich Himmler was interested in mystical, Germanic art that harked back to a tribal past. Another influential Nazi, Alfred Rosenberg, liked the pastoral, romantic style that depicted humble farmers, rural landscapes and blond maidens.

Hitler would have none of it. He loathed Expressionism and modern art whilst pastoral idylls were not serious enough. Goebbels reversed himself and became one of the driving forces behind the Degenerate Art Exhibition, prosecuting the same artworks he had once enjoyed. Rosenberg also let go, albeit reluctantly, whilst Himmler changed tack and stole artworks by the wagonload behind Hitler's back throughout the war.

So How Was "Aryan" Art Defined?

In a sense, the concept of "Aryan" art was defined by what it was not: anything that was ideologically problematic (that did not fit with the extremist beliefs of the regime) was removed until there little left but an academic style that celebrated youth, optimism, power and eternal triumph. Nevertheless, it remained difficult for even the most influential Nazis to understand the selection criteria for art sanctioned by the state.

Take for example Adolf Ziegler, who had been in charge of selecting the artwork to be exhibited in the Great German Art Exhibition. Just before the show opened, Hitler visited in order to inspect the artwork chosen to represent the eternal future of Nazi Germany. He was not pleased with the selection his most loyal followers had made. On the 5th of June, 1937, Goebbels wrote in his diary that the Führer was "wild with rage" and subsequently issued a statement declaring "I will not tolerate unfinished paintings," meaning that the exhibition had to be reconceived at the last minute.

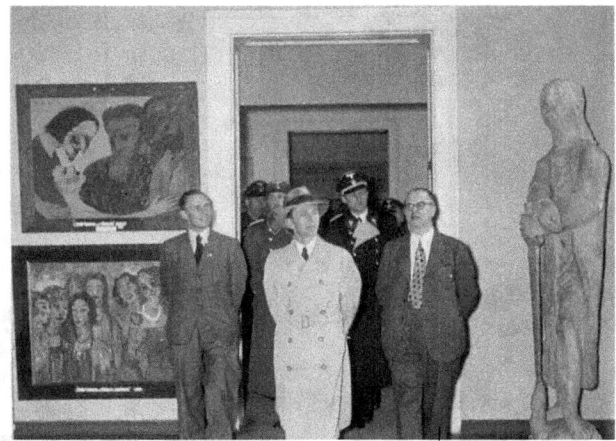

Figure 3. Reich Minister Dr. Goebbels at the exhibition "Degenerate Art." On a Sunday afternoon, the Minister visited the "Haus der Kunst."

Even opportunistic "hard-liners" like Adolf Ziegler, an artist favored by Hitler, were not quite able to fulfill their patron's vision. However, it would not be right to conclude that the criteria for art that represented the "Aryan" state appears to have been based principally on the eye of Adolf Hitler rather than a set of delineated characteristics. Even Hitler's taste was not the ultimate indicator of "Aryan" art: whilst planning what great artworks he would take from the conquered museums of Europe for his never-realized Führer-Museum, he was convinced by his newly appointed museum director that his taste was not up to standard for the world-class museum he envisaged. Rather than firing the man, Hitler deferred to this Dr. Hans Posse, despite the fact that he had recently been fired from his post as museum director in Dresden for endorsing "degenerate art."

What Was Actually on Display in the Two Exhibitions?

The Degenerate Art Exhibition mostly exhibited Expressionism, New Objectivism and some abstract art. Strangely, very few works came from Jewish artists, and a lot of artworks had until recently been favorites of many Nazis. Renowned works by artists such as Ernst Ludwig Kirchner, Karl Schmidt-Rotluff and Ernst Barlach now hung on walls marked with graffiti. The works ranged from quiet and traditional looking, such as Ernst Barlach's *The Reunion (Das Wiedersehen)*, 1926 which showed two poised, realistically carved wooden figures holding each other, to more grotesquely painted works, such as Otto Dix's *War Cripples (Kriegskrüppel)*, 1920: https://www.nga.gov/exhibitions/2006/dada/images/artwork/ 202-739.shtm. This work shows a procession of cartoonesque yet morbid war veterans, painfully moving forward with the aid of push chairs, prosthetic legs and crutches, smoking cheerfully, though one soldier's face is half eaten away, revealing a rictus grin of clenched teeth.

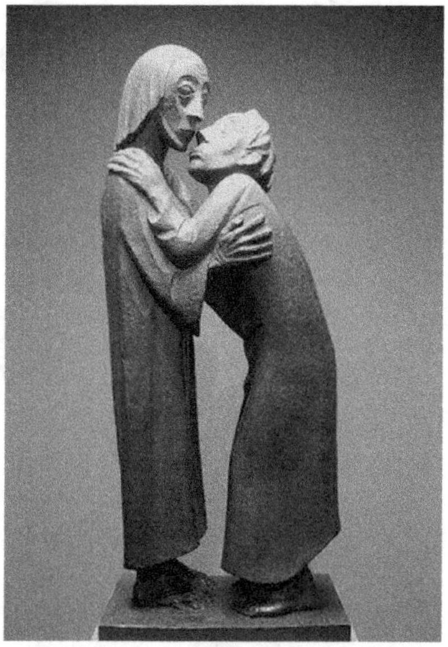

Figure 4. Ernst Barlach, The Reunion (Das Wiedersehen), 1926 mahogany, 90 × 38 × 25 cm, Ernst Barlach Haus, Hamburg

In contrast, the Great German Art Exhibition showed art with the hallmarks of classical tradition, large sculptures of tall and muscular bodies and paintings of heroic soldiers by artists such as Josef Thorak and Arno Breker. Prominent position was given to Breker's *Decathlete ('Zehnkämpfer')* and *Victory ('Siegerin')*, both made in 1936, showing two bronze figures over three metres high, their impersonal facial expressions and perfectly proportioned bodies almost archetypical examples of the classical style.

However, in later editions of the Great German Art Exhibition, works that did not fit the ideals of beauty, youth and optimism crept back in. Realistically painted works depicting soldiers despairing in the trenches by Albert Heinrich and sad, emasciated figures like the bust *Der Walzmeister* by Fritz Koelle began to share the space with oversized muscular bronze men and paintings of serene nude women.

The random nature of Nazi art policy continued after these exhibitions closed. Breker and Thorak, superstars of the Nazi regime, actually had some works branded as degenerate (though this was quickly covered up), whereas the artist Emil Nolde, who joined the Nazi party and was an early and enthusiastic supporter, had been issued a so-called *Malverbot* forbidding him to paint even in the privacy of his own home. He received regular visits from the Gestapo, the secret police, who came to touch his brushes to ensure that they had not been used. Nolde became a water-color painter. The brushes dried a lot faster than with oil paint.

Attributions

CC licensed content, Shared previously

- Munchen, Besichtigung Haus der Deutschen Kunst. **Authored by**: Bundesarchiv, Bild 183-1992-0410-546. **Provided by**: German Federal Archives. **Located at**: https://commons.wikimedia.org/wiki/File:Bundesarchiv_Bild_183-1992-0410-546,_M%C3%BCnchen,_Besichtigung_Haus_der_Deutschen_Kunst.jpg. **License**: *CC BY-SA: Attribution-ShareAlike*

- Ausstellung entartete kunst 1937. **Authored by**: Bundesarchiv, Bild 183-H02648. **Provided by**: German Federal Archives. **Located at**: https://commons.wikimedia.org/wiki/File:Ausstellung_entartete_kunst_1937.jpg. **License**: *CC BY-SA: Attribution-ShareAlike*

- Eichenholz, Ernst Barlach Haus. **Authored by**: Rufus46. **Located at**: https://commons.wikimedia.org/wiki/File:Ernst_Barlach_Das_Wiedersehen_1926_Mahagoni-1.jpg. **License**: *CC BY-SA: Attribution-ShareAlike*

George Bellows

Dr. Beth Harris and Dr. Steven Zucker provide a description, historical perspective, and analysis of George Bellows's *Pennsylvania Station Excavation*.

- https://youtu.be/CIH3VBBL69k

George Bellows, *Pennsylvania Station Excavation*, oil on canvas, c. 1907–08 (Brooklyn Museum)

External Link
View this painting up close in the Google Art Project: • https://www.google.com/culturalinstitute/asset-viewer/pennsylvania-station-excavation/NwGO-JBG7pSUwGQ?projectId=art-project

Attributions

CC licensed content, Shared previously

Grant Wood, American Gothic

Dr. Beth Harris and Dr. Steven Zucker provide a description, historical perspective, and analysis of Grant Wood's *American Gothic*.

- https://youtu.be/vk2GvyNmYD0

Grant Wood, *American Gothic*, 1930, oil on beaver board, 78 × 65.3 cm (30-3/4 × 25-3/4 inches), (The Art Institute of Chicago).

External Link
View this painting up close in the Google Art Project: - https://www.google.com/culturalinstitute/asset-viewer/american-gothic/5QEPm0jCc183Aw?projectId=art-project

Attributions

Georgia O'Keeffe

The Lawrence Tree was painted in the summer of 1929 while O'Keefe was visiting D.H. Lawrence at his Kiowa Ranch during O'Keeffe's first trip to New Mexico; the tree stands in front of the house. Dr. Beth Harris and Dr. Steven Zucker provide a description, historical perspective, and analysis of the work below:

- https://youtu.be/wQq2xOs2BYU

Georgia O'Keeffe, *The Lawrence Tree*, 1929, oil on canvas, 31 × 40 inches, (Wadsworth Atheneum, Hartford).

Edward Hopper, Nighthawks

Dr. Beth Harris and Dr. Steven Zucker provide a description, historical perspective, and analysis of Edward Hopper's *Nighthawks*.

- https://youtu.be/j24uh8cZ3wA

Edward Hopper, *Nighthawks*, 1942, oil on canvas, 84.1 × 152.4 cm / 33-1/8 × 60 inches (The Art Institute of Chicago)

External Link

View this painting up close in the Google Art Project:

- https://www.google.com/culturalinstitute/asset-viewer/nighthawks/6AEKkO_F-9wicw?projec-tId=art-project

---

Near Misses

In place of meaningful interactions, the four characters inside the diner of Edward Hopper's *Nighthawks* are involved in a series of near misses. The man and woman might be touching hands, but they aren't. The waiter and smoking-man might be conversing, but they're not. The couple might strike up a conversation with the man facing them, but somehow, we know they won't. And then we realize that Hopper has placed us, the viewer, on the city street, with no door to enter the diner, and yet in a position to evaluate each of the people inside. We see the row of empty counter stools nearest us. We notice that no one is making eye contact with any one else. Up close, the waiter's face appears to have

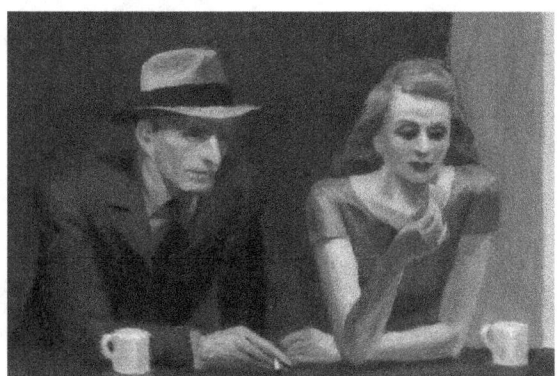

Figure 1. Edward Hopper, Nighthawks, 1942 (detail)

an expression of horror or pain. And then there is a chilling revelation: each of us is completely alone in the world.

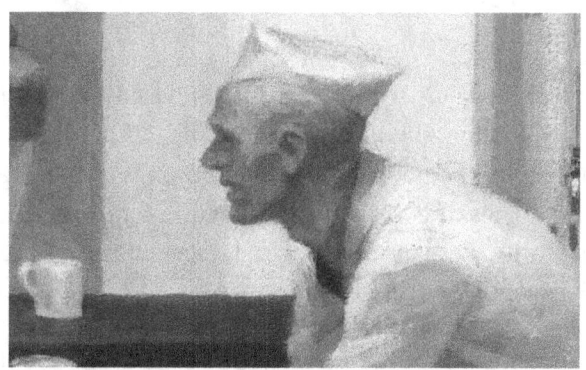

Figure 2. Edward Hopper, Nighthawks, 1942 (detail)

The slickness of the paint, which makes the canvas read almost like an advertisement, and immediate accessibility of the subject matter draws the viewer into Hopper's painting. But he does not tell us a story. Rather than a narrative about men and women out for a festive night on the town, we are invited to ask questions about the characters' ambiguous lives. Are the man and woman a couple? Where are they coming from? Where are they going? Who is the man with his back to us? How did he end up in the diner? What is the waiter's life like? What is causing his distress?

The Light

By setting the scene on one of New York City's oblique corners and surrounding the diner with glass, Hopper was able to exploit stark pictorial devices. First, the fluorescent light flooding the diner is the only light that illuminates the painting; in the absence of a streetlamp, it spills into the night through both windows onto both sides of the street corner. It throws a series of cast shadows onto the sidewalk and apartment buildings, but ultimately draws our attention back to the men and woman inside the diner. The angle also allows him to show the people in a mix of frontal and profile views, heightening the sense that no figure is really communicating with another.

This feeling can be understood by comparing *Nighthawks* to Hopper's earlier painting *Early Sunday Morning:* http://collection.whitney.org/object/46345. Both paintings are set in front of the red brick apartments of New York's Greenwich Village and show us an hour of the day when people are typically not awake. Like *Nighthawks,* which was created at the beginning of America's involvement in World War II, *Early Sunday Morning* was also painted at a historically important moment, the beginning of the Great Depression. But despite their similarities, *Early Sunday Morning* produces a sense of ease in the viewer, not anxiety.

Partially, this is because of the flooding light of dawn. But *Early Sunday Morning,* with its frilly awnings, brightly colored barber's pole, squat fire hydrant, and windows opening to meet the morning sun, presents a world that is about to bustle with life. *Nighthawks* shows the opposite. The windows of the shops and apartments are empty and dark. The only remnants of human activity outside the diner are a cash register in a shop window and a cigar advertisement above the glass pane. There is no clock in the restaurant, but the empty coffee tureens on the back counter betray

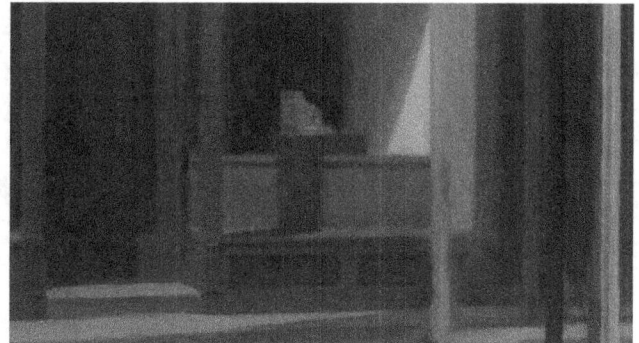

Figure 3. Edward Hopper, Nighthawks, 1942 (detail)

the indecent hour of night. This is a world shut down. Because our characters are awake, they are alienated—not only from each other, but also from civilization itself.

A Timeless Feel

Nighthawks is one of Hopper's New York City paintings, and the artist said that it was based on a real café. Many people have tried to find the exact setting of the painting, but have failed. In his wife's diaries, she wrote that she and Hopper himself both served as models for the people in the painting. Despite these real-life details, the empty composition and flat, abstracting planes of color give the canvas a timeless feel, making it an object onto which one can project one's own reality. Perhaps this is why it has lent itself to so well to many parodies, even appearing as a motif on an episode of *The Simpsons*.

When it was completed the canvas was bought almost immediately by the Art Institute of Chicago where it remains, and has been wildly popular ever since. The painting's modern-day appeal can also be understood because of its ability to evoke a sense of nostalgia for an America of a time gone-by. Despite its inherent universality, the dress of the four people—the woman evoking a pin-up doll, the men in their well-tailored suits and hats, the worker in his soda jerk costume—as well as the "Phillies" advertisement, firmly plant the painting in a simpler past, making it a piece of Americana.

A Subtle Critique

But perhaps *Nighthawks'* enduring popularity can be explained because of its subtle critique of the modern world, the world in which we all live. Despite its surface beauty, this world is one measured in cups of coffee, imbued with an overwhelming sense of loneliness, and a deep desire, but ultimate inability, to connect with those around us.

Frida Kahlo and Diego Rivera

This portrait was painted in San Francisco during the artist's first trip outside of Mexico. She accompanied her husband Diego Rivera who was painting in the United States and would, at the end of the year, be the subject of a retrospecive at The Museum of Modern Art in New York. The banderole carried by the bird above the artist states: "Here you see us, me, Frieda Kahlo, with my beloved husband Diego Rivera, I painted these portraits in the beautiful city of San Francisco, California, for our friend Mr. Albert Bender, and it was the month of April of the year 1931." **Note:** Kahlo changed her German name, Frieda, to Frida.

Dr. Beth Harris and Dr. Steven Zucker provide a description, historical perspective, and analysis of Frida Kahlo's *Frieda and Diego Rivera*

- https://youtu.be/n2HWkDrorRg

Frida Kahlo, *Frieda and Diego Rivera*, 1931, oil on canvas, 39-3/8 × 31 inches or 100.01 × 78.74 cm (San Francisco Museum of Modern Art)

Attributions

CC licensed content, Shared previously

Origins of Abstract Expressionism

What's in a Name?

The group of artists known as Abstract Expressionists emerged in the United States in the years following World War II. As the term suggests, their work was characterized by non-objective imagery that appeared emotionally charged with personal meaning. The artists, however, rejected these implications of the name.

They insisted their subjects were not "abstract," but rather primal images, deeply rooted in society's collective unconscious. Their paintings did not express mere emotion. They communicated universal truths about the human condition. For these reasons, another term—the New York School—offers a more accurate descriptor of the group, for although some eventually relocated, their distinctive aesthetic first found form in New York City.

The rise of the New York School reflects the broader cultural context of the mid-twentieth century, especially the shift away from Europe as the center of intellectual and artistic innovation in the West. Much of Abstraction Expressionism's significance stems from its status as the first American visual art movement to gain international acclaim.

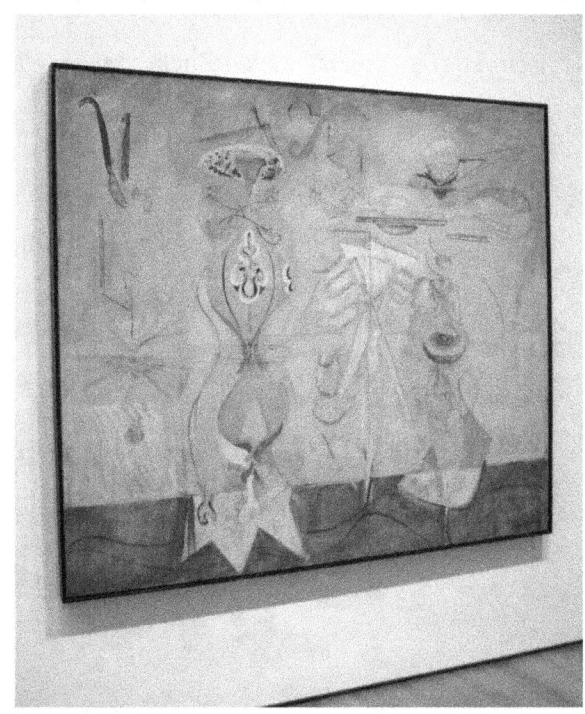

Figure 1. Mark Rothko, Slow Swirl at the Edge of the Sea, 1944, oil on canvas, 191.4 × 215.2 cm (MoMA)

Art for a World in Shambles

Barnett Newman wrote:

We felt the moral crisis of a world in shambles, a world destroyed by a great depression and a fierce World War, and it was impossible at that time to paint the kind of paintings that we were doing—flowers, reclining nudes, and people playing the cello.[1]

Although distinguished by individual styles, the Abstract Expressionists shared common artistic and intellectual interests. While not expressly political, most of the artists held strong convictions based on Marxist ideas of social and economic equality. Many had benefited directly from employment in the Works Progress Administration's Federal Art Project. There, they found influences in Regionalist styles of American artists such as Thomas Hart Benton, as well as the Socialist Realism of Mexican muralists including Diego Rivera and José Orozco.

The growth of Fascism in Europe had brought a wave of immigrant artists to the United States in the 1930s, which gave Americans greater access to ideas and practices of European Modernism. They sought training at the school founded by German painter Hans Hoffmann, and from Josef Albers, who left the Bauhaus in 1933 to teach at the experimental Black Mountain College in North Carolina, and later at Yale University. This European presence made clear the formal innovations of Cubism, as well as the psychological undertones and automatic painting techniques of Surrealism.

Whereas Surrealism had found inspiration in the theories of Sigmund Freud, the Abstract Expressionists looked more to the Swiss psychologist Carl Jung and his explanations of primitive archetypes that were a part of our collective human experience. They also gravitated toward Existentialist philosophy, made popular by European intellectuals such as Martin Heidegger and Jean-Paul Sartre.

Given the atrocities of World War II, Existentialism appealed to the Abstract Expressionists. Sartre's position that an individual's actions might give life meaning suggested the importance of the artist's creative process. Through the artist's physical struggle with his materials, a painting itself might ultimately come to serve as a lasting mark of one's existence. Each of the artists involved with Abstract Expressionism eventually developed an individual style that can be easily recognized as evidence of his artistic practice and contribution.

1. Barnett Newman, "Response to the Reverend Thomas F. Mathews," in Revelation, Place and Symbol (Journal of the First Congress on Religion, Architecture and the Visual Arts), 1969.

What Does it Look Like?

Although Abstract Expressionism informed the sculpture of David Smith and Aaron Siskind's photography, the movement is most closely linked to painting. Most Abstract Expressionist paintings are large scale, include non-objective imagery, lack a clear focal point, and show visible signs of the artist's working process, but these characteristics are not consistent in every example.

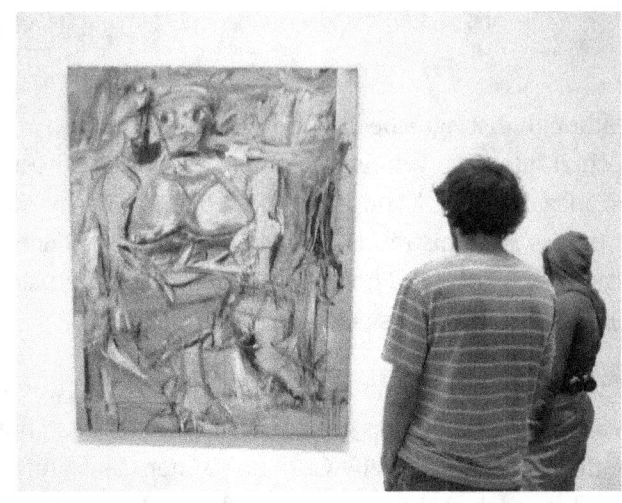

Figure 2. Willem de Kooning, Woman, I, 1950–52, oil on canvas, 192.7 times; 147.3 cm (MoMA)

In the case of Willem de Kooning's *Woman I* (http://www.moma.org/collection/works/79810), the visible brush strokes and thickly applied pigment are typical of the "Action Painting" style of Abstract Expressionism also associated with Jackson Pollock and Franz Kline. Looking at *Woman I,* we can easily imagine de Kooning at work, using strong slashing gestures, adding gobs of paint to create heavily built-up surfaces that could be physically worked and reworked with his brush and palette knife. De Kooning's central image is clearly recognizable, reflecting the tradition of the female nude throughout art history. Born in the Netherlands, de Kooning was trained in the European academic tradition unlike his American colleagues. Although he produced many non-objective works throughout his career, his early background might be one factor in his frequent return to the figure.

In contrast to the dynamic appearance of de Kooning's art, Mark Rothko and Barnett Newman exemplify what is sometimes called the "Color Imagist" or "Color Field" style of Abstract Expressionism. These artists produced large scale, non-objective imagery as well, but their work lacks the energetic intensity and gestural quality of Action Painting.

Figure 3. Mark Rothko, No. 61 (Rust and Blue), 1953. Oil on canvas (1903–1970) Panza Collection. MOCA, LA

Rothko's mature paintings exemplify this tendency. His subtly rendered rectangles appear to float against their background. For artists like Rothko, these images were meant to encourage meditation and personal reflection. Adolph Gottlieb, writing with Rothko and Newman in 1943, explained, "We favor the simple expression of the complex thought."[2]

Barnett Newman's *Vir Heroicus Sublimis* illustrates this lofty goal. In this painting, Newman relied on "zips," vertical lines that punctuate the painted field of the background to serve a dual function. While they visually highlight the expanse of contrasting color around them, they metaphorically reflect our own presence as individuals within our potentially overwhelming surroundings. Newman's painting evokes the eighteenth century notion of the Sublime, a philosophical concept related to spiritual understanding of humanity's place among the greater forces of the universe.

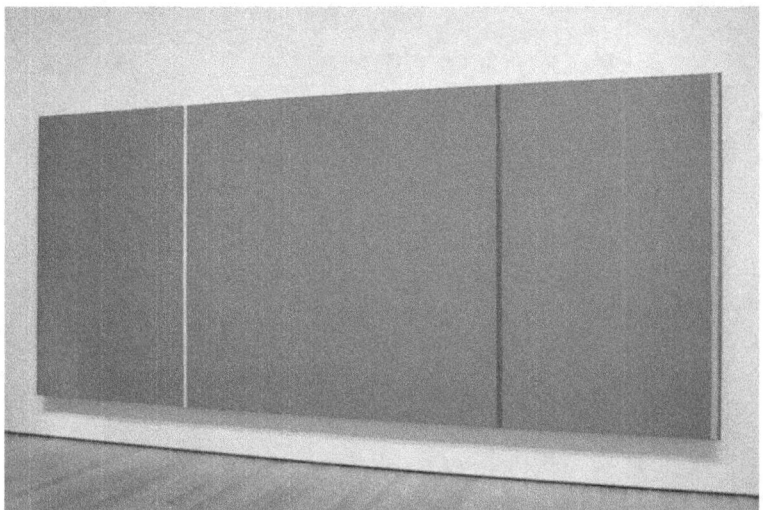

Figure 4. Barnett Newman, Vir Heroicus Sublimis, 1950, MoMA

2. Letter from Mark Rothko and Adolph Gottlieb to Edward Alden Jewell Art Editor, New York Times, June 7, 1943.

Abstract Expressionism's Legacy

Throughout the 1950s, Abstract Expressionism became the dominant influence on artists both in the United States and abroad. The U.S. government embraced its distinctive style as a reflection of American democracy, individualism, and cultural achievement, and actively promoted international exhibitions of Abstract Expressionism as a form of political propaganda during the years of the Cold War. However, many artists found it difficult to replicate the emotional authenticity implicit in the stylistic innovations of de Kooning and Pollock. Their work appeared studied and lacked the same vitality of the first generation pioneers. Others saw the metaphysical undertones of Abstract Expressionism at odds with a society increasingly concerned with a consumer mentality, fueled by economic success and proliferation of the mass media. Such reactions would inevitably lead to the emergence of Pop, Minimalism, and the rise of a range of new artistic developments in the mid twentieth century.

Attributions

Impact of Abstract Expressionism

Click on the link below to view the page "The Impact of Abstract Expressionism" by Kandice Rawlings on Khan Academy (originally developed for Oxford Art Online). Abstract Expressionism had a large effect on how people viewed art. This page takes a look at its influence.

- "The Impact of Abstract Expressionism" by Kandice Rawlings

    ◦ https://www.khanacademy.org/humanities/art-1010/abstract-exp-nyschool/ny-school/a/the-impact-of-abstract-expressionism

Pollock, One: Number 31, 1950

Dr. Beth Harris and Dr. Steven Zucker provide a description, historical perspective, and analysis of Jackson Pollock's *One: Number 31, 1950.*

- https://youtu.be/2JleSka1klc

Jackson Pollock, *One: Number 31, 1950*, Oil and enamel paint on unprimed canvas, 1950 (MoMA)

Attributions

CC licensed content, Shared previously

Pollock's Painting Techniques

In this video from the MoMA, Corey D'Augustine helps us understand Pollock's painting technique.

- https://www.youtube.com/watch?v=EncR_T0faKM

Attributions

Rothko, No. 3/No. 13

Dr. Beth Harris and Dr. Steven Zucker provide a description, historical perspective, and analysis of Mark Rothko's *No. 3/No. 13*.

- https://youtu.be/FnkATpF4O2Q

Mark Rothko, *No. 3/No. 13*, 1949, oil on canvas (MoMA)

Attributions

CC licensed content, Shared previously

Rothko's Painting Technique

In this video from the MoMA, Corey D'Augustine helps us understand Rothko's painting technique.

- https://www.moma.org/multimedia/video/129/689

Attributions

All rights reserved content

Newman, Onement 1

Dr. Beth Harris and Dr. Steven Zucker provide a description, historical perspective, and analysis of Barnett Newman's *Onement I*.

- https://youtu.be/4qgOSBHptLM

Barnett Newman, *Onement I*, 1948, oil on canvas, 27 1/4 × 16 1/4″ (69.2 × 41.2 cm), The Museum of Modern Art

Attributions

de Kooning, Woman I

Dr. Beth Harris and Dr. Steven Zucker provide a description, historical perspective, and analysis of Willem de Kooning's *Woman I.*

- https://youtu.be/WEYKoJTIHcE

Willem de Kooning, *Woman I*, oil on canvas, 1950–52 (MoMA)

Attributions

Robert Motherwell

Dr. Beth Harris and Dr. Steven Zucker provide a description, historical perspective, and analysis of Robert Motherwell's *Elegy to the Spanish Republic No. 57.*

- https://youtu.be/C89z5GncK88

Robert Motherwell, *Elegy to the Spanish Republic No. 57*, 1957-60, oil on canvas, 84 x 109-1/8 inches (San Francisco Museum of Modern Art)

Excerpt from of an interview with Robert Motherwell conducted by Paul Cummings at the Artist's home in Greenwich, Connecticut November 24, 1971

> PAUL CUMMINGS: In the late 1940s you began the Elegy to the Spanish Republic series. Was that title an afterthought on looking back at things?
>
> ROBERT MOTHERWELL: Yes.
>
> PAUL CUMMINGS: How did you develop that? What is it based on?
>
> ROBERT MOTHERWELL: Sometime in the 1940s – I forget when – say, about 1947, when I was still editing books with Wittenborn and Schultz they told me that they'd like to put out an annual about the current scene and would I edit it. I said sure; but I think it should be broader than just painting and sculpture, and that it was too great a responsibility and too great a demand on my time to do it single-handed. I said that I would be glad to do it if I could have some co-editors. The said, "Fine. Who do you want?" I suggested Pierre Chareau as the architectural editor; he was a French architect-in-exile with whom I had worked several years building a studio in East Hampton. I suggested John Cage to deal with music and dance. And Harold Rosenberg to deal with literature; and I would do the painting part. They found that agreeable. We brought out an issue. It was called "Possibilities." The we were working on the second issue. in those days Harold Rosenberg regarded himself as really a poet. He was doing these other things incidentally the way I've always regarded myself as really a painter and doing these other things incidentally. He wrote a very powerful, brutal, I would think Rimbaud-inspired poem. We agreed that I would handwrite the poem in my calligraphy and make a drawing or drawings to go with it and it was to be in black and white. So I began to think not only about getting the brutality and aggression of his poem in some kind of abstract terms but also that this was going to be reproduced in black and white. I worked for weeks getting the amounts. In painting really the whole issue of quality is quantities, is the amounts of black and white or thinness or thickness, fluidity,and whatever. I really conceived something that worked beautifully in black and

white. It must have been at that time that Schultz was killed in the airplane and the whole project was dropped. I stuck the thing in a drawer in East Hampton. A year or two later I moved to New York to a little studio on Fourteenth Street. One day while unpacking I came across it and was able to look at it with detachment. I thought: God, that's a beautiful idea; I should make some paintings on the basis of that kind of structure.

PAUL CUMMINGS: This was on your black and white structure?

ROBERT MOTHERWELL: Yes. One day I realized there was something really obsessional about it, that I would probably make many; that it had taken on a life of its own; and that it would no longer be legitimate to refer it merely to Harold's poem which indeed was the original impulse that it might indeed turn out to be possibly the main statement I would make in painting and therefore I would like to connect this with something that through associations reverberated in my mind as completely and as widely as the concept itself. And belonging to the Spanish Civil War generation I thought of that. I think maybe there was a transitional moment where I thought if it's going to refer to poetry it should be to Lorca [Frederico García Lorca]. In fact, the first Elegy was originally called At Five in the Afternoon from the refrain out to Lorca's poem, the Death of the Bullfighter [Lament for the Death of a Bullfighter (1935)]. Then one of the few times in my life that a lot of people talked to me about a picture was about that picture, and they would say, "I saw the most beautiful picture by you. I can't remember exactly the title. It has something to do with the cocktail hour or something." And suddenly I realized that five in the afternoon in New York means not the death of a bullfighter but a martini. And then I began to grope for a more generalized expression. The original ones were subtitles, I mean Elegy to the Spanish Republic (Granada) or whatever. And then that began to raise questions: does it really look like Granada, and so on.[1]

Attributions

1. *Oral history interview with Robert Motherwell*, 1971 Nov. 24-1974 May 1, Archives of American Art, Smithsonian Institution

Jasper Johns

> One night I dreamed I painted a large American flag, and the next morning I got up and I went out and bought the materials to begin it. And I did. I worked on that painting a long time. It's a very rotten painting—physically rotten—because I began it in house enamel paint, which you paint furniture with, and it wouldn't dry quickly enough. Then I had in my head this idea of something I had read or heard about: wax encaustic.
>
> —Jasper Johns

Salman Khan and Steven Zucker provide a description, historical perspective, and analysis of Jasper Johns's *Flag*.

- https://youtu.be/9bWJt2hjBH0

Jasper Johns, *Flag*, 1954–55 (dated on reverse 1954), encaustic, oil, and collage on fabric mounted on plywood, three panels, 42-1/4 x 60-5/8 inches (107.3 x 153.8 cm), (The Museum of Modern Art).

Attributions

Rauschenberg

Dr. Beth Harris and Dr. Steven Zucker provide a description, historical perspective, and analysis of Robert Rauschenberg's *Bed*.

- https://youtu.be/tvpp2lAD9iY

Robert Rauschenberg, *Bed*, 1955, oil and pencil on pillow, quilt, and sheet on wood supports, 191.1 x 80 x 20.3 cm (The Museum of Modern Art) © 2013 Robert Rauschenberg Foundation

Attributions

Introduction to Photography

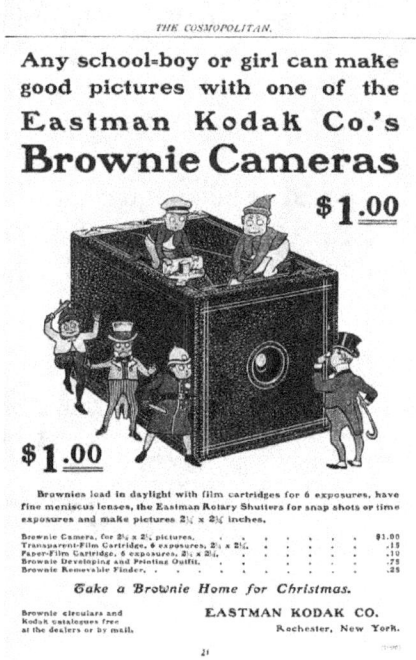

*Figure 1. Eastman Kodak Advertisement for
the Brownie Camera, c. 1900*

Photography undergoes extraordinary changes in the early part of the twentieth century. This can be said of every other type of visual representation, however, but unique to photography is the transformed perception of the medium. In order to understand this change in perception and use—why photography appealed to artists by the early 1900s, and how it was incorporated into artistic practices by the 1920s—we need to start by looking back.

In the later nineteenth century, photography spread in its popularity, and inventions like the Kodak #1 camera (1888) made it accessible to the upper-middle class consumer; the Kodak Brownie camera, which cost far less, reached the middle class by 1900.

In the sciences (and pseudo-sciences), photographs gained credibility as objective evidence because they could document people, places, and events. Photographers like Eadweard Muybridge created portfolios of photographs to measure human and animal locomotion. His celebrated images recorded incremental stages of movement too rapid for the human eye to observe, and his work fulfilled the camera's promise to enhance, or even create new forms of scientific study.

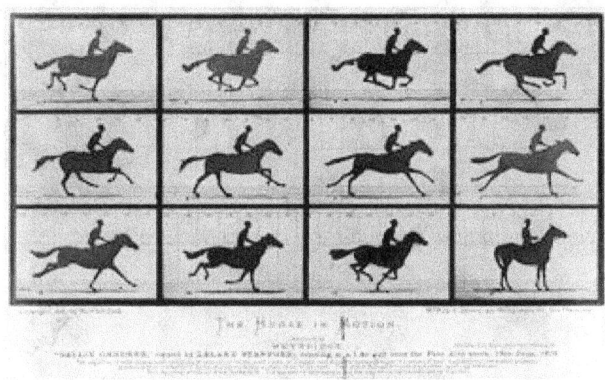

Figure 2. Eadweard Muybridge, Thoroughbred bay mare "Annie G." galloping, Human and Animal Locomotion, plate 626, 1887

In the arts, the medium was valued for its replication of exact details, and for its reproduction of artworks for publication. But photographers struggled for artistic recognition throughout the century. It was not until in Paris's Universal Exposition of 1859, twenty years after the invention of the medium, that photography and "art" (painting, engraving, and sculpture) were displayed next to one another for the first time; separate entrances to each exhibition space, however, preserved a physical and symbolic distinction between the two groups. After all, photographs are mechanically reproduced images: Kodak's marketing strategy ("You press the button, we do the rest,") points directly to the "effortlessness" of the medium.

Since art was deemed the product of imagination, skill, and craft, how could a photograph (made with an instrument and light-sensitive chemicals instead of brush and paint) ever be considered its equivalent? And if its purpose was to reproduce details precisely, and from nature, how could photographs be acceptable if negatives were "manipulated," or if photographs were retouched? Because of these questions, amateur photographers formed casual groups and official societies to challenge such conceptions of the medium. They—along with elite art world figures like Alfred Stieglitz—promoted the late nineteenth-century style of "art photography," and produced low-contrast, warm-toned images like *The Terminal* that highlighted the medium's potential for originality.

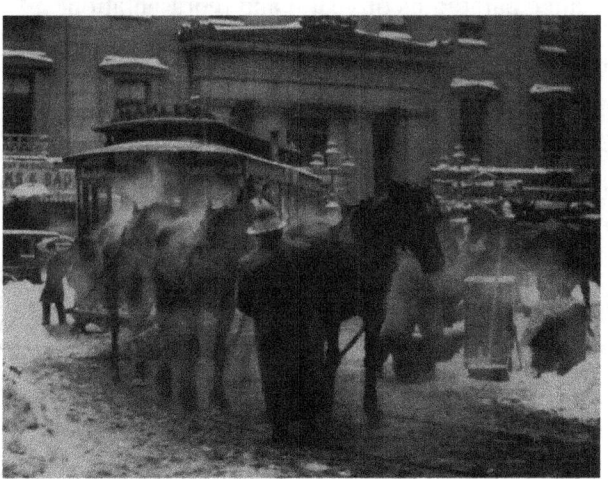

Figure 3. Alfred Stieglitz, The Terminal, photogravure, 1892

So what transforms the perception of photography in the early twentieth century? Social and cultural change—on a massive, unprecedented scale. Like everyone else, artists were radically affected by industrialization, political revolution, trench warfare, airplanes, talking motion pictures, radios, automobiles, and much more—and they wanted to create art that was as radical and "new" as modern life itself. If we consider the work of the Cubists and Futurists, we often think of their works in terms of simultaneity and speed, destruction and reconstruction. Dadaists, too, challenged the boundaries of traditional art with performances, poetry, installations, and photomontage that use the materials of everyday culture instead of paint, ink, canvas, or bronze.

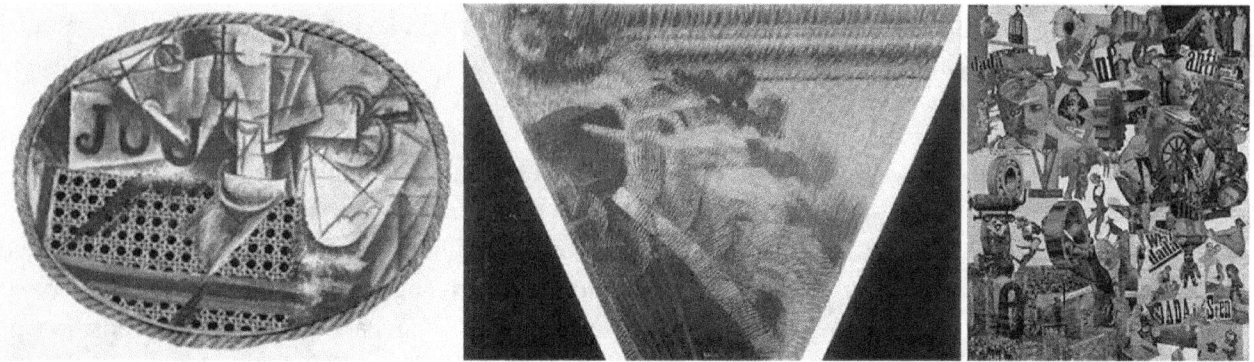

Figure 4. (left) Picasso, Still Life with Chair Caning, 1912, oil, oilcloth and pasted paper on canvas with rope frame; (center) Giacomo Balla, Hand of the Violinist, 1912, oil on canvas; (right) Hannah Höch, Cut with the Kitchen Knife Dada Through the Last Weimar Beer-Belly Cultural Epoch of Germany, 1919–20, photomontage

By the early 1920s, technology becomes a vehicle of progress and change, and instills hope in many after the devastations of World War I. For avant-garde ("ahead of the crowd") artists, photography becomes incredibly appealing for its associations with technology, the everyday, and science—precisely the reasons it was denigrated a half-century earlier. The camera's technology of mechanical reproduction made it the fastest, most modern, and arguably, the most relevant form of visual representation in the post-WWI era. Photography, then, seemed to offer more than a new method of image-making—it offered the chance to change paradigms of vision and representation.

With August Sander's portraits, such as *Secretary at a Radio Station, Pastry Cook* or *Disabled Man*, we see an artist attempting to document—systematically—modern types of people, as a means to understand changing notions of class, race, profession, ethnicity, and other constructs of identity. Sander transforms the practice of portraiture with these sensational, arresting images. These figures reveal as much about the German professions as they do about self-image.

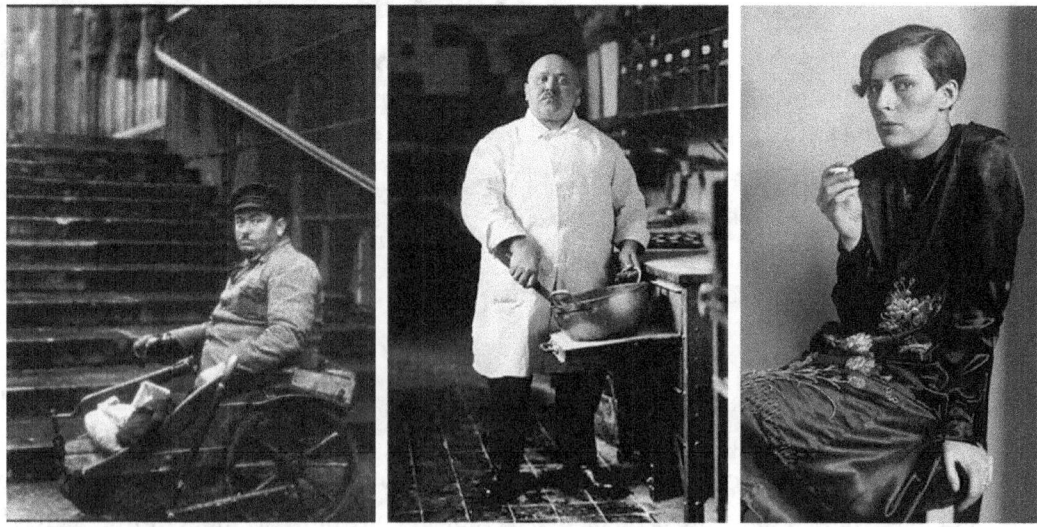

Figure 5. August Sander, Disabled Man, 1926; Pastry Chef, 1928; Secretary at a Radio Station, Cologne, c. 1931

Cartier-Bresson's leaping figure in *Behind the Gare St. Lazare* reflects the potential for photography to capture individual moments in time—to freeze them, hold them, and recreate them. Because of his approach,

Cartier-Bresson is often considered a pioneer of photojournalism. This sense of spontaneity, of accuracy, and of the ephemeral corresponded to the racing tempo of modern culture (think of factories, cars, trains, and the rapid pace of people in growing urban centers).

Umbo's photomontage *The Roving Reporter* shows how modern technologies transform our perception of the world—and our ability to communicate within it. His camera-eyed, colossal observer (a real-life journalist named Egon Erwin Kisch) demonstrates photography's ability to alter and enhance the senses. In the early twentieth-century, this medium offered a potentially transformative vision for artists, who sought new ways to see, represent, and understand the rapidly changing world around them.

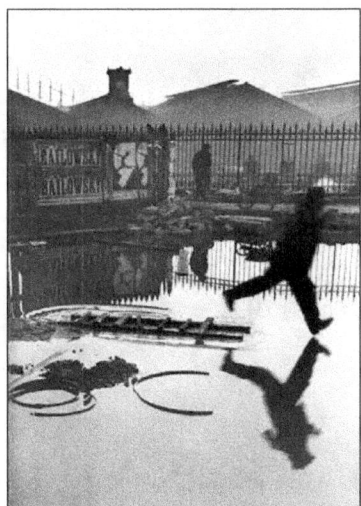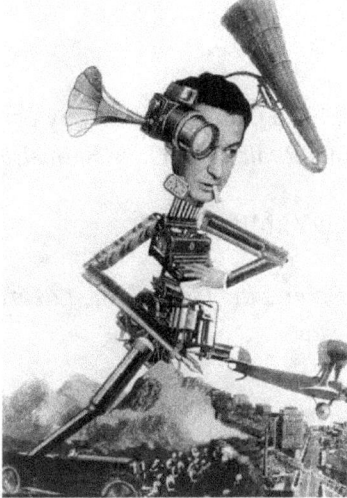

Figure 6. (left) Henri Cartier-Bresson, Behind the Gare St. Lazare, 1932; (right) Umbo (Otto Umbehr), The Roving Reporter, photomontage, 1926

Cartier-Bresson

Dr. Beth Harris and Dr. Shana Gallagher-Lindsay provide a description, historical perspective, and analysis of Henri Cartier-Bresson's *Behind the Gare Saint-Lazare*.

- https://youtu.be/YxMBp4Ef3ek

Henri Cartier-Bresson, *Behind the Gare Saint-Lazare*, Paris, 1932.

Attributions

CC licensed content, Shared previously

Brancusi, Bird in Space

Dr. Beth Harris and Dr. Steven Zucker provide a description, historical perspective, and analysis of Constantin Brancusi's *Bird in Space.*

- https://youtu.be/xWTzH7RV80g

Constantin Brancusi, *Bird in Space*, bronze, limestone, wood, 1928 (MoMA)

Attributions

Frank Lloyd Wright, Guggenheim Museum

Dr. Matthew Postal and Dr. Steven Zucker provide a description, historical perspective, and analysis of the Guggenheim Museum.

- https://youtu.be/JVm-ePTIKR4

Frank Lloyd Wright, Solomon R. Guggenheim Museum, New York City, 1942–1959.

Attributions

Mies van der Rohe, Seagram Building

Dr. Matthew Postal and Dr. Steven Zucker provide a description, historical perspective, and analysis of the Seagram Building.

> **A Note from Dr. Zucker:** In the video I call Le Corbusier a French architect, but he was born in Switzerland and became a French citizen in 1930.

- https://youtu.be/ZyyuflY5k2k

Ludwig Mies van der Rohe, Seagram Building, 375 Park Avenue, New York City (1958)

Attributions

Chapter 14:
1960–Now–Age of
Post-Colonialism Part I

Chapter 14 Overview

What You'll Learn To Do: Examine Contemporary art.

In Chapter 14 we will examine Contemporary art. We will look at how artists like Warhol contributed to the development of Western art. It is imperative to understand Contemporary art in order to see how it impacted later artistic developments.

Learning Activities

The learning activities for this module include:

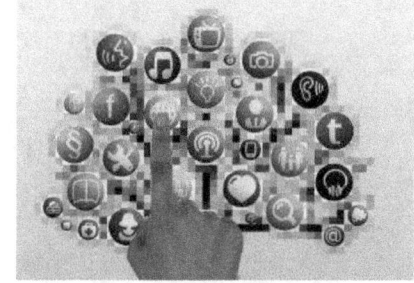

- **Review:** Key Learning Items

The 1960s to Now

- **Watch:** Introduction to Contemporary Art (2 videos: 3:41 and 4:37)

Photography Post 1960

- **Watch:** Diane Arbus (29:24)
- **Watch:** Cindy Sherman (4:22)
- **Watch:** Sherrie Levine (4:25)

The Postwar Figure

- **Watch:** Francis Bacon (5:23)
- **Watch:** Lucian Freud (3:44)

Body as Symbolic Form

- **Read:** Louise Bourgeois

Pop Art

- **Read:** Warhol, Gold Marilyn Monroe (includes a video: 3:14)
- **Watch:** Warhol, Campbell's Soup Cans (7:08)
- **Watch:** Oldenburg, Floor Cake (3:29)
- **Watch:** Lichtenstein, Girl with Ball (?)
- **Watch:** Lichtenstein, Rouen Cathedral Set V (3:09)

Assemblage

- **Watch:** Ed and Nancy Kienholz (5:42)

Postwar German Art

- **Read:** Richter, Uncle Rudi
- **Watch:** Richter, The Cage Paintings (14:27)

Minimalism

- **Read:** Donald Judd (includes a video: 3:49)
- **Watch:** Dan Flavin (2:45)
- **Read:** Robert Morris (includes a video: 2:34)

Process Art

- **Watch:** Eva Hesse, Untitled (3:40)
- **Watch:** Eva Hesse, Untitled (Rope Piece) (3:45)
- **Watch:** Chicago and Benglis (4:42)

Performance Art

- **Read:** Introduction to Performance Art
- **Read:** Joseph Beuys, Fat Chair
- **Watch:** Joseph Beuys, Table with Accumulator (4:14)

Attributions

Key Learning Items

Learning Objectives

After successful completion of this module, you will be able to:

- Understand and apply the concepts and terminology of Contemporary art
- Investigate and apply the fundamental questions we ask when looking at art objects from this movement
- Discuss, collaborate, and generate understanding as to the meaning of Contemporary art
- Assess and evaluate the impact of Contemporary art on the continued evolution of Western art

Key Questions to Ask

While you are reviewing the content of this module, consider the following questions:

- How do we define Postmodernism?
- What types of art have been created since the 1960s?
- How have societal changes affected the art of the later 20-century?

Key Vocabulary Terms

- Postmodernism
- Pop art
- Benday dots
- silk-screen technique
- Assemblage
- Minimalism

- Process art

- Performance art

Here are links to art history glossaries that will help you better understand the above key vocabulary terms.

- ArtLex: Art Dictionary

  - http://www.artlex.com/

- About.com: Art History

  - http://arthistory.about.com/od/glossary/l/bl_Art-Glossary.htm

- Artcyclopedia: A Guide to Fine Art

  - http://www.artcyclopedia.com/

Attributions

CC licensed content, Original

Introduction to Contemporary Art

Little Art Talks provides an introduction to Contemporary Art, as well as resources to help this era of art become more accessible.

- https://youtu.be/YDxrv3g1xXo
- https://youtu.be/IIY-GD3mhfs

Attributions

All rights reserved content

Diane Arbus

This 30 minute documentary *Masters of Photography: Dian Arbus,* provides insights into the photographer's life and work. The documentary was produced in 1972, just one year after Arbus's death.

- https://youtu.be/Q_0sQI90kYI

Cindy Sherman

Dr. Beth Harris and Dr. Shana Gallagher-Lindsay provide a description, historical perspective, and analysis of Cindy Sherman's *Untitled Film Still #21*.

- https://youtu.be/0fPwsLeH8fA

Cindy Sherman, *Untitled Film Still #21*, 1978, gelatin silver print, 7.5 × 9.5 inches (19.1 × 24.1 cm), (MoMA).

Attributions

Francis Bacon

Dr. Beth Harris and Dr. Steven Zucker provide a description, historical perspective, and analysis of Francis Bacon's *Triptych—August 1972*.

- https://youtu.be/JZRY6Eco7BM

Francis Bacon, *Triptych—August 1972*, 1972, oil on canvas, 72 × 61 × 22 in. (183 × 155 × 64 cm), (Tate Modern, London).

Attributions

Lucian Freud

Dr. Beth Harris and Dr. Steven Zucker provide a description, historical perspective, and analysis of Lucian Freud's *Standing by the Rags*.

- https://youtu.be/Nb6EQUS8hDo

Lucian Freud, *Standing by the Rags*, 1988–89, oil on canvas, 66.5 × 54.5 in. (168.9 × 138.4 cm), (Tate Britain, London).

Attributions

CC licensed content, Shared previously

Louise Bourgeois

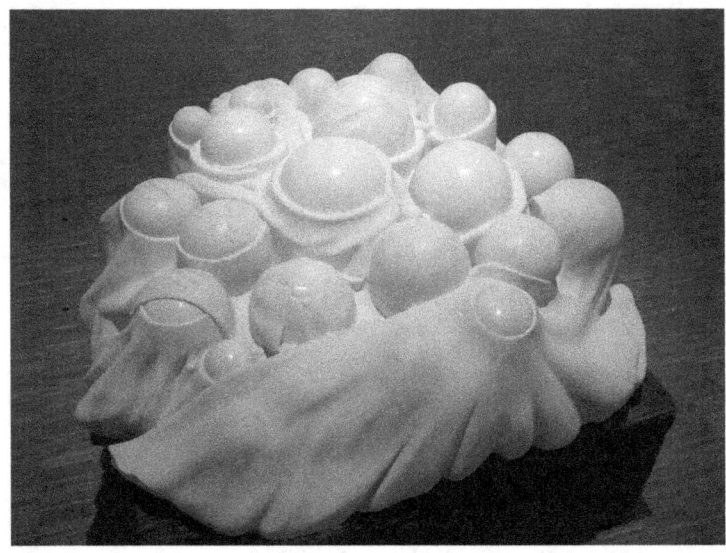

Figure 1. Louise Bourgeois, Cumul I, 1969, white marble on wood base, 22-½ x 50 x 48 inches or 51 x 127 x 122 cm, Centre Pompidou, Musée national d'art moderne, Paris, ©Estate of the artist

The Reality of Three-Dimensional Form

Bulbous mounds, and spherical or oval growths emerge, conflate and disturb. *Cumul I* is a marble sculpture, part of a series, by the late French-born artist, Louise Bourgeois. Cumul, as in, cumulus, is a reference to the forms of rounded clouds. The motif was first developed in drawings but Bourgeois wanted the reality of three-dimensional form, as she thought she could express deeper things in sculpture.

Like so much of Bourgeois' work, *Cumul I* is loaded with entangled metaphors of male and female body parts that are simultaneously abstract and descriptive. Her career breezed over so many significant trends of the 20th century that her work defies identification within any single art movement. Instead, there is an uncompromising personal symbolism throughout her oeuvre (life's work), filled with certain recurring motifs such as vessels, containers, ovoids, body parts, and spiders (a metaphor of her mother's work as a weaver).

Appealing and Disturbing

The sculpture, *Cumul I*, is designed to sit on the floor and be viewed from above. Its forms still shock nearly half a century after its completion. The artist denied any reference to sexual forms in this work, but the association is undeniable. The viewer is confronted with a cluster of mounds that resemble breasts and penises emerging from a rippling fabric. So what then was Bourgeois trying to communicate in this beautifully sculpted marble? What can be understood from a sculpture that is aesthetically appealing and at the same time disturbing?

Bourgeois offered some explanation to her mysterious oeuvre and implied that the Freudian concept of a traumatized childhood was the catalyst for her artistic motives. The artist has confirmed that all of her work found inspiration in her childhood. Scholars have noted that the childhood traumas of having a sick mother and egocentric philandering father who had an affair with her nanny, had a powerful impact on the young Bourgeois who later stated, "My childhood has never lost its magic, it has never lost its mystery, and it has never lost its drama."[1] References to Bourgeois' family, and sexuality, developed over the span of her career into a personal artistic vocabulary.

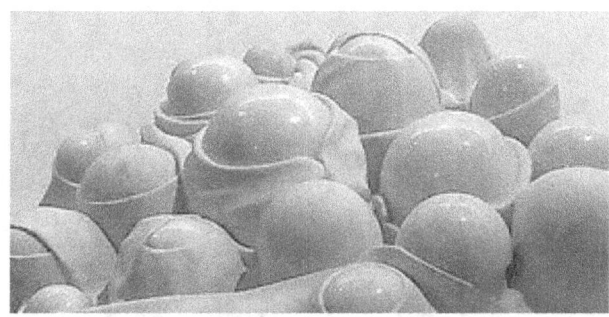

Figure 2. Louise Bourgeois, Cumul I (detail)

Making Sense of *Cumul I*

When we try to make sense of the male and female forms that reveal and conceal themselves simultaneously in *Cumul I*, it can help to remember Bourgeois' childhood. Ambiguity and overlapping gender are characteristics found in many of Bourgeois' sculptures and installations. Her art is deeply personal, confusing, troubling, magical and quite wonderful. She was one of the most significant women artists of the twentieth century.

Attributions

---

1. Louise Bourgeois: Destruction of the Father Reconstruction of the Father, *Writings and Interviews 1923-1997*, edited and with texts by Marie Laure-Bernadac and Hans-Ulrich Obrist, MIT Press, 1998, page 277. The quote is also found in a compilation of Bourgeois' images juxtaposed by text entitled "Album" (http://peterblumgallery.com/books/louise-bourgeois-album) 1994 and published by Peter Blum

Warhol, Gold Marilyn Monroe

Dr. Beth Harris and Dr. Steven Zucker provide a description, historical perspective, and analysis of Andy Warhol's *Gold Marilyn Monroe*.

- https://youtu.be/lXfzq27fGvU

Andy Warhol, *Gold Marilyn Monroe*, 1962, silkscreen ink, silkscreen ink on synthetic polymer paint on canvas, 71.25 × 57 in. (211.4 × 144.7 cm), (MoMA).

Popular Culture, "Popular" Art

At first glance, Pop Art might seem to glorify popular culture by elevating soup cans, comic strips and hamburgers to the status of fine art on the walls of museums. But, then again, a second look may also suggest a critique of the mass marketing practices and consumer culture that emerged in the United States after World War II.

Andy Warhol's *Gold Marilyn Monroe* (1962) clearly reflects this inherent irony of Pop. The central image on a gold background evokes a religious tradition of painted icons, transforming the Hollywood starlet into a Byzantine Madonna that reflects our obsession with celebrity. Notably, Warhol's spiritual reference was especially poignant given Monroe's suicide a few months earlier.

Like religious fanatics, the actress's fans worshipped their idol; yet, Warhol's sloppy silk-screening calls attention to the artifice of Marilyn's glamorous façade and places her alongside other mass-marketed commodities like a can of soup or a box of Brillo pads.

Genesis of Pop

In this light, it's not surprising that the term "Pop Art" first emerged in Great Britain, which suffered great economic hardship after the war. In the late 1940s, artists of the "Independent Group," first began to appropriate idealized images of the American lifestyle they found in popular magazines as part of their critique of British society.[1]

---

1. Critic Lawrence Alloway and artist Richard Hamilton are usually credited with coining the term, possibly in the context of Hamilton's famous collage from 1956, *Just what is it that makes today's home so different, so appealing?* Made to announce the Independent Group's 1956 exhibition "This Is Tomorrow," in London, the image prominently features a muscular semi-nude man, holding a phallically positioned Tootsie Pop.

Pop Art's origins, however, can be traced back even further. In 1917, Marcel Duchamp asserted that any object—including his notorious example of a urinal—could be art, as long as the artist intended it as such. Artists of the 1950s built on this notion to challenge boundaries distinguishing art from real life, in disciplines of music and dance, as well as visual art.

Robert Rauschenberg's desire to "work in the gap between art and life," for example, led him to incorporate such objects as bed pillows, tires and even a stuffed goat in his "combine paintings" that merged features of painting and sculpture. Likewise, Claes Oldenberg created *The Store*, an installation in a vacant storefront where he sold crudely fashioned sculptures of brand-name consumer goods.

These "Proto-pop" artists were, in part, reacting against the rigid critical structure and lofty philosophies surrounding Abstract Expressionism, the dominant art movement of the time; but their work also reflected the numerous social changes taking place around them.

Post-War Consumer Culture Grab Hold (and Never Lets Go)

The years following World War II saw enormous growth in the American economy, which, combined with innovations in technology and the media, spawned a consumer culture with more leisure time and expendable income than ever before. The manufacturing industry that had expanded during the war now began to mass-produce everything from hairspray and washing machines to shiny new convertibles, which advertisers claimed all would bring ultimate joy to their owners.

Significantly, the development of television, as well as changes in print advertising, placed new emphasis on graphic images and recognizable brand logos—something that we now take for granted in our visually saturated world.

It was in this artistic and cultural context that Pop artists developed their distinctive style of the early 1960s. Characterized by clearly rendered images of popular subject matter, it seemed to assault the standards of modern painting, which had embraced abstraction as a reflection of universal truths and individual expression.

Irony and Iron-Ons

In contrast to the dripping paint and slashing brushstrokes of Abstract Expressionism—and even of Proto-Pop art—Pop artists applied their paint to imitate the look of industrial printing techniques. This ironic approach is exemplified by Lichtenstein's methodically painted Benday dots, a mechanical process used to print pulp comics.

As the decade progressed, artists shifted away from painting towards the use of industrial techniques. Warhol began making silkscreens, before removing himself further from the process by having others do the actual printing in his studio, aptly named "The Factory." Similarly, Oldenburg abandoned his early installations and performances, to produce the large-scale sculptures of cake slices, lipsticks, and clothespins that he is best known for today.

Attributions

- Warhol's Gold Marilyn Monroe. **Authored by**: Virginia Spivey. **Provided by**: Khan Academy. **Located at**: https://web.archive.org/web/20140713181454/http://smarthistory.khanacademy.org/pop-art.html. **License**: *CC BY-NC-SA: Attribution-NonCommercial-ShareAlike*

Warhol, Campbell's Soup Cans

Steven Zucker and Sal Khan try to answer why something is qualified as art. They use Andy Warhol, *Campbell's Soup Cans* to illustrate their points.

- https://youtu.be/SdbOrNLcC0I

Andy Warhol, *Campbell's Soup Cans*, 1962, synthetic polymer paint on thirty-two canvases, each 20 × 16 inches (50.8 × 40.6 cm), (The Museum of Modern Art).

Attributions

Oldenburg, Floor Cake

Dr. Beth Harris and Dr. Steven Zucker provide a description, historical perspective, and analysis of Claes Oldenburg's *Floor Cake*.

- https://youtu.be/N-mt2tiRJ7U

Claes Oldenburg, *Floor Cake*, 1962, synthetic polymer paint and latex on canvas filled with foam rubber and cardboard boxes, 58.375 × 114.25 × 58.375 in. (148.2 × 290.2 × 148.2 cm), (MoMA).

Attributions

Lichtenstein, Rouen Cathedral Set V

Dr. Beth Harris and Dr. Steven Zucker provide a description, historical perspective, and analysis of Roy Lichtenstein's *Rouen Cathedral Set V*.

- https://youtu.be/GpwAsXrBJ-Q

Roy Lichtenstein, *Rouen Cathedral Set V*, 1969, oil and magna on canvas, 3 canvases: 63-5/8 × 141-7/8 × 1-3/4 inches (161.61 × 360.36 × 4.45 cm), (SFMOMA).

Attributions

Ed and Nancy Kienholz

Tina Olsen andBruce Guenther provide a description, historical perspective, and analysis of Ed Kienholz and Nancy Reddin Kienholz's *Useful Art #5: The Western Hotel.*

- https://youtu.be/WhGOmAwuQTE

Ed Kienholz and Nancy Reddin Kienholz, *Useful Art #5: The Western Hotel*, 1992 (Portland Art Museum)

Attributions

Richter, Uncle Rudi

"I can't see it. . . . Is it me?" I watched a young woman step closer to the canvas titled, *Uncle Rudi*. She was now physically closer and she was looking hard, but the image kept its distance.

External Link

View this painting on Gerhard Richter's studio website:

- https://www.gerhard-richter.com/en/art/paintings/photo-paintings/death-9/uncle-rudi-5595

Refusing Style

Meaning in Gerhard Richter's art can also keep its distance. The elusiveness of meaning is, in some ways, a central subject of Richter's art. Since the early 1950s, Richter has painted a huge number of subjects in wildly conflicting styles. For most artists, one style emerges and evolves slowly, almost imperceptibly, over the course of their career. This is because artists often continue to work through problems that remain relevant and perhaps, because they achieve a degree of recognition and the market then demands that style. In other words, collectors often want what is known. Artists who abandon their signature style do so at some risk to future sales. Still, some artists do push in startlingly new directions. Willem de Kooning abandoned abstraction for the figure against the advice of his dealer, and Pablo Picasso famously pursued opposing styles simultaneously—think of his volumetric, even bloated Neo-Classicism compared to the collages where he pressed flat every volume in sight.

The Impossibility of Meaning

During Richter's long career, he has produced art in an unprecedented number of conflicting styles starting with the propagandistic Social Realist art he made as a student at the Dresden Art Academy in Communist East Germany. After his move in 1961 to Düsseldorf in the West (via Berlin—the wall was begun the same year), he co-founded a German variant of Pop art which he, somewhat jokingly, termed Capitalist Realism. Since then he has painted high-pitched realism (sometimes blurred just enough to soften the image, or sometimes wiped or scraped beyond all recognition) and produced representations of abstraction (as opposed to abstraction itself). He has explored many of the most pressing visual issues of our time, the relationship of photography to painting, memory and the image, art's role in the representation of war and politics, and perhaps most importantly, the impossibility of fixed meaning.

Image and Ideology

Richter was born in Dresden, Germany on the eve of the Second World War. His two uncles were killed in the war and his father served, but survived. His schizophrenic aunt, Marianne, was murdered by the Nazis as part of their drive to euthanize the sick. Less than a week after his thirteenth birthday, Richter heard some 3,600 British and American planes drop more than half-a-million bombs on Dresden (he then lived just outside the city). 25,000 people were killed in these raids and the Soviets would quickly occupy Eastern Germany. Unlike the idealized, classicized nudes that Adolf Hitler had promulgated, the young Richter was taught Social Realism at the Dresden academy, a celebration of the heroism of communist workers. Once in the West, Richter found that the relationship between image and ideology reversed yet again. Here, images in advertising and popular culture celebrated material wealth and the culture of capitalism. Under the Nazis, under the Soviets, and in the West, Richter saw art used to express political ideology. His art, while deeply concerned with politics and morality, rejects the very possibility of answers, even of the idea that we can know.

Uncle Rudi

Uncle Rudi, the painting the woman had stepped closer to see, is painted in the grays of a black and white photograph. It is small and has the intimacy of a family snapshot. We see a young man smiling proudly and awkwardly. He is clearly self-conscious as he poses in his new uniform. One has the sense that a moment before he was talking to the person behind the camera, likely a friend or family member. Rudi would die fighting soon after the photograph that is the basis for this painting was taken. This is the artist's uncle, the man his grandmother favored and the adult the young Richter was to model himself after. But nothing in this painting is clear. Not the relationship between the artist and his uncle, not the tension between Rudi's innocent awkwardness and his participation in Nazi violence, not even in the relationship between the photograph and Richter's painting. The artist has drawn a dry brush across the wet surface of the nearly finished painting, and by doing this, he obscures the clarity of the photograph, denying us the easy certainty we expect. Richter reminds us that Uncle Rudi, like all images, promise and then fail to bring us closer to the people, things or places represented.

Attributions

CC licensed content, Shared previously

Richter, The Cage Paintings

Robert Storr discusses this series of 6 Cage Paintings by Gerhard Richter that were completed in 2006 and are currently located at the Tate Modern in London.

- https://youtu.be/aOeKj-w-3fY

Attributions

All rights reserved content

Donald Judd

Dr. Beth Harris and Dr. Shana Gallagher-Lindsay provide a description, historical perspective, and analysis of Donald Judd's *Untitled*.

- https://youtu.be/G37C5vKCwH4

Donald Judd, *Untitled*, 1969, ten copper units, each 9 × 40 × 31 inches with 9 inch intervals (Guggenheim Museum, New York)

A Reductive Abstract Art

Although many works of art can be described as "minimal," the name Minimalism refers specifically to a kind of reductive abstract art that emerged during the early 1960s. At the time, some critics preferred names like "ABC," "Boring," or "Literal" Art, and even "No-Art Nihilism," which they believed best summed up the literal presentation and lack of expressive content characterizing this new aesthetic. While scholars have recently argued for a broader definition of Minimalism that would include artists in number of disciplines, the term remains closely linked to sculpture of the period. Donald Judd's *Untitled* (stack pieces) is characteristic in its use of spare geometric forms, repeated to create a unified whole that calls attention to its physical size in relationship to the viewer. Like most Minimalists, Judd used industrial materials and processes to manufacture his work, but his preference for color and shiny surfaces distinguished him among the artists who pioneered the style.

Lack of Apparent Meaning

What most people find disturbing about Minimalism is its lack of any apparent meaning. Like Pop Art, which emerged simultaneously, Minimalism presented ordinary subject matter in a literal way that lacked expressive features or metaphorical content; likewise, the use of commercial processes smacked of mass production and seemed to reject traditional expectations of skill and originality in art. In these ways, both movements were, in part, a response to the dominance of Abstract Expressionism, which had held that painting conveys profound subjective meaning. However, whereas Pop artists depicted recognizable images from kitsch sources, the Minimalists exhibited their plywood boxes, florescent lights and concrete blocks directly on gallery floors, which seemed even more difficult to distinguish as "Art." (One well-known story tells of an art dealer, who visited Carl Andre's studio during the winter and unknowingly burned a sculpture for firewood while the artist was away.) Moreover, when asked to explain his black-striped paintings of 1959, Frank Stella responded, "What you see is what you see." Stella's comment implied that, not only was there no meaning, but that none was necessary to demonstrate the object's artistic value.

Writings

Given these facts, it may seem odd to learn that hundreds of essays and books have been written about Minimalism, many by the artists themselves. It is significant that, although Minimalist art shares similar features, the artists associated with the movement developed their aesthetic ideas from variety of philosophical and artistic influences. Through their writings, Minimalist artists put forth distinctive positions about the work they produced. In addition to his role as a sculptor, Judd was a prominent art critic, and his reviews provide eloquent explanations of his intent—shared by Stella and Dan Flavin—to eliminate the illusionism and "subjective" decision-making of traditional painting. Robert Morris, whose sculpture was influenced by avant-garde dance and performance, published a series of texts, arguing for sculpture to be understood in physical and psychological terms; and, Sol LeWitt introduced the term Conceptual Art to explain the use of seriality and systemic structure in his cubic grid-like forms.

Legacy

In this way, the artists, along with critics and art historians over the past 50 years, have developed a critical discourse that surrounds the art objects, but which is essential to understanding Minimalism itself. Likewise, such artists as Richard Serra, Bernd and Hilla Becher, Maya Lin and Rachel Whiteread, who use Minimalist practice of the early 1960s as a point of departure for their own creative exploration, continue to contribute to the movement's legacy and our understanding of its significance today.

Dan Flavin

Kate Burns and Jillian Punska provide a description, historical perspective, and analysis of Dan Flavin's *Untitled (To Donna) II.*

- https://youtu.be/c6uz8fy1sM4

Dan Flavin, *Untitled (To Donna) II,* 1971, fluorescent light, (Portland Art Museum).

Attributions

Robert Morris

Curator Scott Rothkopf discusses the artist Robert Morris's *Untitled (L-Beams)* (1965), on view in the exhibition Singular Visions.

- https://youtu.be/m6Y6LkZblTk

External Link

View this sculpture on the Whitney Museum of American Art's website:

- http://collection.whitney.org/object/1774

Unfortunately, any photograph of Robert Morris's *L Beams* is going to miss the point if we want to understand the object both in an artistic and material sense. Morris wanted to expose the conditions of perception and display and the fact that these conditions always affect the way we comprehend the art object—sculpture always exists somewhere in relationship to someone at sometime. This specificity, Morris felt, had not been investigated enough, even by the many avant-garde experiments that define Modernism.

By placing two eight-foot fiberglass "L-Beams" in a gallery space (often, he showed three), Morris demonstrated that a division existed between our perception of the object and the actual object. While viewers perceived the beams as being different shapes and sizes, in actuality, they were the same shape and of equal size. In direct opposition to Modernism's focus on the internal syntax of the object, that is, how the object can be understood as something "self-contained," Morris choose instead to examine the external syntax; the theatricality of the object—the way an object extends out from itself into its environment. In his series of essays on sculpture written in the late 1960s, Morris observed how he wanted to make sculpture,

> A function of space, light, and the viewer's field of vision . . . for it is the viewer who changes the shape constantly by his change in position relative to the work. . . . There are two distinct terms: the known constant and the experienced variable.

This last line is revealing as it demonstrates the crux of *L-Beams*. No matter how hard we try, we can't reconcile what we see and what we know. Morris' objects appear one way, "the expierenced variable," but in our minds we identify them to be another, "the known constant."

Informed by theories of the body and perception, including his reading of Maurice Merleau-Ponty's *Phenomenology of Perception* (1945), Morris explored the circumstances of the art object as we actually encounter it. He asked, why do we ignore the space and conditions of display in the presentation of art? Why do we only focus on the object? What about everything that circumscribes it; from its frame, to the wall that it is hung on, to the shape of the space that we put it in.

Like other artists of his generation, Morris pursued an advanced education in art history and earned a Master of Arts degree from Columbia University. Furthermore, Morris was associated with the Judson Dance School, an experimental group of performers who sought to push the conceptual boundaries of dance. These experiences informed Morris's understanding of what art could be, both in relation to the gallery and to history.

In relation to his artistic exploration of perception and space, Morris was explicitly influenced by Hans Namuth's photographs of Jackson Pollock and also by Allan Kaprow's reading of Pollock. Kaprow's essay, "The Legacy of Jackson Pollock" (1958), urged a new generation of artists to adopt the use of "sight, sound, movement [and] people" in order to make their art. Kaprow supported this call with his own brand of theatrical "Happenings," in which he staged bizarre and unplanned events in art galleries, further informing many young artists.

Morris has explained the theories behind his art practice in his teaching and in writing where he has sought to justify his art to a larger audience and enter into the debate surrounding his own practice. In particular, the summer edition of Artforum (1967) included not only Morris's "Notes on Sculpture 3", but also Robert Smithson's "Towards the Development of an Air Terminal Site," Michael Fried's "Art and Objecthood," and Sol LeWitt's "Paragraphs on Conceptual Art." This issue is of utmost importance in understanding Morris's relationship to Modernism, Minimalism, and to Conceptual Art.

Morris's *Untitled (L-Beams)* were shown in the exhibition, "Primary Structures: Younger American and British Sculpture (April 27–June 12, 1966)." This exhibition, which took place at the Jewish Museum in New York, effectively launched Minimalism into the discourse of contemporary art on the international stage. The critical and art historical discussions that followed this exhibition resulted in important debates over the inherent significance of the Minimalist object, the role of the artist in its production, and the role of the viewer in relation to the creation of its meaning.

Attributions

CC licensed content, Shared previously

- Robert Morris, Untitled (L Beams). **Authored by**: Jp McMahon. **Provided by**: Khan Academy. **Located at**: https://web.archive.org/web/20130116124105/http://smarthistory.khanacademy.org/robert-morris-untitled-l-beams.html. **License**: *CC BY-NC-SA: Attribution-NonCommercial-ShareAlike*

All rights reserved content

- Singular Visions: Robert Morris, Untitled (L-Beams), 1965. **Authored by**: WhitneyFocus. **Located at**: https://youtu.be/m6Y6LkZblTk. **License**: *All Rights Reserved.* **License Terms**: Standard YouTube License

Eva Hesse, Untitled

Dr. Beth Harris and Dr. Steven Zucker provide a description, historical perspective, and analysis of Eva Hesse's *Untitled*.

- https://youtu.be/jO1wp-Bx-WE

Eva Hesse, *Untitled*, 1966, enamel paint, string, papier-mâché, elastic cord, (MoMA).

Attributions

CC licensed content, Shared previously

Eva Hesse, Untitled (Rope Piece)

Dr. Beth Harris and Dr. Steven Zucker provide a description, historical perspective, and analysis of Eva Hesse's *Untitled (Rope Piece)*.

- https://youtu.be/-nrSCokEUXg

Eva Hesse, *Untitled (Rope Piece)*, 1970, rope, latex, string, wire, variable dimensions, (Whitney Museum of American Art).

Attributions

CC licensed content, Shared previously

Introduction to Performance Art

When Art Intersects With Life

Many people associate performance art with highly publicized controversies over government funding of the arts, censorship, and standards of public decency. Indeed, at its worst, performance art can seem gratuitous, boring or just plain weird. But, at its best, it taps into our most basic shared instincts: our physical and psychological needs for food, shelter, sex, and human interaction; our individual fears and self-consciousness; our concerns about life, the future, and the world we live in. It often forces us to think about issues in a way that can be disturbing and uncomfortable, but it can also make us laugh by calling attention to the absurdities in life and the idiosyncrasies of human behavior.

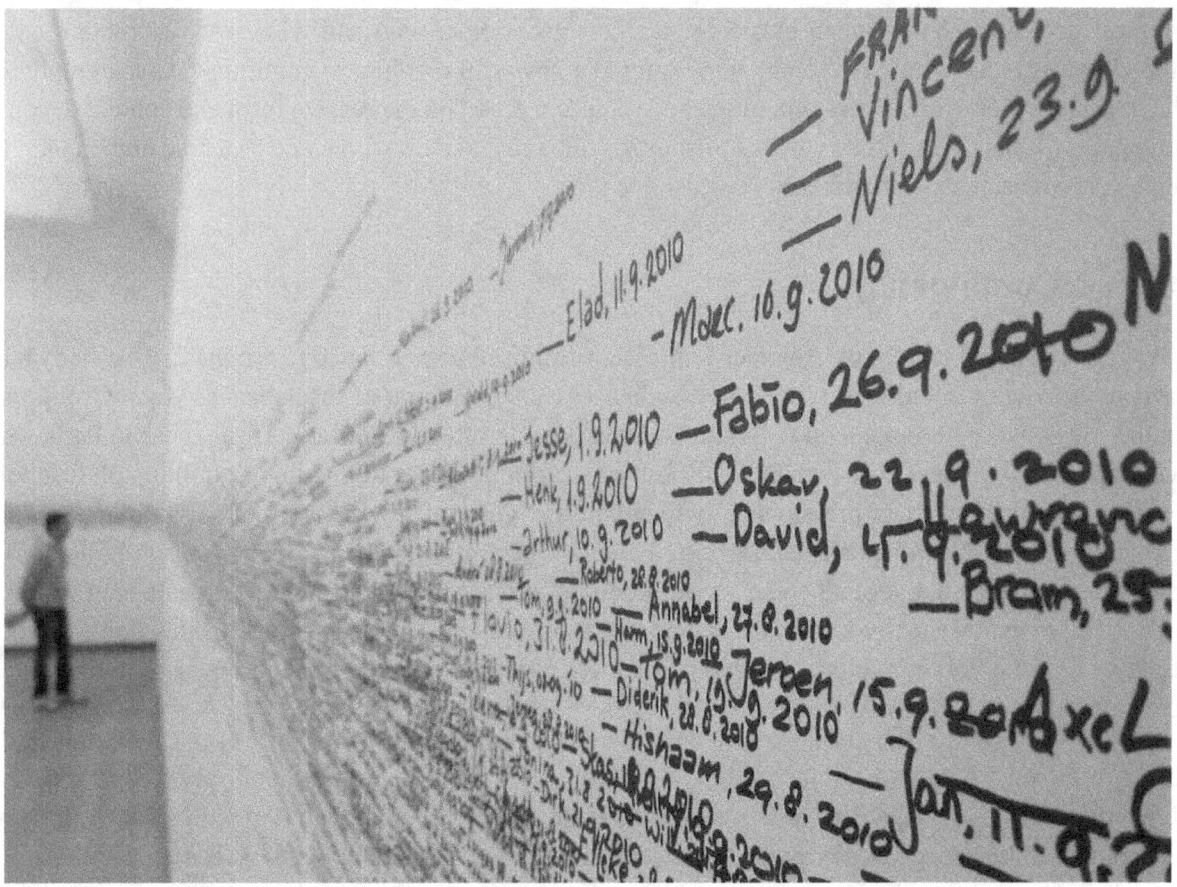

Figure 1. Roman Ondák, Measuring the Universe, 2007, shown enacted at MoMA, 2009

Performance art differs from traditional theater in its rejection of a clear narrative, use of random or chance-based structures, and direct appeal to the audience. The art historian RoseLee Goldberg writes:

> Historically, performance art has been a medium that challenges and violates borders between disciplines and genders, between private and public, and between everyday life and art, and that follows no rules.[1]

Although the term encompasses a broad range of artistic practices that involve bodily experience and live action, its radical connotations derive from this challenge to conventional social mores and artistic values of the past.

Historical Sources

While performance art is a relatively new area of art history, it has roots in experimental art of the late 19th and early 20th centuries. Echoing utopian ideas of the period's avant-garde, these earliest examples found influences in theatrical and music performance, art, poetry, burlesque and other popular entertainment. Modern artists used live events to promote extremist beliefs, often through deliberate provocation and attempts to offend bourgeois tastes or expectations. In Italy, the anarchist group of Futurist artists insulted and hurled profanity at their middle-class audiences in hopes of inciting political action.

Following World War II, performance emerged as a useful way for artists to explore philosophical and psychological questions about human existence. For this generation, who had witnessed destruction caused by the Holocaust and atomic bomb, the body offered a powerful medium to communicate shared physical and emotional experience. Whereas painting and sculpture relied on expressive form and content to convey meaning, performance art forced viewers to engage with a real person who could feel cold and hunger, fear and pain, excitement and embarrassment—just like them.

Action & Contingency

Some artists, inspired largely by Abstract Expressionism, used performance to emphasize the body's role in artistic production. Working before a live audience, Kazuo Shiraga of the Japanese Gutai Group made sculpture by crawling through a pile of mud. Georges Mathieu staged similar performances in Paris where he violently threw paint at his canvas. These performative approaches to making art built on philosophical interpretations of Abstract Expressionism, which held the gestural markings of action painters as visible evidence of the artist's own existence. Bolstered by Hans Namuth's photographs of Jackson Pollock in his studio, moving dance-like around a canvas on the floor, artists like Shiraga and Mathieu began to see the artist's creative act as equally important, if not more so, to the artwork produced. In this light, Pollock's distinctive drips, spills and splatters appeared as a mere remnant, a visible trace left over from the moment of creation.

Shifting attention from the art object to the artist's action further suggested that art existed in real space and real time. In New York, visual artists combined their interest in action painting with ideas of the avant-garde composer John Cage to blur the line between art and life. Cage employed chance procedures to create musical compositions such as 4'33". In this (in)famous piece, Cage used the time frame specified in

---

1. RoseLee Goldberg. *Performance: Live art since the 60s*, New York: Thames & Hudson, 1998, page 20.

the title to bracket ambient noises that occurred randomly during the performance. By effectively calling attention to the hum of fluorescent lights, people moving in their seats, coughs, whispers, and other ordinary sounds, Cage transformed them into a unique musical composition.

The Private Made Political

Drawing on these influences, new artistic formats emerged in the late 1950s. Environments and Happenings physically placed viewers in commonplace surroundings, often forcing them to participate in a series of loosely structured actions. Fluxus artists, poets, and musicians likewise challenged viewers by presenting the most mundane events—brushing teeth, making a salad, exiting the theater—as forms of art. A well-known example is the "bed-in" that Fluxus artist Yoko Ono staged in 1969 in Amsterdam with her husband John Lennon. Typical of much performance art, Ono and Lennon made ordinary human activity a public spectacle, which demanded personal interaction and raised popular awareness of their pacifist beliefs.

In the politicized environment of the 1960s, many artists employed performance to address emerging social concerns. For feminist artists in particular, using their body in live performance proved effective in challenging historical representations of women, made mostly by male artists for male patrons. In keeping with past tradition, artists such as Carolee Schneemann, Hannah Wilke and Valie Export displayed their nude bodies for the viewer's gaze; but, they resisted the idealized notion of women as passive objects of beauty and desire. Through their words and actions, they confronted their audiences and raised issues about the relationship of female experience to cultural beliefs and institutions, physical appearance, and bodily functions including menstruation and childbearing. Their ground-breaking work paved the way for male and female artists in the 1980s and 1990s, who similarly used body and performance art to explore issues of gender, race and sexual identity.

Where Is It?

Throughout the mid-twentieth century, performance has been closely tied to the search for alternatives to established art forms, which many artists felt had become fetishized as objects of economic and cultural value. Because performance art emphasized the artist's action and the viewer's experience in real space and time, it rarely yielded a final object to be sold, collected, or exhibited. Artists of the 1960s and 1970s also experimented with other "dematerialized" formats including Earthworks and Conceptual Art that resisted commodification and traditional modes of museum display. The simultaneous rise of photography and video, however, offered artists a viable way to document and widely distribute this new work.

Performance art's acceptance into the mainstream over the past 30 years has led to new trends in its practice and understanding. Ironically, the need to position performance within art's history has led museums and scholars to focus heavily on photographs and videos that were intended only as documents of live events. In this context, such archival materials assume the art status of the original performance. This practice runs counter to the goal of many artists, who first turned to performance as an alternative to object-based forms of art. Alternatively, some artists and institutions now stage re-enactments of earlier performances in order to recapture the experience of a live event. In a 2010 retrospective exhibition at New York's Museum of Modern Art, for example, performers in the galleries staged live reenactments of works by the pioneering performance artist Marina Abramovic, alongside photographs and video documentation of the original performances.

Don't Try This At Home

New strategies, variously described as situations, relational aesthetics, and interventionist art, have recently begun to appear. Interested in the social role of the artist, Rirkrit Tiravanija stages performances that encourage interpersonal exchange and shared conversation among individuals who might not otherwise meet. His performances have included cooking traditional Thai dinners in museums for viewers to share, and relocating the entire contents of a gallery's offices and storage rooms, including the director at his desk, into public areas used to exhibit art. Similar to performance art of the past, such approaches engage the viewer and encourage their active participation in artistic production; however, they also speak to a cultural shift toward interactive modes of communication and social exchange that characterize the twenty-first century.

Attributions

CC licensed content, Shared previously

Joseph Beuys, Fat Chair

The Artist as "Shaman"

The first encounter with a work by Joseph Beuys is often surprising. Look, for example, at *Fat Chair*, 1964. It is composed of an old, rather ordinary chair with fat placed on the seat.

External Link

View this work on the Whitney Museum of American Art's website:

- http://www.tate.org.uk/art/artworks/beuys-fat-chair-ar00088

Keep in mind, all of the features that fat possesses as a material, and it is clear that a lot of fat and an old chair are not meant to produce feelings of esthetic pleasure. Other materials that Beuys uses in his work: wax, filth, animal hair, and blood, possess similar qualities. Each is a natural material but none are very pleasant in their appearance, structure or smell. Why should artwork be like that? Shouldn't art be "fine" or "beautiful" in some sense?

These works of art are part of Beuys' broader artistic strategy, which can be called "shamanism." Beuys often used natural materials and cult-like ceremonies through which he tried to underline the importance of the irrational and mystical in human beings. With this practice, Beuys tried to oppose the "rational" in contemporary society. He perceived his art as a social mission, needed to heal post-war German society. He wanted to heal, first of all, those who built Auschwitz—that terrible symbol of Nazi horror. This task required an even deeper reform–since in Beuys' eyes, the real source of National Socialism was found in the extreme rationality of modern society.

For Beuys, extreme rationality, efficiency and technocracy, defined the modern era; and although seemingly good, he viewed these trends as extremely dangerous. The Holocaust was only possible because of Germany's rationality, efficiency and functionality coupled with its specific ideological premises. Beuys sought to contrast the Holocaust's rationality with the irrationality he believed could be found in so-called "primitive societies." Irrationality, understood in this way, focused on concrete people, not on abstract or theoretical principles. Beuys suggested that only this could prevent human destruction. "Shamanism" was a part of this "primitive" practice of healing human beings physically, morally, and spiritually.

This shamanistic use of natural materials is meant to underscore man's relation to nature and to a concrete human community in which the practice of healing takes place. These practices do not have an aesthetic purpose and the materials used by Beuys do not pretend to be anything other than what they are—unpleasant, rough natural materials. They are real and do not mislead and this truthfulness yields a kind of beauty.

Attributions

CC licensed content, Shared previously

Chapter 15:
1960–Now–Age of Post-Colonialism Part II

Chapter 15 Overview

What You'll Learn To Do: Examine Contemporary art and its artists.

In Chapter 15 we will continue to examine Contemporary art. We will look at how artists like Hirst contributed to the development of Western art. It is imperative to understand Contemporary art in order to see how it will impact the future.

Learning Activities

The learning activities for this module include:

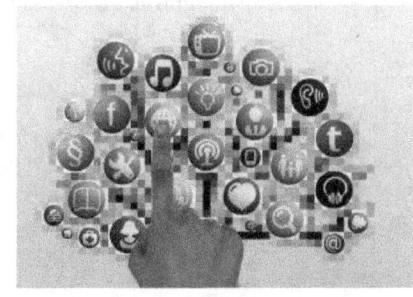

- **Review:** Key Learning Items

Installation Art

- **Read:** Understanding Installation Art

Conceptual Art

- **Read:** Vito Acconci
- **Read:** John Baldessari (includes a video: 3:34)

Institutional Critique

- **Watch:** Hans Haacke (6:37)

Feminist Art

- **Read:** Mary Kelly

Earth Art

- **Read:** Robert Smithson (includes a video: 3:44)

Post-Minimalism

- **Read:** Bruce Nauman

Postmodernism

- **Watch:** Robert Colescott (4:38)

Young British Artists

- **Watch:** Damien Hirst (7:48)

Twenty-First Century

- **Read:** Art in the Twenty-First Century
- **Read:** Ai Weiwei (includes a video: 11:37)

Attributions

Key Learning Items

Learning Objectives

After successful completion of this module, you will be able to:

- Understand and apply the concepts and terminology of Contemporary art
- Investigate and apply the fundamental questions we ask when looking at art objects from this movement
- Discuss, collaborate, and generate understanding as to the meaning of Contemporary art
- Assess and evaluate the impact of Contemporary art on the continued evolution of Western art

Key Questions to Ask

While you are reviewing the content of this module, consider the following questions:

- What are the various types of art produced in the late 20-century?
- How is contemporary art different but also similar to art produced in earlier eras?
- What is the future of art?

Key Vocabulary Terms

- Conceptual art
- installation
- Feminist art
- Earth art
- Post-Minimalism
- Postmodernism

- globalization

Here are links to art history glossaries that will help you better understand the above key vocabulary terms.

- ArtLex: Art Dictionary
  - http://www.artlex.com/
- About.com: Art History
  - http://arthistory.about.com/od/glossary/l/bl_Art-Glossary.htm
- Artcyclopedia: A Guide to Fine Art
  - http://www.artcyclopedia.com/

Attributions

CC licensed content, Original

Understanding Installation Art

Installation art is a complex genre. These works are dependent on their location and how they are displayed. They can involve sounds, lights, and even human beings. Click on the link below to view the article "Understanding Installation Art" developed by *For Dummies*. This article will help you understand exactly what Installation Art is and how it differs from other kinds of art.

- "Understanding Installation Art," by *For Dummies*
  - http://www.dummies.com/how-to/content/understanding-installation-art.html

Vito Acconci

Conceived by performance and conceptual artist Vito Acconci, *Following Piece* (http://www.metmuseum.org/collection/the-collection-online/search/283737) was an activity that took place everyday on the streets of New York, between October 3rd and 25th, 1969. It was part of other performance and conceptual events sponsored by the Architectural League of New York that occurred during those three weeks. The terms of the exhibition "Street Works IV" were to do a piece, sometime during the month, that used a street in New York City. So Acconci decided to follow people around the streets and document his following of them. But why would he do this? Why would Acconci follow random people around New York?

Acconci's work is typical of performance and conceptual art made during this period in the way that he uses his body as the object of his art in order to explore some specific idea. In essence, *Following Piece* was concerned with the language of our bodies, not so much in a private manner, but in a deeply public manner. By selecting a passer-by at random until they entered a private space, Acconci submitted his own movements to the movements of others, showing how our bodies are themselves always subject to external forces that we may or may not be able to control. In his notes that the artist kept during the performance, Acconci wrote:

> Following Piece, potentially, could use all the time allotted and all the space available: I might be following people, all day long, everyday, through all the streets in New York City. In actuality, following episodes ranged from two or three minutes when someone got into a car and I couldn't grab a taxi, I couldn't follow – to seven or eight hours – when a person went to a restaurant, a movie.

In terms of the art work, rather than being just another object that we look at in the gallery, Following Piece was part of the revolution that took place in the art world in the late 1960s that tried to bring art out of the gallery and into the street in order to explore real issues such as space, time, and the human body. Many artists, such as Acconci, used their bodies as their chosen medium. Look at some of Acconci's notes of the period which he wrote before, during and after the event:

- I need a scheme (follow the scheme, follow a person)

- I add myself to another person (I give up control/I don't have to control myself)

- Subjective relationship; subjunctive relationship

- A way to get around. (A way to get myself out of the house.) Get into the middle of things.

- Out of space. Out of time. (My time and space are taken up, out of myself, into a larger system).

All of these ideas were influenced by Acconci's readings. As many other artists of the period, Acconci wanted to get away from specific art problems and engage with social problems. Acconci read books such as Edward Hall's *The Hidden Dimension* (1969), Erving Goffmann's *The Presentation of the Self in Every Day Life* (1959), and Kurt Lewin's *In Principles of Topological Psychological* (1936/1966). All of these books explored the ways in which the individual and the social are interlinked in terms of complex codes that structure the way we act and live everyday.

With regard to the influence on these texts on *Following Piece,* Acconci's use of diagrams specifically refers to Lewin's notion of "field theory": that is, a model that sought to explain human behaviour in terms of relations and in relation to its environment and surroundings. Lewin placed behaviour in a "field" in order to examine it in a theoretical manner. The diagrams drawn by Acconci are an imaginative engagement with this idea of human relations as engaging in a specific field or space. So by following someone around New York, Acconci could perhaps experience what it was like to relinquish self control to others and also explore the intersecting systems that grouped different people together in one field. As we can see from the diagrams, Acconci's intentions were not subjective but much more systematic—they constituted an exploration of the private and public fields that occur in every social space.

Ironically, for all the effort to get out of the gallery, much of Acconci's documentation of *Following Piece,* for example, the texts, photographs (which were taken after the event!), and diagrams, now constitutes a work of art in its own right. MOMA owns several of the photographs of *Following Piece* and other "versions" of this work are also in existence. So, even though Acconci's Following Piece was a performance that occurred in a very specific period (3rd to 25th October, 1969), the reproduction and circulation of the work continues. This fact not only teaches us important things about the nature of performance art and its relationship to the art world, but also how the context of the art work is also never exactly fixed and each time it is presented something new occurs with the work itself.

Attributions

Mary Kelly

Anyone who has been in the unpleasant position of changing a dirty nappy will know that normally your first instinct is to get it as far away from it as possible. So it might seem strange that American artist Mary Kelly (born 1941) took the liners of her son's used cloth nappies, printed them with details of his diet, and displayed them as artworks. Causing some controversy at their debut exhibition, the nappy liners formed the first part of the epic and fascinating *Post Partum Document* (1973–79).

External Link

View this project on Mary Kelly's website. Pay particular attention to the Detail photograph captioned "Perpsex units, white card, sugar paper, crayon / 1 of the 13 units, 35.5 x 28 cm each."

- http://www.marykellyartist.com/post_partum_document.html

Kelly has made works that examine complicated social issues such as the ramifications of war, and the politics of how our identities are constructed. In *Post Partum Document,* she was engaging in a discussion that was happening at the emergence of second-wave feminism about the way in which women worked in the home. At a time where many feminist artists were looking at reclaiming the body through performance—such as Marina Abramovic and Carole Schneeman—or revising history in order to incorporate our foremothers—such as Judy Chicago—Kelly looked more directly at the invisible daily experience of women engaged in domestic labour.

Post Partum Document consists of six sections of documentation that follow the development of Kelly's son, Kelly Barrie, from birth until the age of five. Kelly intricately charts her relationship with her son, and her changing role as a mother by writing on artefacts associated with child care: baby clothes, his drawings, items he collects, and his first efforts at writing. In addition, there are detailed analytical texts that exist in parallel to the objects.

In "Documentation III: Analysed Markings and Diary Perspective Schema," Kelly includes three types of text. She describes them in the documentation that accompanies their exhibition as:

R1 A condensed transcription of the child's conversation, playing it back immediately following the recording session

R2 A transcription of the mother's inner speech in relation to R1, recalling it during a playback later the same day
R3 A secondary revision of R2, one week later, locating the conversation (as object) within a specific time interval (as spatial metaphor) and rendering it "in perspective" (as a mnemic system)

Kelly's documentations that accompany the work are heavily indebted to Lacanian psychoanalysis, which conceives of the unconscious as being structured like a language. This is interesting in relation to *Post Partum Document* because it is so layered with text. The quote above strongly contrasts with extracts taken from column R1 (the transcripts) from the piece dated 27.9.75, which is written in lowercase on a type-writer. They state:

> Come'n do it (wants to fly the kite)
> Down dis, its falling. (I'm pretending to fly the kite)]
> Ask Daddy flying the kite, go ask him (I say Daddy will fly it tomorrow)

We can see how much range there is in the text that she uses. Adding to this, there are the sections in R2 that provide a picture of an adult's day to day interaction with a small child. This column is typed in capital letters, using the aesthetic of the text in order to separate the voices. From the same piece R2 reads:

> I say it would be nice to take it outside as it's very windy but it's also very late so I try to change the subject.
> As I started this game of pretending to fly the kite standing on a chair holding it and making sounds like wind, now I'm stuck with it.
> He remembers promises very well.

Finally, in section R3, Kelly describes her anxiety following an accident in which her son drank liquid aspirin and had to be rushed to hospital. This section is handwritten and is much longer, with candid text that explores the difficulties of childrearing. A part of this section states:

> Sometimes I forget to give him his medicine which makes me feel totally irresponsible or I just feel I wish it was all over i.e. he was 'grown up' but my mother says it never ends the worry just goes on and on

Over the top of all this worry and analysis are Kelly Barrie's drawings. They are typical of the drawings made by a young child, not much more than scribbles on rice paper. However, his lines cut over his mother's careful work; their carelessness seems all the more free when contrasted with her deliberations.

What makes this piece important is the way in which motherhood—so often seen in art history as a sentimental connection between mother and child—is shown as a difficult and complex relationship. Kelly's voice does not overbear her son's, instead it exists in tandem; we see Kelly developing and adapting as much as her child.

This is an extensive project (comprising in total of 139 individual parts) and Kelly's attention to the material qualities of these mundane objects is outstanding. This piece is a central work within feminist art that is still a relevant and a fascinating picture of what motherhood means for women.

Attributions

CC licensed content, Shared previously

- Mary Kelly, Postpartum Document. **Authored by**: Rachel Warriner. **Provided by**: Khan Academy. **Located at**: https://web.archive.org/web/20130425113444/http://smarthistory.khanacademy.org/mary-kellys-postpartum-document.html. **License**: *CC BY-NC-SA: Attribution-NonCommercial-ShareAlike*

Robert Smithson

Dr. Beth Harris and Dr. Shana Gallagher-Lindsay provide a description, historical perspective, and analysis of Robert Smithson's *Spiral Jetty*.

- https://youtu.be/NUu0_Zn55yM

Robert Smithson, *Spiral Jetty*, 1970 (Great Salt Lake, Utah)

A Monument to Paradox and Transience

A loud abrasive buzzing bellows from the nightstand and I raise my head, only to be blinded by the red light emanating from the small—in size, not volume—machine against a backdrop of pure blackness. 4:00 A.M. Oy. I'm immediately beset by the eternal morning conflict: ten more minutes of sleep vs. the rush of adrenaline that wants to start the adventures that await. The latter quickly usurps the former as I realize today is September 25th, a day I've waited for my entire life (metaphorically speaking) and actually been counting down to since the spring. It's Spiral Jetty day.

I bound out of bed, Gianfranco Gorgoni's seminal photograph (http://www.jamescohan.com/artists/estate-of-robert-smithson) of Robert Smithson's iconic earth work on repeat in my head as I shower and "pack" for the daylong adventure that will take me to a remote area of Utah. I meet the rest of my party at the gate at LAX and it's immediately clear from the conversation that we've all arrived at this moment with decades of expectation accumulated. How would the experience compare to the visions (particular to each person) we had all conjured up over the years? Would the jetty "deliver" the transformative experience we all sought? Or would it fall victim to a case of excessively high and unattainable expectations? Time would tell.

But, it would indeed take time. An hour at the airport, followed by an hour plus on the plane, then a two plus hour bus ride over the bumpiest "trail"—it certainly wasn't a road!—imaginable, and ultimately a fifteen minute hike. Nearly eight hours after my day had begun, it came into view. At last, Spiral Jetty.

But . . . it was so, so, so small. That couldn't possibly be it! Naturally the distance made the work appear smaller and it "grew" as we approached, but even as we stood perched on the rocks right above it, it seemed utterly dominated by the landscape. Yet another surprise, the water from the Great Salt Lake no longer permeated the rocks, but was a significant distance beyond. Between the Jetty and the lake, there was a blanket of white—a picture-perfect postcard image of a quiet winter's morn, and yet, the "snow" wasn't melted by the sun blazing down from above. Upon closer inspection, the "snow" was actually crystallized salt that brilliantly reflected the sun's rays and the nearby water.

We walked about the Jetty with the sun hot upon our skin, the smell of the salt air filling our nose and lungs, and the feel of salt crystals on our fingers (having knelt to examine the minerals that carpeted the environ). An all-consuming, olfactory experience. We then decided to make our way across the white blanket to the water's edge, fighting off fears that the salt, which had the distinct characteristics of ice—would "break" and we would plunge into the Great Salt Lake below (which was a physical impossibility since the water wasn't below). From a distance the water had appeared a brilliant blue, but as we neared, gradations of color began to appear—shades of blue, purple, pink, and red—a traveler's mirage, of sorts, and undeniably picturesque.

We found our way up to a piece of land overlooking the jetty and sat down on the rocks to enjoy our sandwiches and "debate" Smithson's intentions and ethical issues in conserving the work with several scholars. One of them compared Smithson's Spiral Jetty to Monet's Rouen Cathedral series which conveyed the same location at various times of day so that he could capture the specific lighting and other nuances of a particular moment. He said, "Smithson's doing that here but he's not doing it on canvas, he's doing it out there in the elements themselves…it has that same type of specificity too it, and yet specificity that is subject to all kinds of permutations." The question was raised about Smithson's vision for the work, his view on its ephemerality, and whether he ever envisioned groups such as ours making the journey out to this incredibly remote location to experience his work.

We were reminded that the physical jetty is only part of the work, which is actually a triad of the "sculpture" in the landscape, an essay by Smithson, and a film documenting the project. But, as time has marched on, the work has become embodied in the minds of the general public in a single photograph, the aforementioned image taken by Gorgoni who hovered about the work in a helicopter and captured the piece from the perfect angle so that it looked colossal, while the hills looked minuscule.

This is due, in large part, to the fact that the jetty became submerged only a few years after it was made, and remained that way for decades. Only in the past ten years has it resurfaced and been "available" for visitation. Though Smithson may not have ever intended or even considered that people would take the time (and trouble) to visit, which begs the question that Loe posed to us, "Who is this work for?" Coolidge said the work was for Gorgoni, that Smithson had literally made it for the photograph. They all agreed that the sculpture itself is the "gesture," but the documentation is every bit as much a part of it.

Up until that moment, the essay, the film, and the Gorgoni photograph were the entirety of my experience with Smithson's Spiral Jetty, which is probably true for all but a small population who've sought out the physical experience of the "gesture." An object whose identity is so deeply intertwined with its documentation is fraught with complexities and paradox, but given interest in ephemerality and entropy, I'd imagine he'd be quite satisfied with the transient nature of his jetty—how it disappears and reappears at nature's will. Such is the foundation for arguing against any conservation of the earth work, and allowing it to emerge and submerge with the tides. And yet, the thought of the work vanishing for another thirty years beneath the lake devastates me. With this debate reeling in my head, I made my way back down to the jetty. If I couldn't be certain the work would be here waiting for my return in the distant future, I'd better take another promenade on the rocks.

This time I separated from my friends, put down my camera, and walked the spiral in absolute silence. Though physically alone, I felt the overwhelming presence of several invisible companions: Mother Nature herself, the spirit of Robert Smithson that is somehow pervades the rocks, and God. I thought about each of them in a way that the loud noise of my crowded, urban existence prohibits. I found the transcendental calm within that often only comes to me upon reading an Emerson poem, hearing a choir sing Amazing Grace, or staring into the floating color-field abyss of a Mark Rothko painting.

I began the walk back to the bus with my colleagues. We found ourselves humbled by the beauty of nature and the power of art, and hailed Smithson for giving us a reason to find our way to this breathtaking place.

On the bumpy ride back towards town, I realized that I had made a pilgrimage in search of a monument, an icon of culture and history, but found pleasure in the aesthetic of transience instead. Spiral Jetty looked nothing like I'd imagined—a.k.a. the Gorgoni photograph – and I'm grateful. Grateful because I saw the work on September 25, 2010 and no one will ever replicate the experience of seeing it on that day, for it reinvents itself with every change of light, tide, and weather.

Attributions

CC licensed content, Shared previously

Bruce Nauman

Bruce Nauman's neon sign, *The True Artist Helps the World by Revealing ?Mystic Truths* (http://www.phil-amuseum.org/collections/permanent/31965.html), asks a multitude of questions with regard to the ?ways in which the twentieth century conceived both avant-garde art and the role of the ?artist in society. If earlier European modernists, such as Mondrian, ?Malevich, and Kandinsky, sought to use art ?to reveal deep-seated truths about the human condition and the role of the artist ?in general, then Bruce Nauman's *The True Artist Helps the World by Revealing ?Mystic Truths* questions such transhistorical and universal ?statements. With regard to this work, Nauman said:

> The most difficult thing about the whole piece for me was the statement. It ?was a kind of test—like when you say something out loud to see if you ?believe it. Once written down, I could see that the statement . . . was on ?the one hand a totally silly idea and yet, on the other hand, I believed it. ?It's true and not true at the same time. It depends on how you interpret it ?and how seriously you take yourself. For me it's still a very strong thought.

By using the mediums of mass culture (neon-signs) and of display (he originally ?hung the sign in his storefront studio), Nauman sought to bring questions? normally considered only by the high culture elite, such as the role and function of art and? the artist in society, to a wider audience. While early European modernists, ?such as Picasso, had borrowed widely from popular culture, they rarely displayed ?their work in the sites of popular culture. For Nauman, both the medium and ?the message were equally important; thus, by using a form of communication ?readily understood by all (neon signs had been widespread in modern industrial society) and by placing this message in the public view, Nauman let everyone ask ?and answer the question.

While it is perhaps the words that stand out most, the symbolism of the spiral (think of Robert Smithson's *Spiral Jetty,* 1969), also deserves attention having been used for centuries in European and other civilizations, such? as megalithic and Chinese art, both as a symbol of time and of nature itself.

Theosophy in interesting in this regard, and since was such an important aspect of the early European Avant-garde. In ?particular, Theosophists believed that all religions are attempts to help humanity? to evolve to greater perfection, and that each religion therefore holds a portion of ?the truth. Through their materials, artists had sought to transform the physical into ?the spiritual. In this sense, Malevich, Mondrian, and Kandinsky sought to use the ?material of their art to transcend it: Nauman, and other of his generation, did not.

Instead, Nauman's work transgresses many genres of art making in that his work explores ?the implications of minimalism, conceptual, performance, and process ?art. In this sense we could call Nauman's art "Post-minimalism," a term coined? by the art critic Robert Pincus-Witten, in his article "Eva Hesse: Post-Minimalism into Sublime" (*Artforum* 10, number 3, November 1971, pages. 35-40). Artists such as Nauman, Acconci, and Hesse, favoured process instead of ?product, or rather the investigation over the end result. However, this is not to ?say they did not produce objects, such as the neon-sign by Nauman, only that ?within the presentation of the object, they also retained an examination of the ?processes that made that specific object.

In this sense, Nauman's neon sign isn't only an object, it's a process, something? that continues to make us think about art, artist, and the role ?that language plays in our conception of both. The words continue to ask this of each beholder who encounters them. Does the artist, the "true ?artist" really "reveal mystical truths"? Or confined to the ?specific culture that it was made in? If we are to believe the statement (remember, it is not? necessarily Nauman's, he merely borrows it from our shared culture), then we might, for example, recognise Leonardo ?da Vinci as a Neo-Platonic artist who showed us ultimate and essential truths through painting. On the other hand, if we reject the statement, then we? would probably recognize the artist as just another producer of a specific set of ?objects, that we call "art."

This type of logic and analytical thinking was influenced by Nauman's reading? of the philosopher Ludwig Wittgenstein's *Philosophical Investigations* (1953).? From Wittgenstein, Nauman took the idea that you put forth a proposition/idea ?in the form of language and then examine its findings, irrespective of its proof or? conclusion. Nauman's "language games," his neon-words, his proposition about? the nature of art and the artist continue to resonant in today's art world, in ?particular with regard to the value we place on the artist's actions and findings.

Attributions

CC licensed content, Shared previously

Damien Hirst

We've already seen this video, but I'd like to rewatch it in its artistic context.

Beth Harris, Sal Khan and Steven Zucker discuss the Damien Hirst sculpture, *The Physical Impossibility of Death in the Mind of Someone Living,* and issues of interpretation.

- https://youtu.be/uDuzy-t7GDA

Damien Hirst, *The Physical Impossibility of Death in the Mind of Someone Living,* 1991, tiger shark, glass, steel, 5% formaldehyde solution, 213 cm × 518 cm × 213 cm (84 in × 204 in × 84 in).

Attributions

CC licensed content, Shared previously

Art in the Twenty-First Century

Click on the link below to view the page "Art in the 21st Century" by Jean Robertson on Khan Academy (originally developed for Oxford Art Online). This page will help you look at art that is being created today and its impact on society.

- "Art in the 21st Century" by Jean Robertson

    ◦ https://www.khanacademy.org/humanities/global-culture/beginners-guide-contemporary-art1/a/art-in-the-21st-century

Attributions

CC licensed content, Original

- Art History II. **Provided by**: Extended Learning Institute of Northern Virginia Community College. **Located at**: http://eli.nvcc.edu/. **License**: *CC BY: Attribution*

Public domain content

- Image of blue i. **Authored by**: OpenClipArtVectors. **Located at**: https://pixabay.com/en/information-circle-icon-blue-160885/. **License**: *Public Domain: No Known Copyright*

Ai Weiwei

Dangerous Art

All art is political in the sense that all art takes place in the public arena and engages with an already existing ideology. Yet there are times when art becomes dangerously political for both the artist and the viewers who engage with that art. Think of Jacques-Louis David's involvement in the French Revolution—his individual investment in art following the bloodshed—and his imprisonment during the reign of terror. If it were not for certain sympathisers, David may well have ended up another victim of the guillotine. Goya is another example of an artist who fell foul of government power. There are instances in the twentieth century when artists have faced down political power directly. Consider the photomontages of John Heartfield. Heartfield risked his life at times to produce covers for the magazine A/Z, which defied both Hitler and the Nazi Party.

Ai Weiwei

The Chinese artist, Ai Weiwei, offers is an important contemporary example. Recently, Weiwei was arrested in China following a crack down by the government on so-called "political dissidents" (a specific category that the Chinese government uses to classify those who seek to subvert state power) for "alleged economic crimes" against the Chinese state. Weiwei has used his art to address both the corruption of the Chinese communist government and its outright neglect of human rights, particularly in the realm of the freedom of speech and thought.

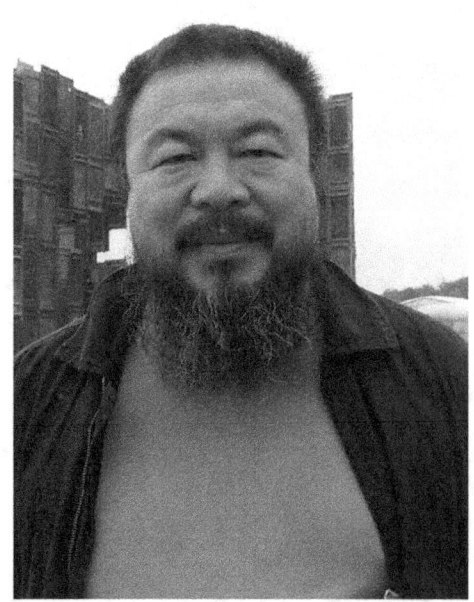

Figure 1. Ai Weiwei

Weiwei has been successful in using the internet (which is severely restricted in China) as a medium for his art. His work is informed by two interconnected strands, his involvement with the Chinese avant-garde group "Stars" (which he helped found in 1978 during his time in the Beijing Film Academy) and the fact that he spent some of his formative years in New York, engaging there with the ideas of conceptual art, in particular the idea of the readymade. Many of the concepts and much of the material that Weiwei uses in his art practice are informed by post-conceptual thinking.

An International Audience

Weiwei has exhibited successfully in the West in many major shows, for example, the 48th Venice Biennale in Italy (1999) and Documenta 12 (2007). He also exhibited *Sunflower Seeds* (October, 2010) in the Turbine Hall in the Tate Modern. In this work, Weiwei filled the floor of the huge hall with one hundred million porcelain seeds, each individually hand-painted in the town of Jingdezhen by 1,600 Chinese artisans. Participants were encouraged to walk over the exhibited space (or even roll in the work) in order to experience the ideas of the effect of mass consumption on Chinese industry and 20th-century China's history of famine and collective work. However, on 16 October, Tate Modern stopped people from walking on the exhibit due to health liability concerns over porcelain dust.

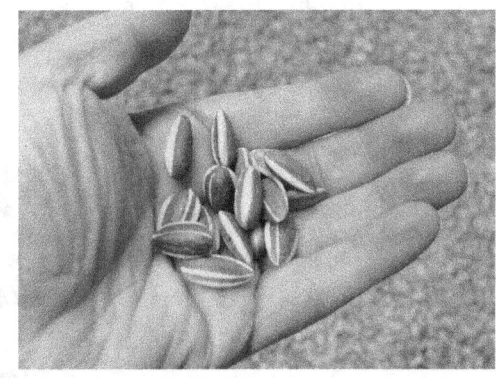

Figure 2. Ai Weiwei, Sunflower Seeds, painted porcelain, 2010

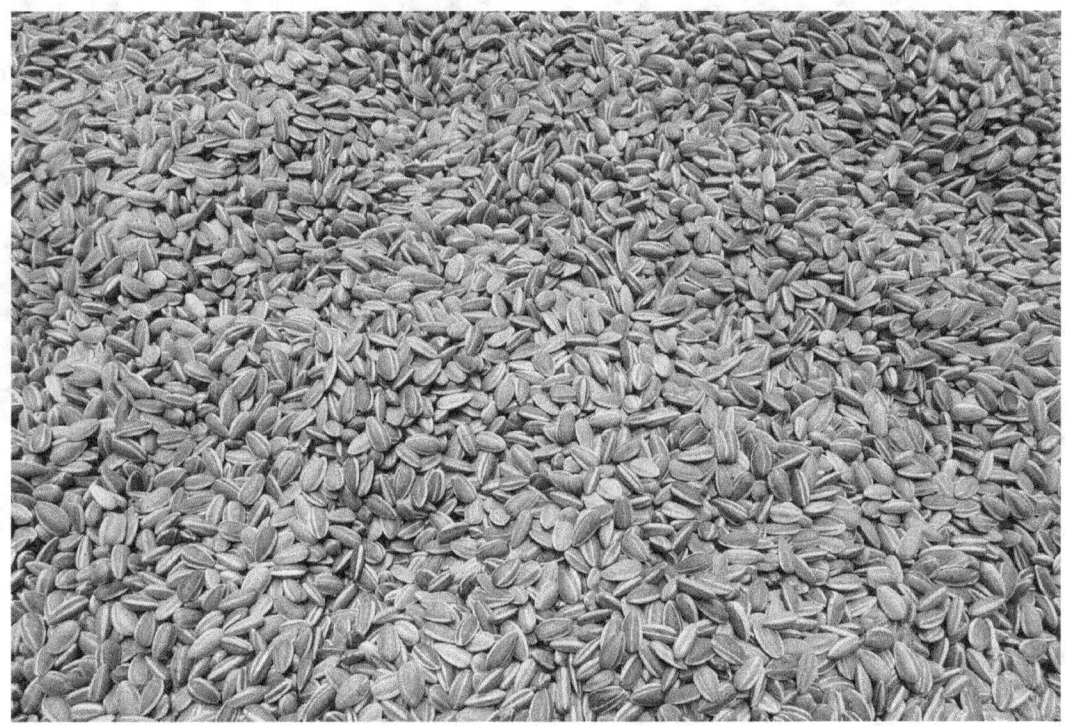

Figure 3. Ai Weiwei, Sunflower Seeds, painted porcelain, 2010

". . . A natural disaster is a public matter."

Perhaps the work that contributed most to Weiwei's current imprisonment and the destruction of his studio was his investigation of corruption in the construction of the schools that collapsed during the 2008 earthquake in Sichuan, China. Like many others, Weiwei investigated how improper material and the contravention of civil engineering laws led to the wholesale destruction of schools (which led in turn to the deaths of thousands of children trapped within them), Weiwei has produced a list of all the victims of the earthquake on his blog. This act is typical Weiwei's use of the internet to communicate information. This information is his "art," in much the way that American artists of the late 1960s used words and ideas as art.

So Sorry

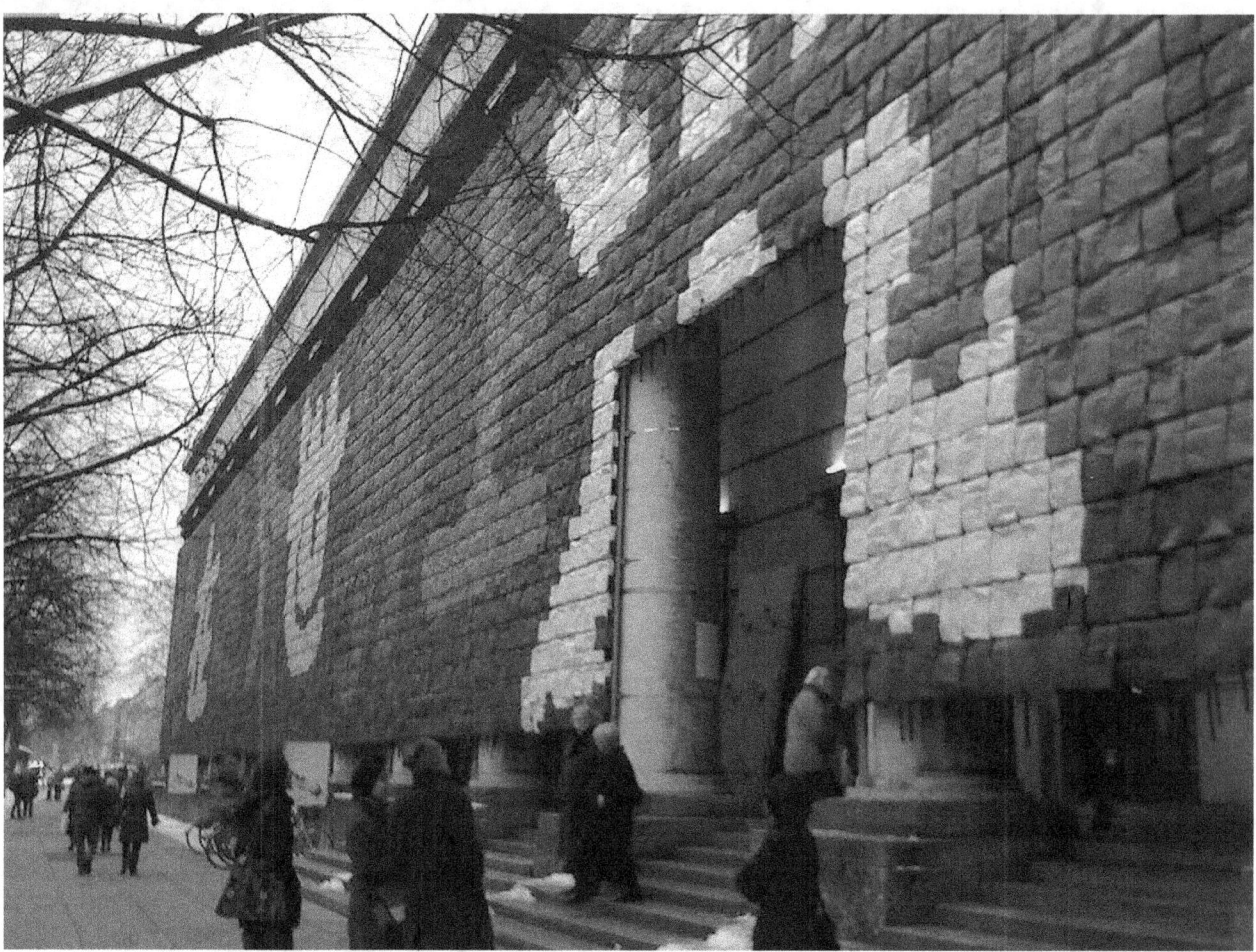

Figure 4. Ai Weiwei, Remembering, backpacks, Haus der Kunst, Munich, 2009

In his retrospective show So Sorry (October 2009 to January 2010, Munich, Germnay), Weiwei created the installation *Remembering* on the façade of the Haus der Kunst.[1] It was constructed from nine thousand children's backpacks. They spelled out the sentence "She lived happily for seven years in this world" in Chinese characters (this was a quote from a mother whose child died in the earthquake). Regarding this work, Weiwei said,

> The idea to use backpacks came from my visit to Sichuan after the earthquake in May 2008. During the earthquake many schools collapsed. Thousands of young students lost their lives, and you could

1. **Historical Note on the Haus der Kunst:** The Haus der Kunst (designed by Paul Ludwig Troost, "first master builder to the führer") was sited by Adolf Hitler and sought to express Nazi ideology by using stone from German quarries and with its references to the work of Klenze and Schinkel. From its opening in 1937, the Haus der Kunst held exhibitions glorifying the "Blood and Soil" propaganda of the Nazi regime.

see bags and study material everywhere. Then you realize individual life, media, and the lives of the students are serving very different purposes. The lives of the students disappeared within the state propaganda, and very soon everybody will forget everything.

The title of the show referred to the apologies frequently expressed by governments and corporations when their negligence leads to tragedies, such as the collapse of schools during the earthquake. Two months before the opening of this exhibition Weiwei suffered a severe beating from Chinese police in Chengdu in August 2009, where he was trying to testify for Tan Zuoren, a fellow investigator of the shoddy construction and the student casualties. Weiwei underwent emergency brain surgery for internal bleeding as a result of the assault.

The Arrest

On April 3rd 2011, Weiwei was arrested at Beijing's airport while while waiting for a flight to Hong Kong. While his detention is broadly believed to be linked to his criticism of the Chinese government, the Chinese Ministry of Foreign Affairs has declared that he is "under investigation for alleged economic crimes." Weiwei's participation in the Jasmine Rallies, a series of peaceful protests which took place all over China in February, no doubt contributed to his arrest.

Weiwei's fate remains unclear, but he reminds us that art still affect us on a deeply political level and can still threaten authoritarian regimes.

While detained, Weiwei sent this video message to be played at TED. At the end of his video, he gave some live remarks.

- https://youtu.be/MVnH8ou3Kd4

Attributions

CC licensed content, Shared previously

- Ai Weiwei, Remembering, and the Politics of Dissent. **Authored by**: JP McMahon. **Provided by**: Khan Academy. **Located at**: https://web.archive.org/web/20130425105453/http://smarthistory.khanacademy.org/ai-weiwei-and-the-politics-of-dissent.html. **License**: *CC BY-NC-SA: Attribution-NonCommercial-ShareAlike*
- Ai Weiwei detained. Here is his TED film. **Authored by**: TED. **Located at**: https://youtu.be/MVnH8ou3Kd4. **License**: *CC BY-NC-ND: Attribution-NonCommercial-NoDerivatives*
- Ai Weiwei. **Authored by**: Hafenbar. **Located at**: https://commons.wikimedia.org/wiki/File:Ai_Weiwei.jpg. **License**: *CC BY-SA: Attribution-ShareAlike*
- Sunflower Seeds by Ai Weiwei, Tate Modern Turbine Hall (handheld). **Authored by**: Loz Pycock. **Located at**: https://flic.kr/p/8JybJj. **License**: *CC BY-SA: Attribution-ShareAlike*
- Sunflower Seeds by Ai Weiwei, Tate Modern Turbine Hall. **Authored by**: Loz Pycock. **Located at**: https://flic.kr/p/8Jy9Vf. **License**: *CC BY-SA: Attribution-ShareAlike*

Public domain content

- Ai Weiwei-So sorry. **Authored by**: Pittigrilli. **Located at**: https://commons.wikimedia.org/wiki/File:Ai_Weiwei-So_sorry.JPG. **License**: *Public Domain: No Known Copyright*